Mirror on America

Essays and Images
from Popular Culture

Mirror on America

Essays and Images
from Popular Culture

FOURTH EDITION

JOAN T. MIMS

ELIZABETH M. NOLLEN
West Chester University

BEDFORD/ST. MARTIN'S   Boston ◆ New York

For Bedford/St. Martin's

Developmental Editor: Adam Whitehurst
Production Editor: Kendra LeFleur
Senior Production Supervisor: Nancy Myers
Marketing Manager: Molly Parke
Editorial Assistant: Erin McGhee
Production Assistant: David Ayers
Copyeditor: Linda McLatchie
Text Design: Claire Seng-Niemoeller and Tom Carling
Cover Art and Design: Billy Boardman
Composition: Macmillan Publishing Solutions
Printing and Binding: R. R. Donnelley & Sons Company

President: Joan E. Feinberg
Editorial Director: Denise B. Wydra
Director of Marketing: Karen R. Soeltz
Director of Editing, Design, and Production: Marcia Cohen
Assistant Director of Editing, Design, and Production: Elise S. Kaiser
Managing Editor: Elizabeth M. Schaaf

Library of Congress Control Number: 2008933114

Manufactured in the United States of America.

4 3 2 1 0 9
f   e   d   c   b   a

For information, write: Bedford/St. Martin's, 75 Arlington Street, Boston, MA 02116 (617-399-4000)

ISBN-10: 0–312–47712–0
ISBN-13: 978–0–312–47712–7

Acknowledgments

Tanzila Ahmed. "100% Indian Hair." Originally posted on www.popandpolitics.com. February 8, 2006. Printed on August 6, 2007. Copyright © 2006 by Tanzila Ahmed. Reprinted by permission of the author. All rights reserved.

Preface for Instructors

If popular culture is a kind of mirror that reflects our multicultural society and its values and preferences, it also forms one of the largest arenas for communication among all members of that society, irrespective of age, gender, ethnicity, or social standing. *Mirror on America: Essays and Images from Popular Culture*, Fourth Edition, gives students the context they need to understand this public dialogue and the critical thinking and writing skills necessary to participate intelligently. Composed primarily of short to medium-length, high interest essays and striking, thought-provoking images, the text's thematic chapters present material that may already be familiar to students in new and thoughtful ways. The text guides their responses and helps them think and write critically about the popular culture surrounding them.

We turned to the subject of popular culture because, after teaching for many years, we became frustrated in our search for a reader that would at once interest and challenge students. Many writing texts underestimate students' social awareness and critical thinking capabilities. *Mirror on America* attempts to address this misconception by coupling thought-provoking editorial guidance with highly readable yet challenging selections of various types and difficulty levels including articles from popular periodicals, essays, cartoons, photographs, paintings, and advertisements.

Beginning with a student-friendly introduction, *Mirror on America* defines popular culture as "that collection of objects, people, events, and places that serves to mirror society and its members and to reflect their values and preferences." Also discussing the importance of reading and writing about popular culture, the introduction stresses that although all components of pop culture may not be of equal quality, they play a crucial role in our daily lives, as well as in our shared social history.

Eight Chapters on Popular Culture

The first chapter, "Active, Involved Reading and the Writing Process: Establishing the Connection," demonstrates the essential link between the reading and writing processes by teaching students to read thoughtfully and to recognize such fundamental issues as audience, tone, and purpose. We think that students who are able to recognize these essentials are more likely to consider them in their own writing. In this chapter we outline for students the various types of questions accompanying each selection and guide them through two sample professional essays. The second half of Chapter 1 leads the student step by step from active reading to self-generated writing and concludes with a student essay written in response to the two professional essays. Chapter 2, "Deconstructing Media: Analyzing an Image," provides guidance on looking critically at images. Several sample images, as well as a student essay analyzing an advertisement, help students to see how they can decode visual media.

Following the initial chapters are six chapters on specific areas of popular culture. Chapters 3 and 4, titled "Define 'American': Reflections on Cultural Identity" and "'How Do I Look?': How Culture Shapes Self-Image," deal with the ways popular culture affects us personally. These are followed by four chapters that deal with areas of culture that affect us in a more global sense: Chapter 5, "What Are You Trying to Say? How Language Works," Chapter 6, "Fantasies for Sale: Marketing American Culture," Chapter 7, "Seeing the Big Picture: Reflecting Culture in Film," and Chapter 8, "American Idols: Representations of American Culture." The chapters on language and icons are new to the Fourth Edition, while the chapter on film has been substantially revised. Also new to this edition is an increased focus on multiculturalism to make the text even more relevant in our rapidly shrinking world. Each thematic chapter has been lengthened to nine essays, and the average length of those essays has increased to offer a bridge to the reading students are doing in their other courses.

Readable, High-Interest Selections

Like the chapter topics, selections were chosen for their currency, high interest, challenging ideas, and readability. They were also chosen with an eye to their ability to generate engaging discussion and writing activities. Selected from sources such as newspapers, magazines, webzines, and essay collections, most readings range from three to five pages—about the same length as the papers that students will be asked to write. In this edition we've included a greater number of longer readings to expose students to more elaborate, fully developed arguments, thus enriching their composition experience. Well-known authors, including Julia Alvarez, Stephen King, and John Leo, write on topics such as American standards of beauty, the appeal of horror movies, and the popularity of body modification.

Paired selections in every chapter model effective arguments. These essays present different—often opposing—stances on a topic, offering an effective way for students to understand the issues at stake and to formulate arguments about them. We think you'll find these readings will generate lively discussion in your classroom.

Striking Visuals

More accurately than other, more traditional texts, *Mirror on America*, Fourth Edition, reflects the students' world by including a wealth of images such as movie stills, paintings, drawings, advertisements, photographs, and cartoons. Every chapter opens with a striking image. These opening visuals are accompanied by questions and prompts for thinking that encourage students to approach the chapter with a critical eye. In several chapters, additional visuals accompany selected essays. These visuals are followed by "Analyzing the Image" questions, which ask students questions about both the composition and the message of the images. The "Focusing on Yesterday, Focusing on Today" visuals and apparatus at the end of each chapter ask students to examine their current culture by comparing and contrasting it with the culture of the past.

Helpful Guidance for Students

The abundant editorial apparatus in *Mirror on America*, Fourth Edition, guides students through the discovery process by asking them carefully wrought questions and by offering them context before and after every chapter and every selection.

At the beginning of each chapter, focused activities guide students to the chapter's topic:

- "Analyzing the Image" questions accompany the chapter-opening visual to stimulate discussion or writing.
- A "Gearing Up" journal and discussion prompt asks students to reflect briefly in writing about the topic for that chapter. This feature may also be used as a homework assignment.
- A brief introduction provides valuable context for the chapter's selections and focuses students' attention more fully on the chapter's topic.
- "Collaborating" activities introduce students to major concerns of the chapter and give them a chance to exchange ideas with their classmates.

Each reading selection is preceded by relevant information and an activity to help frame students' reading:

- An informative headnote to the selection provides students with publication information for the reading and a brief biographical sketch about the selection's author.
- "Thinking Ahead" questions ask students to reflect briefly on the topic of the selection.

Accompanying each reading selection are glosses to explain contexts and terminology that might be unfamiliar to students. Six sets of questions follow each reading. New to the Fourth Edition are two additional "Responding" questions, which provide students with additional suggestions for writing about the essays they've just read.

- "Exercising Vocabulary" questions begin with a list of unfamiliar words for students to look up and incorporate into their personal vocabularies. The remaining questions ask students to derive the meaning of especially interesting words from their context and to apply and compare that meaning to usage in other contexts.
- "Probing Content" questions call for students to engage in thoughtful discussion of the selection's subject.
- "Considering Craft" questions require students to focus on particular techniques used by the writers to accomplish their goals.
- The "Responding to the Writer" question asks students to reflect on some aspect of the reading and to question and comment on the writer's message while connecting it to their own experiences.
- The "Responding to the Topic" question asks students to take a position on a topic raised in the essay.
- The "Responding to Multiple Viewpoints" question asks students to connect two or more essays, generally from the same chapter, in significant ways.
- "Drawing Connections" questions ask students to compare and contrast the way the authors of explicitly paired readings explain their points of view.

Each chapter concludes with "Wrapping Up" activities, including the "Focusing on Yesterday, Focusing on Today" activities discussed earlier.

- "Connecting to the Culture" questions ask students to connect ideas from the essays within or across chapters and to draw their own conclusions. These questions also ask students to reflect on personal experiences similar to those represented in the readings and to consider how their own life experiences are connected to popular culture in general.
- The section "Evaluating and Documenting Sources" at the end of the book offers concise coverage of the new 2009 MLA documentation style. This section features MLA citation models, as well as an annotation of a Web page and an exercise asking students to examine a Web source.

What's New in the Fourth Edition

TEXT SELECTIONS

To keep pace with the ever-changing rhythm of American popular culture, we have included fifty-seven provocative readings, more than two-thirds of which are new. These updated readings offer wide-ranging perspectives on popular culture. The selections encourage students to explore the impact multicultural groups can have on American popular culture, and *Mirror on America* now features more diverse topics and writers. For instance, an essay by Edward Rhymes turns on its head the dominant cultural argument that rap lyrics promote violence and misogyny by carefully analyzing the lyrics in traditionally white heavy metal and hard rock music and raises some insightful questions about the hypocrisy of censorship. Michelle Jana Chan, in "Identity in a Virtual World," discusses the work of photographer Robbie Cooper, whose work examines the way that real people recreate themselves as characters in online games.

TWO NEW CHAPTERS—ON LANGUAGE AND ON AMERICAN ICONS

Chapter 5, "What Are You Trying to Say?: How Language Works" examines the ways that seemingly unconnected topics—whether they are brand names that coin new terms, technology that presents unforeseen opportunities to communicate, or immigration that shapes the way our language evolves—are influencing the ways we write and talk to each other. Another new chapter on American icons, Chapter 8, "American Idols: Representations of American Culture" highlights some of the celebrities, products, pastimes, and symbols that influence collective American identity and represent America to the rest of the world.

MORE WRITING PROMPTS

The fourth edition of *Mirror on America* includes more types of writing prompts than ever, recognizing that student interactions with texts occur at many different levels. Additional writing exercises now follow each reading, and two new categories of prompts, "Responding to the Topic" and "Responding to Multiple Viewpoints," respectively ask students to think beyond one text in order to write about topics from their own perspectives or to consider author perspectives as part of a larger cultural debate.

IMAGE SELECTIONS

Because our students are highly tuned to visual information and their lives are media saturated, we offer students a wide variety of vivid images—twenty-one new to this edition—and ways to understand and respond to them. Chapter 2, "Deconstructing Media: Analyzing an Image," provides students with a framework for reading and writing about visuals. A sample student paper, "Monumental Taste: Using Patriotism to Market Diet

Coke," models the kind of critical analysis students are expected to write. The opening visuals for each chapter, images that are accompanied by "Analyzing the Image" questions, images that accompany selected essays; and the pair of images, "Focusing on Yesterday, Focusing on Today," at the end of each chapter have been carefully updated to focus on such contemporary cultural phenomena as on-line gaming and social networking and the continuing popularity of plastic surgery.

Companion Web Site at bedfordstmartins.com/mirror

Web links throughout the text direct students to the companion Web site, where you and your students will find useful online resources, including TopLinks—a dynamic database of annotated links that relate to each topic in the book and that provide opportunities for further exploration and possible essay ideas. Students may use the online Reading Quizzes to test themselves on the content of each reading. Each quiz offers automatic feedback and immediate scoring, and instructors can track their students' progress.

Student Resources

- *Re:Writing* (bedfordstmartins.com/rewriting): This portal collects the most popular and widely used free online resources from Bedford/St. Martin's in a convenient and easy-to-navigate Web site. Offerings include research and documentation advice, visual analysis exercises, and access to Exercise Central, as well as instructor resources such as bibliographies and online journals.
- *Exercise Central* (bedfordstmartins.com/exercisecentral): The largest collection of editing exercises available online, Exercise Central offers more than 8,000 items, with instant scoring and feedback and an online gradebook for instructors.
- *The Bedford/St. Martin's ESL Workbook*: This ancillary covers grammar issues for multilingual students with varying English-language skills and cultural backgrounds. To reinforce each lesson, instructional introductions are followed by illustrative examples and exercises.

Resources for Instructors

The instructor's manual, *Resources for Teaching* MIRROR ON AMERICA: ESSAYS AND IMAGES FROM POPULAR CULTURE, Fourth Edition, is designed as a practical ancillary offering additional ways to present the material effectively and exercises originating from imaginative alternatives that work well in the classroom. We do not claim to provide all the alternative teaching strategies and resources here. Instead we hope that those we do offer lead to stimulating classroom experiences.

After suggestions on strategies for teaching Chapters 1 and 2, the instructor's manual offers the following material for each additional chapter:

- A brief chapter introduction from the instructor's point of view
- A short discussion of the chapter's opening image
- Comments on "Focusing on Yesterday, Focusing on Today"
- Additional resources

For each selection, the instructor's manual offers additional apparatus:

- A brief introduction to the selection
- "Questions for Discussion"
- "Group Activities"
- "Out of Class Projects"

Through class-testing many of the selections, writing suggestions, and activities in the text, we have found reading and writing about contemporary popular culture to be a highly effective means of teaching students to connect to larger cultural and discourse communities through their own reading and writing. We sincerely hope that you have equally successful classroom experiences as you use *Mirror on America: Essays and Images from Popular Culture*, Fourth Edition, with your own students.

Acknowledgments

We would like to thank Barbara Heinssen for signing this book, thus making our affiliation with Bedford/St. Martin's possible. We have found it a privilege to work with a team of highly competent people at Bedford/St. Martin's, one of the last publishing houses to truly take the time to develop its writers. We especially wish to thank Bedford's past president, Chuck Christensen; its president, Joan Feinberg; its editorial director, Denise Wydra; and its editor in chief in Boston, Karen Henry, for sharing our vision and allowing us to share it with others. Special thanks go to developmental editor Aron Keesbury and his former editorial assistant (now senior editor), Ellen Thibault, for their work on the first edition. Their insight, inventiveness, and general good humor made our collaboration productive and enjoyable. Amanda Bristow, who edited the second edition, and her assistants Karin Halbert and Christina Gerogiannis (now editor), helped transform that edition into an even more relevant and usable textbook by lending their fresh, vibrant perspectives.

We thank Adam Whitehurst, the editor of this edition, for his vital role in giving the book its exciting new focus on multiculturalism. His insights into the most current topics in popular culture have been invaluable.

We appreciate the efforts of editorial assistant Erin McGhee, who helped out with the innumerable details that go into producing a textbook as well as provided instrumental writing help with the updated Instructor's Manual. Our thanks also go to the production team, including Kendra LeFleur, who skillfully engineered and guided the manuscript into book form. Copyeditor Linda McLatchie's suggestions were invaluable. We also wish to recognize the hard work of Linda Finigan, who cleared permissions for all of the images; Stefanie Wortman, who wrote new headnotes and updated existing ones; and Sara Eaton Gaunt, who updated the online reading quizzes. We are very grateful to Sandy Schechter and Richard Lankford, who cleared text permissions for the book. We would also like to thank the following students for their contributions to this edition: Cassandra Dettman, who helped locate essays; Julia Nollen, who helped write apparatus for the film chapter, and to Anabel F. Hart and Robert E. Arthur, two extremely talented young writers who provided the student essays for Chapters 1 and 2.

We also owe a debt of gratitude to a group of people who were instrumental in the revision of this book. We thank our reviewers for their many helpful suggestions: Bob Baron, Mesa Community College; Joy Barta, Independence Community College; Crystal Bickford, Nicholas College; Claudette L. Brassil, Mt. Ararat High School; Christine Bryant, University of Illinois-Urbana Champaign; Joel Dailey, Delgado Community College; Esmeralda Vázquez de Diriye, California State Polytechnic University, Pomona; Susana de la Pena, Moorpark College; Kristin Elsie Graef, Aquinas College; Carey Emmons Crockett, Utah State University; Ellen L. Gorman, Georgetown University; Mary Graham, Cuyamaca College; Jeremiah Hall, California State University, Fullerton; Nainsi J. Houston, Creighton University; Lauren Sewell Ingraham, University of Tennessee at Chattanooga; Jennifer Kluck, South Dakota State University; Dale Leyden, Suffolk County Community College; Tim Melnarik, California State University–San Bernardino; Marilyn Morgan, Brevard Community College–Palm Bay; Heather H. Powers, Indiana University of Pennsylvania; Pam Saalfeld, Northeast Community College; Tracy Schneider, Solano Community College; Anthony Starros, Long Beach Community College; Jennifer Stewart, Indiana University–Purdue University Fort Wayne; Michael Trovato, Ohio State University–Newark; Jason Wohlstadter, Modesto Junior College.

Finally, this book never would have been written had it not been for the many students we have taught over the years in our composition classrooms. With them, we have tested many of the topics, strategies, and activities that comprise this text, and from them we have learned much of what we know about teaching writing and about popular culture today.

Introduction for Students

This is not your usual English textbook. The material focuses on reading and writing about things in your world, like television, movies, music, and technology, often called *popular culture*. Why read and write about popular culture? In order to answer this question, we first need to understand what popular culture is and why it is important.

To arrive at a working definition, we can break the term down into its two components: *popular* and *culture*. In the most general sense, popular means "of the people"—the common people or the population at large, not the elite or chosen few. But more often, popular suggests choice or preference. We usually use this term when we mean something or someone that many ordinary people prefer or value. When you think of popular culture, then, think of the People's Choice Awards as opposed to the Academy Awards.

That brings us to the second term, *culture*. Broadly defined, *culture* refers to the body of beliefs, behaviors, values, and thoughts that influence us every day. It contains not only the good, but also the bad—the high and the low. We normally associate the word *culture*, however, not with the masses—the ordinary man and woman on the street—but with the educated and financially privileged. We think of *Masterpiece* on PBS, not *American Idol*. If a person is cultured, we generally think she possesses good taste, is refined and educated, and is also probably upper-class. If *popular* usually means "chosen by the common people," and *culture* is often associated with the chosen few, then what do these two seemingly contradictory terms mean when they are used together?

We may borrow the Cotton Institute slogan from television commercials to help us arrive at a working definition of popular culture: It is "the fabric of our lives." Pop culture is made up of all the objects, people, events, and places to which most of us readily relate and which comprise a society at any given time, past or present. The objects and people that are widely recognized as symbols of our culture are often referred to as cultural icons. The four components of pop culture—objects, people, events, and places—can be real or imagined. Let's look at some examples:

1. Objects as cultural icons include Barbie dolls, rap songs, television shows, films, clothing, iPods, advertisements, and even Cinderella's glass slipper.

2. People or characters as cultural icons include Paris Hilton, Johnny Depp, Batman, Michael Phelps, the Energizer Bunny, Homer Simpson, and the Aflac Duck.

3. Events, activities, or rituals in popular culture are those that large groups of people participate in or can relate to, including 9/11, the Olympics, the Super Bowl, Thanksgiving dinner, high school proms, Fourth of July fireworks, and the MTV Movie Awards.

4. Places in pop culture are settings that hold special shared meaning for many people and include shopping malls, megaplexes, amusement parks, Mount Rushmore, Las Vegas, Hollywood, the White House, and the Statue of Liberty.

These four elements of popular culture form a mirror in which each of us, as members of a common society, can see ourselves reflected as part of an interconnected, greater whole. At the same time, pop culture not only reflects our tastes and preferences at any given time, past or present, but also plays a role in determining future fads and trends. From the time we get up in the morning until the time we go to bed, and from the time we enter this world until the time we leave it, we are immersed in popular culture. We may agree that not all of its components are of the highest quality or in the best taste, but we would all have to concede that they play an integral part in our daily lives, as well as in our shared social history. Popular culture is part of what makes us all Americans.

It is important to remember that pop culture is not fixed in time. The popular or mass culture of the past may become the high or elite culture of the present, and that same elite culture may simultaneously be repopularized as it is once again embraced by the masses. Consider the case of William Shakespeare. If you read *Macbeth* or *Hamlet* in high school, you probably did not associate those difficult-to-read plays with pop culture. Remember, however, that Shakespeare's plays, much like blockbuster movies today, were extremely popular during the time they were written and enjoyed wide attendance by large, enthusiastic audiences. Shakespeare was tuned in to those audiences, which were made up of all segments of society, from the educated nobility to the illiterate "groundlings," so named because they sat or stood on the ground near the stage. Thus, during his time, Shakespeare's plays were seen as popular entertainment. It was only in later years that his plays were appropriated by learned scholars in universities who sought to analyze them word by word as they continue to do today.

Interestingly enough, as evidence of Shakespeare's popular appeal in the second half of the twentieth century and into the new millennium, entertainment moguls have sought to revitalize his plays by taking them out of the hands of university professors and giving them back to the masses. Not only serious students of Shakespeare but also people who have never read a word of his plays have been able to enjoy his works through both cinematic and live theater productions. Let's examine several of these revisionings of Shakespeare's works from the second half of the twentieth century through the present day.

You may be familiar with *West Side Story*, which recasts *Romeo and Juliet* as the story of a couple struggling to maintain a relationship against a backdrop of gang warfare in a New York City Puerto Rican neighborhood. First the story was a Broadway hit; then a film version was made which drew a much larger audience. Similarly, famed director Baz Luhrmann's 1996 cinematic version of *Romeo and Juliet*, starring Leonardo DiCaprio and Claire Danes, features tough modern gangs, a cross-dressing Mercutio, and a powerful musical score performed by contemporary artists such as Radiohead and Garbage. The 1999 Academy Awards were dominated by the Hollywood blockbuster *Shakespeare in Love*, a rollicking spoof featuring a young Shakespeare with writer's block, played by Joseph Fiennes, who is lovestruck by a beautiful woman, played by Gwyneth Paltrow. Since then, there have been several other popular reincarnations of Shakespeare classics set in contemporary America, featuring young stars like Julia Stiles, Heath Ledger, Amanda Bynes, Ethan Hawke, Catherine Keener, Jet Li, and Aaliyah. These films, which target the teenage market, include *O*, a modern-day retelling of *Othello*; *10 Things I Hate about You*, based on *The Taming of the Shrew*; *She's the Man*, which adapts *Twelfth Night* to a high school setting; *Hamlet* and its satirical play-within-a-play sequel, *Hamlet 2*; and *Romeo Must Die*, yet another retelling of the classic love story *Romeo and Juliet*.

Perhaps the most exciting example of Shakespeare's reaching the masses in much the same way he did in his own day is New York City's Shakespeare in the Park series. The aptly named Public Theater, which celebrated its fiftieth anniversary in 2005, sponsors this series and provides equal accessibility to people of all ages, ethnicities, and educational and income levels. Anyone can see the Shakespeare's plays for free in beautiful Central Park, and tickets or reservations are not required. The public is encouraged to attend rehearsals and even meet the actors, some of whom are Hollywood's brightest stars, such as Meryl Streep, Natalie Portman, Philip Seymour Hoffman, and Denzel Washington. Shakespeare in the Park has become not only a national, but also an international, phenomenon.

Thus Shakespeare is once again finding his way back to the masses. According to The Public Theater's Web site, "The Public is an American theater that embraces the complexities of contemporary society and nurtures both artists and audiences through its commitment to the idea that The Public should be a place of inclusion and a forum for ideas." This sounds a lot like the mission of popular culture studies. Since academics are already studying and writing scholarly articles on the impact of rap music, soap operas, the Internet, films, and video games, which contemporary composers and screenwriters do you think will someday take their place alongside Shakespeare?

Popular culture, then, is that collection of objects, people, events, and places that serves to mirror society and its members and to reflect their values and preferences. By studying pop culture, you gain valuable new insights about yourself and make richer connections to all aspects of the society in which you live. Finally, we hope that you find it not only fulfilling but also fun to read and write about popular culture, a subject with which you are intimately connected every day of your life.

Contents

1 Active, Involved Reading and the Writing Process: Establishing the Connection   1

2 | Deconstructing Media: Analyzing an Image   31

3 | Define "American": Reflections on Cultural Identity   43

4) "How Do I Look?": How Culture Shapes Self-Image   **104**

ANALYZING THE IMAGE:
American Gothic Makeover (PAINTING)   105
Gearing Up   105
Collaborating   106

5   What Are You Trying to Say?: How Language Works

8 American Idols: Representations of American Culture   330

Rhetorical Table of Contents

The rhetorical strategies—analysis, argument, cause and effect, comparison and contrast, definition, description, evaluation, illustration and example, narration, and process analysis—are listed alphabetically for quick reference.

Analysis

Argument

Cause and Effect

Comparison and Contrast

Definition

Description

Evaluation

Illustration and Example

Narration

Process Analysis

Mirror on America

Essays and Images
from Popular Culture

Active, Involved Reading and the Writing Process

Establishing the Connection

If this is a writing course, why is there so much to read in this text? Why is reading the first thing we want to discuss with you?

It's simple, really. People who write well read often. They read to find ideas, both for what to write about and for how to write. Reading makes us think, and good writing requires thought beforehand, during, and afterward. Reading helps us identify things we'd like to model in our own work and things we'll never do, no matter what. Reading opens windows and doors to the world we share and offers mirrors in which we can look at our culture and ourselves.

Reading with a Difference

The kind of reading this discussion involves may not be the kind of reading you are used to. If you think of reading as a sit-still, passive, try-to-stay-awake-until-the-end-of-the-chapter event, you'll need to rethink. Real reading means really getting involved with the text, whether the text is song lyrics, a magazine or newspaper item, a poem, a chapter in a chemistry book, or an essay in this text. The more of your five senses you involve, the better.

GETTING INTO READING

This text includes some things that should make the reading and writing experience more manageable for you and more interesting, too. Each unit begins with an image like a photograph or an advertisement. This opening visual gives you a first glimpse of the chapter's topic and helps you begin to think about that topic. Next is the "Gearing Up" section—a journal and discussion prompt to help you reflect on your previous involvement with that chapter's topic and to get you started writing. Next is introductory text that provides some background thoughts about the chapter and raises some questions to help you relate your own experiences to the topic for reading and discussion. Each chapter also includes a "Collaborating" opening activity that suggests questions for you and your classmates to brainstorm about together before you begin to read and discuss the individual selections in each chapter.

Now you are ready to move on to the reading selections in the chapter. Each essay is introduced by a brief headnote about the selection's writer and the time and place of first publication. Next is "Thinking Ahead," a journal prompt that deals with the topic addressed by that particular reading selection. The reading selection, which may be an essay, an article, or a column from a newspaper, magazine, or Webzine, is next. Five sets of questions follow the reading selection. "Exercising Vocabulary" gives you a chance to explore the use and meaning of some especially relevant words. The first item in this set will always be a vocabulary list, which contains some words from the reading that you may find unfamiliar. Looking up definitions for these terms and writing those definitions in your own words in a vocabulary notebook will help you to expand the number of words at your command when you write or read. The other questions here will challenge you to explore further the history or meaning of interesting words or phrases.

"Probing Content" asks questions about the writer's subject matter. "Considering Craft" questions are about why and how the writer has put together the selection as he or she has chosen to do. Next you'll find three questions to be used as essay prompts. The first, "Responding to the Topic," asks you to examine your own reactions, to relate how the topic affects you personally, as you respond to issues the writer has raised. The second, "Responding to the Writer," asks you to take a position on issues raised by the selection and to defend your point of view. The third, "Responding to Multiple Viewpoints," directs you to develop an essay connecting various sources from within the chapter. For the paired essays in each chapter, you'll find one additional question set, "Drawing Connections," which asks you to compare how the authors of the paired essays make their points about similar topics.

To understand how all these parts work together, let's look at a sample essay. First, read the brief introduction to the essay's subject and author. Many readers may be tempted to skip right over this information because it isn't part of the essay, but that's a mistake. To see why, let's work with the headnote to a sample essay.

Schlock Waves Felt
across U.S. Campuses

Eric L. Wee

The debate about the value of popular culture has been raging for centuries. In the *Washington Post* in June 1998, Eric L. Wee first published this snapshot from the mecca of popular culture studies, the annual conference of the Popular Culture Association and the American Culture Association. By introducing us to some of the presenters and their topics, Wee raises numerous questions about pop culture as an academic discipline. Wee, a former *Washington Post* reporter, is a frequent contributor to the *Washington Post Magazine*. He was a finalist for the Pulitzer Prize in feature writing in 1999 and won a prestigious award for education reporting in 2004.

This headnote offers several important pieces of information. It introduces the occasion that prompted Wee to write—the 1998 Popular Culture Conference—and explains how this author chooses to approach his topic. The headnote also tells us when and where the article first appeared and a little background information about the author so that we can think accurately about his perspective on the topic and the original intended audience. How does the information in the headnote influence your reading?

THINKING AHEAD

Following our sample essay's headnote are a few sentences under the heading "Thinking Ahead." This journal and discussion prompt helps you focus your initial thoughts about the essay's subject. If you have never kept a journal before, you'll find that it's a good way to learn to transfer your thoughts and ideas to paper. Don't worry too much about grammar and spelling as you write in your journal; the important thing here is just to get started writing. These journal notes may be seeds for your more formal essays later. Let's look at a sample journal prompt and one possible response for "Schlock Waves Felt across U.S. Campuses."

> **THINKING AHEAD** To what extent should we examine popular culture? Do the immediacy and relevance of popular culture make up for its lack of historical validity and academic esteem? If popular culture is constantly changing, what value is there in studying it? Are there any life lessons to be learned from studying television shows, movies, music lyrics and videos, advertisements, and other components of everyday life?

Now here is a journal entry written in response to this prompt:

It just seems too easy. If I can learn the same lessons from studying episodes of Grey's Anatomy that I can from reading Leo Tolstoy's novels, why would I wade through all those eight-syllable names? I get it that the same themes from those hundred-year-old novels are being replayed over and over in movies and TV shows — love, death, crime, jealousy. So humanity just keeps repeating the same mistakes. If studying violent movies would help us learn to reduce the violence, then that would be valuable. But what if studying violent movies encourages some people to commit violence and even teaches them new ways to be violent? I can't see a lot of parents wanting to spend money for their kids to take classes where they study Jennifer Lopez and Brad Pitt. It just doesn't seem academic enough.

Remember that everyone's journal response will be different. The task of the journal prompt is to get you to think about a subject in a way that you might not have before, so the writing in your journal won't be a finished product. Your response will be just your initial ideas transferred from your head onto the paper.

READING A SAMPLE ESSAY

Once you have read the introduction to the reading selection and responded to the "Thinking Ahead" journal prompt, you are ready to read the selection itself. But reading doesn't mean you become a spectator. You don't learn about playing a sport just by watching, and you don't learn everything a text has to offer just by letting your eyes wander over the lines. That's why annotating is essential for really involved reading. Annotating means reading and marking the text with a highlighter, pencil, or pen. When you annotate, you open up a dialogue between yourself and the text. You communicate.

Here's how annotating works. Circle any unfamiliar vocabulary words so that you can look them up later. Some may be in the "Exercising Vocabulary" list, but some may not. We explain some unusual words or names, which you probably would not use in your own writing or conversation, at the bottom of the page on which they appear to help you understand what the author is trying to say; be sure to read that information. Underline or highlight important sentences, especially the *thesis*, or main idea, and the *topic sentences* for each paragraph. Mark sentences or phrases that appeal to you or seem especially well worded. Jot down questions in the margin. Draw connections between the author's experiences and your own. Put question marks by whatever you don't accept as true or just don't understand. React to what you're reading!

Here is a copy of our sample essay, "Schlock Waves Felt across U.S. Campuses," with annotations. Don't worry if you would have marked different words and phrases and recorded different comments; that's fine. This is just to show you how one reader has actively read and annotated this essay.

Schlock Waves Felt across U.S. Campuses

ERIC L. WEE

means what? play on "shock"? — (Schlock)

directions based on pop culture— awesome opener!

Go past the 24-screen cineplex playing two shows of *Titanic*. Go past Planet Hollywood. Past the Virgin Megastore. Past McDonald's. 1

Who's they? creates suspense

And then you'll see where they gather. At the Buena Vista Hotel in the heart of Disney World, you'll find the people who are studying 2

Like what? — everything you can't get away from. The professors of popular culture. They see revelations in Calvin Klein underwear ads; they construct new

look up — literary paradigms from R.E.M.[1] lyrics; they analyze porno flicks as if they were fine art. On many campuses, they're scorned by colleagues. But here, they're among friends. Here, for four days in early April, 1,500 members of the Popular Culture Association and the American Culture Associa-

Milton's poem — tion presented papers on such topics as "Godlike Knowledge and Human Understanding in *Paradise Lost* and *Star Trek*"—and they were taken seriously.

Isn't pop culture all about the present?

The study of popular culture, they'll tell you, is the future. As incred- 3
ible as it seems, they may be right.

Who fits in this group?

Drop in on a lecture by Lynnea Chapman King, an English doctoral 4
candidate from Texas Tech University. Her specialty and dissertation topic: "The Films of Generation X." The canon comprises youth-oriented movies made from 1982 to 1997. First she shows a clip from *Fast Times at Ridge-*

great film! — *mont High*, then one from *The Breakfast Club*—all the way up to *Romy and Michele's High School Reunion*. She's grouped the 18 films of the Gen X canon into subgenres, including high school films (*Ferris Bueller's Day Off*), post–high school (*Less Than Zero*) and post-college (*St. Elmo's Fire*).

I can relate! — She talks about how these movies reflect the angst people in their late 20s and early 30s feel about family, their futures and death—and it all seems to be making sense.

Then it hits you: 5

How nice for her! What are her career options?

Ms. Chapman King, age 30, is earning a Ph.D. in *Pretty in Pink*. 6
She's made herself an expert on movies she happens to like. She explains that these are all very significant films, worthy of her scholarship.

Is this worth a degree?

"I think that in 10 years we'll look back and say, 'Yes, I can see 7
that *The Breakfast Club* and, yes, *Reality Bites* and, yes, *Before Sunrise* are a beautiful and valuable reflection of society, and standing alone are examples of good filmmaking.'" There was a time when teaching Plato at

Plato radical?

French for?? — Oxford was considered radical. English literature as a field of study was considered avant-garde on American campuses in the 19th century.

Why? Because it was British?

Still, the old canon provided certain constants. For decades, college 8
students mostly studied the big thinkers and writers who had withstood the

Credibility

true! — test of time. Aristotle, Shakespeare, Wordsworth. But inevitably the people being studied were dead, white, male—and hard to relate to.

The '60s turned everything upside down. Students—and profes- 9
sors—began occupying buildings and issuing demands. Why weren't we

civil rights — studying the histories of nonwhite people? Why was everything from a

Feminist movement — male perspective?

[1] **R.E.M.:** An alternative rock band.

5

[margin right: 10]

Riding this crest of change have been the pop-culture profs. Once the kooky idea of a few people at Bowling Green State University in Ohio, the concept has spread and become institutionalized in colleges nationwide during the past three decades. Traditionalists may still sneer at popular culture studies, but as an academic discipline, it's not about to disappear.

[margin right: Okay, but what's the career path? Where are the jobs?]

[margin left: always about money—student consumers]

[margin right: 11 good word choice]

Students like it. Baby boom–era professors, themselves reared on television, like teaching these classes, too. They're popular—they bring in bodies. And they bring in tuition dollars. "We're no longer in the closet," says Ray Browne, the silver-haired academic who is acknowledged as the godfather of the movement. They used to call him a nut. Now they call him professor emeritus. In 1970, Dr. Browne set up the nation's first popular culture studies program at Bowling Green and also started the Popular Culture Association. Now, just look around. Hundreds of scholars have flocked to Disney World from schools such as Michigan State, Carnegie-Mellon and Virginia Tech. They may not be Ivy League, but pop-culture studies have pervaded those hallowed halls as well. By Dr. Browne's estimate, at least 2 million students are taking pop-culture courses in some form (up from 1 million in 1983).

[margin left: prestigious campuses]

[margin right: This was written in 1998. What's the number for this year? Up or down?]

Of course, not everybody is studying Capt. Kirk. There are some panels here on Depression-era workers and World War II veterans. For too long, scholars ignored everyday people and their everyday lives, Dr. Browne says; academia has been been guilty of arrogant intellectual snobbery.

[margin right: 12 Nice phrase— "ivory tower" thinking]

[margin left: powerful image]

The explosion of mass media has helped fuel popular culture's growth since World War II, creating a nurturing environment for such studies.

[margin right: 13 makes pop culture's growth sound like a wildfire]

Today popular culture invades all of our lives in an unprecedented way: Television, movies and the Internet bombard us with images, archetypes and knowledge. City after city has become almost indistinguishable with look-alike shopping malls.

[margin left: check mythology textbook]

[margin right: 14]

[margin right: remember Mall Rats and Dawn of the Dead]

This mass culture provides brain food for hungry scholars. How much more can be said about Shakespeare after 400 years? But much can be learned from Homer Simpson.

[margin left: or just fast food?]

[margin right: 15]

[margin right: comic books use this theme]

And can we apply Descartes'[2] concept of evil genius to a *Star Trek: The Next Generation* episode? Well, a philosophy professor from Susquehanna University in Pennsylvania is doing just that down the hall.

[margin left: really!]

[margin left: definitely applies!]

[margin right: 16]

Is there any limit to what's legitimate to study here? No, says Dr. Browne. After arguing so long for the study of the mundane, he is not about to start setting limits. Joseph Slade, Ph.D., looks like a distinguished professor. As he stands at the lectern in front of about a dozen fellow academics, he sounds as if he could be giving a discourse on economic theory. But this evening he's lecturing on fetishes. He's just handed out a reading/watching list with titles including *Hidden Obsessions*, *Les Femmes Érotiques* and *Latex*. He switches on the TV. Two women on the screen are appreciating each other.

[margin right: 17]

[margin left: weird topic!]

[margin left: that's being tactful!]

[margin right: What's audience reaction?]

Above the pulsating music, he starts talking about the director's style. "Mostly he's interested in female desire," says Dr. Slade. "The notion is that women are so voracious in their sexual appetite that they will mate with anything."

[margin right: 18]

[margin right: certainly not flattering]

Dr. Slade is director of graduate studies at the University of Ohio's school of telecommunications. He began his porn studies about 27 years ago while a doctoral student at New York University. One night he got sick of working on his dissertation and decided to go walking in Times Square.

[margin left: don't seem to go together]

[margin right: 19]

[margin right: Scholars and porn?]

There he saw the light—specifically the garish neon lights of a triple-X movie house. He watched one hard-core film. Then he watched another. After a third trip, he wrote a paper about the experience. Today, his curriculum vitae describes him as one of America's leading experts on adult film, having analyzed more than 7,000 movies (that's about a dozen a month).

[margin right: 20]

[margin left: like a résumé?]

[margin right: Is this a title you'd want?]

[2]**Descartes:** Seventeenth-century French philosopher and mathematician.

good question!

*But does popular =
worthy of study?*

21   Why study smut?

22   Because, according to Dr. Slade, adult movies portray basic human
nature. And, it's popular. Erotic or hard-core video titles account for $4.2
billion in business, he says. Did you know that we spend as much on adult
movies as we do on hot dogs?

*—money again
—odd comparison*

23   In another conference room, "Hormones and Heartache: Coming of
Age in Pine Valley" is the topic. It's a discussion of the characters in soap
operas, specifically *All My Children.*

*makes sense —
soaps are all over
social issues*

24   Kathy Lyday-Lee, an English professor at Elon College in North
Carolina, is there. She's going to teach a course called "Soap Operas and
Social Issues" this summer. Not that such a class will stick out in a sched-
ule that also includes "The World of NASCAR"[3] and "The Culture and
Business of Nashville."

*Why? Is this a
bad thing?
dig up?*

25   She sees the study of soap operas as a way to teach her students
about social changes as well as broadcasting history. Yet for all the
rational-sounding statements you hear from the conferees, you begin to
sense the real reason they study pop culture is much more simple: They
can't help themselves. After endless years in higher education, constantly
trying to plumb meaning from turgid texts, they can't shut off when they
hit the streets or turn on the tube.

*What does this
last sentence
mean? What does
Eric Wee really
think about value
of pop culture?*

THINKING ABOUT THE READING

After reading and annotating the piece of writing, you are ready to continue the conversation with the text, guided by several sets of questions.
The first set is called "Exercising Vocabulary." The first question here encourages you to locate definitions and think about adding words to your
personal spoken and written vocabulary. Following each word in parentheses is an abbreviation for the part of speech that tells how the word is used
in context—*n.* for *noun, v.* for *verb, adj.* for *adjective,* or *adv.* for *adverb*—so
that you'll know where you might use this word in a sentence. Next is a
number in parentheses; this is the paragraph number in the essay where the
word appears. This allows you to see where and how the writer has used
this word. The words are purposely not defined for you; keep a vocabulary
list in your notebook with definitions that you put into your own words
after reading the dictionary definition. Don't be tempted to simply copy
words from the dictionary onto your notebook page, however. That may
give you penmanship practice, but it won't help your personal vocabulary
grow. Think about building blocks. Someone with more building blocks
can build a more complete castle than someone else with fewer blocks.
Words are the building blocks of essays and conversations. Read what the
dictionary has to say, and write down a definition that makes sense to you.
Then go back and reread the word in context to make sure your definition
fits the author's intent. The objective is for you to be able to use this new
word in your own conversations and writing. Our vocabulary list may
not cover all the words in the selection that you find unfamiliar. Always
feel free to add words you'd like to master from each essay to the list in
your notebook.

[3]**NASCAR:** National Association for Stock Car Auto Racing.

The next questions in the "Exercising Vocabulary" set will require you to examine just a few words or phrases from the selection in close detail. You are asked to draw some conclusions and occasionally to do some detective work to arrive at a meaning for an unfamiliar word.

Here is the "Exercising Vocabulary" section for "Schlock Waves Felt across U.S. Campuses." We have included working definitions that a student might supply for the vocabulary list and possible answers so that you can see how this section works.

EXERCISING VOCABULARY

1. Record your own definition for each word below in your notebook.

    paradigms (n.) (2) *Examples that serve as models.*
    angst (n.) (4) *Anxiety.*
    avant-garde (adj.) (7) *Ahead of its time.*
    archetypes (n.) (14) *Models from which other like things are copied.*

    mundane (adj.) (17) *Ordinary.*
    smut (n.) (21) *Something indecent.*
    plumb (v.) (25) *To examine carefully.*
    turgid (adj.) (25) *Swollen; overblown.*

2. Wee changes a word in a common phrase to create an unusual title for this piece. What is the common phrase? What does it normally describe? What does *schlock* mean? Why has Wee substituted it here?

    The phrase you usually hear is "shock waves," and it is usually used to describe the aftermath of an earthquake. Schlock is a slang word that means something cheap, something not as good as another. Wee uses this word because some people think that popular culture is inferior to classics such as Shakespeare's plays, van Gogh's paintings, or Bach's music.

3. In paragraph 4, Wee uses the word *canon* to talk about a group of "youth-oriented movies." When traditional professors of literature talk about the canon, what do they mean? What usually is included in this canon? What effect does Wee achieve by using the word here?

    The canon usually refers to an officially recognized list of the best of a group. The canon in literature usually refers to famous, accepted works, such as novels by Jane Austen or F. Scott Fitzgerald. Wee uses the really formal word canon here to indicate a group of movies because he's saying that the people who study popular culture feel that this group of movies is just as worthy of serious study as those novels.

The next set of questions is called "Probing Content," and these questions are designed to get you to examine closely what the writer is saying.

Often a second part of the question asks you to think more deeply or to draw a conclusion. Be sure to answer all the parts of each question. You'll remember answers to some of these questions from your first reading, but for others you'll need to reread carefully. Here are "Probing Content" questions for "Schlock Waves Felt across U.S. Campuses" with some suggested answers. Of course, you might think of equally good but different answers.

PROBING CONTENT

1. In paragraph 3, Wee notes that attendees at the Popular Culture Conference will tell you that "the study of popular culture . . . is the future." Why is this statement ironic? Does Wee believe this?

     This statement is ironic because popular culture is all about what's hot right now, not in the future. Wee does seem to think that the study of popular culture, whatever that is at the time, is not going away because of the constant influence of popular culture on our lives (para. 14).

2. What's the problem with studying people who are all "dead, white, male" (para. 8)? What period of time marked a rebellion against such a limited scope to education? How does popular culture relate to opening up the canon?

     We can't relate to dead, white males. In the 1960s, people began to demand a study of people and things that were more representative of themselves and their lives. Pop culture insists that we recognize other artists who might be non-white and female.

3. Who is considered the father of the popular culture studies movement? What did he do to establish the scholastic nature of popular culture? Why did he want to study popular culture?

     Dr. Ray Browne is "the godfather of the movement" (para. 11). He established the first popular culture studies program at a university in Bowling Green, Ohio. Dr. Browne thought that academics needed to get over their "intellectual snobbery" (para. 12) to study what was really important to the common people.

4. What attracts scholars to the study of popular culture? How can this kind of study benefit us all?

     Many people think that everything has already been said about Shakespeare, but applying his themes to new movies is a new area of academic thought. Applying the concepts of old masters to new material makes the old masters relevant to the twenty-first century. Maybe we can learn from their lessons if those lessons fit our generation and our everyday lives.

While the "Probing Content" questions examine what the writer has to say about the subject, the next set of questions, "Considering Craft," encourages you to find out how the writer has packaged that information. You are asked to consider the writer's purpose, audience, language and tone, sentence structure, title, introduction and conclusion, and organization — the very things you must consider when you write your own papers. Here are some sample "Considering Craft" questions for "Schlock Waves Felt across U.S. Campuses" with some possible answers.

CONSIDERING CRAFT

1. Wee begins this commentary by offering directions. Reread paragraph 1. Why does he choose this introduction? Why does he phrase his directions in these terms? How does this introduction set a framework for the essay?

   Wee wants to direct us to the Popular Culture Conference. The directions he uses are all related to popular culture — a multi-screen theater, a restaurant everyone thinks is cool, a music store, and that old standby of pop culture, McDonald's. This introduction sets a framework for the whole essay about the value of popular culture; popular culture guides the direction of our lives.

2. In paragraph 20, Wee remarks that Dr. Joseph Slade "saw the light" while walking in Times Square. In what context is this expression most familiar? What is ironic about this use of language?

   The expression "to see the light" is often used in a religious sense. Here, however, Dr. Slade sees the light while looking at a triple-X movie house, which seems to point to sin, not redemption. And the light that he found led him to view and study pornographic movies.

3. Describe the author's tone in this piece. What does he hope to generate in the reader?

   Wee's tone in this commentary is matter-of-fact. He presents the material and lets the reader draw his or her own conclusions about the merits of studying popular culture. Because he doesn't judge the merits himself, his writing makes the reader weigh the value of studying popular culture and draw his or her own conclusions.

The final section concluding each reading selection offers three writing prompts for essay development: "Responding to the Topic," "Responding to the Writer," and "Responding to Multiple Viewpoints." Here are those questions for our sample essay.

WRITING PROMPTS

Responding to the Topic   If popular culture courses were available on your campus, would you register? What would be the advantages and disadvantages of adding such courses to your schedule? What reaction would you expect from your adviser, family, and friends? Write an essay in which you address these questions.

Responding to the Writer   According to Wee, the study of popular culture as an academic discipline is "not about to disappear" (para. 10). Using support from this essay, write an essay in which you agree or disagree with this statement.

Responding to Multiple Viewpoints   This question will ask you to draw on several selections from either the same or a different chapter. You'll see an example of this type of question after the second essay in this chapter.

Within each chapter, you'll find paired selections that express two different viewpoints about an issue approached in that chapter. These paired selections encourage you to examine several sides of an issue and to weigh the strength of each author's position. Let's read a second essay about studying popular culture.

Pop Culture Studies Turns 25

DAVID JACOBSON

In this essay, David Jacobson traces the relatively short history of a controversial—critics would say dubious—new field of academic study, popular culture studies, started by Ray Browne at Ohio's Bowling Green State University. "Pop Culture Studies Turns 25" was first published in the online magazine *Salon.com* in 1999. Jacobson is a San Francisco-based humorist and journalist whose work appears in such popular publications as *Salon.com, Esquire, Maxim, Details,* and *Life.*

THINKING AHEAD   Who first thought about studying popular culture? Why are scholars attracted to this area of study? What was the motivation? How academic can such study really be?

S omehow you expect Ray Browne to look a little bit more, you know, 1
radical. Maybe an earring as big as a migration tag or one of those Einstein quantum 'fros. After all, he's the godfather of popular culture studies; the founder and still editor in his emeritus[1] years of the *Journal of Popular Culture,* filled with dense analyses of slam-dancing, country music and computer games; the co-founder of the Popular Culture Association, whose 1,000-plus scholars annually present papers on everything from R.E.M. lyrics to porno flicks; the professor who was punted from the English department at Bowling Green State 25 years ago because he was "disgracing the university," but who promptly established the only graduate program and undergraduate major in popular culture in our galaxy; the guy whose career, by his own account, constituted "a kind of class-action suit against conventional points of view and fields of study in the humanities."

But there he is, in all his photos, stolid and blandly groomed, looking 2
like the office manager of some midsized widget[2] company. Yet his embodiment of the average Joe is utterly appropriate. After all, Browne's fundamental notion is that academia should pay the same kind of serious attention to the "common, everyday culture" of the masses—from sitcoms to bestsellers, from rap to lawn ornaments—as it traditionally has to elite stuff.

In the quarter century since Browne founded the popular culture move- 3
ment, it has had wide influence. But no other school has followed Bowling Green State and established a full department, not to mention a library bursting at the seams with romance novels and *Star Trek* memorabilia, and a busy press publishing the history of American skinheads and collections

---

[1]**emeritus:** Retired honorably.
[2]**widget:** A small mechanical device; a gadget.

of soap opera criticism. And even when it's studied under English or mass media, popular culture remains plenty controversial, mocked by the same media that feeds off it, derided by traditionalists hurling jeremiads[3] about pandering and raising important questions about what is worthy of academic attention.

When he boldly confronted tradition, Browne wasn't dabbling in the   4
era's academic anarchy so much as honoring his own roots and character. He was raised by a free-thinking agnostic father in the heart of the Bible Belt—a poor kid in rural Depression-era Alabama who never stopped questioning privilege. In the Army, he saw plenty of the stockade, because "I did not have enough 'Sirs' in my vocabulary," he writes in *Against Academia*, his brief memoir and history of popular culture studies. So it's not surprising that, while Browne cut his academic teeth on more traditional literature and folklore, he ultimately rebelled.

Browne was among the unwashed masses who poured through the col-   5
lege gates sprung open by the G.I. Bill.[4] Like later generations of women, minorities and gays, some of those newcomers noticed that their own culture, in this case that of the vast lower- and middle-class majority, was largely ignored by academics.

To the extent that popular culture was being examined back then, it   6
was through the telescopic lens of history or with the long, cold tongs of the social sciences. But Browne insisted on also looking at contemporary material and applying to it the kind of close, comparative analysis that had previously been reserved for highbrow culture.

Browne and his cohorts insisted that there were alternative and signifi-   7
cant aesthetics afoot below the esoteric radar of traditional scholars.

"People make choices as to what book to read or movie to see, and   8
just as regularly evaluate the experience: This was a good thriller, this is a great party song," writes BGSU pop culture professor Jack Santino in summarizing the program's "socio-aesthetic approach." "These aesthetic criteria are generally unarticulated; it is the task of the researcher to identify them."

Of course, the same folks in and out of academia who criticize post-   9
modern theorists for trivializing the object of study, reducing Shakespeare to a commodified text, also rip pop culture scholars for studying trivial objects, approaching video games as if they held the depths of Shakespeare.

In fact, Browne's most radical argument may be that you can teach   10
critical thinking and gain as good a liberal arts education using pop materials as with the old highbrow ones. "There's just as much glory and virtue in being a Madonna person as in being a Hemingway person," he says. "If you want to study culture through Madonna, it seems to me that's a marvelous opportunity."

---

[3]jeremiads: Expressions of mourning or sorrow (from the book of Jeremiah in the Bible).
[4]G.I. Bill: Congressional legislation that provides money for education and home loans to military veterans.

While a department of popular culture plopped down amid the corn-   11
fields south of Toledo might seem like an intellectual Christo project, it made
political sense. If Browne was the catalyst, the administration at relatively
unknown Bowling Green State was also open to an unorthodox department
that might put them on the academic map.

Popular culture studies rapidly grew in size and notoriety. And BGSU's   12
eight-member faculty now teaches at least 2,000 students a year. Eventually, it set up shop in an uncannily appropriate house built from a 1930s
Montgomery Ward[5] kit. The department was also distinguished by its high
profile in national and even international media attention.

"Some people were delighted by that and some people were embar-   13
rassed by that," says Michael Marsden, who worked with Browne at the
outset and is now dean of liberal arts at Northern Michigan University.

Marsden suffered his share of knocks as a popular culture scholar. After   14
being barraged with faculty criticism when he became a certified Miss Ohio
judge, in order to get "privileged information" for his research on beauty
pageants, he fought back. "I'll file a grievance if you're suggesting there's
some aspect of culture that's forbidden to be studied," he said.

A conference on "the history of roller coasters" at Ohio's famed Cedar   15
Point amusement park garnered accusations that scholars were "squan-
dering taxpayer money and doing foolish things," recalls Marsden. Two
decades later, "that roller coaster course" is still cited by critics knocking
the Bowling Green program.

Yet such criticism still leaves pop culture scholars nonplused. Why   16
should the study of a leisure activity necessarily be a leisurely activity itself?
Department veterans like Professor Christopher Geist say popular culture's
more outrageous, perhaps publicity-seeking past has cast an undeservedly
anti-intellectual image.

While the ever-rebellious Browne still asserts, "I have never come across   17
something that I find worthless," Geist demurs: "I'm not at all afraid to say
some TV rots the brain, but I want to understand why people are drawn
to it."

Given crisscrossing paths of intellectual discovery, given the rise first   18
of American studies, then mass media studies and, more recently, "cultural
studies," it's tough to know how much of pop culture in academia was
spurred by BGSU's program. But sometimes the effect is obvious. In the
1980s, Robert Thompson, a graduate student at Northwestern University,
wrote a paper analyzing the appeal of top TV programs that is a model
of pop culture scholarship. Drawing from studies that concluded that television viewing is characterized by inattention (up to two-thirds of viewers are engaged in other activities while watching), Thompson analyzed
then-top-rated shows like *The Love Boat* and found that they appealed to
their distracted viewers with lots of short scenes and reiterated exposition:

---

[5]**Montgomery Ward:** A department store chain no longer operating.

"A moment's viewing at any time—is enough to get a summary and an update."

As he concluded: "All the things that make these shows appear inartistic—superficial themes, limited character development, low intellectual demand—are really their strong points." [19]

Thompson's paper "*The Love Boat*: High Art on the High Seas" not only predicted the mega-popularity of multi-plot micro-scene shows like *ER* and *Seinfeld*, it launched his career as a pop culture scholar when it was published in Browne's *Journal of American Culture* in 1983. [20]

Looking back over 15 annual conferences of the Popular Culture Association he's attended, Thompson says: "There was room for fans, aficionados[6] and lunatics. To put it bluntly—it was more open and exciting intellectually than most of the established, traditional fields." [21]

Earning his doctorate in TV studies, Thompson founded the Center for the Study of Popular Television at Syracuse University. "I really want to do to TV what English professors did to novels," he says. "I want to engage our culture of choice, popular culture, television, with the same sincerity and seriousness." [22]

At BGSU, there's a bulletin board near the pop culture mailboxes where secretaries tack up media requests for commentary. The department can't afford to return all the long-distance calls. Still, they pour in, highlighting the media's strange relationship with pop culture studies. [23]

Journalists love having a bona fide professor lend guru-esque legitimacy to stories. Last year alone, Browne was quoted in the *Wall Street Journal* about shortening cycles of nostalgia and in the *Buffalo News* on criminality and pro athletes. In the *Los Angeles Times,* he discussed super-tiny cellular phones, and in the *Arizona Republic,* he dissected oversized restaurant servings. [24]

But when pop culture studies is itself the subject, then the media invariably stress the supposedly oxymoronic clang of the professorial and the popular. [25]

"Schlock Waves Felt across U.S. Campuses" went a typical *Dallas Morning News* headline (atop a *Washington Post* feature originally labeled "Pop Goes the Culture") about this year's meeting of the Popular Culture Association. The piece concludes: "They can't help themselves. After endless years in higher education, constantly trying to plumb meaning from turgid texts, they can't shut off when they hit the streets or turn on the tube." [26]

In other words: Academics should stick to old, high-falutin'[7] stuff or the mostly incomprehensible warrens of advanced science. Leave the popular and contemporary to non-egghead journalists who presumably won't over-plumb. [27]

Competitiveness aside, the media's knee-jerk knock on pop studies reflects a disconcerting reality. When the subjects are as opaque to the [28]

---

[6]**aficionados:** Enthusiastic fans.
[7]**high-falutin':** Thinking too highly of oneself; pretentious.

untutored as Milton or Dante, the average citizen has to assume that the academics are scoring fresh, brilliant points in their ivory tower[8] toils. But if the starting point is familiar, then folks can choose to see all the humanities as just a nutty game of intellectual free association.

Some articles in the *Journal of Popular Culture* are rich with insight. A recent piece on slam-dancing truly mines the subject, employing everything from Turner's social drama theory to field observation at nightclubs. It even traces the mosh pit's cultural appropriation by, of all places, Disney World. By contrast a piece in an earlier issue that asks, "If Aristotle were alive today, what books would he read, what television shows would he watch?" (Answers: Tony Hillerman and the defunct *Strange Luck*) just seems like cheesy dorm-room riffing.[9]   29

But whether or not pop culture scholarship is always profound and unique, the media's mockery merely regurgitates conventional wisdom. The *New York Times'* Russell Baker called Thompson's TV studies center at Syracuse "a vision of hell," insisting that TV is trash and that only time can reveal the useful material. Essentially, he implied that this is a supernatural, not an intellectual process: "Until the ages have spoken, [these shows] remain junk."   30

Despite such criticism from the popular press, these days it's tough to find purity in the opposing academic camps. Rebels like Browne and Marsden insist pop culture taught well must be historically and culturally comparative. And a traditionalist like Sanford Pinsker, Shadek Professor of Humanities at Franklin and Marshall College and journal editor of the *National Association of Scholars* ("dedicated to the restoration of intellectual substance"), teaches a course in American humor, drawing on magazine essays from Calvin Trillin and Garrison Keillor. Some might consider that pop studies.   31

Still, there are indelible differences. "You can find the heroic characteristics of *Beowulf* in Batman comics," concedes Pinsker. "But the differences are what's important. The literary texture. The depth of vision."   32

Pop culture scholars would counter that the similarities really are important in helping students make sense of daily life. As Marsden puts it, "Culture changes but it doesn't disappear. It's like energy that just seeks another form."   33

Both sides wheel out the big guns of economic loathing. Browne argues that academics have long traded in arcane knowledge that they have marketed as valuable. Pinsker sees pop culture as dumbing down curricula for mass markets: "Sheer economic facts have a lot more to do with this than Ray Browne ever did. What we need now in colleges are customers and what you do with customers is you make them happy: Here's a product you can sell."   34

---

[8]**ivory tower:** Removed from practical things.
[9]**riffing:** Composing without preparation.

Back at Bowling Green State, the Popular Culture Library reflects the   35
discipline's continued boom and maturation. "We're still taming the frontier here," says head librarian Alison Scott, riding herd on a half-million
items that include "a comprehensive collection of not only Harlequin
romances, but Silhouettes, Heart Songs, Zebras, Intrigues and Candle
Lights."

But the library's hubcap collection has been dispatched to a car mu-   36
seum. The miniature liquor bottles? Also gone. "We didn't have the cars, or
the liquor — or any useful information as to how to place them in a larger
cultural context," says Scott.

And even as Scott gets invited to "speak on the question of comic books   37
in academic libraries, pulp magazines[10] in research libraries," by traditional
librarians taking pop culture more seriously, she seeks to increase BGSU's
19th-century materials.

Scott sounds positively Pinsker-esque when she notes, "We have young   38
students who are just shocked when you infer that there was popular culture
before they were born. And these kids were born in 1980."

EXERCISING VOCABULARY

1. Record your own definition for each word below in your notebook.

punted (v.) (1)	barraged (v.) (14)
pandering (n.) (3)	garnered (v.) (15)
tongs (n.) (6)	nonplused (adj.) (16)
aesthetics (n.) (7)	demurs (v.) (17)
esoteric (adj.) (7)	turgid (adj.) (26)
unarticulated (adj.) (8)	regurgitates (v.) (30)
commodified (adj.) (9)	indelible (adj.) (32)
catalyst (n.) (11)	arcane (adj.) (34)

2. Jacobson notes that Ray Browne might look more radical if he had "one
   of those Einstein quantum 'fros" (para. 1). What is a " 'fro"? Why would
   this indicate a radical person? Why does Jacobson choose Einstein as
   his example?

3. The author uses the word *aesthetics* several times in this piece. What are
   aesthetics? What does Jack Santino mean when he says that Browne's
   popular culture program has a "socio-aesthetic approach" (para. 8)?

4. In paragraph 25, Jacobson refers to the "oxymoronic clang of the professorial and the popular." What is an oxymoron? How well does the
   term apply here? Why?

---

[10] **pulp magazines:** Magazines printed on poor-quality paper.

PROBING CONTENT

1. What has been ironic about the career of Ray Browne? What is ironic about the man himself? How was his frequent incarceration in a U.S. Army stockade a foreshadowing of his life in academia?

2. Explain the odd relationship between the media and popular culture. In what way does this odd relationship benefit both?

3. What did critics cite as their objections to a conference on the history of roller coasters? Why might these same objections be leveled at all popular culture studies?

4. According to Robert Thompson, what's the attraction of studying popular culture? How did Thompson become involved?

CONSIDERING CRAFT

1. Jacobson includes a number of paradoxes in this essay. What is a paradox? Reread paragraphs 3, 9, and 19. How does illuminating these paradoxes further the author's point of view?

2. In paragraph 11, Jacobson refers to the popular culture studies program at Bowling Green as being "like an intellectual Christo project." Who is Christo? What kinds of projects does he do? Why does the author choose this simile? How effective is this word choice?

WRITING PROMPTS

Responding to the Topic   As Michael Marsden notes, "Culture changes but it doesn't disappear. It's like energy that just seeks another form" (para. 33). In what ways does popular culture simply change forms to adapt to a new time and generation? Write an essay examining an example from your own lifetime of a cultural force that has changed form.

Responding to the Writer   As the academic dean of a midsize university, you've been asked by a group of faculty from several disciplines to support the addition of more popular culture courses to the university curriculum. Write a detailed response to this group either supporting or denying their request.

Responding to Multiple Viewpoints   Using evidence from the essays by Wee and Jacobson, write an essay explaining how each author would respond to the rise of interest in popular culture studies in the twenty-first century.

After the paired selections in each chapter, you will find "Drawing Connections" questions that ask you to compare and contrast how the authors of the paired selections explain their points of view on similar topics.

DRAWING CONNECTIONS

1. In "Pop Culture Studies Turns 25," David Jacobson quotes Sanford Pinsker, who argues that the study of pop culture is "dumbing down curricula for mass markets" (para. 34). In "Schlock Waves Felt across U.S. Campuses," Eric L. Wee reveals that one attraction of pop culture studies is that such classes bring in students and thus bring in tuition money. Do you think economics is a driving factor behind the study of popular culture? If this is true, why is it significant?

You'll move through the process of prereading, reading, and postreading described above for each reading selection that your instructor assigns. At the end of all the reading selections in a chapter are several additional features about that chapter's subject called "Wrapping Up." The first is called "Focusing on Yesterday, Focusing on Today." This feature shows you two images, such as a poster and a photograph. One image is an example of popular culture from the past; the other image is an example of contemporary popular culture. Both reflect some aspect of the chapter's subject. The accompanying questions will ask you to think and write about how these two images relate to each other.

Finally, at the end of each chapter are writing suggestions for developing your own essays called "Connecting to the Culture." These writing prompts encourage you to use your own experiences and observations to express your ideas about some aspect of the chapter's topic.

Now it's time to apply the ideas you have been developing while you were reading and answering questions. It's time to write about all the things you have to say.

Writing with a Difference

GETTING INTO WRITING

Writing is often not easy. There are probably a few hundred people for whom writing is as easy as bicycling is for Lance Armstrong. For most of us, though, writing is hard work. Like accurate golf shots, good writing takes practice.

For some of us, the hardest part is just getting started. There is something about blank sheets of paper or computer screens that is downright intimidating. So the first and most important thing is to put something on that paper or screen. If it loosens up your writing hand to doodle in the margins first, then doodle. But eventually (and sometime before 3 a.m. the day the paper is due), it's a good idea to get moving in the right direction.

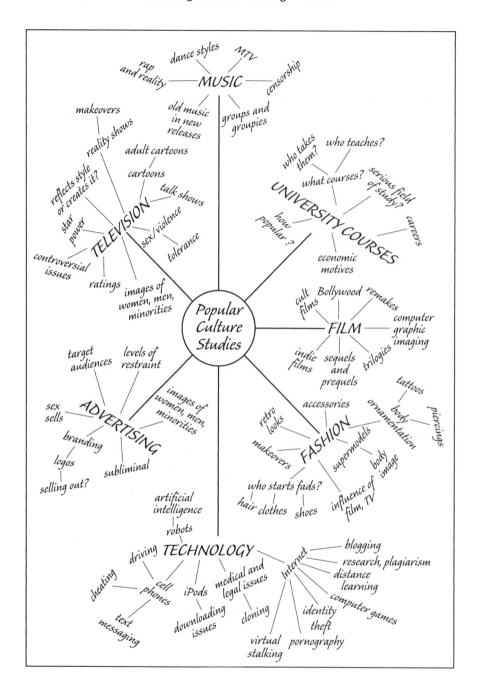

If your creative juices are a little slow to flow, try *brainstorming*. This simply means that you commit to paper whatever ideas related to your topic pop into your head. You don't evaluate them. You just get them down on paper. You don't organize them, reflect on them, or worry about spelling them correctly. You just write them down. There are several popular ways to brainstorm. Lots of people like to do *outlines,* with or without the proper Roman numerals. This method lets you list ideas vertically. Writers who think less in straight lines may want to try *clustering*, also called *webbing*. This is a lot like doodling with intent. Write your subject in the center of your blank page, and circle it. Draw lines radiating out from the center, and at the end of each line write some other words related to your subject. Each of these spokes can have words radiating from it, too. Let's return to our sample paired essays. If a student were brainstorming to write an essay about studying popular culture, one web might look like the one found on page 20.

Planning Purpose, Audience, and Attitude

Before trying to impose any kind of structure or judgment on her random bursts of thought, a good writer has to consider several important things: (1) Why am I writing this paper? (2) For whom am I writing this paper? (3) What is my own attitude about this subject, and how much do I want this attitude reflected in the tone of my paper?

Let's think about your purpose for writing a paper. You think, "I am writing this because I am in this composition class, and the professor said to write an essay." Okay, true, but there's more to purpose than that. Are you hoping to entertain your readers? Inform them? Persuade them to take some action or change an opinion? Your answers to these questions determine how you approach your subject and develop your paper.

Something else that determines how you approach your writing is the intended audience. Who are your readers? How old are they? What are their interests? What do they already know about your topic, and what will you need to explain? Why should this group of people care about your topic? What attitudes do they already hold about this issue? The language you choose is affected by the audience that you expect to reach. An essay about rap music that you are writing for your peers won't need all the explanations that the same essay would need if you were writing it for forty-year-olds.

This is a good time to mention the level of language expected in your writing. How formal or informal should the language be? After all, you're going to be writing about popular culture. However, this does not mean that "street language" is appropriate except in situations like quoting dialogue or song lyrics. All through this first chapter, we've been focusing on popular culture as an academic subject for study, and you're taking an academic course for college credit. *Academic*, in this sense, means adhering to a certain standard or set of rules—in this case, the conventions of standard

English. Maintaining academic language does not mean using large words or long sentences simply because of their length. It does mean applying everything you know about written communication to make your thoughts and ideas come across clearly and accurately to your intended audience—your peers and your professors. Slang or foreign phrases may be appropriate in some of your writing as examples or illustrations of a point, but the language of your essays should be standard English. Remember that poor writing, in this case nonstandard English, obscures thought. Good writing will go a long way toward persuading your audience that you are someone worth listening to.

Once you have determined your purpose and your audience, you are ready to determine the tone of your essay. What is your own attitude toward your subject? To what extent should your writing reflect this attitude to best achieve your purpose for the audience you have identified? Do you want to be completely serious about your subject? Will injecting some humor make your audience more receptive to your writing?

HOOKING THE READER

Once you have some ideas about why you are writing, who your audience is, and your attitude about your subject, the next step is to write a draft. How do you start? Some order has to be made of this potentially useful chaos. Good essays begin with good introductions, so we'll talk about that first. But remember: The introduction doesn't have to be written at this point. Some very good authors write the whole essay and then write the introduction last. That's fine. The introduction has to be at the beginning eventually, but no law says it has to be there in the draft. Too many good essays remain locked in the creators' heads because their writers can't think up an introduction and so never start at all.

At whatever point you are ready to write your introduction, keep in mind one essential thing: If you don't get your audience's attention right away, you lose them. Even though the students who are assigned to read your paper for peer editing will keep reading, and the professor who is paid to read it will do so, other readers need to be involved, or hooked, before they will be receptive to your viewpoint and your ideas. Advertisers figure they have only a precious few seconds to hook you as a potential customer, so they pull out all the stops to grab your attention before you flip that page in the magazine or punch that remote control. As a writer, you have to pull out all the stops to hook your readers. What really nails a reader's attention? This depends on the reader, but some tried-and-true methods work on many readers:

1. First, you might start with a very brief story, also called an *anecdote*. We all love human interest and personal narrative. Make your readers want more information, want answers, and feel curious about what else you'll say.

2. Interesting quotations make good openings, especially if they are startling or are attributed to someone famous. As quotations, though, dictionary definitions are rarely effective as introductions. Statistics can be useful if they are really amazing.

3. A thought-provoking or controversial question can be a good way to get a reader's attention.

IDENTIFYING A THESIS

Besides catching your reader's attention, your introduction may perform another important task: The introduction may house your *thesis statement*. This quick but thorough statement of the main point of the paper may be the first or last sentence of the first paragraph, but it could also be the last sentence of the essay. Where the thesis is located depends on your purpose for writing, your audience, and the effect you wish to create. If you begin with one of the three attention-getters we've mentioned, you'll want to follow up your brief narrative, quotation, or question with a few general statements about your topic, gradually narrowing the focus until you reach your specific thesis, possibly at the end of the first or second paragraph. If you have identified your audience as receptive to your attitude about your subject, then you may choose to state the thesis early in your paper and follow with supporting points that will have your readers nodding in agreement. However, if your purpose is to persuade an audience that is not so likeminded, then you will want to offer convincing proof first and present your thesis later in the paper when readers have already begun to agree with your opinion.

Wherever it occurs, a good thesis can go a long way toward making your essay effective. How do you recognize or create a good thesis statement? First, a good thesis is not simply a fact. Facts don't allow for a lot of fascinating development; they just are. A good thesis expresses the writer's point of view on a topic about which more than one valid opinion exists. Your thesis must be focused. Remember that there's a difference between a subject and a thesis. A subject or topic is what the essay is about—for example, Barbie dolls. A thesis statement expresses the author's attitude about that subject: "Barbie dolls are an expression of society's misguided and demoralizing view of ideal womanhood," or "Barbie dolls are a positive influence on young girls because they indicate the wide variety of career choices available to women today." Everything in your essay must clearly relate to the development of this thesis or main idea.

SUPPORTING THE THESIS

The development of your thesis forms the body of your paper. The major points you wish to make about your thesis become the *topic sentences*, or one-sentence summaries, for various paragraphs. What information do you use for support? Where do you find this information? How much support is enough, and how much is too much?

All the support that anyone can apply to any idea fits into one of two categories: The information is gathered either from personal experience or from a source outside the self. Personal experience knowledge is whatever the writer has gathered through eyewitness encounters in which he has participated directly and personally. Outside source knowledge explains how we know everything else we know. Such outside source knowledge is often informal. We know that it would be painful to fall down a flight of stairs even though we might never have had such an experience and never looked in a medical book to see which body parts would likely be damaged.

However, such outside source knowledge may also be formal and deliberately sought, as when we look up the salaries of professional athletes in *Sports Illustrated* or schedule an interview with the football coach to talk about whether college athletes should be paid. In your writing, you may find it helpful to refer to ideas expressed in the essays in this text. In any case, you must avoid intellectual theft, called plagiarism. Carefully cite the source of the material you are using and put quotation marks around any words taken directly from someone else, whether they are in written or oral form and whether they are expressed in a few words or a few sentences. You can acknowledge sources by using any one of several styles of documentation. Your instructor will let you know which system to use. In the back of this book, you'll find a section called "Evaluating and Documenting Sources" that can help you determine the validity of sources and one way to document them correctly.

ORGANIZING THE CONTENT

The best way to arrange supporting details for your thesis is the one that is best for your purpose and your audience. Some essays begin with a forceful point of support on the first page, and other essays start softly and work up to a big crescendo of convincing examples or argument near the end. You might try sketching out your pieces of support in various arrangements on a sheet of paper to see which order feels most comfortable. Rarely will only one arrangement work. You are looking for whatever organization best moves along your thesis and seems most natural to you.

CONNECTING THE PIECES

The best supporting information in the world won't move your thesis forward if the parts of the paper aren't unified so that your reader can follow your train of thought. Think of the paragraphs of your essay as links in a chain: Each link must be equally strong, no link can be open-ended, and each one must be connected to the link above and the link below. Strong transitional words or phrases can smoothly carry the thesis idea and the reader from one topic sentence and one paragraph to the next one. One way to facilitate this transition process is to use words like *however, nevertheless, furthermore, consequently,* and *in addition.* Another effective transition is to identify a key word or brief phrase in the last sentence of a paragraph and then repeat that word or phrase in the first sentence of the next paragraph. Try to avoid overusing simple and obvious transitions like *first, next,* and *finally* because too many simple transitions may make your ideas seem simplistic.

ARRIVING AT A CONCLUSION

Before you know it, you're ready to arrive at your conclusion. The most important rule about conclusions is to make sure there is one. Do not simply repeat something you have already said, which may lead your readers to believe that you don't respect their intelligence. But do remember that your reader best retains whatever she reads last. The conclusion is your chance to make sure the points you've raised really stick. Therefore, make sure that your main idea — your thesis — is central to your concluding paragraph. Look at how you stated the thesis earlier, and word it a little differently in your conclusion. Some of the same advice that we discussed about introductions applies here: End on a memorable note. Make your essay the one the instructor is still pondering on the ride home.

TITLING THE PAPER AND OTHER FINAL STEPS

If you haven't titled your paper already, you'll want to add a title now. A good title is not just a statement of the subject. It sheds light on which aspects of the subject are covered and how the subject is approached. Like an introduction, a good title also catches a reader's interest. Titles usually are not complete sentences.

Take time to present your paper well. You've worked hard on the ideas. Don't minimize the effect with sloppy margins, inaccurate page numbers, and other unusual printer misdeeds. Remember that your peers and your instructor are evaluating what you have produced, not your intentions.

REVISING THE PAPER

After all this work, surely the paper is ready for the instructor. Not yet. What you have now is a first draft—a fairly complete first draft, admittedly, but still a first draft. You may think it's only the not-so-good writers who go through numerous drafts, but you'd be wrong: Good writers write and rewrite and revise and rewrite. Grammar and spelling errors that seem unimportant by themselves may distract your reader from your carefully prepared chain of ideas. Thankfully, there is a logical pattern to the revising part of the writing process, too.

Start revising with the big things. It's tempting to spell-check first because it's easy and concrete, but that's a mistake for two reasons: (1) Spell-checking is editing, not revising, and (2) You may decide to delete two of the paragraphs you just spent time spell-checking. Ask yourself some hard questions. Does each paragraph contribute to the development of your thesis? If you find a paragraph that doesn't fit under that thesis umbrella, you have only two options: Delete the paragraph, or rewrite the thesis statement to make it broad enough to accommodate the additional material. Are the degree of explanation and the level of language appropriate for your audience? Does each support paragraph carry its own weight, or do some of them seem skimpy and underdeveloped? Does your essay accomplish the purpose you established?

Read the last sentence of each paragraph and the first sentence of the next paragraph. Are your transitions smooth enough? Your reader should get a sense of moving up an escalator, not a sense of being bounced down a staircase, landing with a thud on each topic sentence.

EDITING THE PAPER

Now you are ready to do some editing. Look at the sentences within each paragraph. Are fragments masquerading as sentences? This is a good time to find a quiet spot and read your essay aloud. Once two senses—sight and sound—are involved, you have twice as many opportunities to find anything that's not right yet. It's fine to run the spell-checker at this stage, but if your problem is with usage—like using *to* when you mean *too*—then the spell-checker cannot help you. It's best to keep a dictionary ready and be your own spell-checker. Keep a grammar handbook handy to consult when you are unsure about matters like usage, punctuation, and sentence structure. Remember that your instructor has office hours and that your college or university probably has a tutoring or writing center where you can get help with revising and editing.

PEER EDITING

Once you have completed your own initial revising and editing, your instructor may suggest that your class practice peer editing. No matter how good a writer you are, having someone else take a fresh look at your writing can be beneficial. Here are some general suggestions for specific things to evaluate when you edit a classmate's paper:

1. Read the first paragraph and stop reading. How interested are you in continuing to read? What about the introduction grabs your attention? If you wouldn't be the least bit disappointed if someone took this paper away from you right now, your classmate needs a better introduction. What can you suggest?

2. Continue reading through the first page of the paper. First write down the essay's subject, and then write down the main idea. If you can't find the thesis, make a note of that. If you are unsure of the thesis, write down what you think it might be. Take a minute now to check with the author. If you have identified the thesis correctly, that's fine. If you have identified the wrong message as the thesis, help the author clarify the main idea before you continue reading.

3. Continue reading. Is support for the thesis adequate? Are the examples specific enough? Detailed enough? Frequent enough? If not, make some suggestions. Is the thesis supported to your satisfaction? Why or why not?

4. What is the writer's attitude toward his subject? To what extent is the tone appropriate for the audience? How does the tone advance the writer's purpose or detract from it? When are changes in tone used appropriately or inappropriately?

5. Are there adequate transitions between sentences and paragraphs? Remember, this should feel like a smooth escalator ride. What does the writer do to make sure ideas flow smoothly throughout the paper? Can you easily follow the forward progression of the author's train of thought? If not, suggest some possible revisions.

6. Complete your reading of the essay. What about the final paragraph makes you feel a sense of completion? Is the essay finished, or does it just stop? How effective is the conclusion? What is memorable about it? What would make it stronger?

7. Review the paper now for mistakes in spelling or usage. Make a note of repetitive mistakes, and comment on any awkward points of grammar. Don't attempt to note each error. Be especially alert for the kinds of errors that disrupt the flow of a paper, like fragments, run-ons, comma splices, or sentences that don't make sense.

8. Return the paper to its author and discuss your notes. Leave your notes with the author so that he or she can use them in the final stages of revising and editing. Evaluate the input you have received about your own paper. Resist the urge to be defensive. You are not obligated to make every change suggested, but you should honestly evaluate the comments and use those that seem justified to improve your work.

GAINING FROM THE EFFORT

Writing is like almost anything else: The more you practice, the better you get. We've said the same thing about reading earlier: People who read often and actively read well. The same is true of writing. For some people, writing is fun. For other people, writing is anything but fun. In either case, good writing is hard work. But perhaps no other skill except speech says so much about you to others and has so much to do with how far and how fast you advance in your career. Writing is not just a college skill; writing is a life skill. Your willingness to better your writing ability is directly related to the impression you create, the salary you can expect to earn, and the level of advancement in life you can expect to attain.

Forget the five-paragraph boxes your writing may have been restricted to before now. Remember that formulas work well in math but cramp your style in writing. Swear off procrastination and karate-chop writer's block. There are no topics in this text that you don't already know something about. You have significant things to say. Start writing them down.

A SAMPLE STUDENT ESSAY

Here is a draft of a student essay written in response to a writing prompt associated with the two sample essays in this chapter. Keep in mind that all the writing prompts can be approached from a number of different perspectives. This example reflects one student's decisions about purpose, audience, tone, and writing style.

> **CONNECTING TO THE CULTURE** Ray Browne asserts in "Pop Culture Studies Turns 25," "There's just as much glory and virtue in being a Madonna person as in being a Hemingway person." And Eric L. Wee comments that attendees at the Popular Culture Conference believe that "the study of popular culture . . . is the future." Write an essay in which you either support or argue against the study of popular culture as an academic pursuit. Be sure to include the reasons that popular culture study does or does not merit the time and effort of professors and students and how such study, whether undertaken or avoided, might impact a university education.

The Importance of Reflecting on Popular Culture

ANABEL F. HART

With millions of students enrolled in related classes, popular culture studies are just that--popular. Despite their success among members of my generation, such studies are still often thought of as unworthy of critical analysis in the classroom. In other words, many scholars would not see any value in comparing the public outrage that Janet Jackson's "wardrobe malfunction" triggered to the outrage that Michelangelo sparked by leaving his statue of David totally nude. Who knew in the 1950s that Elvis's controversial gyrating hips would start a movement that continues to this day, more than fifty years later? That is why popular culture studies are important. They allow students and professors to gain new perspective and to reflect on the society in which they live.

In "Schlock Waves Felt across U.S. Campuses," Eric L. Wee states, "There was a time when teaching Plato at Oxford was considered radical. English literature as a field of study was considered avant-garde on American campuses in the 19th century" (para. 7). Such a statement reveals how substantially times have changed and simultaneously demonstrates how every culture experiences its own shock waves of scandal and controversy. Plato stirred up his own controversy with his unorthodox teachings, yet his ideas and ethics withstood the test of time.

Here's a more popular example: When professors ponder cultural genius, the poetry and plays of William Shakespeare often surface. Like Plato, Shakespeare's works have been studied and interpreted worldwide for centuries, and Shakespeare's understanding of human character and his insight into the culture of his time have led to his wide-ranging appeal around the world. In addition, Shakespeare was knowledgeable about other areas of study. His allusions to the Bible, art, law, politics, sports, and history made him popular in his day among a wide cross-section of society. Despite Shakespeare's ability to perceive and explain such things, scholars believe that he was never professionally schooled in these subjects. Such talent makes this author an opportune historical figure to study. He is considered by many to be the greatest poet and dramatist in the history of the English language, and his astonishing popularity is reflected in classrooms around the world. Today, Shakespeare's popularity, not only among students but also among the general public, is further reflected in the many modern dramatic and film adaptations of his works.

However, that does not mean that there aren't prodigious thinkers living today that students may find even more compelling and relevant to their own life experiences. Authors, directors, musicians, and even advertisers have something important to say. Take the novelist J. K. Rowling, for instance. She, like Shakespeare, has won the respect of the masses from Brazil to Japan with her best-selling series of books following the life of a troubled teenaged wizard, Harry Potter. In Rowling's early descriptions, Harry is an awkward boy, plagued by the memory of his troubled past. Throughout the texts, he faces difficulties that many readers, especially young ones, can relate to. In a way, this gives Rowling the advantage over Shakespeare. We students can more easily relate to this contemporary artist who is familiar with the society in which we live. I know I'm more comfortable discussing the virtue of humility in The Sorcerer's Stone than I am talking about either Platonic ideals or notions of familial love and justice in Shakespeare's King Lear.

In "Pop Culture Studies Turns 25," author David Jacobson questions those critics who "rip" popular culture scholars for daring to deemphasize "highbrow" works of art like Shakespeare's plays in favor of close analysis of "unworthy," lowbrow topics like video gaming. Even though such careful study might have once been reserved for authors like Plato and Shakespeare, Jacobson seems to agree with Dr. Ray Browne, the "godfather" of the pop culture studies movement, that "you can teach critical thinking and gain as good a liberal arts education using pop materials as with the old highbrow ones" (para. 10). The same people who disparage the study of "lowbrow subjects" like video games may be uncomfortable with professors who endorse the Harry Potter novels as meaningful literature. However, students today find Rowling's exploration of moral and ethical issues, rather than Shakespeare's, more relevant to their own lives.

Despite Eric L. Wee's concerns, popular culture studies do much more than "bring in bodies" and "tuition dollars" (para. 11). Analysis of the society in which we live will help students gain a better perspective and understanding of the world, resulting in a richer and more relevant educational experience. Is that not the human ideal? Scientists created the scientific method, a means of thinking that orbits around human discovery, in order to apply scientific thinking to everyday situations. Dr. Ray Browne insists that popular culture not be studied in a vacuum. Such an educational philosophy helps professors and students alike reach the goal of all successful teaching: to understand the world around us.

Popular culture studies do merit the time of both the teacher and the learner. By reflecting upon the ever-changing society around us, we gain not only a better understanding of cultural changes and of people's reactions to them, but ultimately a deeper understanding of ourselves. As Ray Browne says in "Pop Culture Studies Turns 25," "There's just as much glory and virtue in being a Madonna person as in being a Hemingway person. . . . If you want to study culture through Madonna, it seems to me that's a marvelous opportunity" (para. 10). It seems that way to me and to millions of other college students, as well.

Deconstructing Media
Analyzing an Image

2

We are a visual culture. We see thousands of visual images every day, yet we pay attention to only a few of them. Vision is our primary way of receiving information from the world around us. There is so much to see that we filter out what we don't need or what doesn't grab our immediate attention. Movie posters try to convince us to see a summertime block-buster, magazine ads try to lure us into buying a particular product, artists and photographers try to get us to feel a certain emotion, while billboards demand our attention no matter where we turn. All visual media compete to send us their messages. The choices we make and the things we buy, even how we perceive and value ourselves, are all affected by the images that are presented to us. You'll discover as you work through this book that American popular culture relies heavily on visual representation; even music is represented visually through the use of music videos. In this text you will see a number of the kinds of visual images you encounter every day—advertisements, photographs, movie stills, comic strips, and cartoons. Learning to "read" these images and discovering what responses they are intended to provoke in us is an important part of understanding our culture.

The Message of Media

Let's picture an imaginary advertisement. The woman is beautiful and graceful. The man appears wealthy and sophisticated. The white sand beach is wide and private; the sparkling blue water is cool and clear; tropical sun-shine bathes the scene. The car in the foreground is a gold-colored luxury convertible. But why aren't the car's tires getting mired in the sand? Why aren't the woman's white shoulders sunburning? In reality, these might be issues you or I would have to think about, but this ad has nothing to do with reality. This is advertising—that shadow world that separates us from our money by luring us into popular mythology.

What mythology? Here's how it goes: Unpopular? Popularity is as easy as changing the brand of jeans you wear. Unsuccessful? You must drive the wrong kind of car. Unattractive? Just wear a new shade of lipstick. Misunderstood? It's not your personality; it's your poor cellular service.

We are in general a well-educated society. Why, then, are we so easily misled? Why do we buy the myths that advertising sells? We buy—and buy and buy and buy—because we desperately want the myths of advertising to be true.

For some time now, our culture has been as visual as we are verbal. We absorb images faster than our brains can process data, but the images remain imprinted in our minds. All those images influence our thoughts and the decisions we make in ways we may never have considered. From the time that we begin to learn to read, we are encouraged to recognize the power of words—to interact with a text, to weigh it for prejudice, to appreciate it with discernment. But images are as powerful as words, and they communicate ideas and impressions that we, as thinking individuals, should *question,* just as we question what we are told or what we read. How can the same skills we use to read be applied to "reading" visual images like billboards, photographs, political cartoons, drawings, paintings, and images on television, movie, and computer screens?

ASKING THE RIGHT QUESTIONS

Effectively deconstructing media images depends on taking those images apart and asking the right questions.

1. What do I see when I look at the image?

     How is color used?

     What is the significance of the layout?

     What are the relative sizes of the objects that compose the image?
2. What is the role of text (any language that accompanies the image)?
3. Where did I first see this image?
4. Who is the target audience?
5. What is the purpose of this image?
6. What is its message?

The easiest questions help solve the mystery of the more difficult ones, so let's think about the obvious. What is really there to be seen when you look at the photo, the ad, or the cartoon strip?

TAKING THE IMAGE APART

Color   Although the images you see in this textbook are reproduced in black and white, most of the media representations around you make careful use of color. When you encounter an image, is your eye drawn to a certain spot on a page by the strength of a color, by the contrast of colors, or by the absence of color? How is color being used to catch your eye and hold your focus on a certain part of the visual?

Layout   Closely related to the use of color is the layout of objects on a page. What relationships are established by how close or how far apart objects or people are placed? What is your eye drawn to first? Sometimes the focal point will be right in the center of the ad or photo and therefore obvious to the viewer. At other times, the object the composer of the image most wants you to appreciate, the one that is central to the image's message, may be easily overlooked. Because English is read from top to bottom and left to right, we tend to look first to the upper left-hand corner of a page. That spot is often used to locate the composer's focal point. At other times the eye may come to rest at the bottom right-hand corner of a page.

Size   The relative size of the people and objects in an image may also help the designer communicate his or her message. A viewer's eye may be drawn to the largest object first, but that may not be where the message lies. To help you see how the relative size of objects can communicate a strong message, look at the photograph titled "To Have and To Hold" in this chapter (p. 35).

Text   Deciding whether a visual image should be accompanied by text or written language is another significant consideration for the photographer, artist, or ad designer. Sometimes the image may be so powerful on its own that text would be an irritating distraction. Think about the photograph of the Marines raising the flag on Iwo Jima during World War II or the shot of the three firefighters raising the flag at Ground Zero in New York City after 9/11. These images speak for themselves. When text is included, other factors have to be examined. How much text is there? Where is it located? How big is the type size? Is more than one font used? Does the text actually deliver the message? Does it enhance the message? Is part of the text a familiar slogan associated with the product like McDonald's "I'm Lovin' It!"? Is a well-known and easily recognized logo or symbol like the Nike Swoosh part of the text? All of these considerations hinge on the importance of the text to the overall message of the visual image.

Location   To properly evaluate a visual image, the discerning viewer must know where the image appeared. Did you see this image on a billboard? On the side of a bus? In the pages of a magazine? Images in *Smithsonian* magazine will have a different purpose than those in *Maxim*. The location of a visual will help you determine the intended target audience.

Target Audience   For whom is this image intended? What are the characteristics of this target audience of viewers? What is the age range? What is their socioeconomic status? What work do they do? Where and how do they live? All this information must be taken into account by the photographer, artist, or designer if the image is to convey its intended message. For example, an ad for baby formula would most likely not hit its target audience if it were placed in *Rolling Stone,* and an ad for a jeweled navel ring in *House Beautiful* probably would not find a receptive audience.

Purpose   Every image has a purpose. If the image is an advertisement on a billboard, on a Web site, or in a magazine, the most obvious question to ask is "What is this ad for?" In today's ads, the answer isn't always readily apparent. The actual object being sold may be a tiny speck on the page or even completely absent. In the imaginary ad described earlier, the product might be the woman's alluring sundress, the man's starched khakis and sports shirt, or the convertible. Or maybe it's an ad for an exotic vacation spot. If the image is a photograph, its purpose may be to commemorate a special moment, object, or person or to illustrate an event or feeling. If the image is a cartoon, its purpose may be to entertain or to make a political or social statement through humor.

Message   "What is the purpose of this image?" may be the most obvious question to ask, but it isn't the most important one. The most important question is "What is the message of this image?" That's a very different question. This question challenges the viewer to probe beyond the obvious visual effects — color, shading, size of objects, text or lack thereof, relative placement of objects — to ferret out the message. This message always seeks to evoke a response from the viewer: Wear this, drink this, click here, think this way, feel this emotion, affirm this value. Using all the information you have assembled by answering the earlier questions, answer this one.

Now you are prepared to deconstruct or "read" the visual images that form such a large part of our popular culture.

READING VISUAL IMAGES

Let's practice with two different types of images: a photograph and a cartoon strip.

Look at the image on page 35 and consider some questions. What do you see in this photograph by Jean-Christian Bourcart? What event is being captured? What do the sizes and positions of the two figures indicate about their relationship? How many modern couples would find this pose an appealing one to place in their wedding albums?

How is color used?   You are seeing this photograph in black and white, but it's easy for your mind to fill in the color here — green grass and greener trees. Even in color, however, the two principal figures would be largely black and white. The white dress of the bride and the black formal wear on the groom let us know right away what event we are viewing. Here the lack of bright color works to emphasize the serious moment being captured on film.

To Have and To Hold

What is the significance of the layout?   Think about the layout and composition of this photograph. Why did Bourcart place the couple outdoors? Perhaps he used a natural setting to reinforce the notion that a wedding is a "natural" cultural ritual. Practically speaking, this shot would have been difficult to frame indoors; the relative depth perception of the two figures is what makes the composition unique.

What is the relative size of the objects that compose the image?   In this particular photo, relative size is the most important feature. Things are not equal. The groom is front and center, dominant, in control. The tiny, fragile doll bride held in his hand resembles the decorative figurine often found atop a wedding cake.

What is the role of text?   No text accompanied the original photograph. The original title in French was "Le Plus Beau Jour de la Vie," which means "the most beautiful day of one's life."

What was the original location of the image?   This photograph appeared in *Doubletake* magazine. Certainly the source is appropriate, since, after the first casual glance, the viewer's eye locks onto the two figures in their unusual pose.

Who is the target audience?   The target audience might include future brides and bridegrooms, anyone interested in photography, or an even wider group of people who are intrigued by the unusual ways that the eye conveys messages about the world and the culture around us.

What is the purpose of this image?   At first glance, this photograph may have been taken to capture an unusual image. Perhaps its intent is to preserve, in a whimsical way, one significant day in the life of a couple. Many families have albums full of wedding photos. But perhaps this photographer had something more serious in mind.

What is the message?   What is the photographer really trying to accomplish? Certainly he has chosen an off-balance approach to arrest our attention. But more is being said. Perhaps Bourcart wishes to tell us what he believes marriage offers young couples. Does he wish to make a statement about male-female relationships? On a day that seems perfect, is there an indication that life won't be "happily ever after" for this bride and groom?

Next let's work on deconstructing a very different type of visual representation, a comic strip.

What do you see when you look at this image?   With a comic strip, the viewer's eyes must travel left to right across the panels, focusing on a number of frames, each of which may offer a visual, text, or both. Often the strip's creator relies on a steady group of repeat readers who over time have learned to appreciate the personalities of the strip's characters and the subtle messages they deliver from the writer.

How is color used?   Although most strips appear in black and white in daily newspapers, many appear in color on Sundays, giving readers a chance to learn more about the characters and the strip's designer. This *Mallard Fillmore* strip appeared in a Sunday newspaper with minimal but effective colorization. Against a light blue background, the duck is green with a yellow bill, and the soda can is a lighter shade of green. We know it's a Sprite can because Mallard says so. The human finger is peach-colored.

What is the significance of the layout?   To some extent, the layout of a cartoon strip is prescribed: It is a series of panels. But the artist still has a great deal of flexibility with layout within the various panels. The most interesting feature in this layout is the shifting view we have of Mallard the duck. At first we see his face, but he turns to the side when addressed by the finger, and by the middle of the strip he has his back to us. We viewers are made to feel outside the conversation, as though we are merely eavesdropping. By the last two panels, Mallard has turned his face to the readers, making us a part of the scam he's pulling.

What is the relative size of the objects that compose the image?   It's certainly no accident that the clearly recognizable "invisible finger of marketing" is as large as Mallard's head in every panel except the final one, when Mallard takes control of the situation. From time to time, as consumers we may feel "under the thumb" of advertising; this comic strip offers a graphic rendering of that concept.

What is the role of text?   As in many comic strips, the text here is crucial to the message. Generally, comic strips rely much more on text than ads or photographs do. The first significant language issue arises in the title of this strip. Mallard Fillmore's name is a play on the name of an American president, Millard Fillmore, whose term of office reflected his own rather lack-luster personality. A mallard is actually one type of duck. We'll pursue the rest of the text when we examine the message of the strip.

What was the original location of this image?   This comic strip is syndicated and appears regularly in many newspapers across the country.

Who is the target audience?   The target audience of this comic strip is not children. Although the duck might catch their eye, the level of sophistication of the humor clearly places this strip beyond their understanding. And certainly a degree of sophistication is required to grasp the irony here. The reader needs to know something about popular culture: What's a Sprite? Nikes? Lugz? What's hip-hop? What's an icon? Knowing that the U.S. government at times pays farmers not to grow certain crops such as soybeans in order not to flood the market and drive prices down explains the fifth panel. Bruce Tinsley, the strip's writer, is not expecting everyone to agree with his opinion, but his target audience is every consumer who is subject to advertising's wiles.

What is the purpose of this image?   Because this is a cartoon strip, we expect it to be entertaining or humorous. To determine if that is its only purpose, let's think about the message.

What is the message?   So what is Tinsley trying to say? Here is an ordinary duck, who might as well be you, the reader, attempting to drink a popular beverage with a powerful marketing firm behind it. According to the finger of advertising, the entire ad campaign designed to elevate Sprite to a new level of "cool" or popularity could be devastated if Sprite were to be associated with this quite ordinary duck. The duck, however, represents the consumer, and he's not as dumb as he looks. He asks to be paid not to harm Sprite's fledgling coolness: He wants to be paid not to drink it. But he plans to take the cash, succumb to the lure of advertising—and buy Nikes or Lugz. What a cycle! What a message! Manufacturers pay advertisers to manufacture an image for a product, and that image alone—not the product—often fuels our wants and loosens our wallets.

WRITING ABOUT AN IMAGE

Using these same questions we have been asking, let's see what one student has to say about decoding a third kind of media, an advertisement.

Monumental Taste: Using Patriotism to Market Diet Coke

Robert E. Arthur

What do I see as I flip through a magazine and come across this advertisement? Mount Tastemore, South Dacola, a revamped version of Mount Rushmore, where the fathers of our nation's history--Washington, Jefferson, Roosevelt, and Lincoln--are all smiling back at me, seeming to be very pleased with the beverage they are holding. There are people lined up at the bottom, many dressed in our nation's colors of red, white, and blue, staring up and pointing excitedly at the iconic landmark. One man, dressed in a blue sweatshirt, is holding a can of the ever-wonderful diet Coke in one hand and pointing eagerly skyward with the other. I focus on the four presidents smiling out at me, all of whom seem to be offering me their diet Cokes. I see the advertisers' way of promoting the cola by revising one of our nation's most recognizable and sacred landmarks. My eyes then drift upward toward the title, "Monumental Taste," which provides a further explanation of the advertisement by its play on words. After being subconsciously persuaded by the ad's graphics, my attention shifts to the text underneath the visual, which reinforces the ad's message, "Mt. Tastemore, South Dacola--the most refreshing tourist attraction in America," and the play on words of the diet Coke logo, "Just for the monumental taste of it!" Finally, my eyes move to the order form for the Special Offer mentioned at the bottom of the page and the legalese that accompanies it. I've been hooked, and this is exactly what the advertisers want.

The advertisement's color scheme not only attracts the eye of the consumer but also furthers the patriotic theme in the ad. The red in the soda cans, the clear blue sky above the presidents' heads, and the large white letters spelling out "Monumental Taste" above the landmark add to this red, white, and blue theme. Also, the adoring spectators lined up at the bottom, many sporting our nation's colors, seem entranced by the remarkable landmark. These colors were wisely chosen by the advertisement's designers. In the U.S. flag, white stands for purity, while red signifies valor and hardiness (and coincidentally is used in many restaurants because it is an appetite stimulant). Finally, blue represents justice, perseverance, and vigilance. Why not showcase these meaningful patriotic colors when trying to sell "all-American" products like diet Coke? After all, few consumers who see this ad will remember that the U.S. government took possession of Mount Rushmore and the surrounding Black Hills region from the Sioux Indians in 1877, only three years after gold was discovered there. However, that isn't what the advertisers want the potential buyer to reflect on here.

While the colors of an advertisement are often responsible for its initial impact on the reader, the text provided with the visual plays a key role in the message to the consumer.

The text, especially the title, "Monumental Taste," provides a better explanation of the ad, using an adjective with both literal and figurative meanings to get the point across in a humorous way. Viewers of all ages can easily recognize the double meaning of the phrase and also pick up on the opinion that not only is this soda's taste remarkable, it's good enough for Honest Abe and his peers, too. Of all of the inhabitants of Mount Tastemore, Lincoln is the only one holding a caffeine-free diet Coke, which is most likely a play on his monumental role in the freeing of thousands of African slaves. The can he is holding is also the only one boasting red, white, and blue lettering, thus furthering the patriotic theme throughout the advertisement. The ad's slogan, "Mt. Tastemore, South Dacola--the most refreshing tourist attraction in America," is another way humor is injected into the text of the advertisement, making it more appealing to those of us who enjoy tastefully humorous things.

In reality, the head of Washington stands as high as a five-story building (about 60 feet). This head would thus be fitting for a person about 465 feet tall. In the advertisement, both the title and the soda cans are much larger in scale than Mt. Tastemore itself. This sizing persuades the reader to focus her attention on these areas first. The twelve people staring up at the presidents are dwarfed by them but are still clearly visible. The text at the bottom of the visual is smaller than that in the title or on the diet Coke cans, but important parts of it are much bigger than that and thus more significant. For example, "Mt. Tastemore, South Dacola--the most refreshing tourist attraction in America," "diet Coke duffel," and "Just for the monumental taste of it!" are significantly larger than the surrounding text.

The purpose of creating such an advertisement is obvious--to persuade people to drink diet Coke. But by offering the duffel bag as an added incentive, the people who see the ad will not only buy diet Coke but will also become living billboards for the product as they carry their diet Coke duffels around with them on their "tasteful" travels. These duffel bags, emblazoned with the huge red letters spelling out the product's name, are an excellent example of effective co-branding.

Advertisements don't need to say, "Buy this product, or you won't be cool." We do that for them. What if the paparazzi catch a celebrity strolling down Rodeo Drive with one of these "haute couture" duffel bags casually thrown over her shoulder? Presto! Fans will rush to order their own duffels, thus becoming walking billboards for the product just as the advertisers intended. For good measure, these consumers will be further influenced by the subliminal message delivered by the small "d" in the brand's name. They will believe that whoever drinks diet Coke will be not only cool but thinner, too. So these proud duffel bag-toting Americans are not only patriotic but cool and thin as well. Soon, as more and more people proudly sport their diet Coke duffels while sipping their diet Cokes, advertisers will enlarge the promotional campaign to extol the soda's fabulous taste to consumers around the globe. Isn't it cool to look and buy "American" even if you don't live here? After all, if this "refreshing" and "monumental" drink is good enough for America's most beloved leaders, it should be good enough for those millions of global consumers who wish to "get a taste of" our popular culture.

You'll have a chance to practice your media-deconstructing skills throughout this text, from the images at the beginning of each chapter to paired images from the past and the present that bring each chapter to a close. Remember to ask yourself the questions we've identified. Look closely—and then look beyond what's on the page to see what's really being communicated.

GEARING UP TO READ IMAGES

Locate an ad, a photograph, or a cartoon strip that appeals to you. Write a brief paragraph stating your initial reaction to the image. Then decode the image by applying the questions identified throughout this chapter. How did your initial impressions change after a careful study of the image?

COLLABORATING

1. Locate a visual image that you think communicates a significant message, and bring it to class. Working with three or four other students, discuss the images you've each chosen, and determine which one is the most effective and why. Then plan and deliver a presentation to your classmates in which your group deconstructs the image you have selected.

2. Working in a small group, assemble a collection of various types of magazines such as music, home and garden, news, sports, and fashion. Analyze the types of ads, photos, and other visuals you find to determine the target audiences. How do the target audiences differ? Evaluate the match between readers of each type of magazine and the products being advertised. Discuss why the advertisers you see chose to invest their marketing dollars in that particular type of magazine. Report your conclusions in a short paper, or present them orally to the rest of the class.

Define "American"
Reflections on Cultural Identity

Analyzing the Image

 The stresses of a "melting pot" culture are clearly revealed in the cover photograph from this 1999 *National Geographic*. While the mother's traditional sari reflects her heritage, the daughter's sleek jump-suit makes a bold statement about her own cultural affiliation: "Like Mother—Not Likely!"

- What does the women's clothing say about them and their cultural identities?

- How would you interpret the facial expressions in this photo?

- What does the mother's and daughter's body language reveal about them?

Research this topic with TopLinks at bedfordstmartins.com/toplinks.

GEARING UP   How would you define "American"? Think about the forces that have helped shape your sense of who you are as a person living in America today. Consider your gender, your sexual preference, your personal appearance, and your ethnicity. How have these forces influenced you? How has your definition of what it means to be an American changed since you were a child?

How do I look to other people? Do I fit in? Do I want to fit in? Will I find my own place in the culture I live in? What should I call myself? Just who am I?

These are questions that all people ask themselves at some time in their lives. Many factors affect people's self-image. One is biological: our gender, our sexual preference, and our physical appearance. The other is cultural and is composed of two segments: the culture of our ancestors and the larger contemporary culture that we participate in, better known as popular culture.

Cultural diversity has become a hot—and sometimes heated—topic in the United States. Should we learn about and celebrate the differences among people of different ethnicities and cultural heritages? Or should we deemphasize those differences and concentrate on the similarities among people? Many people reject the notion that the United States is a melting pot where everyone is simply an "American." Instead, they see America as a salad bowl containing a mix of ethnicities that complement one another and that deserve to maintain their cultural identities within the larger U.S. popular culture. But can too much attention be paid to cultural diversity? Does an appreciation of other ethnic groups unite or further divide us? How do a person's gender and sexual preference enter into the cultural mix?

What happens to members of minority groups when the ideals of their own culture collide with those of the dominant American popular culture? The media are gradually presenting a more accurate reflection of the actual U.S. population, as witnessed by the increasing numbers of models and actors of varying ethnicities and sexual preferences. However, many Americans still feel separated from society's mainstream because they find it difficult to relate to the majority of people who stare out at them from the pages of glossy fashion magazines or from television or movie screens. Those Americans who do not resemble society's supposed role models or live the lifestyle that the media seem to privilege can feel rejected by the mainstream.

The writers in this chapter come from diverse cultural backgrounds and reflect a wide variety of lifestyles. As these authors detail their individual struggles with cultural self-image and awareness, they encourage you to examine the richness of our country's diversity. Reading these essays will help you reflect on what goes into the continual reevaluation and reshaping of your own cultural identity as a man or woman living in the United States today.

COLLABORATING   In groups of four to six students, spend fifteen to twenty minutes discussing the major cultural influences on an individual's self-image as a child and as an adolescent. Consider such influences as ethnicity, gender, sexual preference, home life, peers, teachers, and the media. Make a list of the major influences, and then discuss them as a class.

They've Got to Be Carefully Taught

Susan Brady Konig

This essay is one mother's humorous account of Cultural Diversity Month at her daughter's preschool. Susan Brady Konig was born in Paris, France, in 1962, but was educated in the United States. An experienced journalist, Konig has been an editor for *Seventeen* magazine, has worked as a columnist for the *New York Post*, and has written articles for such wide-ranging publications as the *Washington Post, Us, Travel & Leisure, Ladies' Home Journal,* and the *National Review*. She is currently a regular contributor to *National Review Online.* Her first book, *Why Animals Sleep So Close to the Road (and Other Lies I Tell My Children)*, was published in 2005. "They've Got to Be Carefully Taught" originally appeared in the September 15, 1997, issue of the *National Review.*

> **THINKING AHEAD**   Think back to your early school days. How was the issue of cultural diversity handled? What special occasions were celebrated to highlight diversity issues? How did these events affect your own cultural awareness?

At my daughter's preschool it's time for all the children to learn that they are different from one another. Even though these kids are at that remarkable age when they are thoroughly color blind, their teachers are spending a month emphasizing race, color, and background. The little tots are being taught in no uncertain terms that their hair is different, their skin is different, and their parents come from different places. It's Cultural Diversity Month. 1

I hadn't really given much thought to the ethnic and national backgrounds of Sarah's classmates. I can guarantee that Sarah, being two and a half, gave the subject absolutely no thought. Her teachers, however, had apparently given it quite a lot of thought. They sent a letter asking each parent to contribute to the cultural-awareness effort by "providing any information and/or material regarding your family's cultural background. For example: favorite recipe or song." All well and good, unless your culture isn't diverse enough. 2

The next day I take Sarah to school and her teacher, Miss Laura, anxious to get this Cultural Diversity show on the road, begins the interrogation. 3

"Where are you and your husband from?" she cheerily demands. 4

"We're Americans," I reply — less, I must confess, out of patriotism than from sheer lack of coffee. It was barely 9:00 a.m. 5

"Yes, of course, but where are you from?" I'm beginning to feel like a nightclub patron being badgered by a no-talent stand-up comic.[1] 6

---

[1]**stand-up comic:** A comedian who performs while standing on a stage.

"We're native New Yorkers."   7

"But where are your people from?"   8

"Well," I dive in with a sigh, "my family is originally Irish on both   9
sides. My husband's father was from Czechoslovakia and his mother is
from the Bronx, but her grandparents were from the Ukraine."

"Can you cook Irish?"   10

"I could bring in potatoes and beer for the whole class."   11

Miss Laura doesn't get it.   12

"Look," I say, "we're Americans. Our kids are Americans. We tell them   13
about American history and George Washington and apple pie and all that
stuff. If you want me to do something American, I can do that."

She is decidedly unexcited.   14

A few days later, she tells me that she was trying to explain to Sarah   15
that her dad is from Ireland.

"Wrong," I say, "but go on."   16

"He's not from Ireland?"   17

"No," I sigh. "He's from Queens. I'm from Ireland. I mean I'm   18
Irish—that is, my great-grandparents were. Don't get me wrong, I'm
proud of my heritage—but that's entirely beside the point. I told you we
tell Sarah she's American."

"Well, anyway," she smiles, "Sarah thinks her Daddy's from *Iceland!*   19
Isn't that cute?"

Later in the month, Miss Laura admits that her class is not quite getting   20
the whole skin-color thing. "I tried to show them how we all have different
skin," she chuckled. Apparently, little Henry is the only one who successfully grasped the concept. He now runs around the classroom announcing
to anyone who'll listen, "I'm white!" Miss Laura asked the children what
color her own skin was. (She is a light-skinned Hispanic, which would
make her skin color . . . what? Caramel? Mochaccino?[2]) The kids opted
for purple or orange. "They looked at me like I was crazy!" Miss Laura
said. I just smile.

The culmination of Cultural Diversity Month, the day when the parents   21
come into class and join their children in a glorious celebration of multicultural
disparity, has arrived. As I arrive I see a large collage on the wall depicting the
earth, with all the children's names placed next to the country they are from.
Next to my daughter's name it says "Ireland." I politely remind Miss Laura
that Sarah is, in fact, from America and suggest that, by insisting otherwise,
she is confusing my daughter. She reluctantly changes Sarah's affiliation to
USA. It will be the only one of its kind on the wall.

The mom from Brazil brings in a bunch of great music, and the whole   22
class is doing the samba[3] and running around in a conga line.[4] It's very

---

[2]**mochaccino:** A frothy coffee beverage made from espresso, steamed milk, and chocolate
syrup.

[3]**samba:** A Brazilian dance of African origin; also, the music for this dance.

[4]**conga line:** A Cuban dance of African origin performed by a group, usually in single file,
involving three steps followed by a kick.

cute. Then I get up to teach the children an indigenous folk tune from the culture of Sarah's people, passed down through the generations from her grandparents to her parents and now to Sarah—a song called "Take Me Out to the Ballgame." First I explain to the kids that Sarah was born right here in New York—and that's in what country, Sarah? Sarah looks at me and says, "France." I look at Miss Laura, who just shrugs.

I stand there in my baseball cap and sing my song. The teacher tries to rush me off. I say, "Don't you want them to learn it?" They took long enough learning to samba! I am granted permission to sing it one more time. The kids join in on the "root, root, root" and the "1, 2, 3 strikes you're out," but they can see their teacher isn't enthusiastic.   23

So now these sweet, innocent babies who thought they were all the same are becoming culturally aware. Two little girls are touching each other's hair and saying, "Your hair is blonde, just like mine." Off to one side a little dark-haired girl stands alone, excluded. She looks confused as to what to do next. She knows she's not blonde. Sure, all children notice these things eventually, but, thanks to the concerted efforts of their teachers, these two- and three-year-olds are talking about things that separate rather than connect.   24

And Sarah only knows what she has been taught: Little Henry is white, her daddy's from Iceland, and New York's in France.   25

EXERCISING VOCABULARY

1. Record your own definition for each word below in your notebook.

   badgered (v.) (6)   disparity (n.) (21)
   decidedly (adv.) (14)   collage (n.) (21)
   opted (v.) (20)   concerted (adj.) (24)
   culmination (n.) (21)

2. What does Konig mean when she describes the children in her daughter's class as "color blind" (para. 1)? How does this expression acquire additional meaning when used in the context of this essay?

3. What does Konig's description of Miss Laura's questions as an "interrogation" (para. 3) suggest about the writer's attitude toward the teacher? What kinds of situations or settings do you think of when you hear the word *interrogation*?

4. Why does the writer call "Take Me Out to the Ballgame" an "indigenous folk tune" (para. 22)? What does *indigenous* mean? What kinds of songs are usually referred to as indigenous folk tunes?

PROBING CONTENT

1. The title of this selection is derived from a Rodgers and Hammerstein song "You've Got to Be Carefully Taught" from the musical *South Pacific*. The first lines are "You've got to be taught to hate and fear. You've got to be taught from year to year. It's got to be drummed in your dear little ear. You've got to be carefully taught." Is this title, with its relationship to this popular song, appropriate for this essay? Why or why not?

2. For what reasons does the writer disagree with Miss Laura's strategy? What does she think the students are learning as a result of their classroom activities on diversity?

3. The words *American* or *Americans* are repeated four times in paragraph 13. What does the writer mean when she says that her family is American? To what else besides the geographic location of their home is she referring?

4. Describe the effect of Cultural Diversity Month on the preschool students. From Konig's description, what do the children appear to learn? What positive lessons do they fail to learn?

CONSIDERING CRAFT

1. Find several examples of the writer's use of dialogue in this essay. How does the dialogue affect your attitude about the characters?

2. Describe the writer's tone in this essay. Why does she choose this tone? What kind of response is she hoping to get from the reader as a result?

3. In paragraph 21, the author refers to events at the preschool as "a glorious celebration of multicultural disparity." What word usually appears in place of *disparity*? Why does Konig change the word?

WRITING PROMPTS

Responding to the Topic   In an essay, explore the effects that an emphasis on cultural diversity has had on life in the United States over the last twenty years.

Responding to the Writer   Write an essay in which you agree or disagree with Konig's idea that too much emphasis on cultural diversity may actually separate people of different ethnicities and cultures rather than bring them together.

Responding to Multiple Viewpoints   Compare the position on diversity that Michael Jonas takes in "The Downside of Diversity" with the position that Konig takes in this essay.

For a quiz on this reading, go to bedfordstmartins.com/mirror.

Do I Look Like Public Enemy Number One?

LORRAINE ALI

"Do I Look Like Public Enemy Number One?" is Lorraine Ali's personal account of growing up Arabic in the United States and the prejudices she has faced while living an almost double life—as both an American and an Arab. Ali is a general editor and music critic at *Newsweek,* covering everything from Christian alternative rock to Latino Lone Star rap. Named 1997's Music Journalist of the Year, Ali has been a senior critic for *Rolling Stone* and a contributor to the *New York Times, GQ (Gentleman's Quarterly),* and VH-1's 2002 to 2003 series *One Hit Wonders.* Her music criticism appears in several books, including *Da Capo Best Music Writing 2001: The Year's Finest Writing on Rock, Pop, Jazz, Country, and More* (2001), edited by Nick Hornby and Ben Schafer, and *Kill Your Idols: A New Generation of Rock Writers Reconsiders the Classics* (2004), edited by Jim Derogatis and Carmél Carrillo. In 2002, she won an Excellence in Journalism award from the National Arab American Journalists Association. "Do I Look Like Public Enemy Number One?" was first published in *Mademoiselle* in 1999.

> **THINKING AHEAD** Since the attack on America on September 11, 2001, Arab Americans have been under uncomfortable scrutiny and often unwarranted suspicion. Have terrorist actions by a radical few forever affected our ability to treat all people as the individuals they are? What repercussions will such a shift in thought have on the American way of life?

"You're not a terrorist, are you?" That was pretty much a stock question I faced growing up. Classmates usually asked it after they heard my last name: "Ali" sounded Arabic; therefore, I must be some kind of bomb-lobbing religious fanatic with a grudge against Western society. It didn't matter that just before my Middle Eastern heritage was revealed, my friend and I might have been discussing the merits of rock versus disco, or the newest flavor of Bonne Bell Lip Smacker.[1] 1

I could never find the right retort; I either played along ("Yeah, and I'm going to blow up the math building first") or laughed and shrugged it off. How was I going to explain that my background meant far more than buzz words like *fanatic* and *terrorist* could say? Back in the '70s and '80s, 2

---

[1]**Bonne Bell Lip Smacker:** A brand of flavored lip gloss.

all Americans knew of the Middle East came from television and newspapers. "Arab" meant a contemptible composite of images: angry Palestinian refugees, irate Iranian hostage-takers, extremist leaders like Libya's Muammar al-Qaddafi or Iran's Ayatollah Khomeini, and long gas lines at home. What my limited teenage vernacular couldn't express was that an entire race of people was being judged by its most violent individuals.

Twenty years later, I'm still trying to explain. Not much has changed in the '90s. In fact, now that Russia has been outmoded as Public Enemy Number One, Arabs have been promoted into that position. Whenever a disaster strikes without a clear cause, fingers point toward Islam. When an explosion downed TWA Flight 800, pundits prematurely blamed "Arab terrorists." Early coverage following the Oklahoma City bombing featured experts saying it "showed Middle Eastern traits." Over the next six days there were 150 documented hate crimes against Arab Americans; phone calls to radio talk shows demanded detainment and deportation of Middle Easterners. Last fall, *The Siege* depicted Moslems terrorizing Manhattan, and TV's *Days of Our Lives* showed a female character being kidnapped by an Arabian sultan, held hostage in a harem, and threatened with death if she didn't learn how to belly dance properly. Whatever! 3

My Childhood Had Nothing to Do with Belly Dancing

Defending my ethnicity has always seemed ironic to me because I consider myself a fake Arab. I am half of European ancestry and half Arab, and I grew up in the suburban sprawl of Los Angeles' San Fernando Valley. My skin is pale olive rather than smooth brown like my dad's, and my eyes are green, not black like my sisters' (they got all the Arab genes). Even my name, Lorraine Mahia Ali, saves all the Arab parts for last. 4

I also didn't grow up Moslem, like my dad, who emigrated from Baghdad, Iraq's capital, in 1956. In the old country he wore a galabiya (or robe), didn't eat pork, and prayed toward Mecca five times a day. To me, an American girl who wore short-shorts, ate Pop Rocks,[2] and listened to Van Halen,[3] his former life sounded like a fairy tale. The Baghdad of his childhood was an ancient city where he and his brothers swam in the Tigris River, where he did accounting on an abacus[4] in his father's tea shop, where his mother blamed his sister's polio on a neighbor's evil eye, where his entire neighborhood watched Flash Gordon[5] movies projected on the side of a bakery wall. 5

[2]**Pop Rocks:** A type of fizzy candy popular in the 1970s.
[3]**Van Halen:** A rock musical group first popular in the 1980s.
[4]**abacus:** An ancient device for calculating numbers.
[5]**Flash Gordon:** The hero of a comic book series that originated in 1934 about a space traveler battling evildoers.

My father's world only started to seem real to me when I visited Iraq   6
the summer after fifth grade and stayed in his family's small stucco house. I
remember feeling both completely at home and totally foreign. My sister Lela
and I spoke to amused neighbors in shoddy sign language, sat cross-legged on
the floor in our Mickey Mouse T-shirts, rolling cigarettes to sell at market for
my arthritic Bedouin[6] grandma, and sang silly songs in pidgin[7] Arabic with my
Uncle Brahim. Afterward, I wrote a back-to-school essay in which I referred
to my grandparents as Hajia and Haja Hassan, thinking their names were the
Arab equivalent of Mary Ellen and Billy Bob. "You're such a dumb-ass,"
said Lela. "It just means grandma and grandpa." But she was wrong too. It
actually meant they had completed their Haj duty—a religious journey to
Mecca in Saudi Arabia that millions of Muslims embark on each year.

At home, my American side continued to be shamefully ignorant of all   7
things Arab, but my Arab side began to notice some pretty hideous stereotypes. Saturday-morning cartoons depicted Arabs as ruthless, bumbling, and
hygienically challenged. I'd glimpse grotesque illustrations of Arab leaders
in my dad's paper. At the mall with my mom, we'd pass such joke items as
an Arab face on a bull's-eye. She tried to explain to me that things weren't
always this way, that there was a time when Americans were mesmerized by
Arabia and Omar Sharif[8] made women swoon. A time when a WASP[9] girl
like my mom, raised in a conservative, middle-class family, could be considered romantic and daring, not subversive, for dating my dad. In effect, my
mom belonged to the last generation to think sheiks were chic.

Not so in my generation. My mother tells me that when my oldest sister   8
was five, she said to a playmate that her dad "was an Arab, but not a bad
one." In elementary school, we forced smiles through taunts like, "Hey,
Ali, where's your oilcan?" Teachers were even more hurtful: During roll
call on her first day of junior high, Lela was made to sit through a twenty-
minute lecture about the bloodshed and barbarism of Arabs toward Israel
and the world. As far as I knew, Lela had never shed anyone's blood except
for mine, when she punched me in the nose over a pack of Pixie Sticks.[10]
But that didn't matter. As Arabs, we were guilty by association, even at the
age of twelve.

By High School, I Was Beginning to Believe the Hype

It's awful to admit, but I was sometimes embarrassed by my dad.   9

I know it's every teen's job to think her parents are the most shameful   10
creatures to walk the planet, but this basic need to reject him was exacerbated

---

[6]**Bedouin:** A tent dweller of the desert; a wanderer.
[7]**pidgin:** A simplified form of a language.
[8]**Omar Sharif:** An Egyptian actor best known for his charismatic performances in the films
    Lawrence of Arabia and *Doctor Zhivago*.
[9]**WASP:** Slang term for white Anglo-Saxon Protestant.
[10]**Pixie Sticks:** A type of powdered candy that comes in a paper straw.

by the horrible images of Arabs around me. When he drove me to school, my dad would pop in a cassette of Quran suras (recorded prayers) and recite the lines in a language I didn't understand, yet somehow the twisting, weaving words sounded as natural as the whoosh of the Santa Ana winds through the dusty hills where we lived. His brown hands would rise off the steering wheel at high points of the prayer, the sun illuminating the big white moons of his fingernails. The mass of voices on tape would swell up and answer the Mezzuin[11] like a gospel congregation responding to a preacher. It was beautiful, but I still made my dad turn it down as we approached my school. I knew I'd be identified as part of a culture that America loved to hate.

My dad must have felt this, too. He spoke his native tongue only in the   11
company of Arabic friends and never taught my sisters or me the language, something he would regret until the day he died. His background was a mystery to me. I'd pester him for answers: "Do you dream in English or Arabic?" I'd ask, while he was busy doing dad work like fixing someone's busted Schwinn[12] or putting up Christmas lights. "Oh, I don't know," he'd answer playfully. "In dreams, I can't tell the difference."

Outside the safety of our home, he could. He wanted respect; therefore,   12
he felt he must act American. Though he truly loved listening to Roberta Flack[13] and wearing Adidas sweatsuits, I can't imagine he enjoyed making dinner reservations under pseudonyms like Mr. Allen. He knew that as Mr. Ali, he might never get a table.

Desert Storm Warning

Fifteen years later, "Ali" was still not a well-received name. We were at war   13
with the Middle East. It was January 16, 1991, and Iraq's Saddam Hussein had just invaded Kuwait. I will never forget the night CNN's Bernard Shaw lay terrified on the floor of his Baghdad hotel as a cameraman shot footage of the brand-new war outside his window. I was twenty-six and working for a glossy music magazine called *Creem*. When the news broke that we were bombing Baghdad in an operation called Desert Storm, I went home early and sat helpless in my Hollywood apartment, crying. Before me on the TV was a man dressed in a galabiya, just like the kind my dad used to wear around the house, aiming an ancient-looking gun turret toward our space-age planes in the sky. He looked terrified, too. With every missile we fired, I watched the Baghdad I knew slip away and wondered just who was being hit. Was it Aunt Niama? My cousin Afrah?

Back at work, I had to put up with "funny" faxes of camels, SCUD   14
missiles, and dead Arabs. To my colleagues, the Arabs I loved and respected

[11]**Mezzuin:** An Islamic cantor who sings to lead worshipers in prayer.
[12]**Schwinn:** A popular bicycle manufacturer.
[13]**Roberta Flack:** A jazz and pop singer who first gained popularity in the early 1970s.

were now simply targets. Outside the office, there was a virtual free-for-all of racist slogans. Arab-hating sentiment came out on bumper stickers like "Kick Their Ass and Take Their Gas." Military footage even documented our pilots joking as they bombed around fleeing civilians. They called it a turkey shoot. A turkey shoot? Those were people.

Arabs bleed and perish just like Americans. I know, because two years   15 before we started dropping bombs on Baghdad, I watched my father die. He did not dissolve like a cartoon character, nor defy death like a Hollywood villain. Instead, chemotherapy shrunk his 180-pound body down to 120, turned his beautiful skin from brown to ashen beige, and rendered his opalescent[14] white fingernails a dull shade of gray. When he finally let go, I thought he took all the secrets of my Arabness with him, all the good things America didn't want me to know. But I look in the mirror and see my father's wide nose on my face and Hajia's think lines forming between my brows. I also see my mom's fair skin, and her mother's high cheekbones. I realize it's my responsibility to somehow forge an identity between dueling cultures, to focus on the humanity, not the terror, that bridges both worlds.

EXERCISING VOCABULARY

1. Record your own definition for each word below in your notebook.

stock (adj.) (1)	mesmerized (v.) (7)
retort (n.) (2)	subversive (adj.) (7)
composite (n.) (2)	exacerbated (v.) (10)
outmoded (v.) (3)	pseudonyms (n.) (12)
pundits (n.) (3)	forge (v.) (15)
shoddy (adj.) (6)	

2. In paragraph 2, the author regrets "what my limited teenage vernacular couldn't express." What does *vernacular* mean? What is the purpose of a group having its own vernacular?

3. Ali states that "now that Russia has been outmoded as Public Enemy Number One, Arabs have been promoted into that position" (para. 3). What is ironic about her use of the word *promoted* in this context?

4. What does it mean to possess and to give the "evil eye"? How does Ali's inclusion of this phrase in paragraph 5 contribute to your understanding of the gap between her life and the early life of her father?

PROBING CONTENT

1. In Ali's opinion, how did television enhance the image of the "bad Arab"?

---

[14]**opalescent:** Reflecting an iridescent light.

2. What elementary school experience stimulated Ali's awareness of her family's cultural heritage? How did that experience color her everyday thinking?

3. What examples does Ali provide to show how carefully she and her family tried to keep their two cultures from clashing?

CONSIDERING CRAFT

1. In paragraph 5, what strong images does Ali choose to represent her American childhood? What images represent her father's childhood? How does her inclusion of these images convey the gap between her father's culture and the one in which she was raised?

2. How does Ali use her personal experience to make a broad statement about how people of one culture relate to those from a different background? How effective is this writing strategy?

WRITING PROMPTS

Responding to the Topic   Explain how Ali's phrase "dueling cultures" (para. 15) has taken on a very different meaning since this essay was first published in 1999. In light of recent events, what would you say to Ali about her effort "to focus on the humanity, not the terror" (para. 15), that bridges Middle Eastern and American cultures?

Responding to the Writer   In paragraph 8, Ali asserts that she and her family have been made "guilty by association." In an essay, identify and explore the history surrounding another cultural group that has been made "guilty by association."

Responding to Multiple Viewpoints   Write an essay in which you explore how the efforts of the teacher in "They've Got to Be Carefully Taught" would be received by Ali and by Julia Alvarez.

For a quiz on this reading, go to bedfordstmartins.com/mirror.

I Want to Be Miss America

JULIA ALVAREZ

In "I Want to Be Miss America," Julia Alvarez examines an American tra-dition from an outsider's point of view. After moving to the United States from the Dominican Republic at the age of ten, Alvarez and her sisters watched the Miss America pageant for clues about how to look more "American."

A prolific writer, Alvarez has published eighteen books, including *How the Garcia Girls Lost Their Accents* (1991), winner of the PEN/Oakland Award, and *In the Time of the Butterflies* (1994), a National Book Critics Circle Finalist. *In the Time of the Butterflies* was made into a 2001 fea-ture film produced by and starring Salma Hayek, with Marc Anthony and Edward James Olmos. Alvarez's *Before We Were Free* (2002) won the 2004 Pura Belpré Medal for narrative from the American Library Association. Other recent works, *In the Name of Salomé* (2000), *A Cafecito Story* (2001), and *How Tía Lola Came to Stay* (2001), also won top book and media awards. She has recently published a novel, *Saving the World* (2006), and a nonfiction book, *Quinceañera: Coming of Age in the USA* (2007). Alvarez currently teaches creative writing at Middlebury College in Vermont. "I Want to Be Miss America" was first published in her collection of essays *Something to Declare* (1999).

> **THINKING AHEAD** Within every culture, there are some firmly held beliefs about what constitutes "beauty." How are these ideals a reflection of the values of the culture? When have you ques-tioned any of the beauty ideals in your own culture? What caused you to begin to question them?

A s young teenagers in our new country, my three sisters and I searched 1 for clues on how to look as if we belonged here. We collected magazines, studied our classmates and our new TV, which was where we discovered the Miss America contest.

Watching the pageant became an annual event in our family. Once a 2 year, we all plopped down in our parents' bedroom, with Mami and Papi presiding from their bed. In our nightgowns, we watched the fifty young women who had the American look we longed for.

The beginning was always the best part—all fifty contestants came 3 on for one and only one appearance. In alphabetical order, they stepped forward and enthusiastically introduced themselves by name and state. "Hi! I'm! Susie! Martin! Miss! Alaska!" Their voices rang with false cheer. You could hear, not far off, years of high-school cheerleading, pom-poms, bleachers full of moon-eyed boys, and moms on phones, signing them up for all manner of lessons and making dentist appointments.

There they stood, fifty puzzle pieces forming the pretty face of America, 4 so we thought, though most of the color had been left out, except for one, or possibly two, light-skinned black girls. If there was a "Hispanic," she usually looked all-American, and only the last name, López or Rodríguez, often mispronounced, showed a trace of a great-great-grandfather with a dark, curled mustache and a sombrero charging the Alamo.[1] During the initial roll-call, what most amazed us was that some contestants were ever picked in the first place. There were homely girls with cross-eyed smiles or chipmunk cheeks. My mother would inevitably shake her head and say, "The truth is, these Americans believe in democracy—even in looks."

We were beginning to feel at home. Our acute homesickness had passed, 5 and now we were like people recovered from a shipwreck, looking around at our new country, glad to be here. "I want to be in America," my mother hummed after we'd gone to see *West Side Story*,[2] and her four daughters chorused, "OK by me in America." We bought a house in Queens, New York, in a neighborhood that was mostly German and Irish, where we were the only "Hispanics." Actually, no one ever called us that. Our teachers and classmates at the local Catholic schools referred to us as "Porto Ricans" or "Spanish." No one knew where the Dominican Republic was on the map. "South of Florida," I explained, "in the same general vicinity as Bermuda and Jamaica." I could just as well have said west of Puerto Rico or east of Cuba or right next to Haiti, but I wanted us to sound like a vacation spot, not a Third World country, a place they would look down on.

Although we wanted to look like we belonged here, the four sisters, our 6 looks didn't seem to fit in. We complained about how short we were, about how our hair frizzed, how our figures didn't curve like those of the bathing beauties we'd seen on TV.

"The grass always grows on the other side of the fence," my mother 7 scolded. Her daughters looked fine just the way they were.

But how could we trust her opinion about what looked good when she 8 couldn't even get the sayings of our new country right? No, we knew better. We would have to translate our looks into English, iron and tweeze them out, straighten them, mold them into Made-in-the-U.S.A. beauty.

So we painstakingly rolled our long, curly hair round and round, using 9 our heads as giant rollers, ironing it until we had long, shining shanks, like our classmates and the contestants, only darker. Our skin was diagnosed by beauty consultants in department stores as sallow; we definitely needed a strong foundation to tone down that olive. We wore tights even in the summer to hide the legs Mami would not let us shave. We begged

---

[1] **the Alamo:** Former Franciscan mission in San Antonio, Texas, where Texans lost a heroic battle in the Texas war of independence against Mexico.
[2] ***West Side Story:*** Broadway musical (1957) and film (1961) that featured clashes between rival gangs in a modern-day Romeo and Juliet story.

for permission, dreaming of the contestants' long, silky limbs. We were ten, fourteen, fifteen, and sixteen—merely children, Mami explained. We had long lives ahead of us in which to shave.

We defied her. Giggly and red-faced, we all pitched in to buy a big tube 10 of Nair[3] at the local drugstore. We acted as if we were purchasing contraceptives. That night we crowded into the bathroom, and I, the most courageous along these lines, offered one of my legs as a guinea pig. When it didn't become gangrenous or fall off as Mami had predicted, we creamed the other seven legs. We beamed at each other; we were one step closer to that runway, those flashing cameras, those oohs and ahhs from the audience.

Mami didn't even notice our Naired legs; she was too busy disapprov- 11 ing of the other changes. Our clothes, for one. "You're going to wear that in public!" She'd gawk, as if to say, What will the Americans think of us?

"This is what the Americans wear," we would argue back. 12

But the dresses we had picked out made us look cheap, she said, like 13 bad, fast girls—gringas without vergüenza, without shame. She preferred her choices: fuchsia skirts with matching vests, flowered dresses with bows at the neck or gathers where you wanted to look slim, everything bright and busy, like something someone might wear in a foreign country.

Our father didn't really notice our new look at all but, if called upon 14 to comment, would say absently that we looked beautiful. "Like Marilina Monroe." Still, during the pageant, he would offer insights into what he thought made a winner. "Personality, Mami," my father would say from his post at the head of the bed, "Personality is the key," though his favorite contestants, whom he always championed in the name of personality, tended to be the fuller girls with big breasts who gushed shamelessly at Bert Parks.[4] "Ay, Papi," we would groan, rolling our eyes at each other. Sometimes, as the girl sashayed back down the aisle, Papi would break out in a little Dominican song that he sang whenever a girl had a lot of swing in her walk:

Yo no tumbo caña,
Que la tumba el viento,
Que la tumba Dora
Con su movimiento!

("I don't have to cut the cane,
The wind knocks it down,
The wind of Dora's movement
As she walks downtown.")

My father would stop on a New York City street when a young woman 15 swung by and sing this song out loud to the great embarrassment of his

[3]**Nair:** A brand of hair-removal lotion.
[4]**Bert Parks:** Longtime host of the Miss America pageant.

daughters. We were sure that one day when we weren't around to make him look like the respectable father of four girls, he would be arrested.

My mother never seemed to have a favorite contestant. She was an ex-beauty herself, and no one seemed to measure up to her high standards. She liked the good girls who had common sense and talked about their education and about how they owed everything to their mothers. "Tell that to my daughters," my mother would address the screen, as if none of us were there to hear her. If we challenged her — how exactly did we not appreciate her? — she'd maintain a wounded silence for the rest of the evening. Until the very end of the show, that is, when all our disagreements were forgotten and we waited anxiously to see which of the two finalists holding hands on that near-empty stage would be the next reigning queen of beauty. How can they hold hands? I always wondered. Don't they secretly wish the other person would, well, die?

My sisters and I always had plenty of commentary on all the contestants. We were hardly strangers to this ritual of picking the beauty. In our own family, we had a running competition as to who was the prettiest of the four girls. We coveted one another's best feature: the oldest's dark, almond-shaped eyes, the youngest's great mane of hair, the third oldest's height and figure. I didn't have a preferred feature, but I was often voted the cutest, though my oldest sister liked to remind me that I had the kind of looks that wouldn't age well. Although she was only eleven months older than I was, she seemed years older, ages wiser. She bragged about the new kind of math she was learning in high school, called algebra, which she said I would never be able to figure out. I believed her. Dumb and ex-cute, that's what I would grow up to be.

As for the prettiest Miss America, we sisters kept our choices secret until the very end. The range was limited — pretty white women who all really wanted to be wives and mothers. But even the small and inane set of options these girls represented seemed boundless compared with what we were used to. We were being groomed to go from being dutiful daughters to being dutiful wives with hymens intact. No stops along the way that might endanger the latter; no careers, no colleges, no shared apartments with girlfriends, no boyfriends, no social lives. But the young women on-screen, who were being held up as models in this new country, were in college, or at least headed there. They wanted to do this, they were going to do that with their lives. Everything in our native culture had instructed us otherwise: girls were to have no aspirations beyond being good wives and mothers.

Sometimes there would even be a contestant headed for law school or medical school. "I wouldn't mind having an office visit with her," my father would say, smirking. The women who caught my attention were the prodigies who bounded onstage and danced to tapes of themselves playing original compositions on the piano, always dressed in costumes they had sewn, with a backdrop of easels holding paintings they'd painted. "Overkill," my older sister insisted. But if one good thing came out of our watching this yearly parade of American beauties, it was that subtle permission we all felt as a family: a girl could excel outside the home and still be a winner.

Every year, the queen came down the runway in her long gown with a   20
sash like an old-world general's belt of ammunition. Down the walkway
she paraded, smiling and waving while Bert sang his sappy song that made
our eyes fill with tears. When she stopped at the very end of the stage and
the camera zoomed in on her misty-eyed beauty and the credits began to
appear on the screen, I always felt let down. I knew I would never be
one of those girls, ever. It wasn't just the blond, blue-eyed looks or the
beautiful, leggy figure. It was who she was—an American—and we were
not. We were foreigners, dark-haired and dark-eyed with olive skin that
could never, no matter the sun blocks or foundation makeup, be made into
peaches and cream.[5]

Had we been able to see into the future, beyond our noses, which we   21
thought weren't the right shape; beyond our curly hair, which we wanted to
be straight; and beyond the screen, which inspired us with a limited vision
of what was considered beautiful in America, we would have been able to
see the late sixties coming. Soon, ethnic looks would be in. Even Barbie,
that quintessential white girl, would suddenly be available in different
shades of skin color with bright, colorful outfits that looked like the ones
Mami had picked out for us. Our classmates in college wore long braids like
Native Americans and embroidered shawls and peasant blouses from South
America, and long, diaphanous skirts and dangly earrings from India. They
wanted to look exotic—they wanted to look like us.

We felt then a gratifying sense of inclusion, but it had unfortunately   22
come too late. We had already acquired the habit of doubting ourselves as
well as the place we came from. To this day, after three decades of living in
America, I feel like a stranger in what I now consider my own country. I am
still that young teenager sitting in front of the black-and-white TV in my
parents' bedroom, knowing in my bones I will never be the beauty queen.
There she is, Miss America, but even in my up-to-date, enlightened dreams,
she never wears my face.

EXERCISING VOCABULARY

1. Record your own definition for each word below in your notebook.

   acute (adj.) (5)   aspirations (n.) (18)
   sallow (adj.) (9)   prodigies (n.) (19)
   gawk (v.) (11)   sappy (adj.) (20)
   sashayed (v.) (14)   diaphanous (adj.) (21)
   inane (adj.) (18)   gratifying (adj.) (22)

2. Define the word *quintessential* and then explain why Alvarez calls Barbie
   "that quintessential white girl" (para. 21).

---

[5]**peaches and cream:** A complimentary description of Caucasian skin.

3. In her final sentence, why does Alvarez refer to her adult dreams as "enlightened"? How have her dreams changed since her childhood? How truly enlightened are her dreams?

PROBING CONTENT

1. When Alvarez explains where her family came from, what geographic reference points does she use to help friends locate the Dominican Republic? Why does she choose these landmarks instead of others?

2. Why don't the Alvarez girls trust the opinion of their mother about what looks good? Why is their father's opinion also suspect?

3. What hopes for the future were Alvarez and her sisters expected to have? How were these expectations at odds with the plans of some of the Miss America contestants? How did this difference make the girls feel?

4. How did a change in the appearance of Barbie dolls mirror what Alvarez saw at college? How does Alvarez feel about this development?

CONSIDERING CRAFT

1. Why does Alvarez put an exclamation point after every word of the contestant's introduction in paragraph 3? What does this unusual punctuation achieve?

2. In paragraph 4, Alvarez writes, "There they stood, fifty puzzle pieces forming the pretty face of America . . . though most of the color had been left out." How does this figurative language reinforce the main idea of her essay?

3. Reread paragraph 13. Explain the irony in the last sentence. Why does Alvarez use irony here?

4. How does Alvarez's concluding paragraph differ in tone from the first paragraph of her essay? What message does this difference in tone convey to the reader?

WRITING PROMPTS

Responding to the Topic   Do you identify with the strong need of Alvarez and her sisters "to look as if we belonged" (para. 1)? Why are some people so motivated not to express and celebrate their differences but to simply "fit in"?

Responding to the Writer   Write an essay in which you explore numerous expressions of American culture to prove or disprove Mami's assertion that "Americans believe in democracy—even in looks" (para. 4).

Responding to Multiple Viewpoints   In an essay, compare Alvarez's struggles to "fit in" with those experienced by Lorraine Ali in "Do I Look Like Public Enemy Number One?"

For a quiz on this reading, go to bedfordstmartins.com/mirror.

There She Was

ANALYZING THE IMAGE

This photograph shows the contestants in the 1924 Miss America pageant. At that time, women represented their cities, not their states. Compare these contestants with those you have seen on television.

1. Are these early Miss America contestants representative of the American population as a whole at that time? Why or why not?

2. How do the women in the photograph compare to today's contestants? How are they similar? How are they different?

3. What effect have women's changing roles in society had on these differences?

4. Would the Alvarez sisters find a role model among these young women? Why or why not?

Will the Last Gay Bar in Laguna Beach Please Turn Out the Lights?

SHAWN HUBLER

Shawn Hubler has been at the *Los Angeles Times* since 1989, first as a re-porter and feature writer, then as a columnist, and now as a staff writer. This feature, sparked by the movement to save a landmark gay bar, was first published in the *Los Angeles Times* in March 2007.

> **THINKING AHEAD** Are gay bars and gay neighborhoods unnecessary relics of the past? Why or why not? What recent cultural shifts have greatly impacted the lives and options of gays and les-bians? How significant is preserving the character of a community? Explain your response.

The bungalow at Pacific Coast Highway and Cress Street used to be a   1
happy hour beacon in Laguna Beach. Young men holding hands, Will-and-Grace[1] types, the occasional gaggle of curious straights, the random lesbian couple—all would gather on weekends at Woody's at the Beach, a cottage-y gay bar. By midnight, the party would spread down the block to the venerable Boom Boom Room, with its dancing and drag queens, and to Bounce, a smaller joint across the street.

Sometimes neighbors complained. Sometimes tourists gawked and hol-   2
lered. But the scene, like the town's art galleries and surf shops, was part of the area's character and history. Before Laguna Beach was conjuring images of drama-prone television teens and oceanfront mansions, it was the city that elected America's first openly gay mayor. Its incidence of AIDS was, for a time, among the highest per capita in the nation. The Boom Boom Room is where Rock Hudson and Paul Lynde and Bette Midler once partied. Woody's, under one owner or another, had been gay for two generations.

The block-long promenade between them was like a miniature West   3
Hollywood in the heart of once-conservative Orange County, and locals insisted the town wouldn't be itself if it went away.

Then the Boom Boom Room was sold to a billionaire with plans to   4
eventually turn the site into a boutique hotel. Within a year, the owners of Woody's got an offer to cash out. A family-owned Mexican restaurant took over the space. Down went the fence that hid the back patio. In came the highchairs. When the new Avila's El Ranchito opened last month, leaving

[1]Will-and-Grace: Refers to a television show about a gay Manhattan attorney and his straight female best friend.

the Boom, as it is locally known, to boom alone into an uncertain future on its side of the highway, the block took on the feel of both a beginning and an ending.

And now, though the margaritas at the new place are both popular and delicious, the talk of the town is what will become of the local gay scene. Or, as a quipster at a coffeehouse put it one recent morning: "Will the last gay bar in Laguna please turn out the lights?"

Laguna Beach isn't alone in its evolution. From South Beach to San Francisco, progress and economics are creating similar debates.

Though gay neighborhoods are thriving in some cities—Houston, for example—other, more settled enclaves are changing fast. The Castro district in San Francisco has had to make room for more and more straight families. In West Hollywood, straight college kids have infiltrated gay bars, sometimes by the busload, and one of the biggest concerns is what a city official has termed "heterosexualization."

Matt Foreman, executive director of the National Gay and Lesbian Task Force, has watched the development with mixed feelings. "The loss of these enclaves does hurt and is something to be deeply concerned about," he says.

On the other hand, much of the change is being driven by inexorable forces. The Internet, he explains, has made it less important for gays and lesbians to go to special bars and communities to meet each other. And the once-blighted neighborhoods that were settled by gays—often because they felt unwelcome elsewhere—now are so gentrified, in many cases, that younger people can't afford them.

"Property values go up and straight families move in and gay people move on," Foreman says, "either because they want to capitalize on their investment or simply can't afford to live there anymore."

And underlying it all may be an even bigger factor: the power of acceptance, says UCLA demographer Gary Gates. The post-HIV era and the debate over same-sex marriage, he says, have brought about a major shift in public attitudes and "a fairly big coming-out process."

As a senior research fellow at UCLA's Williams Institute on Sexual Orientation Law and Public Policy, Gates published an analysis of recent U.S. Census data. Between 2000 and 2005, he says, the census showed a 30 percent increase in the number of same-sex couples, and a big part of the reason appears to be that these couples felt freer to report their existence. In some states in the Midwestern heartland, for example, the increase was as much as 81 percent.

The data, Gates says, paint a more diverse picture than ever before of the nation's gay and lesbian population—and present a far more diverse map of where they are living. Among other things, the numbers show an apparent out-migration of same-sex couples from gay enclaves such as San Francisco into less expensive suburbs and nearby cities such as San Jose, Oakland and Berkeley.

In Orange County, gay organizations report similar movement: "The   14
gayest town in Orange County is still overwhelmingly Laguna," says Jon
Stordahl, vice chair of the board of directors of the Center Orange County, a
gay, lesbian, bisexual and transgender service organization. "But the second-
gayest is Aliso Viejo, a new community just over the hill with more entry-
level housing."

Gay night life has changed too, Stordahl says. Though several of the   15
county's gay-only bars have closed in the last year, they have been supplanted by suburban clubs in Orange, Irvine and Costa Mesa that have
reached out to their new market with special nights for gay patrons.

"Success comes at a price," he says, "and part of that success is that the   16
old institutions that catered to us because we had no place to go—maybe
we don't need so much anymore."

That's slim comfort for Fred Karger, who during a recent lunch hour   17
sat in a booth at what used to be Woody's, eating a chicken quesadilla. No,
he is not the last gay man in Laguna—the 2000 census shows only four
cities in California with a higher proportion of same-sex households. But
he's worried: "You're not going to have people moving in if there's no life
here—no gay life."

Karger is a 57-year-old retired marketing and public relations consultant   18
who has split his time between Los Angeles and Laguna Beach for a decade.
When word got out last year that the Boom Boom Room might close, he
founded an organization called Save the Boom!!! to do something about it. . . .
The group presented the City Council with nearly six thousand signatures
on a petition begging the city to intercede and keep the bar open.

The council expressed sympathy but took no action. . . .   19

Still, Karger and others say, there is more at stake in Laguna Beach   20
than buff guys and cold beers, and it's not a gay-or-straight worry. The
fear of too much change too quickly has, in recent years, become a sort of
official town motif. As recently as a decade ago, Laguna Beach could
regard itself as a bohemian hangout, more Bolinas than Bel-Air. Now when
tourists think of the town, they're more likely to picture rich reality-show
kids than alternative lifestyles and artists.

The median home price has risen to $1.5 million. Boogie boards make   21
way for Botox parties at the high school's annual silent auction. And the
new Lagunans—the ones investing millions of dollars in their tear-down
beach shacks—aren't as tolerant of bars in general as were the less uptight
old-timers.

Joel Herzer, the former owner of Woody's, says a key reason he decided   22
to sell—aside from his desire to spend more time in Palm Springs, where
his partner lives and gay business is thriving—was a push by surrounding
homeowners to ban nonresidential parking, which would have profoundly
impacted his business.

"People move to this little beach community and say they don't want   23
it to change, and then the first thing they do is try to make it into Mission
Viejo," he says.

Thus, Karger's quest to save the granddaddy of Laguna's gay bars—an   24
offbeat one maybe, but then again, his adopted community once was an
offbeat place. And when a town like Laguna Beach loses its gay soul, he
asks, who'll be left to save it from total straightness?

He pauses as the lunch plates are cleared by a young gay waiter   25
who jokes that he hasn't been to the Boom Boom Room since the
days when he'd sneak in as a teenager. In the background, a toddler
shouts—"BABABABABA!!"—at his mother and father at the next table.

In the lunch-hour sunshine, it's hard to remember what this place   26
looked like when it was still Woody's, before it became just a nice lunch
spot somewhere between where we're going and where we've been.

EXERCISING VOCABULARY

1. Record your own definition for each word below in your notebook.

   venerable (adj.) (1)   inexorable (adj.) (9)
   gawked (v.) (2)   supplanted (v.) (15)
   conjuring (v.) (2)   intercede (v.) (18)
   enclaves (n.) (7)   bohemian (adj.) (20)

2. In paragraph 1, the author refers to "the occasional gaggle of curious
   straights." What animal group is called a gaggle? What are the implications of this term when applied to humans? What images does this
   colorful language evoke?

3. Explain what the author means in paragraph 7 by the term
   heterosexualization.

4. What happens to a neighborhood that has been "gentrified" (paragraph
   9)? How does the noun *gentry* relate to the idea of gentrification? In the
   context of this selection, how is gentrification a positive or a negative
   development?

PROBING CONTENT

1. Why were neighbors of the Laguna Beach gay bar scene willing to tolerate
   places like Woody's and the Boom Boom Room?

2. According to UCLA demographer Gary Gates, what factors have brought
   about "a fairly big coming-out process" (para. 11) for gays? What demographics support his conclusion?

3. Briefly describe several changes cited in this selection that have less-
   ened the need for gay bars and communities.

CONSIDERING CRAFT

1. Describe the author's tone in this selection. How does this tone reinforce the essay's purpose?

2. Read the title of this selection. How does Hubler's title choice foreshadow the essay's content? What feelings do you think he hopes to create in readers by using this title?

3. In paragraph 20, Hubler notes that as Laguna Beach changes, "boogie boards make way for Botox parties." What are boogie boards, and with what culture are they associated? What is Botox, and for what is it used? What kind of person might attend Botox parties? How does this expression reflect the changes happening in Laguna Beach?

WRITING PROMPTS

Responding to the Topic   Using this selection as a guide, write an essay in which you focus on one town or one neighborhood from your own experience that is evolving from its old personality and appearance to something different. Describe the changes in detail, and explore the reasons behind the transformation.

Responding to the Writer   If you lived in Laguna Beach, would you join Fred Karger's "Save the Boom!!!" movement? Write an essay in which you defend your decision to join or not to join. Write to persuade others in your community to adopt your position.

Responding to Multiple Viewpoints   Write an essay in which you use information from "Will the Last Gay Bar in Laguna Beach Please Turn Out the Lights?" to support or refute Michael Jonas's thesis in "The Downside of Diversity."

For a quiz on this reading, go to bedfordstmartins.com/mirror.

Globalization vs. Americanization

ANDREW LAM

Andrew Lam is an editor for *New America Media* and a commentator for NPR's *All Things Considered*. Born in South Vietnam, Lam has written a book on the Vietnamese diaspora, *Perfume Dreams*, which won a PEN/Beyond Margins Award. In "Globalization vs. Americanization," he argues that the spread of cultures around the world does not necessarily mean a McDonald's on every corner. The essay first appeared on the Internet news service *Alternet.*

> **THINKING AHEAD** How has living in the twenty-first century blurred the distinctions among cultures? Is national origin as fundamentally important to our sense of identity as it once was? Why or why not? What factors have most strongly impacted your own sense of cultural identity?

A friend, well traveled and educated, recently predicted the evils of global- 1
ization in very simple terms. "Everyone will be eating at McDonald's, listening to Madonna, and shopping at mega-malls," he prophesied. "It'll be absolutely awful."

What I told him then is that globalization is not the same as Americaniza- 2
tion, though sometimes it's hard for Americans to make that distinction. The most crucial aspect of globalization is the psychological transformation that's affecting people everywhere.

Let me offer my own biography as an example. I grew up a patriotic 3
South Vietnamese living in Vietnam during the war. I remember singing the national anthem, swearing my allegiance to the flag and promising my soul and body to protect the land and its sacred rice fields and rivers. Wide-eyed child that I was, I believed every word.

But then the war ended and I, along with my family (and eventually 4
a couple of million other Vietnamese), betrayed our agrarian[1] ethos and land-bound sentiments by fleeing overseas to lead a very different life.

Almost three decades later, I make a living traveling between East 5
Asia and the United States of America as an American journalist and writer. My relatives, once all concentrated in Saigon, are scattered across three continents, speaking three and four other languages, becoming citizens of several different countries. Once sedentary and communal and bound by a singular sense of geography, we are now bona fide[2]

---

[1]**agrarian:** Having to do with agriculture.
[2]**bona fide:** Genuine; real.

cosmopolitans who, when we get online or meet in person, still marvel at the difference between our past and our highly mobile if intricately complex present.

Yesterday my inheritance was simple — the sacred rice fields and rivers that defined who I was. Today, Paris and Hanoi and New York are no longer fantasies but my larger community, places to which I feel a strong sense of connection due to familial relationships and friendships and personal ambitions. Once great, the distances are no longer daunting but simply a matter of rescheduling. 6

I am hardly alone. There's a transnational revolution taking place, one right beneath our very noses. The Chinese businessman in Silicon Valley[3] is constantly in touch with his Shanghai mother on a cell phone while his high-tech workers build microchips and pave the information superhighway for the rest of the world. The Mexican migrant worker moves his family back and forth, one country to the other, treating the borders as if they were mere nuisances, and the blond teenager in Idaho is making friends with the Japanese girl in Osaka in a chatroom, their friendship easily forged as if time and space and cultural barriers have been breached by their lilting modems and the blinking satellites above. 7

The differences between my friend's view and my propositions are essentially the differences between a Disney animation and a Michael Ondaatje novel, say, *The English Patient*. Disney borrows world narratives (*Mulan* and *The Little Mermaid*) for backdrops, but it rewrites all complicated stories toward a singular outcome: happily ever after. It disembowels complexity, dismisses tragedy, forces differences into a blender and regurgitates formulaic platitudes. 8

Ondaatje's novel, on the other hand, is a world rooted in numerous particularities. It's a world where people from dissimilar backgrounds encounter one another and are trying, by various degrees of success and failure, to connect and influence each other. And it's a world complicated by memories and ambitions and multiple connections and displacements. Its unique and rounded characters refute simplification. 9

So McDonald's golden arches and mega-malls may be proliferating in every major metropolis across the world, but so are Thai and Vietnamese restaurants! Many other original cultures and languages and traditions continue to thrive. Think Bombay movies, Buddhist monks in Bangkok, Balinese dancers in Bali — these will not simply wash away because CNN and MTV are accessible now to the peasant in his mud hut. 10

While there's no denying that America is the sole supreme power in this post–Cold War era, America and all things American are not the end point. As we look at the world through our own prism, we tend to forget that we ourselves have dramatically changed in an age of open systems. 11

Koreatown in Los Angeles and Chinatown in San Francisco and the Cuban community in Miami are, after all, not places created for nostalgic 12

[3]**Silicon Valley:** Center of the U.S. software industry, located in California.

purposes but vibrant and thriving ethnic enclaves. They are changing the American landscape itself—a direct challenge to the old ideas of melting pot and integration. And Islam and Buddhism are the two fastest growing religions in America.

To want to be rooted is a deep human desire, of course, but to be dis- 13 placed and uprooted, alas, is a human condition—Man's fate. All over the world, people are moving from language to language, from culture to culture, sensibility to sensibility, negotiating across time zones and continents. It's a world that resists simplification. Man's identity is in conflict, has become both the cause of pain and fear for some and the source of enormous inspiration for others. I am inclined, of course, to be on the side of the latter.

The new man's talent is the ability to overcome paralysis of the many 14 conflicting selves by finding and inventing new connections between them. He holds opposed ideas in his head without going crazy. He resists the temptation to withdraw into a small shell of separatism and fundamentalism and xenophobia. He learns instead to hear others and respect differences and, in the process, transcends paradox. He sees the world with its many dimensions simultaneously. Geography for him may be memory and logistics, but it's no longer destiny.

EXERCISING VOCABULARY

1. Record your own definition for each word below in your notebook.

   ethos (n.) (4)   platitudes (n.) (8)
   sedentary (adj.) (5)   refute (v.) (9)
   regurgitates (v.) (8)   proliferating (v.) (10)

2. Lam states that certain communities have become "ethnic enclaves" (para. 12). What is an enclave? How do these communities challenge old ideas?

3. In paragraph 14, the author notes that the "new man" refuses to fall prey to xenophobia. What is a phobia? If a person has xenophobia, what is his or her concern?

PROBING CONTENT

1. How does Lam explain globalization? How does this term differ from Americanization? Why is this distinction difficult for Americans to grasp?

2. What did people share who were "bound by a singular sense of geography" (para. 5)? What has negated this shared feeling?

3. In paragraph 7, the author discusses the "transnational revolution" happening today. What is this revolution? Why is it occurring at this point in history?

CONSIDERING CRAFT

1. Opening essays with quotations is a popular method of introduction. How well does the initial quotation in paragraph 1 set the tone for the essay that follows? Does it matter that the quotation is not from an authority or a recognized source? Why?

2. Explain what Lam means in paragraph 7 when he writes of a Chinese businessman in Silicon Valley, "His high-tech workers build microchips and pave the information superhighway for the rest of the world." How does this use of figurative language enhance Lam's writing?

3. Lam feels that Disney's view of the world "disembowels complexity, dismisses tragedy, forces differences into a blender and regurgitates formulaic platitudes" (para. 8). How does this use of figurative language, coupled with some unfamiliar words, enhance or detract from his argument?

4. In paragraphs 8 and 9, Lam compares a friend's view and his own to the difference between Disney movies and a famous author's novel. How effectively does this comparison make his point?

WRITING PROMPTS

Responding to the Topic   To what extent do you consider yourself a citizen of the world? Write an essay in which you explore your own globalization experiences or those you'd like to have in the future. Include how such experiences contribute to your sense of cultural identity.

Responding to the Writer   Lam believes that "man's identity is in conflict" as a result of globalization (para. 13). Write an essay in which you support or argue against this assertion, using both your own experience and Lam's global and psychological transformation to prove your point.

Responding to Multiple Viewpoints   In an essay, compare how Michael Jonas in "The Downside of Diversity" and Lam in "Globalization vs. Americanization" view the continuing relevance of the idea of "the American melting pot."

For a quiz on this reading, go to bedfordstmartins.com/mirror.

Naming Our Destiny

ARNOLD M. KEE

Arnold M. Kee is a writer who works by day as the manager of Fellowship Administration for the National Consortium for Graduate Degrees for Minorities in Engineering and Science. Previously, he worked for the Institute for Higher Education Policy. His essay "Naming Our Destiny," originally published in 2001 on PopPolitics.com, concerns his struggle to find a name for his son that reflects his identity as an African American.

> **THINKING AHEAD**   To what extent has your family heritage impacted the opportunities you have had in life so far? In what ways do you expect your cultural identity to impact your future? Why? How important is having a sense of one's cultural identity?

C hoosing a name for our first son required a value synthesis. Between 1 my wife and I, one of us wanted an African name to link him to our cultural heritage. The other preferred a more culturally neutral name, to shield our son's résumé or school applications from prejudice. The crossroads of class-oriented and cultural values made me seriously question if we had truly become "bourgeois,"[1] or had we become what some African Americans call "bougie" (pronounced with a soft "g"). Finding the answer would not only clarify my professional mission, it would help us chart the course we want our growing family to follow.

There is a difference between the terms "bourgeois" and "bougie." 2 Bourgeois is an observation identifying a true commitment to frugality, the accumulation of significant material wealth and the preservation of the aristocracy and similar capitalist values. Bougie is a commentary characterizing certain African Americans as mostly concerned with the *appearance* of wealth. It also suggests a mask covering one's true culture.

In some ways, the name we chose for our son was a mask since his eth- 3 nic identity would not be readily apparent. But our deliberations involved more than appearance. When we pored over Web sites and books containing more than twenty thousand names and genealogies, we talked about the symbolism each potential name would carry. Old Testament names were strong candidates because they were derived from virtues like faith, dedication and hard work; by giving him my middle name, which reaches back several generations, it tied him to family tradition. Admittedly, we did give up some of our heritage by not choosing an African name. Yet bougie did not fully explain the reasons for our choice.

---

[1]**bourgeois:** Middle class; marked by commercial interests.

So how about bourgeois? Neither of us has an aristocratic background,   4
nor are we conservative on fiscal policy. We both attended reputable universities, but we're still working on accumulating material wealth. Moreover, our views on social policy seem much too progressive to mesh with
the stodginess[2] evoked by the bourgeois adjective. So bourgeois didn't seem
applicable either.

Still pondering the answer, I was listening to National Public Radio   5
when David Brooks was discussing his book *Bobos in Paradise: The New
Upper Class and How They Got There* (Simon and Schuster, 2000). Brooks
explained that "bobos" are those among the educated elite who attempt
to reconcile bourgeois ideals with bohemian[3] ones (i.e., promote artistic
or cultural expression, question the status quo and serve the disenfranchised[4]). They might also appear to be contradictory at first. Using phrases
like "compassionate conservatism," "smart growth," and "natural hair
color" without irony, they can articulate the link between two (seemingly)
opposing concepts.

Brooks's analysis of the bobo lifestyle can be broken into three cat-   6
egories: environment, personal history and attitude. A bobo environment
includes expensive stores that provide shoppers the opportunity to pay
above-market prices for items made to look old, simple or "earthy." High-
end furniture stores like Ethan Allen or Pottery Barn fit this category with
their rustic and Shaker[5] styles. The personal history of bobos is marked by
high professional achievement based not on family wealth, but on education,
ambition and hard work.

The bobo attitude or world view shapes their environment and guides   7
their personal histories. It moderates their bourgeois taste for expensive
specialty markets with "organic" production or "Old World" cooking. It
balances the hubris that might accompany an elite college degree with community service or understatement ("I went to a small university in New
Haven"). The richer bobos become, the harder they try to find bohemian
ways to express their financial success.

As I listened more closely, I thought perhaps Brooks had captured the   8
disparate ideas I was trying to reconcile. Then a female caller asked him
whether he had attempted to apply his thesis to African Americans; he con-
fessed he hadn't. Thus, I've decided to try to answer the question, believing
it might clarify my perspective on our family's values in the process.

By examining his book, I discovered that upwardly mobile African   9
Americans and bobos share the same spirit. For example, as members from
each group move up the social ladder, many legitimize their success by
channeling it into social causes. My own values seem to be a composite of
the interconnections between the two cultures, but it's worth first taking a
look at the rise of the black bourgeoisie.

---

[2]**stodginess:** Being dull or boring.
[3]**bohemian:** Unconventional.
[4]**disenfranchised:** Deprived of a right.
[5]**Shaker:** Sect that practices a rustic communal life.

Merging Africa and America

Africans who crossed the Atlantic in the 1700s did not bring luggage. How-   10
ever, memories of their old lives were stowed away in their African names.
But when they arrived in the New World, those names were replaced with
European ones, triggering an ongoing process of African redefinition in
America.

Olaudah Equiano exhibited an early attempt at redefinition. He was a   11
slave captured in Northern Nigeria and brought to America around 1755.
His first name, which means "favored," "having a loud voice," and "well
spoken," turned out to be prophetic. It was illegal for slaves to read, but he
found a way to master English and write a narrative in 1789 that recounted
his Atlantic crossing and his introduction to slavery. In one passage he
wrote, "My [new] captain and master called me Gustavus Vassa. I at that
time began to understand him a little, and refused to be called so . . . and
when I refused to answer to my new name, it gained me many a cuff;[6] so
at length I submitted, and was obliged to bear the present name, by which
I have been known ever since."

Equiano forged a new identity out of his African memory and European   12
present; the result was an assimilation formula many African Americans
after him followed to varying degrees. He wrote that he "imbibed their
spirit, and imitated their manners," but he then directed his growing literary
talent toward the Abolition[7] cause.

Perhaps more difficult to reconcile were dual racial identities. A great   13
number of biracial (or less favorably, mulatto) children were born during
slavery, often the result of rape. Their lighter skin generally meant they
would be exempt from grueling fieldwork and would instead perform do-
mestic work. It also meant they would receive a second-hand education of
bourgeois values. By working in the "big house" they were exposed to the
conversations and activities concerning the business of slavery. Hence, they
were white and black, privileged and enslaved.

Some biracial progeny simply accepted the privilege that came with   14
their lighter skin and conferred its benefits upon their "darker" family
members. Others created a separate society, from which sprung a set of
values and traditions still within the spectrum of black culture. For others
still, there was no true reconciliation. They either muted African memories
and "passed" for white or were rejected by their extended family. This
last group lived in a type of cultural exile. In his novel *Autobiography
of an Ex-Colored Man* (Sherman, French & Co., 1912), James Weldon
Johnson described such a dilemma: "Sometimes it seems to me that I have
never really been a Negro, that I have been only a privileged spectator of
their inner life; at other times I feel that I have been a coward, a deserter
and I am possessed by a strange longing for my mother's people." (The
character's mother was black; his father, white.)

[6]**cuff:** Slap.
[7]**Abolition:** The movement to eliminate slavery in the United States.

Questioning Education

Unshackled but not unfettered, free black men and women seeking education found incongruity between it and their self-image. On one hand, education could mean liberation of the mind and preparation for new opportunities. On the other hand, the education they received often advanced European ideals that conflicted with black realities. For example, Western Civilization courses recorded Africa as the "dark continent" or periods of glory for African nations as the "dark ages." African American contributions to history were overlooked or downplayed. Psychological studies of blacks depicted them as sociopaths, genetically prone to commit crime. 15

The question posed to would-be scholars then was: "Does academic excellence in the context of a society that holds African Americans in low regard mean acceptance of anti-black ideals?" Author Carter G. Woodson believed the segregated educational system prepared black students for second-class living. In his landmark book, *The Mis-Education of the Negro* (Africa World Press, Inc., 1933), he wrote: "When you control a man's thinking you do not have to worry about his actions. . . . You do not need to send him to the back door. He will go without being told. In fact, if there is no back door, he will cut one for his special benefit. His education makes it necessary." 16

Conversely, pioneer educators such as Mary McLeod Bethune, W. E. B. Du Bois, Anna Julia Cooper and Booker T. Washington had a more utilitarian[8] outlook. "Education has the irresistible power to dissolve the shackles of slavery," Bethune said. Based on this belief, she went on to build Florida's Bethune-Cookman College. Washington founded Tuskegee University in Alabama. But whether education for blacks was a means to an end or a way to challenge European thought, the quest for education engendered intense introspection. 17

As many doctors, lawyers, educators and other professionals emerged from historically black institutions, they legitimized their education by discussing how it would help their communities. Returning to their native communities to begin private practice, black professionals took pride in providing services that blacks previously found inaccessible. 18

To Be Gifted, Black and Bourgeois

As the black bourgeoisie emerged in the mid-twentieth century, its members started living in enclaves that grew into exclusive communities: Highland Beach, Maryland; Baldwin Park, California; or Oak Bluffs in Martha's Vineyard. These communities also practiced their own form of discrimination by excluding blacks who did not have the proper pedigree. 19

---

[8]**utilitarian:** Practical.

While membership generally guaranteed a financially rewarding professional life, it still could not protect wealthy blacks from the fallout of racial discrimination.

In his trenchant, if not caustic, book *Black Bourgeoisie* (Free Press, 1957), former Howard University Prof. E. Franklin Frazier analyzed the lifestyle of African Americans who had "made it" when school desegregation was occurring. He found that financial or professional success, coupled with their rejection of (and by) white society, led to destructive attempts at personal reconciliation. Instead of using social activism to balance their success, blacks purchased yachts, mansions and cars to mitigate their rejection. Instead of looking at their "blackness" as a context to celebrate the obstacles they had overcome, they saw it as the last obstacle preventing them from true success. The adoption of these "white manners" created other problems, as some were left feeling empty, yet filled with self-hatred.   20

The difficulty in finding equilibrium between bourgeois success and bohemian connections persisted into the late 1980s. When Lois Benjamin interviewed a hundred prominent African Americans for her book *The Black Elite: Facing the Color Line in the Twilight of the Twentieth Century* (Nelson Hall, Inc., 1991), she found that successful corporate executives worried about being labeled "Uncle Toms."[9]   21

Though a misnomer, the term stung when used against blacks accused of trading their ethnic and racial identity for acceptance within a white business environment. Still, they knew they had to stifle progressive ideals if they wanted to be considered for the same positions as whites. Despite their knotted existence, some black corporate executives claimed they could successfully combine their influence with social consciousness. Some tutored children in distressed communities. Others made significant financial or professional contributions to organizations such as the National Urban League and the NAACP.   22

Building upon both Frazier and Benjamin's work, Lawrence Otis Graham has painted the most current picture of the black bourgeoisie in *Our Kind of People: Inside America's Black Upper Class* (HarperCollins, 1999). In observations and interviews, Graham found that elitist attitudes and materialism, which Frazier noted in the 1950s, were still prevalent among the black elite. School reputation, house size, and, to a large extent, the shade of their skin determined which blacks qualified as one of "our kind." And yet Graham, who grew up as one of "our kind" and who also admitted getting a "de-negroidizing" nose job, fervently defended the social conscience of his colleagues. He recounted numerous examples of how exclusive organizations to which he belonged contributed to the well being of their communities.   23

For many of the blacks described within Graham's book, acceptance to the invitation-only inner sanctum of blacks was not only a means to   24

---

[9]**Uncle Toms:** Blacks who seek the approval of whites; from Harriet Beecher Stowe's *Uncle Tom's Cabin.*

success, but success itself. Those who belonged to exclusive black social organizations like Jack and Jill (for young adults), Boulé (for professional men), or Girlfriends (professional women) defended their membership, saying it positioned them for educational and professional opportunities. While that pursuit may in fact lead to material benefits, it is clear that acceptance into such groups is also an end unto itself. Graham notes that negative opinion followed those who mistakenly attended the wrong colleges, joined the wrong Greek organizations, or moved to the wrong neighborhood.

Resolving Incongruities

Reviewing centuries of African American identity and redefinition made   25
it clear that the questions my wife and I asked ourselves about our identity had been raised long ago. Phrases in our lexicon[10] like "Give back to the community," "Remember where you came from" and, more recently, "Keep it real," or pejoratives[11] like "Uncle Tom" and "Oreo" (synonymous with bougie) indicated that many other African Americans were seeking answers to those questions.

This enhanced perspective, however, now provided answers for me: First,   26
none of the terms—bobo, bougie or black bourgeoisie—fully described us. Our high educational and professional standards might appear bougie to those who don't know our true motivations, but we will not change those standards because of appearances. We share the bobo attitude (financial success must blend with social conscience), but we have not yet achieved the financial success typical bobos have enjoyed. Likewise, our community, Prince George's County in Maryland, is still trying to make itself suitable for bobos. Though we have a few interesting bookstores and restaurants, we lack Old World bakeries, Ethan Allen stores and other high-end retail.

Our lives intersect with some of the social structures upon which the   27
black bourgeoisie draw their strength. For instance, my wife went to a prominent historically black college. Also, the church where we were married is known for its network of black professionals. We know the success of the people with whom we interact in these places inspires other young blacks, but we don't share the elitism that genealogically separates one "kind" of successful black from another. Our friendships cross economic boundaries and are based on mutual feelings of respect, not who will help us gain entry into the inner sanctum.

To be a successful black couple in America is to accept some bourgeois   28
values. We maintain thriftiness in order to save money to buy a home. And we help preserve the aristocracy by working at or buying products from Fortune 500 companies instead of starting our own. So we'll just keep on making sure each morning we recognize the couple we see in the mirror.

---

[10]**lexicon:** Vocabulary of a group.
[11]**pejoratives:** Negative remarks; remarks that discourage.

With these answers we could look back on our son's name and feel at peace   29
with our decision. We chose his first name, Spencer, because it seemed to con-
note dignity and individuality. We chose his second name, Madison, because
his father, grandfather and great-grandfather share it. And despite the fact his
name is not identifiably African, our attitudes, experiences and extended family will cause it to take on African American meaning. The clarity these answers provide for our family's mission comes at a great time because Spencer
is now taking his first steps. Likewise, our newly tested convictions made us
more confident when naming his younger brother, Sterling. Over time, each
will come to understand the history, complexity and optimism they represent.

EXERCISING VOCABULARY

1. Record your own definition for each word below in your notebook.

   frugality (n.) (2)   progeny (n.) (14)
   genealogies (n.) (3)   trenchant (adj.) (20)
   articulate (v.) (5)   caustic (adj.) (20)
   hubris (n.) (7)   mitigate (v.) (20)
   assimilation (adj.) (12)   misnomer (n.) (22)
   imbibed (v.) (12)   prevalent (adj.) (23)

2. Kee writes that selecting his oldest son's name "required a value synthesis" (para. 1). What is a synthesis? How can values be synthesized?
   Why was this necessary for Kee and his wife?

3. Explain what the author means by the phrase "unshackled but not unfettered" (para. 15). First define these two adjectives. Then examine and
   explain how Kee uses them here. What point is he making?

4. In this essay, Kee discusses groups and relationships that would give his
   family access to "the inner sanctum" (para. 27). What is a sanctum? With
   what is the word usually associated? What does it mean in this context?

PROBING CONTENT

1. What event in Kee's life caused him to focus so closely on his own cultural identity? Why did this event cause such serious reflection?

2. Explain David Brooks's concept of "bobos." What distinguishes bobos
   from other people? Describe their lives. In what ways are bobos alike
   and different from other African Americans?

3. In what different ways have biracial African Americans regarded their
   heritage? What options were open to them? Why?

4. How did "blacks accused of trading their ethnic and racial identity for
   acceptance" (para. 22) reconcile their economic success with their social
   consciences? Why was this necessary?

CONSIDERING CRAFT

1. Why does Kee choose the title "Naming Our Destiny" for this essay? What dual meaning does this title have?

2. In paragraph 1, Kee notes that "between my wife and I, one of us wanted an African name [for our son]." Why doesn't Kee identify which of the two of them wanted an African name? How does this ambiguity continue throughout the essay?

3. In paragraph 10, Kee uses irony to enforce a point. What is the ironic language in this paragraph? What does this sentence mean? How effectively does this language choice make Kee's point?

4. In the first and the final paragraphs of the selection, Kee creates a framework around his entire essay. How does he accomplish this? How does this stylistic choice shape his writing? What does it contribute to the reader's understanding of Kee's approach to his subject?

WRITING PROMPTS

Responding to the Topic Shakespeare wrote, "What's in a name?" According to Kee, there is much significance in a name. From your own experience, write an essay revealing how significant a person's name is in shaping his or her destiny. Cite specific examples of names that you believe have helped or hindered their recipients.

Responding to the Writer Lawrence Otis Graham, in his book *Our Kind of People*, pursues the idea that membership in certain organizations not only may translate into improved economic status but also may be "an end unto itself" (para. 24). In an essay, agree or disagree with this assertion. Reference specific organizations that you believe may contribute to or be perceived to contribute to a person's acceptance and opportunities to advance.

Responding to Multiple Viewpoints In "Naming Our Destiny," Kee traces "the rise of the black bourgeoisie" (para. 9) in a brief history of blacks in America. Write an essay in which you explain whether the findings reported by Michael Jonas in "The Downside of Diversity" are a logical continuation of the history Kee delivers or a step backward. Use evidence from both essays to support your thesis.

For a quiz on this reading, go to bedfordstmartins.com/mirror.

People Like Us

DAVID BROOKS

David Brooks is a columnist for the *New York Times* and a commentator for
The NewsHour with Jim Lehrer. He is the author of *Bobos in Paradise: The
New Upper Class and How They Got There* (2000) and *On Paradise Drive:
How We Live Now (and Always Have) in the Future Tense* (2004). In 2006,
he was a visiting professor at Duke University's Terry Sanford Institute of
Public Policy. "People Like Us" was first published in the *Atlantic Monthly*
in 2003.

> **THINKING AHEAD**   Since you've been in school, what
> opportunities have you had to interact with people from racial,
> cultural, ethnic, religious, or social backgrounds different from your
> own? To what extent have you taken advantage of these opportunities?
> Why? How has such interaction affected your ideas?

M aybe it's time to admit the obvious. We don't really care about diversity   1
all that much in America, even though we talk about it a great deal.
Maybe somewhere in this country there is a truly diverse neighborhood in
which a black Pentecostal minister lives next to a white antiglobalization
activist, who lives next to an Asian short-order cook, who lives next to
a professional golfer, who lives next to a postmodern-literature professor
and a cardiovascular surgeon. But I have never been to or heard of that
neighborhood. Instead, what I have seen all around the country is people
making strenuous efforts to group themselves with people who are basi-
cally like themselves.

Human beings are capable of drawing amazingly subtle social distinc-   2
tions and then shaping their lives around them. In the Washington, D.C.,
area Democratic lawyers tend to live in suburban Maryland, and Republican
lawyers tend to live in suburban Virginia. If you asked a Democratic lawyer
to move from her $750,000 house in Bethesda, Maryland, to a $750,000
house in Great Falls, Virginia, she'd look at you as if you had just asked
her to buy a pickup truck with a gun rack and to shove chewing tobacco
in her kid's mouth. In Manhattan the owner of a $3 million SoHo loft
would feel out of place moving into a $3 million Fifth Avenue apartment.
A West Hollywood interior decorator would feel dislocated if you asked
him to move to Orange County. In Georgia a barista[1] from Athens would
probably not fit in serving coffee in Americus.

---

[1]**barista:** One who is considered to have professional expertise in the preparation of coffee
   drinks; from the Italian for "bartender."

It is a common complaint that every place is starting to look the same.   3
But in the information age, the late writer James Chapin once told me,
every place becomes more like itself. People are less often tied down to
factories and mills, and they can search for places to live on the basis of
cultural affinity. Once they find a town in which people share their values,
they flock there, and reinforce whatever was distinctive about the town
in the first place. Once Boulder, Colorado, became known as congenial
to politically progressive mountain bikers, half the politically progressive
mountain bikers in the country (it seems) moved there; they made the place
so culturally pure that it has become practically a parody of itself.

But people love it. Make no mistake—we are increasing our happi-   4
ness by segmenting off so rigorously. We are finding places where we are
comfortable and where we feel we can flourish. But the choices we make
toward that end lead to the very opposite of diversity. The United States
might be a diverse nation when considered as a whole, but block by block
and institution by institution it is a relatively homogeneous nation.

When we use the word *diversity* today, we usually mean racial integra-   5
tion. But even here our good intentions seem to have run into the brick
wall of human nature. Over the past generation reformers have tried hero-
ically, and in many cases successfully, to end housing discrimination. But
recent patterns aren't encouraging: According to an analysis of the 2000
census data, the 1990s saw only a slight increase in the racial integration
of neighborhoods in the United States. The number of middle-class and
upper-middle-class African American families is rising, but for whatever
reasons—racism, psychological comfort—these families tend to congregate
in predominantly black neighborhoods.

In fact, evidence suggests that some neighborhoods become more seg-   6
regated over time. New suburbs in Arizona and Nevada, for example,
start out reasonably well integrated. These neighborhoods don't yet have
reputations, so people choose their houses for other, mostly economic reasons. But as neighborhoods age, they develop personalities (that's where
the Asians live, and that's where the Hispanics live), and segmentation
occurs. It could be that in a few years the new suburbs in the Southwest
will be nearly as segregated as the established ones in the Northeast and
the Midwest.

Even though race and ethnicity run deep in American society, we should   7
in theory be able to find areas that are at least culturally diverse. But here,
too, people show few signs of being truly interested in building diverse
communities. If you run a retail company and you're thinking of opening
new stores, you can choose among dozens of consulting firms that are quite
effective at locating your potential customers. They can do this because
people with similar tastes and preferences tend to congregate by ZIP code.

The most famous of these precision marketing firms is Claritas, which   8
breaks down the U.S. population into sixty-two psycho-demographic clus-
ters, based on such factors as how much money people make, what they
like to read and watch, and what products they have bought in the past.

For example, the "suburban sprawl" cluster is composed of young families making about $41,000 a year and living in fast-growing places such as Burnsville, Minnesota, and Bensalem, Pennsylvania. These people are almost twice as likely as other Americans to have three-way calling. They are two and a half times as likely to buy Light n' Lively Kid Yogurt. Members of the "towns & gowns" cluster are recent college graduates in places such as Berkeley, California, and Gainesville, Florida. They are big consumers of DoveBars and *Saturday Night Live*. They tend to drive small foreign cars and to read *Rolling Stone* and *Scientific American*.

Looking through the market research, one can sometimes be amazed 9 by how efficiently people cluster—and by how predictable we all are. If you wanted to sell imported wine, obviously you would have to find places where rich people live. But did you know that the sixteen counties with the greatest proportion of imported-wine drinkers are all in the same three metropolitan areas (New York, San Francisco and Washington, D.C.)? If you tried to open a motor-home dealership in Montgomery County, Pennsylvania, you'd probably go broke because people in this ring of the Philadelphia suburbs think RVs are kind of uncool. But if you traveled just a short way north, to Monroe County, Pennsylvania, you would find yourself in the fifth motor-home-friendliest county in America.

Geography is not the only way we find ourselves divided from people un- 10 like us. Some of us watch Fox News, while others listen to NPR. Some like David Letterman, and others—typically in less urban neighborhoods—like Jay Leno. Some go to charismatic[2] churches; some go to mainstream churches. Americans tend more and more often to marry people with education levels similar to their own and to befriend people with backgrounds similar to their own.

My favorite illustration of this latter pattern comes from the first, 11 noncontroversial chapter of *The Bell Curve*. Think of your twelve closest friends, Richard J. Herrnstein and Charles Murray write. If you had chosen them randomly from the American population, the odds that half of your twelve closest friends would be college graduates would be six in a thousand. The odds that half of the twelve would have advanced degrees would be less than one in a million. Have any of your twelve closest friends graduated from Harvard, Stanford, Yale, Princeton, Caltech, MIT, Duke, Dartmouth, Cornell, Columbia, Chicago or Brown? If you chose your friends randomly from the American population, the odds against your having four or more friends from those schools would be more than a billion to one.

Many of us live in absurdly unlikely groupings because we have orga- 12 nized our lives that way.

It's striking that the institutions that talk the most about diversity often 13 practice it the least. For example, no group of people sings the diversity

[2]**charismatic:** Guided by the power of the Holy Spirit.

anthem more frequently and fervently than administrators at just such elite universities. But elite universities are amazingly undiverse in their values, politics and mores.[3] Professors in particular are drawn from a rather narrow segment of the population. If faculties reflected the general population, 32 percent of professors would be registered Democrats and 31 percent would be registered Republicans. Forty percent would be evangelical Christians. But a recent study of several universities by the conservative Center for the Study of Popular Culture and the American Enterprise Institute found that roughly 90 percent of those professors in the arts and sciences who had registered with a political party had registered Democratic. Fifty-seven professors at Brown were found on the voter-registration rolls. Of those, fifty-four were Democrats. Of the forty-two professors in the English, history, sociology and political-science departments, all were Democrats. The results at Harvard, Penn State, Maryland and the University of California at Santa Barbara were similar to the results at Brown.

What we are looking at here is human nature. People want to be around 14 others who are roughly like themselves. That's called community. It probably would be psychologically difficult for most Brown professors to share an office with someone who was pro-life, a member of the National Rifle Association, or an evangelical Christian. It's likely that hiring committees would subtly—even unconsciously—screen out any such people they encountered. Republicans and evangelical Christians have sensed that they are not welcome at places like Brown, so they don't even consider working there. In fact, any registered Republican who contemplates a career in academia these days is both a hero and a fool. So, in a semi-self-selective pattern, brainy people with generally liberal social mores flow to academia, and brainy people with generally conservative mores flow elsewhere.

The dream of diversity is like the dream of equality. Both are based on 15 ideals we celebrate even as we undermine them daily. (How many times have you seen someone renounce a high-paying job or pull his child from an elite college on the grounds that these things are bad for equality?) On the one hand, the situation is appalling. It is appalling that Americans know so little about one another. It is appalling that many of us are so narrow-minded that we can't tolerate a few people with ideas significantly different from our own. It's appalling that evangelical Christians are practically absent from entire professions, such as academia, the media and filmmaking. It's appalling that people should be content to cut themselves off from everyone unlike themselves.

The segmentation of society means that often we don't even have argu- 16 ments across the political divide. Within their little validating communities, liberals and conservatives circulate half-truths about the supposed awfulness of the other side. These distortions are believed because it feels good to believe them.

[3]**mores:** Beliefs and customs of a particular group.

On the other hand, there are limits to how diverse any community   17
can or should be. I've come to think that it is not useful to try to hammer
diversity into every neighborhood and institution in the United States. Sure,
Augusta National[4] should probably admit women, and university sociology
departments should probably hire a conservative or two. It would be nice
if all neighborhoods had a good mixture of ethnicities. But human nature
being what it is, most places and institutions are going to remain culturally
homogeneous.

It's probably better to think about diverse lives, not diverse institutions.   18
Human beings, if they are to live well, will have to move through a series
of institutions and environments, which may be individually homogeneous
but, taken together, will offer diverse experiences. It might also be a good
idea to make national service a rite of passage for young people in this
country: it would take them out of their narrow neighborhood segment and
thrust them in with people unlike themselves. Finally, it's probably important for adults to get out of their own familiar circles. If you live in a coastal,
socially liberal neighborhood, maybe you should take out a subscription
to *The Door*, the evangelical humor magazine; or maybe you should visit
Branson, Missouri.[5] Maybe you should stop in at a megachurch.[6] Sure, it
would be superficial familiarity, but it beats the iron curtains that now separate the nation's various cultural zones.

Look around at your daily life. Are you really in touch with the broad   19
diversity of American life? Do you care?

EXERCISING VOCABULARY

1. Record your own definition for each word below in your notebook.

strenuous (adj.) (1)	congregate (v.) (5)
congenial (adj.) (3)	fervently (adv.) (13)
parody (n.) (3)	undermine (v.) (15)
segmenting (v.) (4)	appalling (adj.) (15)
homogeneous (adj.) (4)	validating (adj.) (16)

2. In paragraph 2, the author writes, "A West Hollywood interior decorator would feel dislocated" if he were asked to move to Orange County,
   California. With what do we usually associate the term *dislocated*? Why
   does Brooks choose to use that word here? How does it help to convey
   his message?

---

[4]**Augusta National:** Golf club in Augusta, Georgia, that is the official site of the Masters
   Golf Tournament.
[5]**Branson, Missouri:** Vacation center popular with older people and featuring Las Vegas–
   style shows.
[6]**megachurch:** Protestant congregation with a very large number of weekly attendees, often
   nondenominational and generally conservative.

3. Brooks states that people "search for places to live on the basis of cultural affinity" (para. 3). Explain the term *cultural affinity*. How does this tendency affect neighborhoods and communities?

4. Who would be included in a "towns & gowns" community (para. 8)? What "gowns" are referred to here? What would the use of such an expression reveal about a community?

PROBING CONTENT

1. Explain Brooks's statement that, over time, "every place becomes more like itself" (para. 3). How does this theory relate to the idea of the American melting pot?

2. How has what Brooks refers to as "the brick wall of human nature" (para. 5) impacted social integration? What trends does Brooks see developing as a result?

3. What does Brooks maintain is lost when people relate to others like themselves? What long-term effects might this behavior create?

4. Why does Brooks support the idea of required national service? How would such a requirement benefit the country and the participating individuals?

CONSIDERING CRAFT

1. What kind of imagery is Brooks creating in paragraph 2 when he writes that "she'd look at you as if you had just asked her to buy a pickup truck with a gun rack and to shove chewing tobacco in her kid's mouth"? What point is he making? How does this language make his point?

2. In paragraph 13, Brooks focuses on a paradox at elite universities. What is a paradox? What is the paradox that Brooks notes here? How is this paradox expressed on campuses across the United States?

3. Brooks writes that national service should become "a rite of passage" (para. 18). What does this expression mean? Name some cultural rites of passage with which you are familiar. How would national service fit the definition of a rite of passage?

4. In paragraph 18, Brooks writes that even "superficial familiarity" "beats the iron curtains that now separate the nation's various cultural zones." What was the Iron Curtain? How appropriate and effective is Brooks's use of this metaphor?

WRITING PROMPTS

Responding to the Topic   Using your own experience, write an essay in response to the questions "Are you really in touch with the broad diversity of American life? Do you care?" (para. 19). Provide specific examples that support your response.

Responding to the Writer   Write an essay in which you either support or refute Brooks's assertion that "any registered Republican who contemplates a career in academia these days is both a hero and a fool" (para. 14). To obtain material for your essay, interview a number of your instructors who are willing to discuss with you their political opinions and experience as faculty at your institution.

Responding to Multiple Viewpoints   Compare Brooks's ideas about neighborhoods and their populations with those expressed by Shawn Hubler in "Will the Last Gay Bar in Laguna Beach Please Turn Out the Lights?"

For a quiz on this reading, go to bedfordstmartins.com/mirror.

Mongrel America

Gregory Rodriguez

Gregory Rodriguez is a columnist for the *Los Angeles Times*, and his work has also appeared in the *New York Times, the Wall Street Journal*, and the *Washington Post*. He is an Irvine Senior Fellow and the Director of the California Fellows Program for the New America Foundation. In 2007, he published *Mongrels, Bastards, Orphans, and Vagabonds: Mexican Immigration and the Future of Race in America*. The following essay is an excerpt from that book.

> **THINKING AHEAD** How important are racial categories in our society today? To whom are they important? When are they important? Have they gained or lost significance over the last twenty years? Why?

A re racial categories still an important—or even a valid—tool of government policy? In recent years the debate in America has been between those who think that race is paramount and those who think it is increasingly irrelevant, and in the next election cycle this debate will surely intensify around a California ballot initiative that would all but prohibit the state from asking its citizens what their racial backgrounds are. But the ensuing polemics[1] will only obscure the more fundamental question: What, when each generation is more racially and ethnically mixed than its predecessor, does race even mean anymore? If your mother is Asian and your father is African American, what, racially speaking, are you? (And if your spouse is half Mexican and half Russian Jewish, what are your children?) 1

Five decades after the end of legal segregation, and only thirty-six years after the Supreme Court struck down anti-miscegenation[2] laws, young African Americans are considerably more likely than their elders to claim mixed heritage. A study by the Population Research Center, in Portland, Oregon, projects that the black intermarriage rate will climb dramatically in this century, to a point at which 37 percent of African Americans will claim mixed ancestry by 2100. By then more than 40 percent of Asian Americans will be mixed. Most remarkable, however, by century's end the number of Latinos claiming mixed ancestry will be more than two times the number claiming a single background. 2

Not surprisingly, intermarriage rates for all groups are highest in the states that serve as immigration gateways. By 1990 Los Angeles County 3

[1]**polemics:** Fierce attacks on the opinions of others.
[2]**anti-miscegenation:** Opposition to marriage between people of different races.

had an intermarriage rate five times the national average. Latinos and Asians, the groups that have made up three-quarters of immigrants over the past forty years, have helped to create a climate in which ethnic or racial intermarriage is more accepted today than ever before. Nationally, whereas only 8 percent of foreign-born Latinos marry non-Latinos, 32 percent of second-generation and 57 percent of third-generation Latinos marry outside their ethnic group. Similarly, whereas only 13 percent of foreign-born Asians marry non-Asians, 34 percent of second-generation and 54 percent of third-generation Asian Americans do.

Meanwhile, as everyone knows, Latinos are now the largest minority   4
group in the nation. Two-thirds of Latinos, in turn, are of Mexican heritage. This is significant in itself, because their sheer numbers have helped Mexican Americans do more than any other group to alter the country's old racial thinking. For instance, Texas and California, where Mexican Americans are the largest minority, were the first two states to abolish affirmative action: When the collective "minority" populations in those states began to outnumber whites, the racial balance that had made affirmative action politically viable was subverted.

Many Mexican Americans now live in cities or regions where they are   5
a majority, changing the very idea of what it means to be a member of a "minority" group. Because of such demographic changes, a number of the policies designed to integrate nonwhites into the mainstream—affirmative action in college admissions, racial set-asides in government contracting—have been rendered more complicated or even counterproductive in recent years. In California cities where whites have become a minority, it is no longer clear what "diversity" means or what the goals of integration policies should be. The selective magnet-school program of the Los Angeles Unified School District, for example, was originally developed as an alternative to forced busing—a way to integrate ethnic minority students by encouraging them to look beyond their neighborhoods. Today, however, the school district is 71 percent Latino, and Latinos' majority status actually puts them at a disadvantage when applying to magnet schools.

But it is not merely their growing numbers (they will soon be the   6
majority in both California and Texas, and they are already the single largest contemporary immigrant group nationwide) that make Mexican Americans a leading indicator of the country's racial future; rather, it's what they represent. They have always been a complicating element in the American racial system, which depends on an oversimplified classification scheme. Under the pre-civil-rights formulation, for example, if you had "one drop" of African blood, you were fully black. The scheme couldn't accommodate people who were part one thing and part another. Mexicans, who are a product of intermingling—both cultural and genetic—between the Spanish and the many indigenous peoples of North and Central America, have a history of tolerating and even reveling in such ambiguity. Since the conquest of Mexico, in the sixteenth century, they have practiced *mestizaje*—racial and cultural synthesis—both in their own country and

as they came north. Unlike the English-speaking settlers of the western frontier, the Spaniards were willing everywhere they went to allow racial and cultural mixing to blur the lines between themselves and the natives. The fact that Latin America is far more heavily populated by people of mixed ancestry than Anglo America is the clearest sign of the difference between the two outlooks on race.

Nativists[3] once deplored the Mexican tendency toward hybridity. In the mid-nineteenth century, at the time of the conquest of the Southwest, Secretary of State James Buchanan feared granting citizenship to a "mongrel race." And in the late 1920s Representative John C. Box, of Texas, warned his colleagues on the House Immigration and Naturalization Committee that the continued influx of Mexican immigrants could lead to the "distressing process of mongrelization" in America. He argued that because Mexicans were the products of mixing, they harbored a relaxed attitude toward interracial unions and were likely to mingle freely with other races in the United States.   7

Box was right. The typical cultural isolation of immigrants notwithstanding, those immigrants' children and grandchildren are strongly oriented toward the American melting pot. Today two-thirds of multiracial and multiethnic births in California involve a Latino parent. *Mexicanidad*, or "Mexicanness," is becoming the catalyst for a new American cultural synthesis.   8

In the same way that the rise in the number of multiracial Americans muddles U.S. racial statistics, the growth of the Mexican American mestizo[4] population has begun to challenge the Anglo American binary view of race. In the 1920 census Mexicans were counted as whites. Ten years later they were reassigned to a separate Mexican "racial" category. In 1940 they were officially reclassified as white. Today almost half the Latinos in California, which is home to a third of the nation's Latinos (most of them of Mexican descent), check "other" as their race. In the first half of the twentieth century Mexican American advocates fought hard for the privileges that came with being white in America. But since the 1960s activists have sought to reap the benefits of being nonwhite minorities. Having spent so long trying to fit into one side or the other of the binary system, Mexican Americans have become numerous and confident enough to simply claim their brownness—their mixture. This is a harbinger of America's future.   9

The original melting-pot concept was incomplete: It applied only to white ethnics (Irish, Italians, Poles and so forth), not to blacks and other nonwhites. Israel Zangwill, the playwright whose 1908 drama *The Melting Pot* popularized the concept, even wrote that whites were justified in avoiding intermarriage with blacks. In fact, multiculturalism—the ideology that promotes the permanent coexistence of separate but equal cultures in one place—can be seen as a by-product of America's exclusion of African   10

[3]**Nativists:** Those who favor people native to an area as opposed to immigrants.
[4]**mestizo:** Someone of mixed racial heritage, often a combination of Mexican and Caucasian.

Americans from the melting pot; those whom assimilation rejected came to reject assimilation. Although the multicultural movement has always encompassed other groups, blacks gave it its moral impetus.

But the immigrants of recent decades are helping to forge a new   11 American identity, something more complex than either a melting pot or a confederation of separate but equal groups. And this identity is emerging not as a result of politics or any specific public policies but because of powerful underlying cultural forces. To be sure, the civil-rights movement was instrumental in the initial assault on racial barriers. And immigration policies since 1965 have tended to favor those immigrant groups — Asians and Latinos — who are most open to intermarriage. But in recent years the government's major contribution to the country's growing multiracialism has been — as it should continue to be — a retreat from dictating limits on interracial intimacy and from exalting (through such policies as racial set-asides and affirmative action) race as the most important American category of being. As a result, Americans cross racial lines more often than ever before in choosing whom to sleep with, marry, or raise children with.

Unlike the advances of the civil-rights movement, the future of racial   12 identity in America is unlikely to be determined by politics or the courts or public policy. Indeed, at this point perhaps the best thing the government can do is to acknowledge changes in the meaning of race in America and then get out of the way. The Census Bureau's decision to allow Americans to check more than one box in the "race" section of the 2000 Census was an important step in this direction. No longer forced to choose a single racial identity, Americans are now free to identify themselves as mestizos — and with this newfound freedom we may begin to endow racial issues with the complexity and nuance they deserve.

EXERCISING VOCABULARY

1. Record your own definition for each word below in your notebook.

paramount (adj.) (1)	reveling (v.) (6)
viable (adj.) (4)	catalyst (n.) (8)
subverted (v.) (4)	binary (adj.) (9)
demographic (adj.) (5)	impetus (n.) (10)
rendered (v.) (5)	exalting (v.) (11)
indigenous (adj.) (6)	nuance (n.) (12)

2. Explain the concept of *mestizaje* (para. 6). How does this term define the outlook on race prevalent in Latin America? How is this outlook at odds with the Anglo American viewpoint?

3. In paragraph 7, Rodriguez uses the term *hybridity*. What association is usually made with the noun *hybrid*? How is a hybrid created? How effective is the author's use of the term here to convey his point?

4. Rodriguez asserts that the willingness of Mexican Americans to acknowledge their mixed heritage is "a harbinger of America's future" (para. 9). Define the term *harbinger.* How does this word depict what the author wishes to explain?

PROBING CONTENT

1. According to Rodriguez, what are the trends regarding interracial marriages? In what areas of the United States do such marriages occur most frequently? Why?

2. How has the identification of a "minority group" become more difficult recently in some cities and states? What have been some unexpected consequences of the population shifts that have occurred?

3. Explain multiculturalism as Rodriguez defines it. How does multiculturalism relate to the "melting pot" idea? According to Rodriguez, what group is most responsible for the rise of multiculturalism? Why?

4. What initiated the breakdown of racial barriers? What forces will propel this breakdown into the future? How has this shift occurred?

CONSIDERING CRAFT

1. Explain the title of this essay. With what is the word *mongrel* usually associated? How does the connotative meaning of this word differ from its denotative meaning? How well does this title fit the author's thesis?

2. Where is Rodriguez's thesis statement located in this selection? Why does he locate it there? How does its location affect your reading of the selection?

3. Look at the transitions between Rodriguez's paragraphs in this essay. By skillfully using transitions, he has moved his discussion forward carefully and smoothly. Cite several instances of effective transitions in this essay, and explain how Rodriguez uses them to make his thoughts flow seamlessly.

WRITING PROMPTS

Responding to the Topic   You or someone you know may have family members of different cultural backgrounds. In an essay, explore the impact of mixed heritage on an American family. What are the benefits and the disadvantages?

Responding to the Writer   In an essay, argue for or against identifying one's race or cultural identity on documents such as census forms, college applications, student loan or scholarship applications, and others you choose to discuss.

Responding to Multiple Viewpoints   What advice would Rodriguez give to Arnold Kee as Kee and his wife consider names for their son ("Naming Our Destiny")?

DRAWING CONNECTIONS

1. How might David Brooks, author of "People Like Us," respond to Rodriguez's questions about what race really means in the United States today ("Mongrel America," para. 1)? How do Brooks's conclusions about diversity support or contradict Rodriguez's data showing a more frequent rate of intermarriage? Use text from each of the essays to support your response.

2. In "People Like Us," David Brooks contends that "the United States might be a diverse nation when considered as a whole, but block by block and institution by institution it is a relatively homogeneous nation" (para. 4). Rodriguez argues just the opposite, that "Americans cross racial lines more often than ever before in choosing whom to sleep with, marry, or raise children with" ("Mongrel America," para. 11). How will it be possible for America to be richly integrated in the bedroom but widely segregated in neighborhoods and communities? Which of these two authors do you believe paints a more accurate picture, based on your own experience? Defend your response with evidence from the essays.

For a quiz on this reading, go to bedfordstmartins.com/mirror.

The Downside of Diversity

MICHAEL JONAS

Michael Jonas is acting editor for *CommonWealth* magazine, published by a nonprofit public policy think tank in Boston, Massachusetts. He also writes a weekly column on local politics for the *Boston Globe*. "The Downside of Diversity" was first published in the *Boston Globe* in August 2007. In this article, Jonas discusses research by a Harvard political scientist that challenges commonly held beliefs about the value of civic diversity.

> **THINKING AHEAD** How beneficial do you believe diversity is to the quality of life in a community? What are the advantages of being surrounded by a very diverse population? What are the drawbacks?

1   It has become increasingly popular to speak of racial and ethnic diversity as a civic strength. From multicultural festivals to pronouncements from political leaders, the message is the same: our differences make us stronger.

2   But a massive new study, based on detailed interviews of nearly thirty thousand people across America, has concluded just the opposite. Harvard political scientist Robert Putnam—famous for *Bowling Alone*, his 2000 book on declining civic engagement—has found that the greater the diversity in a community, the fewer people vote and the less they volunteer, the less they give to charity and work on community projects. In the most diverse communities, neighbors trust one another about half as much as they do in the most homogenous settings. The study, the largest ever on civic engagement in America, found that virtually all measures of civic health are lower in more diverse settings.

3   "The extent of the effect is shocking," says Scott Page, a University of Michigan political scientist.

4   The study comes at a time when the future of the American melting pot is the focus of intense political debate, from immigration to race-based admissions to schools, and it poses challenges to advocates on all sides of the issues. The study is already being cited by some conservatives as proof of the harm large-scale immigration causes to the nation's social fabric. But with demographic trends already pushing the nation inexorably toward greater diversity, the real question may yet lie ahead: how to handle the unsettling social changes that Putnam's research predicts.

5   "We can't ignore the findings," says Ali Noorani, executive director of the Massachusetts Immigrant and Refugee Advocacy Coalition. "The big question we have to ask ourselves is, what do we do about it; what are the next steps?"

The study is part of a fascinating new portrait of diversity emerging   6
from recent scholarship. Diversity, it shows, makes us uncomfortable — but
discomfort, it turns out, isn't always a bad thing. Unease with differences
helps explain why teams of engineers from different cultures may be ideally
suited to solve a vexing problem. Culture clashes can produce a dynamic
give-and-take, generating a solution that may have eluded a group of people
with more similar backgrounds and approaches. At the same time, though,
Putnam's work adds to a growing body of research indicating that more
diverse populations seem to extend themselves less on behalf of collective
needs and goals.

His findings on the downsides of diversity have also posed a chal-   7
lenge for Putnam, a liberal academic whose own values put him squarely
in the pro-diversity camp. Suddenly finding himself the bearer of bad
news, Putnam has struggled with how to present his work. He gathered
the initial raw data in 2000 and issued a press release the following year
outlining the results. He then spent several years testing other possible
explanations.

When he finally published a detailed scholarly analysis in June in the   8
journal *Scandinavian Political Studies*, he faced criticism for straying from
data into advocacy. His paper argues strongly that the negative effects of
diversity can be remedied and says history suggests that ethnic diversity
may eventually fade as a sharp line of social demarcation.

"Having aligned himself with the central planners intent on sustaining   9
such social engineering, Putnam concludes the facts with a stern pep talk,"
wrote conservative commentator Ilana Mercer, in a recent *Orange County
Register* op-ed[1] titled "Greater diversity equals more misery."

Putnam has long staked out ground as both a researcher and a civic   10
player, someone willing to describe social problems and then have a hand
in addressing them. He says social science should be "simultaneously rigorous and relevant," meeting high research standards while also "speaking to
concerns of our fellow citizens." But on a topic as charged as ethnicity and
race, Putnam worries that many people hear only what they want to.

"It would be unfortunate if a politically correct progressivism were to   11
deny the reality of the challenge to social solidarity posed by diversity," he
writes in the new report. "It would be equally unfortunate if an ahistorical
and ethnocentric conservatism were to deny that addressing that challenge
is both feasible and desirable."

Putnam is the nation's premier guru of civic engagement. After studying   12
civic life in Italy in the 1970s and 1980s, Putnam turned his attention to
the United States, publishing an influential journal article on civic engagement in 1995 that he expanded five years later into the best-selling *Bowling
Alone*. The book sounded a national wake-up call on what Putnam called

---

[1]op-ed: In a newspaper, a page opposite the editorials.

a sharp drop in civic connections among Americans. It won him audiences with presidents Bill Clinton and George W. Bush and made him one of the country's best known social scientists.

Putnam claims the United States has experienced a pronounced decline in "social capital," a term he helped popularize. Social capital refers to the social networks — whether friendships or religious congregations or neighborhood associations — that he says are key indicators of civic well-being. When social capital is high, says Putnam, communities are better places to live. Neighborhoods are safer; people are healthier; and more citizens vote.   13

The results of his new study come from a survey Putnam directed among residents in forty-one U.S. communities, including Boston. Residents were sorted into the four principal categories used by the U.S. Census: black, white, Hispanic, and Asian. They were asked how much they trusted their neighbors and those of each racial category, and questioned about a long list of civic attitudes and practices, including their views on local government, their involvement in community projects and their friendships. What emerged in more diverse communities was a bleak picture of civic desolation, affecting everything from political engagement to the state of social ties.   14

Putnam knew he had provocative findings on his hands. He worried about coming under some of the same liberal attacks that greeted Daniel Patrick Moynihan's landmark 1965 report on the social costs associated with the breakdown of the black family. There is always the risk of being pilloried[2] as the bearer of "an inconvenient truth," says Putnam.   15

After releasing the initial results in 2001, Putnam says he spent time "kicking the tires really hard" to be sure the study had it right. Putnam realized, for instance, that more diverse communities tended to be larger, have greater income ranges, higher crime rates and more mobility among their residents — all factors that could depress social capital independent of any impact ethnic diversity might have.   16

"People would say, 'I bet you forgot about X,'" Putnam says of the string of suggestions from colleagues. "There were twenty or thirty X's."   17

But even after statistically taking them all into account, the connection remained strong: Higher diversity meant lower social capital. In his findings, Putnam writes that those in more diverse communities tend to "distrust their neighbors, regardless of the color of their skin, to withdraw even from close friends, to expect the worst from their community and its leaders, to volunteer less, give less to charity and work on community projects less often, to register to vote less, to agitate for social reform more but have less faith that they can actually make a difference, and to huddle unhappily in front of the television."   18

---

[2]**pilloried:** Publicly punished or exposed to ridicule.

"People living in ethnically diverse settings appear to 'hunker   19
down'—that is, to pull in like a turtle," Putnam writes.

In documenting that hunkering down, Putnam challenged the two domi-   20
nant schools of thought on ethnic and racial diversity, the "contact" theory
and the "conflict" theory. Under the contact theory, more time spent with
those of other backgrounds leads to greater understanding and harmony
between groups. Under the conflict theory, that proximity produces tension
and discord.

Putnam's findings reject both theories. In more diverse communities,   21
he says, there were neither great bonds formed across group lines nor
heightened ethnic tensions, but a general civic malaise.[3] And in perhaps
the most surprising result of all, levels of trust were not only lower between groups in more diverse settings but even among members of the
same group.

"Diversity, at least in the short run," he writes, "seems to bring out the   22
turtle in all of us."

The overall findings may be jarring during a time when it's become   23
commonplace to sing the praises of diverse communities, but researchers in
the field say they shouldn't be.

"It's an important addition to a growing body of evidence on the   24
challenges created by diversity," says Harvard economist Edward
Glaeser.

In a recent study, Glaeser and colleague Alberto Alesina demonstrated   25
that roughly half the difference in social welfare spending between the
United States and Europe—Europe spends far more—can be attributed
to the greater ethnic diversity of the U.S. population. Glaeser says lower
national social welfare spending in the United States is a "macro" version
of the decreased civic engagement Putnam found in more diverse communities within the country.

Economists Matthew Kahn of UCLA and Dora Costa of MIT reviewed   26
fifteen recent studies in a 2003 paper, all of which linked diversity with
lower levels of social capital. Greater ethnic diversity was linked, for example, to lower school funding, census response rates, and trust in others.
Kahn and Costa's own research documented higher desertion rates in the
Civil War among Union Army soldiers serving in companies whose soldiers
varied more by age, occupation and birthplace.

Birds of different feathers may sometimes flock together, but they are   27
also less likely to look out for one another. "Everyone is a little self-conscious
that this is not politically correct stuff," says Kahn.

So how to explain New York, London, Rio de Janiero, Los Angeles—   28
the great melting-pot cities that drive the world's creative and financial
economies?

---

[3]**malaise:** Lack of a sense of well-being.

The image of civic lassitude dragging down more diverse communities　29
is at odds with the vigor often associated with urban centers, where ethnic
diversity is greatest. It turns out there is a flip side to the discomfort diversity can cause. If ethnic diversity, at least in the short run, is a liability for
social connectedness, a parallel line of emerging research suggests it can
be a big asset when it comes to driving productivity and innovation. In
high-skill workplace settings, says Scott Page, the University of Michigan
political scientist, the different ways of thinking among people from different cultures can be a boon.

"Because they see the world and think about the world differently than　30
you, that's challenging," says Page, author of *The Difference: How the
Power of Diversity Creates Better Groups, Firms, Schools, and Societies.*
"But by hanging out with people different than you, you're likely to get
more insights. Diverse teams tend to be more productive."

In other words, those in more diverse communities may do more bowl-　31
ing alone, but the creative tensions unleashed by those differences in the
workplace may vault those same places to the cutting edge of the economy
and of creative culture.

Page calls it the "diversity paradox." He thinks the contrasting pos-　32
itive and negative effects of diversity can coexist in communities, but
"there's got to be a limit." If civic engagement falls off too far, he says,
it's easy to imagine the positive effects of diversity beginning to wane as
well. "That's what's unsettling about his findings," Page says of Putnam's
new work.

Meanwhile, by drawing a portrait of civic engagement in which more　33
homogeneous communities seem much healthier, some of Putnam's worst
fears about how his results could be used have been realized. A stream
of conservative commentary has begun—from places like the Manhattan Institute and *The American Conservative*—highlighting the harm the
study suggests will come from large-scale immigration. But Putnam says
he's also received hundreds of complimentary e-mails laced with bigoted
language. "It certainly is not pleasant when David Duke's[4] Web site hails
me as the guy who found out racism is good," he says.

In the final quarter of his paper, Putnam puts the diversity challenge　34
in a broader context by describing how social identity can change over
time. Experience shows that social divisions can eventually give way to
"more encompassing identities" that create a "new, more capacious sense
of 'we,'" he writes.

Growing up in the 1950s in a small Midwestern town, Putnam knew　35
the religion of virtually every member of his high school graduating class
because, he says, such information was crucial to the question of "who was
a possible mate or date." The importance of marrying within one's faith,

---

[4]**David Duke:** Former Grand Wizard of the Knights of the Ku Klux Klan.

he says, has largely faded since then, at least among many mainline Protestants, Catholics and Jews.

While acknowledging that racial and ethnic divisions may prove more   36
stubborn, Putnam argues that such examples bode well for the long-term prospects for social capital in a multiethnic America.

In his paper, Putnam cites the work done by Page and others, and uses   37
it to help frame his conclusion that increasing diversity in America is not only inevitable, but ultimately valuable and enriching. As for smoothing over the divisions that hinder civic engagement, Putnam argues that Americans can help that process along through targeted efforts. He suggests expanding support for English-language instruction and investing in community centers and other places that allow for "meaningful interaction across ethnic lines."

Some critics have found his prescriptions underwhelming. And in offer-   38
ing ideas for mitigating his findings, Putnam has drawn scorn for stepping out of the role of dispassionate researcher. "You're just supposed to tell your peers what you found," says John Leo, senior fellow at the Manhattan Institute, a conservative think tank. "I don't expect academics to fret about these matters."

But fretting about the state of American civic health is exactly what   39
Putnam has spent more than a decade doing. While continuing to research questions involving social capital, he has directed the Saguaro Seminar, a project he started at Harvard's Kennedy School of Government that promotes efforts throughout the country to increase civic connections in communities.

"Social scientists are both scientists and citizens," says Alan Wolfe, director   40
of the Boisi Center for Religion and American Public Life at Boston College, who sees nothing wrong in Putnam's efforts to affect some of the phenomena he studies.

Wolfe says what is unusual is that Putnam has published findings as a   41
social scientist that are not the ones he would have wished for as a civic leader. There are plenty of social scientists, says Wolfe, who never produce research results at odds with their own worldview.

"The problem too often," says Wolfe, "is people are never uncomfortable   42
about their findings."

EXERCISING VOCABULARY

1. Record your own definition for each word below in your notebook.

homogenous (adj.) (2)	provocative (adj.) (15)
demographic (adj.) (4)	lassitude (n.) (29)
inexorably (adv.) (4)	wane (v.) (32)
vexing (adj.) (6)	mitigating (adj.) (38)
demarcation (n.) (8)	

2. According to Jonas, Putnam is concerned about "an ahistorical and eth-nocentric conservatism" (para. 11). How does the meaning of the word *historical* change when the prefix *a* is added? What do the two halves of the word *ethnocentric* mean? What is the implication when this prefix and suffix are combined?

3. In paragraph 12, Jonas refers to Putnam as "the nation's premier guru of civic engagement." What is a guru? Name several other individuals who have been referred to as gurus. How does Jonas justify bestowing this title on Putnam?

4. Putnam delayed releasing the final results of his study to allow him-self to spend time "kicking the tires really hard" (para. 16). What does this expression mean literally, and in reference to what is it usually used? When it is used figuratively, as it is here, what does it mean?

PROBING CONTENT

1. According to Jonas, why might a culturally diverse team of experts be able to solve a problem that a team from similar backgrounds could not solve? How would Scott Page from the University of Michigan respond?

2. Based on Robert Putnam's research, what is the downside of living in a diverse community? Why may diverse communities present "a bleak picture of civic desolation" (para. 14)?

3. Explain Putman's concept of "social capital" (para. 13).

4. What is Putnam's position on the increasing diversity in America? What can Americans do to make that diversity productive?

CONSIDERING CRAFT

1. The original subtitle of this selection was "A Harvard political scientist finds that diversity hurts civic life. What happens when a liberal scholar unearths an inconvenient truth?" When you read "an inconvenient truth," what comes to mind? If Jonas is making a deliberate effort to link Putnam's research results with another very public concern, how effective is this strategy? What is that concern?

2. You may be familiar with the expression "Birds of a feather flock to-gether." Jonas bends that saying to suit his purpose here and writes, "Birds of different feathers may sometimes flock together, but they are also less likely to look out for one another" (para. 27). What does Jonas achieve by varying the wording of an expression with which many

readers will already be familiar? Does this provide greater clarity for you, or does it create confusion? In what way?

3. In this selection, Jonas delivers the majority of what many readers will perceive as "bad news" first before mitigating that bad news with hope for the future. Is this a wise pattern of organization for his content? Why or why not?

4. In paragraph 4, Jonas questions the future of "the American melting pot." What is the origin of that expression? How does its use here further Jonas's argument?

WRITING PROMPTS

Responding to the Topic   Using your personal experience, write an essay exploring the assertion that "virtually all measures of civic health are lower in more diverse settings" (para. 2).

Responding to the Writer   Robert Putnam delayed releasing the final results of his study because the results contradicted his own beliefs. Write an essay in which you support or reject Putnam's decision to share his research findings in spite of their controversial nature.

Responding to Multiple Viewpoints   Compare the viewpoint of Jonas in this essay with that of Shawn Hubler in "Will the Last Gay Bar in Laguna Beach Please Turn Out the Lights?" on the value and "social capital" of diverse neighborhoods.

For a quiz on this reading, go to bedfordstmartins.com/mirror.

Wrapping Up Chapter 3

CONNECTING TO THE CULTURE

1. Think about celebrities who have helped shape your cultural identity. They might be models, sports figures, musicians, or television personalities. They might have had positive, negative, or mixed influences on you. Write an essay in which you trace the influence these people have had on your cultural identity.

2. Since you have been attending college, what new cultural influences have you experienced? Have they been positive, negative, or mixed? To what extent have you been influenced? In what ways have these influences changed you?

3. What influence has your particular cultural group had on the formation of your self-image? Give specific examples.

4. Imagine yourself as a current or future parent and identify some negative cultural influences on the formation of cultural identity in children. Detail how you would attempt to curb those influences.

5. What role do you think television plays in shaping and reinforcing our ideas about people of cultures or races different from our own? Cite specific examples of television shows to support your points.

Focusing on Yesterday, Focusing on Today

Norman Rockwell's art for *The Saturday Evening Post* has long been considered a staple of American popular culture. This New England artist rendered the everyday moments that have defined our society, catching our humanity and our frailty in a way that everyone can relate to and few other artists can match. In this iconic 1943 painting, *Freedom from Want*, Rockwell captures a moment familiar to many Americans, the extended family gathered around the table celebrating Thanksgiving. The song lyrics "Over the river and through the woods to Grandmother's house we go" may come to mind as we seem to be invited into this happy gathering by the smiling figures around the table.

Freedom from Want

This contemporary drawing by Charlie Powell titled *One Big Happy Family* (Salon.com, 2004) captures a "family" moment similar to Rockwell's but with a distinctly different cast of characters. As we examine these diverse figures gathered around the table, we find ourselves composing our own story about the scene depicted and the probable dinner table conversation.

Both images celebrate that distinctly American holiday, Thanksgiving. Why is this ironic in the case of the Powell drawing? Who's missing from the Norman Rockwell painting? From the Powell drawing? As you consider the two images, reflect on these questions: What is the image of American life and culture represented by each? How do these visuals reflect the changes in American culture across the sixty-plus years that separate them? What has remained the same? How accurate are the titles of the two images? To what extent does either of these visuals represent the Thanksgiving celebrations that your family has experienced? How do your family's cultural traditions compare with those suggested by the two visuals?

One Big Happy Family

4 "How Do I Look?"

How Culture Shapes Self-Image

Analyzing the Image

This illustration accompanied the May 31, 2004, *U.S. News & World Report* cover story titled "Makeover Nation." Its inspiration is Grant Wood's iconic oil painting *American Gothic,* which features a serious-looking farm couple standing in front of their gothic-style farmhouse. Recently, Wood's painting has appeared in the opening credits of the popular television show *Desperate Housewives.* It also inspired a poster for the reality television show *The Simple Life*, which starred Paris Hilton and Nicole Richie.

- Why did the artist choose the painting *American Gothic* for his inspiration?

- What modern touches did the artist add to Wood's painting?

- Why did the artist make the changes he did?

- What message about current American culture does this visual convey?

Research this topic with TopLinks at bedfordstmartins.com/toplinks.

GEARING UP Think about the forces that have shaped the image you project to the world. Make a list of the major influences on your personal style. These might include people you know, television and movie actors, fashion models, makeover shows, advertisements, magazines, Web sites, or even music videos. Then think about specific times during your teen years when you were satisfied or dissatisfied with the way you appeared to others. Why did you feel the way you did? How did these feelings affect you? To what extent do you still feel the effects today?

We are aware of how we look to others from the time we are toddlers. "What a pretty little girl" or "What a big strong boy" echoes in our ears and in our minds. At an early age, we begin to realize that there are very specific feminine and masculine ideals of beauty and behavior. Although these may be somewhat culture-specific, all Americans, regardless of ethnicity, quickly discover that the dominant ideal is represented by young, attractive men or women with toned bodies, winning personalities, and a great sense of style. Think about the Abercrombie & Fitch models frolicking on the beach, the famous faces selling Revlon cosmetics, or the curvaceous Victoria's Secret models lounging in sexy lingerie. Think, too, of the movie stars, television actors, and sports stars you watch and have possibly come to idolize. Do you feel that their good looks and confidence often contribute substantially to their success? Hasn't research shown that attractive people have an edge over those judged less attractive when all other attributes are equal? Is it an accident that the great majority of American presidents have been more than six feet tall and that tall men are more successful than short men in the world of business? Even in the virtual world, it is rare to find overweight avatars.

Most of us never have and never will look like these "beautiful" people. Luckily, for many of us, our appearance does not become a major lifelong obsession. Though we may have grown up playing with Barbie or Ken (in their WASP or ethnic versions), we didn't grow up thinking we had to look like them or like the contestants on *America's Next Top Model* or the star of *The Bachelor*. Even though most people find the teenage years difficult because that is when we begin to discover who we are, we generally grow into fairly confident adults who are comfortable in our own skins. Most of us have decided to make the most of our good features and to downplay or simply live with the less-than-perfect ones.

For some people, however, the search for the perfect look becomes a distracting, even life-threatening, obsession. In an effort to improve the bodies they were born with or to reverse the march of time, men and women alike have succumbed to some form of makeover madness like fad diets and exercise programs, steroids and liposuction, Botox and collagen injections, and extreme body modification and cosmetic surgery. In this chapter, you will read selections by a variety of authors about their own struggles with or reflections on self-image. Some of the essays are humorous, and some are serious. All, however, should make you reflect on not only the image you see in the mirror every morning, but also the image you want others to see. Additionally, these readings should encourage you to reflect on those cultural influences that have helped shape who you are, how you see yourself, and how others see you.

> **COLLABORATING**   In groups of four to six students, discuss the question "What makes people attractive?" Brainstorm a list of ten attributes for men and ten for women. Then study your lists to determine how many of these qualities relate to body image and how many to behavior. Share your observations with the rest of the class.

My Inner Shrimp

GARRY TRUDEAU

Garry Trudeau's humorous essay "My Inner Shrimp" examines the impact of body image on the fragile self-esteem of a teenager. Trudeau is well known for his comic strip *Doonesbury*, for which he won a Pulitzer Prize in 1975. He has contributed articles to *The New Yorker*, *The New Republic*, *Harper's*, the *Washington Post*, *Time*, and the *New York Times*. "My Inner Shrimp" first appeared in the *New York Times Magazine* on March 31, 1997.

> **THINKING AHEAD**   Describe a time when you were dissatisfied with the way you looked, when your "inner" and "outer" body image were at odds. How did this affect you?

For the rest of my days, I shall be a recovering short person. Even from my lofty perch of something over six feet (as if I don't know within a micron), I have the soul of a shrimp. I feel the pain of the diminutive, irrespective of whether they feel it themselves, because my visit to the planet of the teenage midgets was harrowing, humiliating, and extended. I even perceive my last-minute escape to have been flukish,[1] somehow unearned — as if the Commissioner of Growth Spurts had been an old classmate of my father.

My most recent reminder of all this came the afternoon I went hunting for a new office. I had noticed a building under construction in my neighborhood — a brick warren[2] of duplexes, with wide, westerly-facing windows, promising ideal light for a working studio. When I was ushered into the model unit, my pulse quickened: The soaring, twenty-two-foot living room walls were gloriously aglow with the remains of the day. I bonded immediately.

Almost as an afterthought, I ascended the staircase to inspect the loft, ducking as I entered the bedroom. To my great surprise, I stayed ducked: The room was a little more than six feet in height. While my head technically cleared the ceiling, the effect was excruciatingly oppressive. This certainly wasn't a space I wanted to spend any time in, much less take out a mortgage on.

Puzzled, I wandered down to the sales office and asked if there were any other units to look at. No, replied a resolutely unpleasant receptionist, it was the last one. Besides, they were all exactly alike.

---

[1]**flukish:** Relating to good or bad luck.
[2]**warren:** A mazelike place where one could easily become lost.

"Are you aware of how low the bedroom ceilings are?" I asked.   5

She shot me an evil look. "Of course we are," she snapped. "There were   6
some problems with the building codes. The architect knows all about the
ceilings.

"He's not an idiot, you know," she added, perfectly anticipating my   7
next question.

She abruptly turned away, but it was too late. She'd just confirmed   8
that a major New York developer, working with a fully licensed architect,
had knowingly created an entire twelve-story apartment building virtually
uninhabitable by anyone of even average height. It was an exclusive highrise
for shorties.

Once I knew that, of course, I couldn't stay away. For days thereafter,   9
as I walked to work, some perverse, unreasoning force would draw me
back to the building. But it wasn't just the absurdity, the stone silliness of
its design that had me in its grip; it was something far more compelling.
Like some haunted veteran come again to an ancient battlefield, I was revisiting
my perilous past.

When I was fourteen, I was the third-smallest in a high school class of   10
one hundred boys, routinely mistaken for a sixth grader. My first week of
school, I was drafted into a contingent of students ignominiously dubbed
the "Midgets," so grouped by taller boys presumably so they could taunt
us with more perfect efficiency. Inexplicably, some of my fellow Midgets refused to be diminished by the experience, but I retreated into self-pity. I sent
away for a book on how to grow tall, and committed to memory its tips on
overcoming one's genetic destiny—or at least making the most of a regret-
table situation. The book cited historical figures who had gone the latter
route—Alexander the Great, Caesar, Napoleon (the mind involuntarily
added Hitler). Strategies for stretching the limbs were suggested—hanging
from door frames, sleeping on your back, doing assorted floor exercises—all
of which I incorporated into my daily routine (get up, brush teeth, hang from
door frame). I also learned the importance of meeting girls early in the day,
when, the book assured me, my rested spine rendered me perceptibly taller.

For six years, my condition persisted; I grew, but at nowhere near the   11
rate of my peers. I perceived other problems as ancillary, and loaded up
the stature issue with freight shipped in daily from every corner of my
life. Lack of athletic success, all absence of a social life, the inevitable run-
ins with bullies—all could be attributed to the missing inches. The night
I found myself sobbing in my father's arms was the low point; we both
knew it was one problem he couldn't fix.

Of course what we couldn't have known was that he and my mother   12
already had. They had given me a delayed developmental timetable. In my
seventeenth year, I miraculously shot up six inches, just in time for graduation and a fresh start. I was, in the space of a few months, reborn—and
I made the most of it. Which is to say that thereafter, all of life's disappointments, reversals, and calamities still arrived on schedule—but blissfully
free of subtext.

Once you stop being the butt, of course, any problem recedes, if only to   13
give way to a new one. And yet the impact of being literally looked down
on, of being *made* to feel small, is forever. It teaches you how to stretch,
how to survive the scorn of others for things that are beyond your control.
Not growing forces you to grow up fast.

Sometimes I think I'd like to return to a high-school reunion to surprise   14
my classmates. Not that they didn't know me when I finally started catching
up. They did, but I doubt they'd remember. Adolescent hierarchies have a
way of enduring; I'm sure I am still recalled as the Midget I myself have
never really left behind.

Of course, if I'm going to show up, it'll have to be soon. I'm starting   15
to shrink.

EXERCISING VOCABULARY

1. Record your own definition for each word below in your notebook.

   diminutive (adj.) (1)   compelling (adj.) (9)
   harrowing (adj.) (1)   contingent (n.) (10)
   ascended (v.) (3)   ignominiously (adv.) (10)
   excruciatingly (adv.) (3)   taunt (v.) (10)
   resolutely (adv.) (4)   ancillary (adj.) (11)
   perverse (adj.) (9)   calamities (n.) (12)

2. In the opening sentence, Trudeau refers to himself as a "recovering short person." What type of person do you usually think of when you hear the word *recovering*? How does the author's word choice prepare you for the subject of this essay?

3. In paragraph 12, Trudeau explains that when he was seventeen, "all of life's disappointments, reversals, and calamities still arrived on schedule—but blissfully free of subtext." What is a subtext? What is the subtext to which the author is referring in this sentence?

4. Trudeau states that "adolescent hierarchies have a way of enduring" (para. 14). What is a hierarchy? Give an example. What does he mean when he refers to adolescent hierarchies? Give some examples from your own experience to explain your response.

PROBING CONTENT

1. What effect did the author's visit to the new apartment building have on him? Why did it affect him this way?

2. What problem did Trudeau have in high school? How did he react to the nickname he was given? How did his reaction differ from that of others with the same problem? How did he attempt to overcome this problem?

3. What happened when Trudeau was seventeen? How did this affect his outlook on life?

4. Has Trudeau completely overcome his high school anxiety? Support your response with material from his essay.

CONSIDERING CRAFT

1. Trudeau is a well-known cartoonist. Describe his tone in this essay. How does he use humor to drive home his argument? Refer to several specific examples, including the title.

2. In paragraph 9, the author describes himself as a "haunted veteran come again to an ancient battlefield, . . . revisiting my perilous past." Examine this comparison. What kind of figure of speech is it? How effective is its use here?

3. Trudeau's use of irony often enhances his writing. In paragraph 10, he writes, "some of my fellow Midgets refused to be diminished by the experience." How is this statement ironic? What effect does he achieve by using irony here?

WRITING PROMPTS

Responding to the Topic   How do you respond to Trudeau's obsession with his "inner shrimp"? Do you empathize with him? If so, why? Or do you think he makes too much of his problem, especially because many will say that he should have grown out of it? In your response, make sure to include any personal experiences that have influenced your thinking.

Responding to the Writer   Trudeau believes that "height matters." Write an essay in which you argue for or against this idea. Include numerous specific examples.

Responding to Multiple Viewpoints   Trudeau ("My Inner Shrimp"), Dan Barden ("My New Nose"), Alice Walker ("Beauty: When the Other Dancer Is the Self"), and Grace Suh ("The Eye of the Beholder") all write about physical features that made them feel different or "other." To what extent has society in the past decade become more accepting of difference? Consider the role of the media (television, film, newspaper and magazine stories, and the Internet) when forming your response.

For a quiz on this reading, go to bedfordstmartins.com/mirror.

Venus Envy

Patricia McLaughlin's column "Ask Patsy" has appeared on TotalWoman.com since its launch in April 2000. Her syndicated style column appears in more than two hundred newspapers nationwide. She has also published feature stories and essays in the *Washington Post, Mirabella,* the *American Scholar,* the *New York Times Magazine,* and *Rolling Stone.* In this essay, first published in the *Philadelphia Inquirer Magazine* on November 5, 1995, McLaughlin draws candid and often humorous parallels with women's long-standing worries about their looks.

> **THINKING AHEAD** How much does gender influence people's concern with their personal appearance? Which specific things about appearance most concern men? Which things most concern women? Compare the amount of time you think men and women devote to looking their best.

It used to be that what mattered in life was how women looked and what men did—which, to many women and other right-thinking people, didn't seem fair. Now, thanks to the efforts of feminists (and a lot of social and economic factors beyond their control) what women do matters more. 1

Meanwhile, in a development that's almost enough to make you believe in the Great Seesaw of Being, how men look is also beginning to carry more weight. Men are having plastic surgery to get rid of their love handles[1] and tighten their eye bags and beef up their chins and flatten their bellies and even (major wince) bulk up their penises. They're dyeing their hair to hide the gray. They're buying magazines to find out how to lose those pesky last five pounds. 2

Naturally, women who always envied the way men never had to suffer to be beautiful think they're making a big mistake. (What next: too-small shoes with vertiginous heels?) But maybe they don't exactly have a choice. 3

The key to how men feel about how they look, says Michael Pertschuk, who's writing a book about it, is social expectation: What do they think folks expect them to look like? And how far do folks expect them to go to look that way? 4

You think of anorexia and bulimia as disorders that strike teenage girls, but men get them, too—not many, but "a bit more" than used to, according to Pertschuk, a psychiatrist who sees patients (including men) 5

---

[1]**love handles:** Excess fat around the waist; also called a spare tire.

with eating disorders. Because eating disorders virtually always start with a "normal" desire to lose weight and look slimmer, the increase among men suggests that men are worrying about their looks more than they used to.

Pertschuk has also worked with the dermatologists and plastic surgeons 6 at the Center for Human Appearance at the University of Pennsylvania to screen candidates for cosmetic surgery, and he says "there are certainly more male plastic surgery patients," which suggests the same thing: "It's become more culturally accepted or expected for men to be concerned about their appearance."

And no wonder, when you look at the media. Stephen Perrine, articles 7 editor at *Men's Health*, a magazine that in the last six years has built a circulation as big as *Esquire*'s and *GQ*'s put together, says the mass media "in the last five to seven years has really changed the way it portrays men." Whether you look at Calvin Klein's[2] underwear ads or that Diet Coke commercial where the girls in the office ogle the shirtless construction hunk, "men are more and more portrayed as sex objects. So they're feeling the way women have for many, many years: 'Oh, that's what's expected of me? That's what I'm supposed to look like?' " And they—some of them, anyway—rush to live up to those expectations.

Which—wouldn't you know?—turns out to be a heck of a lot easier 8 for them than it ever was for women: "It's easier for men to change their bodies," Perrine says, "easier to build muscle, easier to burn fat." Besides, the male physical ideal is more realistic to begin with: A man "who's healthy and works out . . . will look like Ken, but a woman can exercise till she's dead, and she's not going to look like Barbie," Perrine says.

Ken? Is that really what women want? 9

Maybe some women. Me, I get all weak in the knees when I see a guy 10 running a vacuum, or unloading a dishwasher without being asked. Not that Calvin Klein is ever going to advertise his underwear on a cute guy with a nice big electric broom.

But what women want isn't the point. 11

Used to be, Pertschuk says, men who had plastic surgery said they were 12 doing it for their careers: They wouldn't get promoted if they looked old and fat and tired. Now they say the same thing women do: "I want to feel better about myself." In other words, they look at their love handles or eye bags or pot bellies or saggy chins and feel inadequate and ugly and unworthy, just the way women have been feeling all along about their hips, stomachs, thighs, breasts, wrinkles, etc.

That's new: For more men, self-regard has come to hinge not just on 13 what they do, but on what they see in the mirror. And it's easier to change that than the values that make them feel bad about it.

---

[2]**Calvin Klein:** An American fashion designer known for his classic style.

EXERCISING VOCABULARY

1. Record your own definition for each word below in your notebook.

   wince (n.) (2)
   vertiginous (adj.) (3)
   ogle (v.) (7)

2. What does the adjective *pesky* (para. 2) mean? This word sounds like the noun *pest.* What characteristics do pests and pesky things share? In what way could the last five pounds of a diet be pesky?

3. Check your definition for *vertiginous.* Using that definition as a starting point, explain what a person who suffers from vertigo fears. How does the phrase "too-small shoes with vertiginous heels" (para. 3) relate to what McLaughlin is saying here?

PROBING CONTENT

1. According to McLaughlin, what three changes in men's behavior show that they are worrying more about their looks than they used to? How are these changes a reaction to what is happening in our society?

2. Why does McLaughlin say that it is easier for men to conform to a cultural ideal than it is for women? Where do these cultural ideals come from?

3. According to Michael Pertschuk, why did men in the past say they were altering their appearance by such methods as plastic surgery? How have the reasons men give for having plastic surgery changed? What does this change indicate about our culture?

CONSIDERING CRAFT

1. Who is Venus? How does knowing who she is help you understand the deliberate play on words in this essay's title?

2. How do McLaughlin's quotes from Michael Pertschuk and Stephen Perrine help make her point? If she wanted to use other sources, what would she gain by quoting them directly instead of just summing up their opinions?

3. What is the effect of having paragraphs 9 and 11 each be only one sentence long? What makes this strategy successful?

4. In her conclusion, McLaughlin restates her thesis. How does this kind of conclusion benefit the reader? How does it benefit the writer?

WRITING PROMPTS

Responding to the Topic Based on your personal experience and your knowledge of the opposite sex, to what extent do you believe that men and women agonize about personal appearance and are willing to suffer for it? Write an essay in which you answer these questions.

Responding to the Writer McLaughlin argues that men are now more concerned than ever before with their appearance. Write an essay in which you agree or disagree with her position. Make sure to provide specific examples.

Responding to Multiple Viewpoints Write an essay in which you compare the way plastic surgeons are portrayed in McLaughlin's "Venus Envy" and Dan Barden's "My New Nose." Use examples from both texts.

For a quiz on this reading, go to bedfordstmartins.com/mirror.

100% Indian Hair

TANZILA AHMED

Tanzila Ahmed is an activist, writer, and founder of South Asian American Voting Youth, a national nonprofit organization that encourages political participation. Her essays have appeared on the Web sites *Wiretap* and *Pop + Politics*, where "100% Indian Hair" appeared in February 2006. She graduated from the University of Southern California and currently lives in Los Angeles.

THINKING AHEAD Many of the products you use and the fashions you wear originate in other cultures. How much thought have you given to this reality? Reflect on an occasion when you or someone you know has adopted a look borrowed from another culture. What were the reasons for adopting this look? Describe the reactions to this new look.

E very time I drive down La Brea here in L.A., I always do a double 1 take when I cross Pico. There is this huge red sign in front of a store in a strip mall that says, "100% Indian Hair." As a South Asian woman, I find this sign ridiculously strange and wonder just what exactly would happen if I walked into the store. Would they turn me away? Would they kidnap me into the back room for a hair hijacking? Should I start collecting the hair out of my drain and bring it in for some extra money to pay for grad school? What is it about my kind of hair that makes beauty shops so excited about advertising that they have "100% Indian Hair"?

I am reminded of a former African American co-worker of mine every 2 time I think of hair weaves. I remember the first time she told me she was getting hair extensions in her hair, how she was so excited and ecstatically told me, "I'm paying more money for my extensions because it's real human hair!"

I was mortified. "Whose human hair is it?!?!" 3

She thought about it for a minute. "You know, I don't know. I just 4 know it's human hair."

I was seriously grossed out by this thought. I likened it to using old nail 5 clippings and gluing them onto someone else's nail. You see, in the process of getting hair extensions, one gets long strands of hair, sometimes fake, sometimes real. These strands are then placed into people's hair to give the appearance of longer, fuller hair overnight. The hair can be braided in, glued in, sewed in, or clamped in. People pay a lot of money to get this hair placed into their own. But the thing that they don't know is where this human hair comes from.

Why Indian hair? Because our hair is the best. No, for real, that's what 6
the research shows. Indian hair is thicker than European hair and thinner
than Chinese hair. Once treated, it is less prone to breaking. The best kind
of hair is long and untreated, with all the cuticles[1] in the same direction. It
is collected in plaits.[2] Where, oh where, can you find such hair?

Well, the Web research shows that plaits of hair in India are cut off for 7
weddings or offered to a god at religious temples. This hair is then collected
by "hair factories" that buy it for 15 rupees (25 cents) per gram. This one
hair retailer based out of Chennai says, "Indian women donate their hair as
an offering to their god as a sign of modesty. It is their understanding that it
will be sold by the monks for a substantial sum of money that will be used
to finance schools, hospitals and other publicly favored facilities."

I have some serious problems believing this. First of all, I don't remem- 8
ber an Indian wedding I've attended or a Bollywood[3] movie I've seen where
the hair was cut off the women. Secondly, women in India are ridiculously
vain about their hair and will spend hours going through the ritual of soak-
ing their hair in warm coconut oil and shampooing twice. A woman would
have to be desperate and really in need of the 15 rupees per gram to cut
her hair. Thirdly, supposing that women cut off their hair at the temple as
an offering to a god. I'm not so sure that they'd be happy in knowing that
their hair is really going around the world to be weaved into someone's hair
for $50 a plait.

OK, here comes the speech. The thing that disturbs me about the whole 9
hair trade is the "south corrupts the south" mentality; that is, women of
color in the United States are the ones benefiting from the exploitation of
women of color in South Asia. How can women consciously get human
hair weaved into their own without knowing where the hair came from?
Or that it came from the exploitation of other women of color? It's the
same way people of color will go to Wal-Mart to buy their clothes without consciously thinking of the people of color who created the clothes in
sweatshops. Where's the solidarity, people?

I'm all about looking good and spending the money on making that 10
happen. I'm also totally aware that I have cream of the crop hair that is the
envy of all, and whatever I say will be met with, "What do you care? You
have 100 percent Indian hair." I also understand that there is a whole culture of getting hair weaves that I am not a part of, and that by telling people
not to get hair weaves anymore I am inflicting my cultural values on theirs.
I get it. But I do think that, as one woman of color to another woman of
color, it is important to know the truth about 100 percent human hair, that
this hair was actually alive and had a life before it entered into a weave.

As for me, I'm going to start collecting the hair off my pillow and see if 11
I can make some money with my 100 percent Indian hair.

[1]**cuticles:** The outermost layers of hair shafts that overlap like shingles.
[2]**plaits:** Braids of hair.
[3]**Bollywood:** The name given to Indian film; a combination of Bombay and Hollywood.

EXERCISING VOCABULARY

1. Record your own definition for each word below in your notebook.

   ecstatically (adv.) (2)
   mortified (adj.) (3)
   exploitation (n.) (9)

2. What are sweatshops (para. 9)? How does the term *sweatshop* reflect the working conditions within? Who usually works in sweatshops? How much do they get paid? In which areas are sweatshops located?

3. What does the word *solidarity* mean (para. 9)? How does its prefix reflect its meaning? Name some groups of people who feel a sense of solidarity.

4. What does the expression "the cream of the crop" mean (para. 10)? Where did this term originate?

PROBING CONTENT

1. What does Ahmed's coworker say about her new weave? How does the author respond to this comment?

2. What does a hair retailer from Chennai claim about its product? Why does the writer find it difficult to believe these claims?

3. Describe what Ahmed means by "the 'south corrupts the south' mentality" (para. 9). What does she think of this kind of thinking?

4. What does the writer mean when she says that she is "inflicting [her] cultural values" on other people (para. 10)? Which people is she speaking of? How does this make her feel?

CONSIDERING CRAFT

1. Ahmed poses four questions in the first paragraph of her essay. Why does she do this? How does this strategy affect the reader's approach to this essay?

2. Find each appearance of the phrase "100% Indian Hair" in the essay. Describe its effect each time it is used. Why is this placement of the title phrase important?

3. In paragraph 9, Ahmed writes, "OK, here comes the speech." What does she mean by this? How effective is this transition?

4. Describe the writer's tone in the final paragraph of the essay. Why does she adopt this tone? How does it affect your reading?

WRITING PROMPTS

Responding to the Topic Ahmed asks us to consider the social and political implications of fashion and urges us to think about the real people behind those fashion trends. Write an essay in which you explore a fashion trend that originated in a culture different from your own. Consider questions such as the following: Who inspired this look? Who created it? Why has this fashion trend been so popular? Who wears it? Have there been any controversies surrounding this fashion trend? Why?

Responding to the Writer In her essay, Ahmed writes that she is aware that she is "inflicting [her] cultural values" on others when she tells them not to get hair weaves (para. 10). Write an essay in which you agree or disagree with her statement. Examine whether fashion reflects cultural values and whether people have the right to tell others how to look. Make sure to cite specific examples in your writing.

Responding to Multiple Viewpoints How would Grace Suh ("The Eye of the Beholder") and John Leo ("The 'Modern Primitives'") respond to Ahmed's social concerns in her essay "100% Indian Hair"? What would they think of "the speech" she gives in paragraph 9 when she speaks of what she terms "the 'south corrupts the south' mentality"?

For a quiz on this reading, go to bedfordstmartins.com/mirror.

Girls Going Mild(er)

JENNIE YABROFF

Jennie Yabroff is a freelance writer who is based in New York. She has written stories for many leading publications, including the *New York Times*, *Salon*, and *Newsweek*, where the following article was first published in 2007. Although we often hear about young women pushing the limits of "decency" with their clothing choices, Yabroff looks instead at how some women are pushing back against this idea by dressing more traditionally.

> **THINKING AHEAD**   Think about your own personal style. Would you call it "wild" or "mild" or a combination of the two? Why? What affects your clothing choices? Reflect on a time when you changed your normal style to fit a particular situation. How did this make you feel?

Consider the following style tips for girls: Skirts and dresses should fall no more than four fingers above the knee. No tank tops without a sweater or jacket over them. Choose a bra that has a little padding to help disguise when you are cold. These fashion hints may sound like the prim mandates of a 1950s "health" film. But they are from the Web site of Pure Fashion, a modeling and etiquette program for teen girls whose goal is "to show the public it is possible to be cute, stylish and modest." Pure Fashion has put on thirteen shows in 2007 featuring six hundred models. National director Brenda Sharman estimates there will be twenty-five shows in 2008. It is not the only newfangled outlet for old-school ideas about how girls should dress: ModestApparelUSA.com, ModestByDesign.com and DressModestly.com all advocate a return to styles that leave almost everything to the imagination. They cater to what writer Wendy Shalit claims is a growing movement of "girls gone mild"—teens and young women who are rejecting promiscuous "bad girl" roles embodied by Britney Spears, Bratz Dolls and the nameless, shirtless thousands in *Girls Gone Wild* videos. Instead, these girls cover up, insist on enforced curfews on college campuses, bring their moms on their dates and pledge to stay virgins until married. And they spread the word: In Pennsylvania, a group of high-school girls "girlcotted" Abercrombie & Fitch for selling T-shirts with suggestive slogans (WHO NEEDS BRAINS WHEN YOU HAVE THESE?). Newly launched *Eliza* magazine bills itself as a "modest fashion" magazine for the seventeen- to thirty-four-year-old demographic. Macy's has begun carrying garments by Shade clothing, which was founded by two Mormon women wanting trendy, but not-revealing, clothes. And Miss Utah strode the runway of the 2007 Miss America pageant in a modestly cut one-piece swimsuit. (She didn't win the crown.) According to Shalit, whose new book *Girls Gone Mild* was published last month, this "youth-led rebellion" is a welcome corrective to our licentious, oversexed times. But is the new modesty truly a revolution, or is it merely an inevitable reaction to a culture of increased female sexual empowerment, similar to the backlash against flappers in the 1920s and second-wave feminists in the 1970s?

Shalit has made a career of cataloging the degradations of our culture   2
while championing crusades of virtue. Her first book, *A Return to Modesty*, argued that chastity was hot—and informed readers she intended to remain a virgin until her wedding night. Shalit says she was inundated with letters and e-mail from girls dismayed by cultural pressure to be "bad." She began a Web site, ModestyZone.net—there are at least a dozen similar ones today—and started collecting information from three thousand e-mail exchanges between 1999 and 2006. "There's a dawning awareness that maybe not everyone participating in these behaviors is happy with them, so let's not assume everyone doing this is empowered," she says. She blames the usual suspects: media, misguided feminist professors, overly permissive parents. Sharman also points a finger at Moms Gone Wild. "It used to be that moms would control the way their daughters dressed. But now we have this *Desperate Housewives* culture, and the moms are as influenced by the media as the kids," she says. "They've lost the sense of encouraging their daughters to be ladylike." Pure Fashion, which is affiliated with the Roman Catholic organization Regnum Christi, aims to "help young ladies make better choices," says Sharman.

This is not the first time women have been asked to make these choices.   3
During a century of tumult over the roles and rights of women, fashion and sexual expression have remained lightning rods for controversy. The forward-thinking women of the 1920s who cut their hair, threw out their corsets, and dared to smoke in public were the Britney Spearses and Paris Hiltons of their day, says Joshua Zeitz, author of *Flapper: A Madcap[1] Story of Sex, Style, Celebrity, and the Women Who Made America Modern*. "Everything is relative—girls weren't wearing thongs or getting bikini waxes, but they were coming to school in knee-length skirts, wearing lipstick and smoking," Zeitz says. "The concern at the time was that the culture was sexualizing young girls. The backlash came during the Great Depression, when you see a movement to get women back into the home, in part to correct this culture of licentiousness."

The most recent attempt to turn back the clock may be a reaction to yet   4
another sexual revolution: "Gays and lesbians are becoming mainstreamed, women make up more than half of college populations, they're becoming full partners in the workplace and there's a general cultural deconstruction[2] of what gender means," Zeitz says. "We go through waves of progress and reaction, but you can never bottle these things back up for real."

[1]**Madcap:** Crazy; zany.
[2]**deconstruction:** The questioning of traditional assumptions.

Another explanation may be the mainstreaming of conservative reli- 5
gious values. Just as WHAT WOULD JESUS DO? bracelets enjoyed a cultural
moment on par with rubber LIVE STRONG bands, faith-based programs like
Pure Fashion (which theoretically answers the question "What Would Mary
Wear?") are gaining acceptance in the culture at large. Most modest-clothing
Web sites have religious underpinnings,[3] from Mormon to Christian to
Muslim, but attract nonreligious customers as well. Shalit is an Orthodox
Jew, now married to a rabbi, and many girls she profiles see religion as
motivating. "Since the good girl today is often socially ostracized, a lot of
girls naturally find solace in their faith in God," she says.

What makes the movement unique, according to Shalit, is that it's the 6
adults who are often pushing sexual boundaries, and the kids who are
slamming on the brakes. "Well-meaning experts and parents say that they
understand kids' wanting to be 'bad' instead of 'good,'" she writes in her
book. "Yet this reversal of adults' expectations is often experienced not as
a gift of freedom but a new kind of oppression." Which just may prove
that rebelling against Mom and Dad is one trend that will never go out of
style.

EXERCISING VOCABULARY

1. Record your own definition for each word below in your notebook.

   prim (adj.) (1)   backlash (n.) (1)
   mandates (n.) (1)   degradations (n.) (2)
   etiquette (adj.) (1)   chastity (n.) (2)
   advocate (v.) (1)   inundated (v.) (2)
   cater (v.) (1)   affiliated (v.) (2)
   promiscuous (adj.) (1)   tumult (n.) (3)
   demographic (n.) (1)   ostracized (v.) (5)
   licentious (adj.) (1)   solace (n.) (5)

2. Yabroff calls fashion and sexual expression "lightning rods for controversy" (para. 3). What is a lightning rod? What purpose does it serve?
   How does it work? What does the author mean in this metaphor?

3. In paragraph 2, Yabroff writes that Wendy Shalit has championed "crusades of virtue." What were the Crusades? When did they take place?
   What image does Shalit hope to bring to mind by using the phrase
   "crusades of virtue"?

4. Yabroff uses the terms "mainstreamed" (para. 4) and "mainstreaming"
   (para. 5) in her essay. What does it mean to "mainstream" someone or
   something? In what setting is this term generally used?

---

[3]underpinnings: Foundations.

PROBING CONTENT

1. Describe the new modesty movement. How do its members dress? How do they act?

2. Yabroff cites women such as Wendy Shalit and Brenda Sharman who promote the modesty movement. Whom or what do they blame for what they consider immodest dress and behavior?

3. During what historical period were women faced with choices about what they would wear and how they would act? What choices did some of these women make?

4. According to Wendy Shalit, whom Yabroff quotes in the final paragraph of the essay, what makes the current modesty movement "unique"?

CONSIDERING CRAFT

1. Describe the play on words in the title of the essay. How effective is this rhetorical strategy?

2. Yabroff quotes other writers extensively in her essay. Why does she do this? How does this affect your reading of the essay?

3. Yabroff quotes Wendy Shalit, who claims that it is "the kids who are slamming on the brakes" (para. 6). In what context is this phrase normally used? What does it mean here?

4. Why does Yabroff end her essay with a play on words? What is it? How does it work in the essay?

WRITING PROMPTS

Responding to the Topic   In an essay, explore the extent to which your personal style reflects your beliefs and values. Be sure to include specific examples to support your ideas.

Responding to the Writer   Write an essay in which you agree or disagree with Shalit's assertion that adults are to blame when their attempts to understand young people's longings to be "bad" create "a new kind of oppression" (para. 6).

Responding to Multiple Viewpoints   How would the parents in the essays by Garry Trudeau ("My Inner Shrimp"), Alice Walker ("Beauty: When the Other Dancer Is the Self"), and Grace Suh ("The Eye of the Beholder") respond to the claim made in Yabroff's essay about the effect parents can have on their children's personal identity? Supply examples to support your argument.

For a quiz on this reading, go to bedfordstmartins.com/mirror.

Identity in a Virtual World

MICHELLE JANA CHAN

Michelle Jana Chan is a travel writer for CNN, *Newsweek*, and the *Daily Telegraph*. She also writes hotel reviews for the Web site *Travel Intelligence*, and she founded a travel publishing company that produces guides for weekend travelers. "Identity in a Virtual World" appeared on CNN.com on June 14, 2007.

> **THINKING AHEAD** Online alter egos are called avatars. Do you have or would you like to have an avatar? Why? What would your avatar look like? Would it be human or nonhuman? What would be its gender, its name, its race, and its age? Why would you make these choices when you create your avatar?

There's more to someone's identity than a social security number, pass- 1
port photo and set of fingerprints, but it's difficult to define exactly what else it is. Is it what the public sees or the inner self? Some would argue that virtual identity is a truer reflection of self than someone's image in the real world.

Photographer Robbie Cooper has studied the relationship between 2
gamers' real and online identities, taking photographs of the two images for the book he co-authored, *Alter Ego: Avatars and Their Creators*. Cooper fuses together real portraits and virtual images of dozens of gamers and investigated if people's digital representations in role-playing environments were an echo of their true selves.

Cooper says it was initially tough to get people to volunteer for the 3
book, which essentially took the mask off the character. "It was extremely difficult going to chat rooms and trying to persuade people I was really a photographer and doing this project," he explains. "But then I posted web pages on fan sites associated with certain games, asking people to apply with a picture of themselves and their avatar and I was quite surprised. We were getting fifty e-mails a day."

He confesses he doesn't completely understand why some people came 4
forward, especially when they highlighted how much they enjoyed the anonymity of the online world. "It's a bit ironic," Cooper says. "There was a professor who teaches public policy and law at Seoul University in South Korea. In the game world, he plays a little girl and he said he wanted to maintain the illusion, yet he's sitting there posing for my book. My feeling about it is you might create a character and enjoy the anonymity of it at first, but that character then becomes a bigger part of your life."

Who's Who?

In a virtual world, online identity is potentially much more flexible than real   5
identity, allowing easily changes in race, class, gender, age, socio-economic
background and even species. It offers freer self-definition, including multiple
identities and shared identity, within worlds lacking behavior guidelines or
prescribed etiquette.

Cooper says, if there was a general trend, the online identities people   6
chose were "less ordinary" than their real selves. "In the virtual world,
they either had more powers or better looks. I tried hard to find someone
who deliberately played a fat avatar and I couldn't find anyone—although
apparently they do exist. It does seem like in almost every case, the avatar
is bigger, better, faster, it can fly, it has abilities the person doesn't have in
the real world."

Nick Yee studies immersive virtual reality[1] at Stanford University,   7
California, and says there are measurable trends in character creation.
"One of my studies showed that introverts generally describe their avatars
as idealized versions of themselves," Yee says. "Another observation is that
in games where people can gender-bend, men are much more likely to than
females."

But Yee concedes there's not necessarily a deep psychological reason   8
for everything. "It could be that it's harder for men to explore different
gender roles in real life. But the most common reasons I hear from men are
that female avatars are treated better in games, that they are more often
given free gifts, and if they are going to stare at a character for twenty
hours a week, they would rather look at a female!"

Blurring the Lines

Studies do suggest virtual environments can be a way of expressing a dif-   9
ferent side of personalities or escaping the social constraints of real life. But
Yee says, even though online characters are not bound by rules, they tend
to self-regulate how they look and often mirror human behavior in the real
world.

"I've found the more flexibility there is," Yee says, "the more limita-   10
tions come in. Take Second Life.[2] It's a place where you can get away from
your first life, but it ends up looking exactly like suburban America. Second
Life bores me because it feels like my backyard."

As Cooper was taking photos for the book *Alter Ego*, co-author Tracy   11
Spaight was conducting interviews of the subjects. Spaight agrees that
human characteristics and behavior patterns are present throughout the

[1]**immersive virtual reality:** A hypothetical future technology in which the virtual and real
 worlds will be indistinguishable to the user.
[2]**Second Life:** A popular video game that allows its players to live in an alternate universe.

virtual world. "We bring a lot of ourselves into the game space, the appropriate norms, what's considered proper and not proper," Spaight says. "I mean, if you just got up and logged off from the game, if you didn't wave or bow or say goodbye, that would be rude."

Yee says he can be scared or sickened by what he sees in the online   12
world. "When we have all the freedom that we could want, what's strange is how much we insist on being in bodies that we're used to and spend time doing suburban activities like shopping," he says. "In the virtual world, we even exaggerate the superficiality of what we're used to, like stereotypical female anatomies. That's what really fascinates me about these worlds. They trap us even more."

EXERCISING VOCABULARY

1. Record your own definition for each word below in your notebook.

anonymity (n.) (4)   introverts (n.) (7)
prescribed (adj.) (5)   concedes (v.) (8)
etiquette (n.) (5)

2. What does it mean to "gender-bend" (para. 7)? With whom do we associate this term? What is its connotative meaning?

3. In her essay, Chan cites a book entitled *Alter Ego*. What does the term mean? Why is the title particularly fitting, given the book's subtitle?

4. In paragraph 11, Chan speaks of appropriate "norms." What is a norm? List other words that share the prefix *norm*. Give several examples of behavioral norms in the game space.

PROBING CONTENT

1. According to the essay, how can an online identity be more "flexible" than real identity? How do avatars usually differ from their real-life counterparts? Provide specifics in your response.

2. What effect does the lack of rules have on the virtual world and its inhabitants? Why?

3. According to Chan, why do men often choose female avatars for themselves?

4. Nick Yee states that virtual worlds "trap us even more" (para. 12). More than what? In what ways?

CONSIDERING CRAFT

1. In paragraph 2, Chan describes Robbie Cooper's experiment to discover whether people's avatars were "an echo of their true selves." How can an online identity echo a real one?

2. Chan writes that Cooper said that at first it was difficult to persuade the subjects in his experiment to take "the mask off the character" (para. 3). Why does Chan use the word *mask*? To what kind of a mask is she referring? How effective is her word choice here?

3. In most of her essay, Chan summarizes and quotes from the findings of other people. Why did she make this choice? In what way does this help or hinder her in getting her own ideas across?

4. In paragraph 9, Chan suggests that we are attracted to virtual reality because in it we can evade "the social constraints of real life." What are some of these constraints? Why would we choose to avoid them?

WRITING PROMPTS

Responding to the Topic   If you could live in a virtual world, would you? Write an essay in which you detail the advantages and the disadvantages of shedding the life you now lead for a virtual one.

Responding to the Writer   Nick Yee argues that the virtual identities that some people adopt "trap" them in identities very similar to their "real-world" ones (para. 12). Write an essay in which you agree or disagree with his opinion. Make sure to cite specific examples from your own experience or that of others.

Responding to Multiple Viewpoints   Dan Barden, Alice Walker, and Garry Trudeau all struggle with personal identity. What kinds of avatars might these authors have created before they came to terms with their personal images? Describe these avatars in detail, including what they might look like and how they might act.

For a quiz on this reading, go to bedfordstmartins.com/mirror.

Me and My Avatar

ANALYZING THE IMAGE

This "split-screen" photograph is one of three that accompanied Michelle Jana Chan's essay "Identity in a Virtual World." The photo first appeared in *Alter Ego*, a book written by Robbie Cooper and discussed by Chan in her essay. Pictured here are South Korean gamer Choi Seang Rak, professor of law at Seoul University and his avatar Uroo Ahs.

1. Compare the two parts of the photograph. How are they different? How are they similar?

2. What surprises you about the avatar that Choi Seang Rak created for himself? What image is he trying to portray through Uroo Ahs?

3. How does the layout of the photograph mirror the idea of an alter ego or a split personality? How effective is this visual composition?

4. How does seeing this photograph affect your reading? Pay particular attention to paragraph 4 in which Chan discusses Robbie Cooper's impression of Choi Seang Rak and Uroo Ahs.

The "Modern Primitives"

JOHN LEO

This essay by John Leo first appeared in the July 31, 1995, edition of *U.S. News & World Report*. Leo, whose weekly column appeared in *U.S. News & World Report* and 150 newspapers from 1988 to 1995, has also written for the *New York Times* and *Time* magazine and is the author of *Two Steps Ahead of the Thought Police* (1998) and *Incorrect Thoughts: Notes on Our Wayward Culture* (2000). He is now a writer and contributing editor for the Manhattan Institute's *City Journal*. "The 'Modern Primitives'" examines the renewed popularity of body modification.

> **THINKING AHEAD** When you think of body modification like piercing or tattooing, who comes to mind? A friend? A movie star? A musician? A gang member? What image do you have of people with piercings or tattoos? Do you have a piercing or tattoo, or have you considered getting one? What was your motivation? What effect did you want to achieve? What reactions did your piercing or tattoo elicit from other people?

The days when body piercers could draw stares by wearing multiple 1 earrings and a nose stud are long gone. We are now in the late baroque phase[1] of self-penetration. Metal rings and bars hang from eyebrows, noses, nipples, lips, chins, cheeks, navels and (for that coveted neo-Frankenstein[2] look) from the side of the neck.

"If it sticks out, pierce it" is the motto, and so they do, with special attention 2 to genitals. Some of the same middle-class folks who decry genital mutilation in Africa are paying to have needles driven through the scrotum, the labia, the clitoris, or the head or the shaft of the penis. Many genital piercings have their own names, such as the ampallang or the Prince Albert. (Don't ask.)

And, in most cases, the body heals without damage, though some women 3 who have had their nipples pierced report damage to the breast's milk ducts, and some men who have been Prince Alberted no longer urinate in quite the same way.

What is going on here? Well, the mainstreaming-of-deviancy thesis 4 naturally springs to mind. The piercings of nipples and genitals arose in the homosexual sadomasochistic[3] culture of the West Coast. The Gauntlet,

---

[1]**late baroque phase:** A period of ornate, richly ornamented decoration.
[2]**Frankenstein:** Refers to an unnamed monster created from parts of dead bodies by Dr. Victor Frankenstein in Mary Shelley's 1818 novel *Frankenstein, or The Modern Prometheus*.
[3]**sadomasochistic:** Relating to the association of sexual pleasure with the inflicting and receiving of pain.

founded in Los Angeles in 1975, mostly to do master and slave piercings, now has three shops around the country that are about as controversial as Elizabeth Arden[4] salons. Rumbling through the biker culture and punk, piercing gradually shed its outlaw image and was mass marketed to the impressionable by music videos, rock stars and models.

The nasty, aggressive edge of piercing is still there, but now it is coated 5 in happy talk (it's just body decoration, like any other) and a New Age[5]-y rationale (we are becoming more centered, reclaiming our bodies in an anti-body culture). Various new pagans, witches and New Agers see piercing as symbolic of unspecified spiritual transformation. One way or another, as Guy Trebay writes in the *Village Voice*, "You will never find anyone on the piercing scene who thinks of what he's doing as pathological."

The yearning to irritate parents and shock the middle class seems to 6 rank high as a motive for getting punctured repeatedly. Some ask for dramatic piercings to enhance sexual pleasure, to seem daring or fashionable, to express rage, or to forge a group identity. Some think of it as an ordeal that serves as a rite of passage, like ritual suspension of Indian males from hooks in their chests.

Piercing is part of the broader "body modification" movement, which 7 includes tattooing, corsetry, branding and scarring by knife. It's a sign of the times that the more bizarre expressions of this movement keep pushing into the mainstream. The current issue of *Spin* magazine features a hair-raising photo of a woman carving little rivers of blood into another woman's back. "Piercing is like toothbrushing now," one of the cutters told *Spin*. "It's why cutting is becoming popular." Slicing someone's back is a violent act. But one of the cutters has a bland justification: People want to be cut "for adornment, or as a test of endurance, or as a sacrifice toward a transformation." Later on we read that "women are reclaiming their bodies from a culture that has commodified starvation and faux sex." One cuttee says: "It creates intimacy. My scars are emotional centers, signs of a life lived."

But most of us achieve intimacy, or at least search for it, without a 8 knife in hand. The truth seems to be that the sadomasochistic instinct is being repositioned to look spiritually high-toned. Many people have found that S&M[6] play "is a way of opening up the body-spirit connection," the high priest of the body modification movement, Fakir Musafar, said in one interview.

Musafar, who has corseted his waist down to nineteen inches and mortified 9 his flesh with all kinds of blades, hooks and pins, calls the mostly twentyish people in the body modification movement "the modern primitives." This is another side of the movement: the conscious attempt to repudiate Western

---

[4]**Elizabeth Arden:** A company that produces beauty products and owns beauty spas.
[5]**New Age:** A spiritual movement that stresses the unity and practice of all belief systems despite their differences.
[6]**S&M:** Sadomasochistic.

norms and values by adopting the marks and rings of primitive cultures. In some cases this is expressed by tusks worn in the nose or by stretching and exaggerating holes in the earlobe or nipple.

Not everyone who pierces a nipple or wears a tongue stud is buying into this, but something like a new primitivism seems to be emerging in body modification, as in other areas of American life. It plugs into a wider dissatisfaction with traditional Western rationality, logic and sexual norms, as well as anger at the impact of Western technology on the natural environment and anger at the state of American political and social life. 10

Two sympathetic analysts say: "Amidst an almost universal feeling of powerlessness to 'change the world,' individuals are changing what they have power over: their own bodies. . . . By giving visible expression to unknown desires and latent obsessions welling up from within, individuals can provoke change." 11

Probably not. Cultural crisis can't really be dealt with by letting loose our personal obsessions and marking up our bodies. But the rapid spread of this movement is yet another sign that the crisis is here. 12

EXERCISING VOCABULARY

1. Record your own definition for each word below in your notebook.

   decry (v.) (2)
   deviancy (n.) (4)
   rationale (n.) (5)
   centered (adj.) (5)
   reclaiming (v.) (5)
   pathological (adj.) (5)
   bland (adj.) (7)

   commodified (v.) (7)
   faux (adj.) (7)
   mortified (v.) (9)
   repudiate (v.) (9)
   latent (adj.) (11)
   welling (v.) (11)

2. In paragraph 1, Leo speaks of "that coveted neo-Frankenstein look." What does the verb *to covet* mean? What then does the word *coveted* mean? What does the prefix *neo* mean? Describe a neo-Frankenstein look.

3. Paragraph 4 refers to "the mainstreaming-of-deviancy thesis." What does the verb *to mainstream* mean? How can you apply that meaning of *mainstream* to Leo's phrase?

PROBING CONTENT

1. In what cultures or among what groups of people did body piercing first become popular in the United States? What was its significance?

2. Explain the broader movement of which, according to Leo, body piercing is a part.

3. Before Leo explains what he means by the "new primitivism" (para. 10), he offers several other motives for body modification. What are these?

4. How effectively does the writer think body modification deals with "cultural crisis" (para. 12)? Why is this true?

CONSIDERING CRAFT

1. The title is an oxymoron, or a phrase made up of seeming opposites. Explain how people with tattoos or body piercings can be both modern and primitive.

2. Why does Leo mention several other motives for body modification and then dismiss them in favor of the idea that "a new primitivism" (para. 10) is the major motive?

3. What effect do Leo's many graphic examples of body modification have on you? Why does he include them?

4. Describe the writer's attitude toward his subject. What is the tone of this essay? How difficult is the vocabulary? Based on this information, for what audience do you think Leo is writing?

WRITING PROMPTS

Responding to the Topic   You probably know several people who have body piercings or tattoos, and you might have them yourself. What were their or your motives for these body modifications? What images did they or you want to project? Did these body modifications produce the anticipated results?

Responding to the Writer   In paragraph 10, Leo claims that "a new primitivism" "plugs into a wider dissatisfaction with traditional Western rationality, logic and sexual norms, as well as anger at the impact of Western technology on the natural environment and anger at the state of American political and social life." Respond to this statement in an essay. Be sure to provide specific examples.

Responding to Multiple Viewpoints   In "The 'Modern Primitives,'" Leo writes that "The yearning to irritate parents and shock the middle class seems to rank high as a motive for getting punctured repeatedly" (para. 6). How would adherents of the new modesty movement described in Jennie Yabroff's "Girls Going Mild(er)" respond to Leo's claim?

For a quiz on this reading, go to bedfordstmartins.com/mirror.

Body Rites

ANALYZING THE IMAGE

Examine this contemporary advertisement for Body Rites, an Austin, Texas, "piercing, branding, and scarification" center located inside a tattoo parlor. For some, to express oneself today requires more than wardrobe enhancement; it requires body modification.

1. Why did the ad designer choose to use the split image?

2. What function does the text in this ad serve?

3. Why are so many people today exploring fashion trends beyond clothing, like piercing or tattooing?

My New Nose

DAN BARDEN

Dan Barden's fiction and essays have appeared in *GQ* (*Gentlemen's Quarterly*), *Details*, and various literary magazines. His first long work, *John Wayne: A Novel*, was published in 1998. He is currently an associate professor at Butler University in Indianapolis, where he teaches creative writing and fiction writing. In "My New Nose," which appeared in *GQ* magazine in May 2002, Barden takes a humorous but candid journey "to the center of his face."

> **THINKING AHEAD**   What do you think of men who have cosmetic surgery to improve their looks? How does your response compare to your opinion of women who have cosmetic surgery?

Until several months ago, I had a thuggish nose. It looked like I got hit 1 real hard. Collapsed in the middle, it leaned a lot toward the left. It made people think I was tougher than I was, or aiming to be. Once, in a bar in San Francisco, an old drunk asked me if I'd been a boxer. When I lied and said yes, he told me I must have lost a lot. That's the sort of nose I had.

I got it from a run-in with a surgeon who was supposed to correct a 2 deviated septum, which made my breathing difficult. But the operation was botched, and I came out looking like a prizefighter. That operation—when I was 19—was the most pain I've ever experienced, hands down. Months later I found that my breathing had only gotten worse.

Eventually, I made peace with my nose. I found that I *liked* looking like 3 a thug. The nose turned me into the kind of Irish Catholic guy who might fit in at the squad room on *NYPD Blue*. Without the nose, I came to think, I might have been just another guy who missed the boat to blandly handsome by about twenty minutes. I believed my nose was my destiny—my dark, Irish, bar-fighting heritage somehow rising to the surface of my face. It didn't matter that I'd never been in a fistfight. The nose was a projection of who I might have been if I weren't, in fact, me. I was almost convinced I *was* the nose. I don't know how many times I've puffed up my chest in front of some fellow who could easily crush me, thereby avoiding a fight. That was the nose talking.

But then a few things happened that I think of as the beginning of the end 4 of the old nose. I married a good woman. I started—brace yourself—wearing loafers. I shaved my goatee. It was at that point that I started to wonder, What if I wanted to pretend to be something other than what I always thought I should be? I watch way too many movies, and I began to worry about the distinction between a character actor and a leading man. Most guys with faces like mine are character actors. What if I wanted to be a lead? When I say *lead*, I don't mean being out there fighting for the spotlight. I mean leading the way leading men do, almost invisibly. John Wayne used to say that being a lead was less fun than people thought: Everybody else got to show off, and he had to stand there, alone, at the center of it all. Being a lead is like being the straight man—the fellow who stands around and lets everyone else do their shtick.

My old nose was my shtick, a song and dance I did for years. I wanted   5
to drop it all and lead, for once. I wanted to be so out in front of things that I became invisible.

So I decided to get a nose job. Rhinoplasty. The big fix. I made an ap-   6
pointment with a cosmetic surgeon, telling him the precise sort of nose I wanted. Neurotically, I explained to him the difference between an "Irish" nose and a "Caucasian" nose. I can't believe I said that. The bottom line was that I didn't want a perfect little Anglican nose, but one that fit my rangy[1] face. I had walked around for twenty years with a sponge of meat above my mouth, but I was terrified of a perfect nose.

The surgery went smoothly this time. I had no real pain, just an   7
unpleasant swollen feeling. As I recovered, I wondered, floating in the Vicodin[2] clouds, whether I had betrayed some cosmic rule by changing my flesh. A friend, talking about his wife's plastic surgery, once told me that our bodies were nothing more than vehicles for our souls. He asked me whether I would live my whole life in the same dented car just because I was born in it. Well, maybe I should. Even if I could, did I have the *right* to try to change myself from a character actor into a lead?

It was a week or so before I could see the thing. My doctor snipped at   8
some sutures, removed the splint and told me that my new nose had cartilage from one of my ears. I kept him talking for a while to postpone the moment of truth. After he removed the cowl, he held up a mirror—just like in the movies—and I was amazed by the absolute straightness of the thing though it was a little bulbous at the end, the way my ancestors would want it. It was, indeed, a leading man's nose.

In some ways, the new nose is bigger than the old nose, but this time   9
like the prow of a ship that cuts through the world more neatly. As my nose settled (and I began to breathe through it as well as my doctor promised I would), I noticed something: I stopped looking at the nose, almost as soon as it arrived. It immediately stopped being the focus of my face—it disappeared as a concern to me. My doctor put it best: "It's not that it's aesthetically such a better nose," he said, "but trauma is no longer the first thing someone thinks when they look at your face."

Something else happened as I got used to the nose: I could feel my   10
persona shifting. It was a little scary. Actually, it felt like I was shifting in

[1]**rangy:** With ample room.
[2]**Vicodin:** A pain-killing medication.

the direction of *not* having a persona. This felt weirdly powerful. I was no longer looking at my nose but at the absence of two decades of built-up defenses.

Psychologically, my nose had become the emblem for all that held me back, and I had had to deal with it. Some people will tell you that's an inside job. Years of psychotherapy, spiritual growth—blah, blah, blah. Of course, they're right, but I believe rhinoplasty can also be a kind of spiritual growth. It has taught me how to be, or how to begin to be, self-effacing—the man who can lead and disappear at the same time. Certainly, it has helped me physically. After I settled into my new nose, I suddenly yearned to get into shape. I'd been swimming before the operation, but after the surgery it just kicked in. My stroke became this thing of beauty. Part of the reason I'm swimming, I'm sure, is vanity—I want a nice body to go with my nice face—but it's also more mystical than that. I feel like I'm being charmed back to some state before anything went wrong, before trauma. I'm starting over, in a way, but no one's looking at my face. 11

I saw my doctor again recently. He's a great man—both a technician and an artist—and people should write poems about him, the way Yeats wrote poems about Byzantine³ goldsmiths. Who has more to say about the turn of this century than a man who gives people new faces? 12

When I tried to explain to him the way I feel about my new nose, he talked about a "fixation on structure," how the service he provides is often to eliminate the structure and therefore the fixation. I would have thought this a load of crap if it weren't now the story of my life. 13

In the same conversation, he also reminded me of the nineteenth-century fondness for dueling scars, which I had totally forgotten about. Once upon a time, when men dueled, it was so fashionable to have saber scars on your face that some men actually faked them. Maybe that's what happened to me. I'm just glad I don't need to fake it anymore. 14

EXERCISING VOCABULARY

1. Record your own definition for each word below in your notebook.

   cowl (n.) (8)
   bulbous (adj.) (8)
   aesthetically (adv.) (9)
   persona (n.) (10)

   emblem (n.) (11)
   self-effacing (adj.) (11)
   fixation (n.) (13)

2. What does the idiomatic expression "missed the boat" mean (para. 3)? How might the writer have "missed the boat to blandly handsome" (para. 3)? How does the word *blandly* qualify the word *handsome* here?

---

³**Byzantine:** Relating to the ornate painting and decorative style developed during the Byzantine empire.

3. In paragraph 4, Barden writes, "Being a lead is like being the straight man—the fellow who stands around and lets everyone else do their shtick." In what context do you normally hear the terms *lead, straight man*, and *shtick*? What is a straight man? What is shtick? What do these terms mean as they are used in the essay?

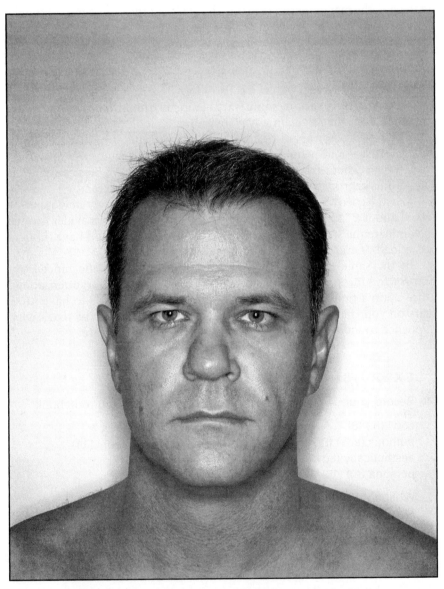

Losing the Trauma: The Author Before and After Surgery

PROBING CONTENT

1. What does Barden mean when he says that "my nose had become the emblem for all that held me back" (para. 11)?

2. How does the author describe what his nose looked like before surgery? What specific words does he use and why?

3. Describe what happened to make Barden consider "the beginning of the end of the old nose" (para. 4). What impact did the old nose have on his self-image?

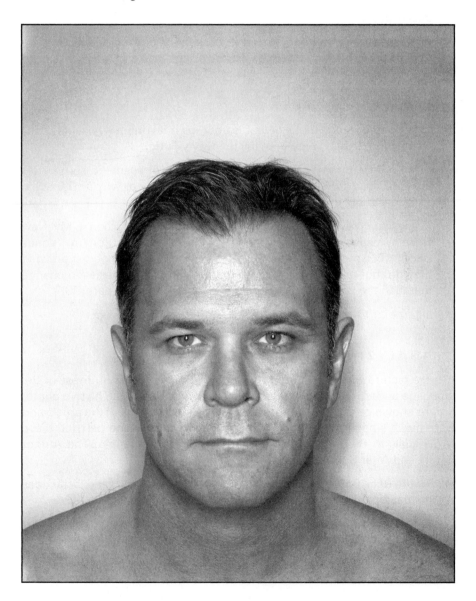

4. How does the author react to his "new nose" directly after surgery? How does his reaction change later on? Why?

CONSIDERING CRAFT

1. Barden alludes to actors and acting several times during the essay. Examine two or three examples. Why does he include these references?

2. The author quotes his cosmetic surgeon several times during the essay. Find two or three examples. Why does Barden use this strategy? How effective is it?

3. Why does the essay end with a discussion of dueling scars? How do they relate to the subject of the essay?

WRITING PROMPTS

Responding to the Topic   What is your least favorite physical feature? In an essay, explain why you feel the way you do.

Responding to the Writer   Has your opinion of cosmetic surgery for men changed after reading "My New Nose"? Why or why not? Explain your reasoning in an essay.

Responding to Multiple Viewpoints   How would Barden ("My New Nose") respond to Patricia McLaughlin's final assertion in "Venus Envy," "For more men, self-regard has come to hinge not just on what they do, but on what they see in the mirror. And it's easier to change that than the values that make them feel bad about it" (para. 13)?

For a quiz on this reading, go to bedfordstmartins.com/mirror.

ANALYZING THE IMAGE

A large picture of the author with a bandaged face takes up most of the first page of Barden's article as it originally appeared in *GQ*. The two photographs shown on pp. 136–37 appeared on the second page of the article and were much smaller than the first image. The caption accompanying these two visuals in the original article reads "Losing the Trauma: The Author Before and After Surgery."

1. Where does Barden mention "trauma" in the essay? What exactly does he mean by the term?

2. What differences do you see between his *before* and *after* shots? How significant are these differences?

3. Why include the photographs with the essay? How do they affect your reading?

The Eye of the Beholder

GRACE SUH

Grace Suh is a native of Seoul, Korea, but she was raised in Wisconsin and Chicago. She works as an editor and writing coach in New York City. Her work has appeared in the *New York Times, Smock Magazine,* and the *Asian Pacific American Journal.* She has been awarded fellowships by the Overbrook Foundation and the Edward F. Albee Foundation. This essay appears in *Echoes: New Korean American Writings* (2003), edited by Elaine H. Kim and Laura Hyun Yi Kang. By reading Suh's description of her makeover, which first appeared in *A. Magazine* in 1992, we become passengers on her journey to selfhood.

> **THINKING AHEAD**   Reflect on a time when you did something solely to fit in with a certain group. What was the outcome? To what extent did your efforts achieve the desired effect?

Several summers ago, on one of those endless August evenings when the sun hangs suspended just above the horizon, I made up my mind to become beautiful. 1

It happened as I walked by one of those mirrored glass-clad office towers, and caught a glimpse of my reflection out of the corner of my eye. The glass on this particular building was green, which might have accounted for the sickly tone of my complexion, but there was no explaining away the limp, ragged hair, the dark circles under my eyes, the facial blemishes, the shapeless, wrinkled clothes. The overall effect—the whole being greater than the sum of its parts—was one of stark ugliness. 2

I'd come home from college having renounced bourgeois suburban values, like hygiene and grooming. Now, home for the summer, I washed my hair and changed clothes only when I felt like it, and spent most of my time sitting on the lawn eating mini rice cakes and Snickers[1] and reading dogeared[2] back issues of *National Geographic.* 3

But that painfully epiphanous day, standing there on the hot sidewalk, I suddenly understood what my mother had been gently hinting these past months: I was no longer just plain, no longer merely unattractive. No, I had broken the Unsightliness Barrier. I was now UGLY, and aggressively so. 4

And so, in an unusual exertion of will, I resolved to fight back against the forces of entropy.[3] I envisioned it as reclamation work, like scything 5

---

[1]**Snickers:** A candy bar.
[2]**dogeared:** With page corners turned down.
[3]**entropy:** In physics, the tendency of things to move toward disorder.

down a lawn that has grown into meadow, or restoring a damaged fresco.[4] For the first time in ages, I felt elated and hopeful. I nearly sprinted into the nearby Neiman Marcus. As I entered the cool, hushed, dimly lit first floor and saw the gleaming counters lined with vials of magical balm, the priest-esses of beauty in their sacred smocks, and the glossy photographic icons of the goddesses themselves—Paulina, Linda, Cindy, Vendella—in a wild, reckless burst of inspiration I thought to myself, Heck, why just okay? Why not BEAUTIFUL?

At the Estée Lauder[5] counter, I spied a polished, middle-aged woman   6 whom I hoped might be less imperious than the aloof amazons at the Chanel counter.

"Could I help you?" the woman (I thought of her as "Estée") asked.   7

"Yes," I blurted. "I look terrible. I need a complete makeover—skin,   8 face, everything."

After a wordless scrutiny of my face, she motioned me to sit down and   9 began. She cleansed my skin with a bright blue mud masque and clear, tingling astringent and then applied a film of moisturizer, working extra amounts into the rough patches. Under the soft pressure of her fingers, I began to relax. From my perch, I happily took in the dizzying, colorful swirl of beautiful women and products all around me. I breathed in the billows of perfume that wafted through the air. I whispered the names of products under my breath like a healing mantra:[6] cooling eye gel, gentle exfoliant,[7] nighttime neck area reenergizer, moisture recharging intensifier, ultra-hydrating complex, emulsifying[8] immunage. I felt immersed in femininity, intoxicated by beauty.

I was flooded with gratitude at the patience and determination with   10 which Estée toiled away at my face, painting on swaths of lip gloss, blush, and foundation. She was not working in vain, I vowed, as I sucked in my cheeks on her command. I would buy all these products. I would use them every day. I studied her gleaming, polished features—her lacquered nails, the glittering mosaic of her eyeshadow, the complex red shimmer of her mouth, her flawless, dewy skin—and tried to imagine myself as impeccably groomed as she.

Estée's voice interrupted my reverie, telling me to blot my lips. I stuck   11 the tissue into my mouth and clamped down, watching myself in the mir-ror. My skin was a blankly even shade of pale, my cheeks and lips glaringly bright in contrast. My face had a strange plastic sheen, like a mannequin's. I grimaced as Estée applied the second lipstick coat: Was this right? Didn't I look kind of—fake? But she smiled back at me, clearly pleased with her work. I was ashamed of myself: Well, what did I expect? It wasn't like she had anything great to start with.

[4]**fresco:** A painting that is created on wet plaster.
[5]**Estée Lauder:** A manufacturer of expensive cosmetics.
[6]**mantra:** A secret word chanted repeatedly in prayer or incantation.
[7]**exfoliant:** A mixture that causes peeling off in layers.
[8]**emulsifying:** Making a suspension of two liquids that do not mix, such as oil and water.

"Now," she announced, "Time for the biggie—Eyes." 12

"Oh. Well, actually, I want to look good and everything, but, I mean, I'm sure you could tell, I'm not really into a complicated beauty routine." My voice faded into a faint giggle. 13

"So?" Estée snapped. 14

"Sooo." I tried again, "I've never really used eye makeup, except, you know, for a little mascara sometimes, and I don't really feel comfortable—" 15

Estée was firm. "Well, the fact is that the eyes are the windows of the face. They're the focal point. An eye routine doesn't have to be complicated, but it's important to emphasize the eyes with some color, or they'll look washed out." 16

I certainly didn't want that. I leaned back again in my chair and closed my eyes. 17

Estée explained as she went: "I'm covering your lids with this champagne color. It's a real versatile base, 'cause it goes with almost any other color you put on top of it." I felt the velvety pad of the applicator sweep over my lids in a soothing rhythm. 18

"Now, being an Oriental, you don't have a lid fold, so I'm going to draw one with this charcoal shadow. Then, I fill in below the line with a lighter charcoal color with a bit of blue in it—frosted midnight—and then above it, on the outsides of your lids, I'm going to apply this plum color. There. Hold on a minute. Okay. Open up." 19

I stared at the face in the mirror, at my eyes. The drawn-on fold and dark, heavy shadows distorted and reproportioned my whole face. Not one of the features in the mirror was recognizable, not the waxy white skin or the redrawn crimson lips or the sharp, deep cheekbones, and especially, not the eyes. I felt negated; I had been blotted out and another face drawn in my place. I looked up at Estée, and in that moment I hated her. "I look terrible," I said. 20

Her back stiffened. "What do you mean?" she demanded. 21

"Hideous. I don't even look human. Look at my eyes. You can't even see me!" My voice was hoarse. 22

She looked. After a moment, she straightened up again, "Well, I'll admit, the eyeshadow doesn't look great." She began to put away the pencils and brushes. "But at least now you have an eyelid." 23

I told myself that she was a pathetic, middle-aged woman with a boring job and a meaningless life. I had my whole life before me. All she had was the newest Richard Chamberlain[9] miniseries. 24

But it didn't matter. The fact of the matter was that she was pretty, and I was not. Her blue eyes were recessed in an intricate pattern of folds and hollows. Mine bulged out. 25

---

[9]**Richard Chamberlain:** An actor who starred in the television program *Dr. Kildare* in the 1960s and in the television miniseries *Shogun* and *The Thorn Birds* in the 1980s.

I bought the skincare system and the foundation and the blush and the lip   26
liner pencil and the lipstick and the primer and the eyeliner and the eyeshad-
ows—all four colors. The stuff filled a bag the size of a shoebox. It cost a lot.
Estée handed me my receipt with a flourish, and I told her, "Thank you."

In the mezzanine[10] level washroom, I set my bag down on the counter   27
and scrubbed my face with water and slimy pink soap from the dispenser.
I splashed my face with cold water until it felt tight, and dried my raw skin
with brown paper towels that scratched.

As the sun sank into the Chicago skyline, I boarded the Burlington   28
Northern Commuter[11] for home and found a seat in the corner. I set the
shopping bag down beside me, and heaped its gilt boxes and frosted glass
bottles into my lap. Looking out the window, I saw that night had fallen.
Instead of trees and backyard fences I saw my profile—the same reflection,
I realized, that I'd seen hours ago in the side of the green glass office building. I did have eyelids, of course. Just not a fold. I wasn't pretty. But I was
familiar and comforting. I was myself.

The next stop was mine. I arranged the things carefully back in the rect-   29
angular bag, large bottles of toner and moisturizer first, then the short cylinders of masque and scrub and powder, small bottles of foundation and
primer, the little logs of pencils and lipstick, then the flat boxed compacts of
blush and eyeshadow. The packages fit around each other cleverly, like pieces
in a puzzle. The conductor called out, "Fairview Avenue," and I stood up.
Hurrying down the aisle, I looked back once at the neatly packed bag on the
seat behind me, and jumped out just as the doors were closing shut.

EXERCISING VOCABULARY

1. Record your own definition for each word below in your notebook.

   stark (adj.) (2)   scrutiny (n.) (9)
   renounced (v.) (3)   wafted (v.) (9)
   bourgeois (adj.) (3)   reverie (n.) (11)
   icons (n.) (5)   mannequin (n.) (11)
   imperious (adj.) (6)   distorted (v.) (20)
   aloof (adj.) (6)   recessed (v.) (25)

2. What is an epiphany? How is Suh's day of beauty "painfully epiphanous" (para. 4)?

3. In paragraph 4, Suh says that she "had broken the Unsightliness Barrier."
   In the fields of science and engineering, what other barrier can be broken?
   Why does the writer choose this image?

---

[10]**mezzanine:** A low-ceilinged story between two main stories of a building.
[11]**Burlington Northern Commuter:** A commuter train that ran from Chicago to the city's
   northern suburbs.

4. Suh refers to famous models in paragraph 5 as "goddesses" and to their pictures as "icons." How are these two words used in a religious sense? How does that affect your reading of this paragraph?

PROBING CONTENT

1. What causes Suh to get a makeover? What feelings lead her to make this decision?

2. On which facial feature does Estée focus? What is the significance of this? What does it say about Estée's ideas about beauty?

3. What is the writer's reaction to the makeover? Whom does she think she looks like now?

4. What causes Suh to leave the makeup behind her on the commuter train? What does she feel like after she does this?

5. What lesson do you think Suh learns from her experience at Neiman Marcus?

CONSIDERING CRAFT

1. Of what common saying does the title of the essay remind you? How does this saying relate to the general message of the essay?

2. How does Suh's tone or attitude change as she begins to describe the cosmetic counters at Neiman Marcus? Why does it change? Why does Suh call the saleswomen "priestesses of beauty" (para. 5)? What does this indicate about her opinion of them? Of American culture as a whole?

3. Reread paragraphs 9 and 10, in which Suh uses many examples of specialized language, or jargon, from the beauty industry—including "exfoliant," "ultra-hydrating complex," and "emulsifying immunage." What is the effect of Suh's use of such language? Describe in detail how she communicates her "reverie" in these paragraphs.

4. The saleswoman calls Suh "an Oriental" (para. 19). What does Suh achieve by using this word? What is the difference between this term and the currently more culturally acceptable term "Asian American"?

5. Reread the dialogue in paragraphs 12 through 16. What effect does this exchange have on your understanding of the essay's message?

WRITING PROMPTS

Responding to the Topic   Have you or a person you know ever had a makeover or considered having one? Have you ever watched a television show that featured a makeover? Write an essay in which you describe one of these scenarios and its outcome.

Responding to the Writer   As a Korean American, Suh details her struggle to conform to a Western ideal of beauty. Write an essay in which you argue the pros and cons of adopting a mainstream look.

Responding to Multiple Viewpoints   John Leo ("The 'Modern Primitives'"), Dan Barden ("My New Nose"), and Jennie Yabroff ("Girls Going Mild[er]") all present examples of the difficult decisions some people make that affect the ways in which others perceive them. Write an essay in which you examine the reasons people might decide to make significant changes in their appearance or behavior. Explore how these changes might affect the way others perceive them. Use material from these three essays to support your ideas.

For a quiz on this reading, go to bedfordstmartins.com/mirror.

Beauty: When the Other Dancer Is the Self

ALICE WALKER

Alice Walker was born in 1944 in Georgia, the youngest of eight children. She is best known for her novel *The Color Purple* (1982), which in 1983 won both the Pulitzer Prize for Fiction and the National Book Award. It was later made into a film nominated for eleven Academy Awards and most recently was adapted as a Broadway musical produced by Oprah Winfrey. A prolific and varied writer, Walker has produced eight novels, three collections of short stories, numerous volumes of poetry, and three collections of essays. Her work has been included in many anthologies. In 2002, she published an update of her early work *Langston Hughes, American Poet*, a biography for children. Her most recent novel, *Now Is the Time to Open Your Heart*, was published in 2004. "Beauty: When the Other Dancer Is the Self" first appeared in her essay collection *In Search of Our Mothers' Gardens: Womanist Prose* (1983). It has become an iconic description of one amazing woman's struggle to accept herself—flaws and all.

> **THINKING AHEAD**   Think of a time when you or someone you know—a friend or a fictional character—suffered a disfiguring or debilitating injury. What was the person's response to this injury? How did that response change over time?

It is a bright summer day in 1947. My father, a fat, funny man with   1
beautiful eyes and a subversive wit, is trying to decide which of his eight children he will take with him to the county fair. My mother, of course, will not go. She is knocked out[1] from getting most of us ready: I hold my neck stiff against the pressure of her knuckles as she hastily completes the braiding and then beribboning of my hair.

My father is the driver for the rich old white lady up the road. Her name   2
is Miss Mey. She owns all the land for miles around, as well as the house in which we live. All I remember about her is that she once offered to pay my mother thirty-five cents for cleaning her house, raking up piles of her magnolia leaves, and washing her family's clothes, and that my mother—she of no money, eight children, and a chronic earache—refused it. But I do not think of this in 1947. I am two and a half years old. I want to go everywhere my daddy goes. I am excited at the prospect of riding in a car. Someone has told me fairs are fun. That there is room in the car for only three of us doesn't faze me at all. Whirling happily in my starchy frock, showing off my

---

[1]**knocked out:** Fatigued; tired out; exhausted.

biscuit-polished[2] patent-leather[3] shoes and lavender socks, tossing my head in a way that makes my ribbons bounce, I stand, hands on hips, before my father. "Take me, Daddy," I say with assurance, "I'm the prettiest!"

Later, it does not surprise me to find myself in Miss Mey's shiny black car, sharing the back seat with the other lucky ones. Does not surprise me that I thoroughly enjoy the fair. At home that night I tell the unlucky ones all I can remember about the merry-go-round,[4] the man who eats live chickens, and the teddy bears, until they say: that's enough, baby Alice. Shut up now, and go to sleep. 3

It is Easter Sunday, 1950. I am dressed in a green, flocked,[5] scalloped-hem dress (handmade by my adoring sister, Ruth) that has its own smooth satin petticoat and tiny hot-pink roses tucked into each scallop. My shoes, new T-strap patent leather, again highly biscuit-polished. I am six years old and have learned one of the longest Easter speeches to be heard that day, totally unlike the speech I said when I was two: "Easter lilies/pure and white/blossom in/the morning light." When I rise to give my speech I do so on a great wave of love and pride and expectation. People in the church stop rustling their new crinolines.[6] They seem to hold their breath. I can tell they admire my dress, but it is my spirit, bordering on sassiness (womanishness), they secretly applaud. 4

"That girl's a little *mess*," they whisper to each other, pleased. 5

Naturally I say my speech without stammer or pause, unlike those who stutter, stammer, or, worst of all, forget. This is before the word "beautiful" exists in people's vocabulary, but "Oh, isn't she the *cutest* thing!" frequently floats my way. "And got so much sense!" they gratefully add . . . for which thoughtful addition I thank them to this day. 6

It was great fun being cute. But then, one day, it ended. 7

I am eight years old and a tomboy.[7] I have a cowboy hat, cowboy boots, checkered shirt and pants, all red. My playmates are my brothers, two and four years older than I. Their colors are black and green, the only difference in the way we are dressed. On Saturday nights we all go to the picture show, even my mother; Westerns are her favorite kind of movie. Back home, "on the ranch," we pretend we are Tom Mix,[8] Hopalong Cassidy,[9] Lash LaRue[10] (we've even named one of our dogs Lash LaRue); we chase each other for hours rustling cattle, being outlaws, delivering damsels from distress. Then 8

---

[2]biscuit-polished: Greased with a biscuit and made shiny.
[3]patent-leather: Leather with a hard, shiny surface.
[4]merry-go-round: An amusement park ride featuring brightly colored animals to sit on; a carousel.
[5]flocked: Having a raised velvety pattern.
[6]crinolines: Stiff petticoats designed to make a skirt stand out.
[7]tomboy: A young girl who enjoys vigorous activities traditionally associated with males.
[8]Tom Mix: An actor in 1930s Western films.
[9]Hopalong Cassidy: An actor in Western films and television series from the 1930s through the 1950s.
[10]Lash LaRue: An actor in Western films in the 1940s, known as the King of the Bullwhip.

my parents decide to buy my brothers guns. These are not "real" guns. They shoot "BBs," copper pellets my brothers say will kill birds. Because I am a girl, I do not get a gun. Instantly I am relegated to the position of Indian. Now there appears a great distance between us. They shoot and shoot at everything with their new guns. I try to keep up with my bow and arrows.

One day while I am standing on top of our makeshift "garage"—pieces 9 of tin nailed across some poles—holding my bow and arrow and looking out toward the fields, I feel an incredible blow in my right eye. I look down just in time to see my brother lower his gun.

Both brothers rush to my side. My eye stings, and I cover it with my 10 hand. "If you tell," they say, "we will get a whipping. You don't want that to happen, do you?" I do not. "Here is a piece of wire," says the older brother, picking it up from the roof; "say you stepped on one end of it and the other flew up and hit you." The pain is beginning to start. "Yes," I say. "Yes, I will say that is what happened." If I do not say this is what happened, I know my brothers will find ways to make me wish I had. But now I will say anything that gets me to my mother.

Confronted by our parents we stick to the lie agreed upon. They place 11 me on a bench on the porch and I close my left eye while they examine the right. There is a tree growing from underneath the porch that climbs past the railing to the roof. It is the last thing my right eye sees. I watch as its trunk, its branches, and then its leaves are blotted out by the rising blood.

I am in shock. First there is intense fever, which my father tries to break 12 using lily leaves bound around my head. Then there are chills: my mother tries to get me to eat soup. Eventually, I do not know how, my parents learn what has happened. A week after the "accident" they take me to see a doctor. "Why did you wait so long to come?" he asks, looking into my eye and shaking his head. "Eyes are sympathetic," he says. "If one is blind, the other will likely become blind too."

This comment of the doctor's terrifies me. But it is really how I look that 13 bothers me most. Where the BB pellet struck there is a glob of whitish scar tissue, a hideous cataract, on my eye. Now when I stare at people—a favorite pastime, up to now—they will stare back. Not at the "cute" little girl, but at her scar. For six years I do not stare at anyone, because I do not raise my head.

Years later, in the throes[11] of a mid-life crisis, I ask my mother and sister 14 whether I changed after the "accident." "No," they say, puzzled. "What do you mean?"

What do I mean? 15

I am eight, and, for the first time, doing poorly in school, where I have 16 been something of a whiz since I was four. We have just moved to the place where the "accident" occurred. We do not know any of the people around us because this is a different county. The only time I see the friends I knew is when we go back to our old church. The new school is the former state penitentiary. It is a large stone building, cold and drafty, crammed to

[11]**throes:** Difficult or painful struggles.

overflowing with boisterous, ill-disciplined children. On the third floor there is a huge circular imprint of some partition that has been torn out.

"What used to be here?" I ask a sullen girl next to me on our way past it to lunch.   17

"The electric chair," says she.   18

At night I have nightmares about the electric chair, and about all the people reputedly "fried" in it. I am afraid of the school, where all the students seem to be budding criminals.   19

"What's the matter with your eye?" they ask, critically.   20

When I don't answer (I cannot decide whether it was an "accident" or not), they shove me, insist on a fight.   21

My brother, the one who created the story about the wire, comes to my rescue. But then brags so much about "protecting" me, I become sick.   22

After months of torture at the school, my parents decide to send me back to our old community, to my old school. I live with my grandparents and the teacher they board. But there is no room for Phoebe, my cat. By the time my grandparents decide there *is* room, and I ask for my cat, she cannot be found. Miss Yarborough, the boarding teacher, takes me under her wing, and begins to teach me to play the piano. But soon she marries an African—a "prince," she says—and is whisked away to his continent.   23

At my old school there is at least one teacher who loves me. She is the teacher who "knew me before I was born" and bought my first baby clothes. It is she who makes life bearable. It is her presence that finally helps me turn on the one child at the school who continually calls me "one-eyed bitch." One day I simply grab him by his coat and beat him until I am satisfied. It is my teacher who tells me my mother is ill.   24

My mother is lying in bed in the middle of the day, something I have never seen. She is in too much pain to speak. She has an abscess in her ear. I stand looking down on her, knowing that if she dies, I cannot live. She is being treated with warm oils and hot bricks held against her cheek. Finally a doctor comes. But I must go back to my grandparents' house. The weeks pass but I am hardly aware of it. All I know is that my mother might die, my father is not so jolly, my brothers still have their guns, and I am the one sent away from home.   25

"You did not change," they say.   26

Did I imagine the anguish of never looking up?   27

I am twelve. When relatives come to visit I hide in my room. My cousin Brenda, just my age, whose father works in the post office and whose mother is a nurse, comes to find me. "Hello," she says. And then she asks, looking at my recent school picture, which I did not want taken, and on which the "glob," as I think of it, is clearly visible, "You still can't see out of that eye?"   28

"No," I say, and flop back on the bed over my book.   29

That night, as I do almost every night, I abuse my eye. I rant and rave at it, in front of the mirror. I plead with it to clear up before morning. I tell it I hate and despise it. I do not pray for sight. I pray for beauty.   30

"You did not change," they say.   31

I am fourteen and baby-sitting for my brother Bill, who lives in Boston.   32
He is my favorite brother and there is a strong bond between us. Understanding my feelings of shame and ugliness he and his wife take me to a
local hospital, where the "glob" is removed by a doctor named O. Henry.
There is still a small bluish crater where the scar tissue was, but the ugly
white stuff is gone. Almost immediately I become a different person from
the girl who does not raise her head. Or so I think. Now that I've raised
my head I win the boyfriend of my dreams. Now that I've raised my head
I have plenty of friends. Now that I've raised my head classwork comes
from my lips as faultlessly as Easter speeches did, and I leave high school
as valedictorian,[12] most popular student, and *queen*, hardly believing my
luck. Ironically, the girl who was voted most beautiful in our class (and
was) was later shot twice through the chest by a male companion, using
a "real" gun, while she was pregnant. But that's another story in itself.
Or is it?

"You did not change," they say.   33

It is now thirty years since the "accident." A beautiful journalist comes to   34
visit and to interview me. She is going to write a cover story for her magazine that focuses on my latest book. "Decide how you want to look on the
cover," she says. "Glamorous, or whatever."

Never mind "glamorous," it is the "whatever" that I hear. Suddenly   35
all I can think of is whether I will get enough sleep the night before the
photography session: if I don't, my eye will be tired and wander, as blind
eyes will.

At night in bed with my lover I think up reasons why I should not   36
appear on the cover of a magazine. "My meanest critics will say I've sold
out," I say. "My family will not realize I write scandalous books."

"But what's the real reason you don't want to do this?" he asks.   37

"Because in all probability," I say in a rush, "my eye won't be straight."   38

"It will be straight enough," he says. Then, "Besides, I thought you'd   39
made your peace with that."

And I suddenly remember that I have.   40

I remember: 41

I am talking to my brother Jimmy, asking if he remembers anything   42
unusual about the day I was shot. He does not know I consider that day the
last time my father, with his sweet home remedy of cool lily leaves, chose
me, and that I suffered and raged inside because of this. "Well," he says,
"all I remember is standing by the side of the highway with Daddy, trying
to flag down[13] a car. A white man stopped, but when Daddy said he needed
somebody to take his little girl to the doctor, he drove off."

I remember: 43

I am in the desert for the first time. I fall totally in love with it. I am   44
so overwhelmed by its beauty, I confront for the first time, consciously, the

---

[12]**valedictorian:** The student who has the highest rank in his or her class and delivers the
graduation speech.

[13]**flag down:** To signal to stop.

meaning of the doctor's words years ago: "Eyes are sympathetic. If one is blind, the other will likely become blind too." I realize I have dashed about the world madly, looking at this, looking at that, storing up images against the fading of the light. *But I might have missed seeing the desert!* The shock of that possibility—and gratitude for over twenty-five years of sight—sends me literally to my knees. Poem after poem comes—which is perhaps how poets pray.

On Sight

I am so thankful I have seen
The Desert
And the creatures in the desert
And the desert Itself.

The desert has its own moon
Which I have seen
With my own eye.
There is no flag on it.
Trees of the desert have arms
All of which are always up
That is because the moon is up
The sun is up
Also the sky
The stars
Clouds
None with flags.

If there *were* flags, I doubt
the trees would point.
Would you?

But mostly, I remember this: 45

I am twenty-seven, and my baby daughter is almost three. Since her birth 46 I have worried about her discovery that her mother's eyes are different from other people's. Will she be embarrassed? I think. What will she say? Every day she watches a television program called *Big Blue Marble*. It begins with a picture of the earth as it appears from the moon. It is bluish, a little battered-looking, but full of light, with whitish clouds swirling around it. Every time I see it I weep with love, as if it is a picture of Grandma's house. One day when I am putting Rebecca down for her nap, she suddenly focuses on my eye. Something inside me cringes, gets ready to try to protect myself. All children are cruel about physical differences, I know from experience, and that they don't always mean to is another matter. I assume Rebecca will be the same.

But no-o-o-o. She studies my face intently as we stand, her inside and 47 me outside her crib. She even holds my face maternally between her dimpled little hands. Then, looking every bit as serious and lawyerlike as her father, she says, as if it may just possibly have slipped my attention: "Mommy, there's a *world* in your eye." (As in, "Don't be alarmed, or do anything crazy.") And then, gently, but with great interest: "Mommy, where did you *get* that world in your eye?"

For the most part, the pain left then. (So what, if my brothers grew   48
up to buy even more powerful pellet guns for their sons and to carry real guns themselves. So what, if a young "Morehouse man"[14] once nearly fell off the steps of Trevor Arnett Library because he thought my eyes were blue.) Crying and laughing I ran to the bathroom, while Rebecca mumbled and sang herself off to sleep. Yes indeed, I realized, looking into the mirror. There *was* a world in my eye. And I saw that it was possible to love it: that in fact, for all it had taught me of shame and anger and inner vision, I *did* love it. Even to see it drifting out of orbit in boredom, or rolling up out of fatigue, not to mention floating back at attention in excitement (bearing witness, a friend has called it), deeply suitable to my personality, and even characteristic of me.

That night I dream I am dancing to Stevie Wonder's[15] song "Always"   49
(the name of the song is really "As," but I hear it as "Always"). As I dance, whirling and joyous, happier than I've ever been in my life, another bright-faced dancer joins me. We dance and kiss each other and hold each other through the night. The other dancer has obviously come through all right, as I have done. She is beautiful, whole and free. And she is also me.

EXERCISING VOCABULARY

1. Record your own definition for each word below in your notebook.

faze (v.) (2)	penitentiary (n.) (16)
sassiness (n.) (4)	sullen (adj.) (17)
relegated (v.) (8)	crater (n.) (32)
makeshift (adj.) (9)	scandalous (adj.) (36)
cataract (n.) (13)	dashed (v.) (44)

2. In paragraphs 12 and 44, Walker quotes her doctor as saying, "Eyes are sympathetic. If one is blind, the other will likely become blind too." In what other context do we generally use the word *sympathetic*? What does it mean?

3. Walker writes that "Miss Yarborough, the boarding teacher, takes me under her wing" (para. 23). What does it mean to offer someone board? What is the situation of the boarding teacher? What does it mean to take someone under one's wing? Where does this image originate?

---

[14]**Morehouse man:** A student at Morehouse College, Atlanta, Georgia, the only all-male, historically black institution of higher learning in the United States.
[15]**Stevie Wonder:** An African American singer, pianist, and songwriter who is blind.

PROBING CONTENT

1. What happens that causes Walker to stop being "cute" (para. 7)? What role do her brothers play in this incident?

2. Describe the author before the "accident." What are her outstanding characteristics? How does she relate to those around her?

3. Describe Walker after the accident. How does she change both physically and psychologically?

4. When does Walker begin to regain her confidence? What role does her brother Bill play in this?

5. In paragraph 47, Rebecca says, "Mommy, there's a *world* in your eye." What does the child mean? Where does Rebecca get this idea? How does the child's reaction affect her mother?

CONSIDERING CRAFT

1. What is the significance of the title? Why does Walker choose a dance metaphor?

2. Why does Walker insert the poem "On Sight" within her essay (para. 44)? How does this affect your reading?

3. Why does the author repeat certain phrases throughout the essay? Find two or three examples and discuss their use in the essay.

4. Examine several examples of achronological order in Walker's essay. Why do you think she chooses to present her narrative in this manner?

WRITING PROMPTS

Responding to the Topic   Think about people with a physical disability whom you have known personally or have seen on television or in the movies. Write an essay in which you describe how they dealt with their condition and your reaction to them.

Responding to the Writer   Walker's essay details her struggle to come to terms with her physical difference and to finally see herself as beautiful. Children and their reactions to her eye play a significant role in her struggle with self-image. Write an essay in which you argue that children play either a primarily positive or a primarily negative role in the formation of others' perceptions of themselves.

Responding to Multiple Viewpoints   Both Walker and Dan Barden ("My New Nose") detail the epiphanies they experienced concerning their self-image in their essays. Compare their experiences. How are they similar? How are they different?

DRAWING CONNECTIONS

1. How does the saying "Beauty is in the eye of the beholder" apply to Grace Suh's "The Eye of the Beholder" and Walker's "Beauty: When the Other Dancer Is the Self"? Write an essay in which you answer this question by using examples from both essays.

2. In the final paragraph of her essay, Walker describes the dancer as "beautiful, whole and free" and adds that "she is also me." How do the adjectives Walker uses to describe her new self-image apply to Grace Suh in "The Eye of the Beholder"?

3. In both Walker's and Grace Suh's essays, a woman's eye plays a central role. Consider the lessons that both Walker and Suh learned about themselves and about others. Also explore the importance of societal and cultural pressures on both women's struggle to become comfortable with their personal images.

For a quiz on this reading, go to bedfordstmartins.com/mirror.

Wrapping Up Chapter 4

CONNECTING TO THE CULTURE

1. If, as Patricia McLaughlin ("Venus Envy") and Dan Barden ("My New Nose") argue, men are now more concerned than ever before with their appearance, what elements in our society are most responsible for this heightened awareness? To what extent are the media (television, movies, magazines, newspapers, and the Internet) responsible? What consequences do you expect? What changes in advertising or new products support this thesis?

2. Think about the people who have helped shape your self-image, both inner and outer. These may be people you know personally or celebrities you have never actually met. These people may have been positive role models for you, helping you to set goals for yourself, or negative influences showing you what you did not want to become. In an essay, explore how one or several of these people have influenced you.

3. Different cultures have different ideals of beauty. Do some research on another country whose beauty ideals are different from those in the United States. In an essay, examine the differences you have found and relate how the standard of beauty affects the members of the culture you selected.

4. Ideals of beauty and fashion have changed throughout history in the United States. Pick a specific historical period and research how these ideals were defined for men or women during that time. Then write an essay in which you compare the ideals of that historical period to today's ideals of beauty and fashion. Use specific examples and visuals from the time period you have researched.

Focusing on Yesterday, Focusing on Today

People young and old, male and female, have been writing diaries and keeping journals for centuries. Some of these records, such as those written by famous novelists, explorers, or government leaders, have become important public documents. However, most diaries and journals remain distinctly private. Whether writers use a pen and paper or a computer keyboard, they normally record their innermost thoughts in a "room of one's own" such as a bedroom or a study. Indeed it is considered taboo to invade a person's space by reading his or her diary or journal.

In these days of Web cams and social-networking Web sites like MySpace, Facebook, and YouTube, the "Dear Diary" dialogue has grown into a very public conversation with dozens, hundreds, or even thousands of other people. And many of those people who are viewing the person in front of the Web cam or the face on Facebook may be complete strangers who live around the globe.

"Dear Diary"

How are the activities pictured in these visuals similar? How are they different?

What are the advantages and disadvantages of keeping diaries or journals the "old-fashioned" way like the young woman in the photograph?

Why have Web cams and Web sites like MySpace, Facebook, and YouTube become so popular? Why do so many people use them? What are the disadvantages or even dangers of using Web cams or social-networking Web sites?

MySpace Is Your Space

5 What Are You Trying to Say?

How Language Works

Analyzing the Image

The age of computers has caused a functional reevaluation of the definition of language. What conveys meaning? Words don't actually have to be involved at all. Symbols, icons, emoticons, and images all convey meaning in ways that were not even contemplated twenty years ago.

- What exactly are you looking at here? What comprises the image? What different interpretations are possible?

- Is this language? If so, what is it saying? How do the symbols convey meaning?

- How many people would understand this message? Why?

Research this topic with TopLinks at bedfordstmartins.com/toplinks.

GEARING UP   Is English your first language? Whether it is or isn't, what do you remember about learning to speak English? By whom were you taught? What early words did you use? Do you speak another language now? Would you like to be fluent in another language? Which one? Why?

For human beings, language skills may be our most significant acquisition. We learn early to be vocal to get what we want. However, short of a bout of bad laryngitis, most of us take for granted the fluency and frequency with which we employ language to communicate our needs and desires. We don't spend much time considering how words — or which words — become part of our common linguistic currency. Unlike the French government, the U.S. government bureaucracy doesn't include a committee whose sole function is to attempt to regulate the language. American English is very eclectic; we adopt words from just about everywhere. Consider the words *hors d'oeuvres, kayak, moped, zeitgeist, jihad, raccoon, queso, fjord, aardvark, sauna, kosher, phobia, Fahrenheit, kindergarten, smorgasbord, macho, chef, genre, cul-de-sac, karate,* and *apartheid.*

In spite of being so welcoming to words from other languages, we engage in animated debate over whether the native speakers of those languages should continue to use their mother tongues exclusively when they live in the United States. Should immigrants assimilate culturally and linguistically, or should they strive to retain their own culture's customs and language? Language is, after all, an innate part of cultural identity. Is bilingual education a benefit to students new to the American school system, or is it a hindrance not in their best interest?

Should everyone who wants to be an American live and work and play in English?

And exactly which English would we have newcomers learn? There's the casual English with which we interact with friends, and there's the standard English our professors and bosses expect us to master. Have today's thumb-jumping text messagers lost the ability to distinguish between language for MySpace and language appropriate for someone else's space, like the classroom or the workplace? To what extent has text messaging replaced face-to-face communication? What happens when all emotions have been reduced to emoticons?

It's impossible to separate our language from our popular culture. An entire category of words bombarding our speech habits comes from advertising. When does a product name become so commonplace that is begins to represent all things of that type (Kleenex, for example)? Even parts of speech undergo metamorphosis. How many nouns have recently become verbs, not through *Webster*, but through daily usage? "How long have you been officed in that building downtown?" "Why don't you just Google it?" "I'll text you about the party." And although computers may not be able to replicate themselves yet, they have spawned their own vocabulary: "blogging," "virtual reality," and "surfing the Web," for example.

The selections in this chapter explore these ideas and other language-related assumptions in ways that may cause you to really think about the words you speak and those you hear.

> **COLLABORATING**   In groups of three or four students, make a list of all the ways you can think of to communicate with another person. List the advantages and disadvantages of each method. Have each member of the group defend his or her favorite method, and then poll your classmates to see which method of communication they prefer. Brainstorm together about how communication may change over the next twenty years.

Like

PATRICIA T. O'CONNER

Patricia T. O'Conner is the author of *Woe Is I: The Grammarphobe's Guide to Better English in Plain English* (1996) and *Words Fail Me: What Everyone Who Writes Should Know about Writing* (1999) as well as the coauthor, with Stewart Kellerman, of *You Send Me: Getting It Right When You Write Online* (2002). Her most recent book is *Woe Is I Jr.* (2007), an illustrated book on grammar for kids. She gained experience with grammar in her fifteen years as an editor for the *New York Times*. This essay first appeared in the July 15, 2007, edition of the *New York Times* as part of the regular *On Language* column.

> **THINKING AHEAD** Listen to the students around you in the bookstore, classroom, hallways, or cafeteria. How many times do you hear someone use the word *like*, not as a verb but as an interruption in speech? How often do you do this yourself? How did *like* become a fixture in our conversations?

ike is a friendly word. As a verb, it gives off affectionate vibes. In other 1
parts of speech, it's a mensch[1] as well, emphasizing what things have in common, not what separates them. But there's another *like* in the air, a gossipy usage that has grammar purists—and many parents of teenagers—climbing the walls.

This upstart *like* is the new *say*, and users (or abusers, depending on 2
which side you take) find it a handy tool for quoting or paraphrasing the speech of others, often with sarcasm or irony. Linguists call it the "quotative[2] *like*," but any 16-year-old can show you how it works.

For example, *like* can introduce an actual quotation ("She's like, 'What 3
unusual shoes you're wearing!'") or paraphrase one ("She's like, my shoes are weird!").

Or it can summarize the inner thoughts of either the quoter or the quotee 4
("She's like, yeah, as if I'd be caught dead in them! And I'm like, I care what you think?").

Like even lets a speaker imitate the behavior of the person being quoted 5
("She's like . . ." and the speaker smirks and rolls her eyes).

This *like* is not to be confused with the one that sticklers[3] see as a mean- 6
ingless verbal tic ("The band was, like, outrageous!"). Linguists would argue,

---

[1]**mensch:** Someone honest and reliable.
[2]**quotative:** Related to a quotation.
[3]**sticklers:** People who insist on adherence to the rules.

however, that even that one has its uses — to emphasize something ("I was, like, exhausted!") or to hedge a statement ("We had, like, six hours of homework!").

But back to the *like* that's used as a marker to introduce quotes (real or   7
approximate) as well as thoughts, attitudes and even gestures. Parents may gnash their teeth, but language scholars like *like*.

"It's a shame this poor little usage gets such a bum rap," says Jennifer   8
Dailey-O'Cain, an associate professor at the University of Alberta in Canada and one of several people interviewed by e-mail for this column. Dailey-O'Cain, who has published an often-cited study on the use of *like*, says, "It's innovative, it serves a particular function and it does specific things that you can't duplicate with other quotatives."

The other quoting words commonly used in speech are *say*, of course,   9
along with *go* ("He goes, 'Give me your wallet'") and *all* ("I'm all, 'Sure, dude, it's yours'"). But *like* definitely has legs. In just a generation or so it has spread throughout much of the English-speaking world.

O.K., the new *like* is hot and it's useful, but is it legit? Aren't some rules   10
of grammar or usage being broken here?

Linguists and lexicographers[4] say no. It's natural, they say, for words   11
to take on new roles. In this case, a "content word" (one that means something) has become a "function word" (one that has a grammatical function but little actual meaning). Academics call the process "grammaticalization." It's one of the ways language changes.

So is the new *like* proper English? Well, the latest editions of *The American*   12
Heritage Dictionary of the English Language and *Merriam-Webster's Collegiate Dictionary* now include it as a usage heard in informal speech. That's not a ringing endorsement, but it's not a condemnation either.

As for me, I'm convinced that this is a useful, even ingenious, addition to   13
informal spoken English. But let's be honest. For now, at least, it smacks of incorrectness to a great many people. In writing my grammar book for kids, I wrestled with this problem. In the end, I suggested that the usage is O.K. in informal conversation but not for situations requiring your best English.

Contrary to popular opinion, *like* is not exclusively a kid thing. Grown-   14
ups use it too, men and women about equally, according to Dailey-O'Cain.

"Part of what inspired my study was the fact that my mother (who was   15
in her 50s at the time) used to complain about other people using *like*," she says. "But once I started pointing it out to her every single time she used it herself, she stopped making those kinds of criticisms!"

The linguist Geoffrey Pullum, an author of *The Cambridge Grammar of*   16
the English Language, finds the usage "quite logical and reasonable." And he agrees that it's not confined to youngsters. "My former student Jessica Maki caught her 65-year-old aunt, who grew up in North Carolina, saying, 'I'm like, don't answer the telephone!'"

---

[4]**lexicographers:** Persons who write or edit a dictionary.

Yet part of the resistance to *like* may be due to its youthful rep. "People 17
see it as associated with teenagers," says Arnold Zwicky, a visiting professor
of linguistics at Stanford. "In general, variants associated with young people
tend to be disdained."

Another unfounded assumption about *like* is that it's used by the less 18
educated among us. "A lot of people are going to say that the variant just
'sounds uneducated,' and no amount of factual evidence is likely to counter
this judgment," Zwicky says. "Here we have another factor contributing
to people's disdain for the quotative *like*, especially in their own children:
nobody wants their kids to sound uneducated."

I've always believed that young people are capable of knowing when 19
to use formal versus informal, written versus spoken English. Zwicky's experience with *like*-mindedness seems to bear this out. "It's a specifically
spoken form," he says. "I don't see it in writing, even from my students
who are heavy users of it in speech, except when they're producing writing
that they intend to sound like speech."

A word to parents: Loosen up. You may be using *like* this way yourselves 20
without even realizing it. I have a confession to make. My husband caught me
in the act only the other day. He was like, "Did you hear what you just said?"

EXERCISING VOCABULARY

1. Record your own definition for each word below in your notebook.

   purists (n.) (1)   innovative (adj.) (8)
   upstart (adj.) (2)   ingenious (adj.) (13)
   linguists (n.) (2)   variants (n.) (17)
   smirks (v.) (5)   disdained (adj.) (17)
   tic (n.) (6)

2. What does it mean "to hedge a statement" (para. 6)? What function does a
   real hedge serve? When the noun is used as a verb, what does it mean?

3. What does the expression "to gnash one's teeth" mean? What is this
   expression's source? What does O'Conner's use "to gnash one's teeth"
   in paragraph 7 communicate to the reader?

4. What is O'Conner saying about the usage of *like* when she writes that this
   word "definitely has legs" (para. 9)? What kind of figurative language is
   she using here?

PROBING CONTENT

1. What is one use of *like* that scholars favor? Why do they like *like* in this
   usage?

2. Explain the difference between a "content word" and a "function word"
   (para. 11). What is the process called by which a content word evolves
   into a function word?

3. Explain two reasons mentioned in this essay why some people resist using *like* in its new sense.

CONSIDERING CRAFT

1. In her first two sentences, O'Conner sets the tone for her essay and establishes her position on her topic. How does she accomplish this? What tone does she establish? To what extent are this tone and her point of view consistent throughout the essay?

2. O'Conner quotes a number of sources in her essay. Identify three of them and explain how their inclusion furthers the author's purpose and supports her thesis.

3. The author deliberately raises points of view that are different from her own. How does she handle these opposing viewpoints? What does she accomplish by including them?

WRITING PROMPTS

Responding to the Topic   With what groups do you associate frequent use of the word *like* in conversation? Write an essay in which you profile, from your own experience, the frequent user of *like* and the ways in which use of this word reflects his or her personality.

Responding to the Writer   O'Conner states, "I've always believed that young people are capable of knowing when to use formal versus informal, written versus spoken English" (para. 19). Write an essay in which you agree or disagree with her position. Use specific examples to support your thesis.

Responding to Multiple Viewpoints   The noted historian David McCullough, speaking to Boston College's class of 2008, urged the graduates, "Please, please do what you can to cure the verbal virus that seems increasingly rampant among your generation."* One of the words he specifically asked them to give up was *like.* O'Conner would hate to see this little word go. Write an essay in which you agree with either McCullough or O'Conner. Be sure to defend your position with sufficient supporting details.

For a quiz on this reading, go to bedfordstmartins.com/mirror.

*Quoted in *Austin American-Statesman,* American Digest, May 26, 2008, page G1.

Corporate Names and Products Creep into Everyday Language

GENEVA WHITE

Geneva White is a reporter and columnist for the *Northwest Herald* in the Greater Chicago area. In this article, which appeared in the *Northwest Herald* in 2007, White discusses all the ways we incorporate brand names into our everyday language, sometimes without even realizing we've done so.

> **THINKING AHEAD**   In your own speech, think about brand names you employ to represent everything of that type (Band-Aid, for example). Make a list of these. Now add to your list other brand names used generically that you've heard on television or in movies. How do proper nouns become common nouns in our vocabulary?

We "Google" ex-boyfriends and ex-girlfriends. 1

We "Netflix" DVDs. 2

Before heading to parties, we often "Mapquest" the directions. 3

And rather than miss our favorite television shows, we "TiVo" them. 4

What has become of the English language? Linguists insist this integration of corporate names, products and services into our everyday speech is nothing new. 5

Dennis Baron, a professor of English and linguistics, points out that in the 1980s, we were "Xeroxing" copies. Older generations likely remember the days when all cameras were called "Kodaks." 6

"This is one of the ways that language naturally works," said Baron, who teaches at the University of Illinois in Champaign. "Common inventions, technologies and products become embedded in the language and extend their use to other areas. That's how language changes and spreads." 7

Scott Osmundson, 31, said he finds himself incorporating words that originated with the Internet. 8

"Yeah, I say 'Google it,'" said Osmundson, of Johnsburg. "With how big the Internet has gotten it was bound to happen." 9

Osmundson said his friends have told him to "YouTube" videos. "MySpace me" is another expression he's heard people say. 10

"We're starting to lose the English language," Osmundson said. "Especially with texting and how people abbreviate words now." 11

As the English language evolves, new words must be added to *Merriam-Webster's Collegiate Dictionary*. Among the latest words appearing in the 12

163

dictionary's 11th edition, set to be released this fall, are *DVR* (Digital Video Recorder), *speed dating, sudoku*[1] and *telenovela.*[2]

"Webster is constantly adding new words to the dictionary," said   13
Heather Brown, assistant chair of the English department at Woodstock High School. "If you notice, most of those are technology driven."

So far, Brown, who teaches creative writing and American literature,   14
hasn't seen students use terms such as "Googling" in their papers.

"But it's definitely in their lexicon when they're talking with each   15
other," she said.

Frequent use of a word not only helps it get into the dictionary. The   16
practice can also put a product's copyright at stake.

"It's tricky for [corporations]," Baron said. "They want the names of   17
their products to be on everybody's lips, but they don't want it to be used as a generic [word]. They don't want all tissues to be Kleenex."

Ironically, just because a word ends up in the dictionary, it's still not neces-   18
sarily O.K. to use on school papers, college entrance exams and cover letters.

"'*Ain't*' has been in the dictionary for some time," Brown said. "We   19
still don't allow it."

Renee Woods of Crystal Lake said "Google" often comes up in her   20
conversations.

"My friend just 'Googled' herself," said Woods, 25. "That's weird."   21

EXERCISING VOCABULARY

1. Record your own definition for each word below in your notebook.

   integration (n.) (5)   incorporating (v.) (8)
   embedded (v.) (7)   lexicon (n.) (15)

2. In paragraph 17, Dennis Baron is quoted as saying that businesses want their products to be popular but don't really want that product's name "to be used as a generic." What does *generic* mean? What part of speech is the word as Baron uses it? Give an example of *generic* used as a different part of speech. Why does the author add a final word in brackets that wasn't part of the original quote?

3. Who are linguists? What does the study of linguistics involve? Why are linguists' ideas important to this essay?

PROBING CONTENT

1. What is one way that language evolves, according to Professor Dennis Baron?

2. According to Professor Heather Brown, how much of the new Internet-inspired vocabulary is making its way into students' writing?

---

[1]*sudoku*: A puzzle completed on a grid using numbers and the application of logic.
[2]*telenovela*: Melodrama miniseries made popular in Latin America.

3. To what area are most of the new words in *Merriam-Webster's Collegiate Dictionary* related? Why is this the case?

CONSIDERING CRAFT

1. In this relatively brief selection, White quotes four sources. How does this affect your reading of her essay? What observations can you make about the credentials of White's sources? Why do you think she chose these particular sources?

2. How does White incorporate her topic into the introduction to catch the reader's attention? What can you learn from her introduction that you can apply to your own writing?

3. In this selection, what strategy does White use to prove the point that "the integration of corporate names, products and services into our everyday speech is nothing new" (para. 5)?

WRITING PROMPTS

Responding to the Topic   Write an essay in which you discuss some changes you personally have noted in the language we use daily. Elaborate on the reasons for these changes. Be sure to use specific examples to support your argument.

Responding to the Writer   Dennis Baron states, "This is one of the ways that language naturally works" (para. 7). Scott Osmundson, however, complains, "We're starting to lose the English language" (para. 11). Whose viewpoint is more accurate? Write an essay in which you defend one of these positions.

Responding to Multiple Viewpoints   How would the teachers of English to non-native speakers in Caitlin Miner-Le Grand's "More Than Language" react to the infiltration of product and brand names into English? Would having to consider these new words make the teachers' jobs easier or more difficult? Why? Write an essay in which you explore these ideas.

For a quiz on this reading, go to bedfordstmartins.com/mirror.

More Than Language

CAITLIN MINER-LE GRAND

Caitlin Miner-Le Grand is a communications associate for the Council of the Americas, an international business organization. She has coauthored essays for *Salon* and *Voices Unabridged,* an Internet magazine on human rights for women. "More Than Language" appeared in *Wiretap* in November 2006.

> **THINKING AHEAD**   To what extent is it possible or desirable to teach American English to non-native speakers without injecting some American culture? From what sources do you think people in other countries derive their opinions about what it means to be an American? How accurate are their preconceptions?

On the first day of class, Trudi Connolly marched in, clambered to the 1
top of her desk, took off her cowboy boots and forced thirty Chinese teenagers to shout "I don't understand!" This was their introduction to their new English teacher, a 20-year-old American who had come to China for two months during her summer vacation from college.

The culture clash was immediate, and calculated. With little teacher 2
training, Connolly was betting on a combination of English grammar and dialogue on American culture as the most effective way to reach Chinese adolescents already versed in pop-punk and Hollywood movies.

"I try to set up my classroom as a microcosm for how I understand 3
American life as opposed to Chinese life: often less structured, more free-form, less clarity of meaning and purpose, more different opinions," said Connolly. "Many of them had never had any serious interaction with Westerners before, and by forcing them to acknowledge me as a discrete individual, I think that many of them loosened their grip on their generalities."

This involved showing pictures of her family and friends, and talking 4
about her life in the United States. It wasn't always what her students expected to hear. In one example, they were surprised to hear that there are homeless people in the United States — they expected everyone to be rich. "When we think of both the worst and best stereotypes of ourselves, this is the image they have of us," Connolly said, ticking off "gun-toting," "self-centered," and "generous."

Rachel Greenwald's students, meanwhile, were already living in the 5
United States when they started taking her English class last spring, offered through Mixteca, a non-profit organization based in Sunset Park, Brooklyn, that offers services to the neighborhood's large Latin American population.

Some of her students had been in the United States for over twenty years without mastering the language or the social customs.

For Danielle Renwick, teaching English was the easiest way to pay the rent when she moved down to Buenos Aires, Argentina, this fall after graduating from college. After a quick certification course, she found work at American Express, a U.S.-based company operating in Argentina. The company pays for their employees to take English classes, since language skills are crucial for conducting international business.

These three young Americans taught on separate continents under vastly different circumstances. But one thing they have in common is that they all found themselves navigating the fine lines between teaching a language and explaining American culture. All three had students who had taken some form of English classes beforehand, or at least had some passing familiarity; in today's globalized world, it is becoming increasingly rare to find someone with absolutely no exposure to English.

While Mandarin Chinese claims the largest number of native-born speakers worldwide, English has the most second-language learners, in addition to its hefty number of native speakers. It has acquired lingua franca[1] status, helped along by technological advances such as the Internet.

Intersection of Language and Culture

While the exact definition of culture varies, most theorists agree that it can essentially be boiled down to the behaviors and beliefs of a certain group. The United States has been beaming its culture out into the world for the past century, through its music, movies, TV shows, and video games. Global politics aside, many perceive American culture to be a globally homogenizing force.

The intersection of language and culture has been debated for years. Connolly, who is now pursuing a Master's degree in comparative literature in New York City, firmly believes that the two are inseparable. She remembers looking through her Chinese middle school students' English textbooks and finding a lesson that taught them to say "the family are in the living room." This prompted a discussion of students' cultural conceptions on the nature of a family, whether it should be understood as a single unit or the sum of its individual members.

"Sometimes you just have to stab forward, but I do try to include in any discussions of grammar at least a few pointers about how grammatical rules produce and reveal the ways in which we understand the world," said Connolly.

Renwick, armed with grammar exercise sheets provided by her certification school, believes that English could be taught simply as a language, untied from the moorings of its speakers' culture, but that that would get dull.

[1]**lingua franca:** A common language.

"I don't have the idea that I'm teaching U.S. culture, but it comes out," 13
said Renwick. "I'm teaching grammar, but it's within a greater context."
For one exercise, she says she brought in an article on her small Wisconsin
hometown, so that her students could understand her origins while practicing
their vocabulary and comprehension.

Many of Greenwald's students in Brooklyn wanted to learn English as 14
a way of understanding their children, who jump comfortably in and out
of contemporary American culture. "I want to know what my daughter is
saying on the phone when she talks to boys at night," Greenwald remembers
one of them saying.

Subtle social differences, like how most people in the United States 15
neglect to say good morning, puzzled her students. "You can't just give
someone rules and exercises that don't have any connection to the culture
and the life they're living," said Greenwald, who found herself explaining
video game jargon and slang. "It won't stick."

Lessons Learned

One of Connolly's most successful lessons involved teaching a roomful 16
of 14-year-old Chinese students to sing Billy Joel's "Piano Man." "We
wanted to use materials with a sort of pluralistic, democratic edge, and
'Piano Man' has such a diversity of human beings in it, we thought this
would be a useful way to discuss differences of lifestyle," said Connolly.
She described her materials as hodge-podge, but with an eye toward the
bigger picture.

Connolly says she caught her students off-guard by agreeing with them 17
when they said they believed the United States and China were on a collision
course as the world's current superpowers. But she asserted that whatever
happened was, in large part, up to them, "specifically, as upper-class, educated, English-speakers." Political dissent was also heavily discussed in her
classroom, and her students often got their first taste of open criticism—both
of the U.S. and the Chinese systems.

American politics get a lot of press around the world, to varying degrees 18
of complexity. Halfway through teaching her class the morning after the
recent midterm elections, Renwick realized she hadn't found time to check
the results. One of her Argentine students broke down the results exactly,
adding that two races were still in contention. As opposed to Connolly's
Chinese preteens, the Argentinean adults grasped the plurality of political
discussion within the United States.

Living within the United States, however, Greenwald's students were 19
often apolitical. One of her students came to class excitedly talking about
the Army recruiter who had tried to enlist her son, and all the benefits
that an Army career entailed. Greenwald tried to provide context for the
recruiter's glowing description of Army life, such as the high possibility
that her son would be sent to a warzone.

"If you don't speak English, how can you demand the rights that go   20
along with your American experience?" said Greenwald, adding, "I was
much more political about it than most of them were interested in. They
were like, 'eh, ok.'"

Worried about sounding trite, she said she wants them to undergo the   21
same process that early American immigrants did. She says that most people
don't realize how much influence Latin American immigrants already
exert on U.S. culture, from music to a higher demand for Latin American
products in grocery stores, to the fact that even here students' Hasidic Jewish
employers have learned bits of Spanish to communicate. "It's almost like
the reverse of our idea of globalization," she says. Teaching her students
to communicate in English was not just a question of assimilation; instead,
Greenwald believes, it opened up the possibility of their interacting with
and further diversifying American culture.

All three young women jumped into teaching English with little or no   22
training, and admitted to feeling daunted, especially in the beginning. While
they do not share a common approach, they do agree on one thing: for their
students, they were not only English teachers but also cultural ambassadors.

In a world where television screens across the globe are inundated   23
with American programs like *Desperate Housewives* and *Baywatch*, many
may feel that they already have an understanding, perhaps too much so, of
Amercian culture. Renwick said that one of her main goals was to present
a different side of the United States. Greenwald and Connolly agreed.

"Just having a more finely tuned, flexible way to compare the cultures   24
was a major step in the right direction," concluded Connolly.

EXERCISING VOCABULARY

1. Record your own definition for each word below in your notebook.

   discrete (adj.) (3)   trite (adj.) (21)
   homogenizing (adj.) (9)   assimilation (n.) (21)
   jargon (n.) (15)   daunted (adj.) (22)
   pluralistic (adj.) (16)   inundated (v.) (23)

2. Trudi Connolly calls her classroom "a microcosm for how I understand American life as opposed to Chinese life" (para. 3). What is a microcosm? Explain how a classroom could fulfill this function.

3. Trudi Connolly describes her teaching materials as "hodge-podge" (para. 16). What does this expression mean? How does using materials other than textbooks reflect Connolly's attitude about the relationship between culture and language?

4. Rachel Greenwald, teaching non-native English-speakers within the United States, worries about her students being "apolitical" (para. 19). How is the common word *political* changed by the prefix *a*? What potentially harmful effects could this attitude have for her students?

PROBING CONTENT

1. What surprised Trudi Connolly's students about people in the United States? What stereotypical images did her students have about Americans? Where do these ideas originate?

2. Trudi Connolly and Danielle Renwick both express their opinions about the deliberate injection of American culture into language teaching. Explain the position each takes and how each teacher puts that to use in her classroom.

3. What language has the most second-language learners? What modern advances have helped this number grow?

4. How do the approaches that these three young women use to teach English to non-native speakers differ? On what point do all three agree?

CONSIDERING CRAFT

1. How effective is Miner-Le Grand's introduction? Why? What attributes of this introduction could be applied to any essay?

2. What does Miner-Le Grand accomplish by including the teaching experiences of three women in this selection rather than focusing in more depth on the story of just one of them? How does this approach support her thesis?

3. Miner-Le Grand states that Danielle Renwick "believes that English could be taught simply as a language, untied from the moorings of its speakers' culture, but that that would get dull" (para. 12). What is usually tied to moorings? How does this metaphor work to explain Renwick's approach to teaching non-native speakers?

WRITING PROMPTS

Responding to the Topic Where have you lived besides the United States? Which languages other than English do you speak? Write an essay in which you explore the impact of learning to live among members of another culture. If you have had this opportunity, use your own experience. If you have not yet had this experience, write about what you would hope to learn and how you would go about the learning process.

Responding to the Writer Miner-Le Grand states, "Global politics aside, many perceive American culture to be a globally homogenizing force" (para. 9). Write an essay in which you agree or disagree with this assertion. Use specific references from this essay and other sources to support your thesis.

Responding to Multiple Viewpoints   In her essay "In the Language of Our Ancestors," Mindy Cameron introduces the "language nest" concept for language instruction. Write an essay in which you explore the possibility of this concept being used by any or all of the English teachers whose stories are told in "More Than Language." What challenges and opportunities would be associated with its introduction to and use with their students?

For a quiz on this reading, go to bedfordstmartins.com.

Snapshots

No...*clocks.* DO YOU HAVE CLOCKS?

It's a good thing Chuck raised his voice, because Pedro understood loud English.

Loud English

ANALYZING THE IMAGE

This cartoon aptly depicts the stereotype of the "ugly American" that Americans who travel abroad must constantly try to disprove. If someone spoke Russian to you in a loud voice, would that clarify the meaning of his or her words?

1. Look closely at the cartoon. What attributes of the speaker are stereotypical?

2. Interpret the expression on the face of the man behind the pottery stand. What might he be thinking?

3. Read the caption and then explain the irony.

Rule of Thumbs: Love in the Age of Texting

NATALIE Y. MOORE

Natalie Moore is a reporter for Chicago Public Radio's South Side Bureau and coauthor of the book *Deconstructing Tyrone: A New Look at Black Masculinity in the Hip Hop Generation* (2006). She has worked for newspapers in Detroit, St. Paul, and Jerusalem, and her articles have been published in *Essence*, *Bitch*, the *Chicago Sun-Times*, and the *Chicago Tribune*. This op-ed piece was originally published in the *Washington Post* in September 2007.

> **THINKING AHEAD** How involved are you with text messaging? Where does it fit for you in the list of ways to communicate— before telephoning but after face-to-face conversations, or in some other order? If you don't text message now, would you like to do so? Why?

I once had a boyfriend who was Mr. Text-o-Rama.

He never wanted to talk, but he always wanted to text. To him, the only way to communicate was via thumb.

I remember a Saturday afternoon I spent with a female friend when I didn't have my cellphone handy. By the evening, I had a logjam of text messages from him. The final mess of a message inquired whether our relationship was over because of my "lack of communication."

I called him. He didn't answer.

And so it went. During our relationship, he sent me curt texts reeking of attitude. He sent texts that had the elocution[1] of an August Wilson soliloquy. If I tried to actually call him to work something out, he'd fire off a snippy "You're busy. I'll talk to you later." It got so I wished I could string him up by his thumbs.

Looking back, I see that relationship as the embodiment of how technology is slowly killing romance. It's draining the courting out of courtship. And frankly, I'm ready to hit "delete" on the whole thing.

A flirtatious text here and there is fine, but a text of more than one hundred characters? That's overkill (not to mention hard to read). When the time comes, I don't want to see the words "will u marry me" in one-point font. Call me old-fashioned, but I wonder what's so "advanced" about these so-called advancements in communication. When they're abused, they can

---

[1]**elocution:** The art of speaking well in front of others.

make a caveman's grunt seem refined. The same gadgets that allow you to be in touch all the time sometimes mask the fact that you never really touched at all.

"Texting is a way of life," says etiquette expert Joy Weaver, "but it cannot 8 replace the human voice or touch." Tell me about it.

The relationship began sweetly enough. We met through mutual friends 9 and quickly took a liking to each other. We visited museums and book-stores and camped out at dive bars. I liked that he was so expressive and open. And I had never dated a guy who liked to communicate quite so much in so many ways.

"I love you." 10

I looked down at my cellphone and read the text message. It was the first 11 time he'd expressed those dreamy words. My heart fluttered. I immediately speed-dialed him back to hear him say it out loud.

He didn't answer. "Call you later," he texted me back. 12

At the time, I was too giddy to notice—or care—how weird that was, 13 or how even weirder the many scenarios that followed were: being forced to boost the allotment on my mobile text-messaging plan. So much passive aggression delivered via tiny rectangular pieces of plastic.

My thumbs becoming so tired. 14

Initially, texting with him was thrilling. Wherever I was—on assign- 15 ment, at the airport, out with friends—his sweet messages triggered but-terflies. It was like talking, or flirting, but better. We were always only a few keystrokes away from communicating at any time, night or day.

But soon that became the problem. 16

On the day of my birthday bash, he texted me that he was "uncomfort- 17 able" with our relationship and that we needed to talk before the party.

Say what? We hadn't had a fight. I called him. No answer. I called again 18 and again and again. Finally, he answered with some lame excuse. I'm still not sure exactly what the problem was.

Repeat scenario. Add water and stir. He often seemed unable to articu- 19 late what made him mad or uneasy. But that didn't stop him from firing off messages accusing me of not communicating. Me. The girl who likes to hear or see the person she's talking to.

The final few weeks before we broke things off were a blur, one long 20 string of digitally delivered angst. Once upon a time, drunken dialing could ruin a relationship. Ha. Try getting drunken, misspelled texts at 3 a.m.

What was I to make of this? According to Barb Iverson, a professor of 21 new media at Columbia College Chicago, the latest technology revolution means that there are now two kinds of people in the world: "digital im-migrants" and "digital natives." The digital immigrants came of age before the technology revolution and they struggle to adapt to the new language, rituals and protocol. The digital natives instinctively emote through their thumbs and don't consider a relationship "official" until their Facebook or MySpace profile says it is.

Then there are the Gen-Xers like me who are somewhere in between. 22

In the United States, we have come fairly late to the texting game. The 23
Chinese, who embraced this technology years before it arrived here, send
300 billion text messages a year, and the number is rising. Half the 13- to
15-year-olds in Australia own cellphones. In Japan, some experts have noted
that thumbs are growing physically bigger and people are now using that
digit—and not the index finger—to point and ring doorbells. Texting is so
prevalent that Japanese teenagers are called the "tribe of the thumb."

Anthropologist Bella Ellwood-Clayton studied texting and dating in 24
the Philippines, which she calls the texting capital of the world. In a 2005
study, she detailed how it works: A man might send an innocuous text message to a woman. If she replies quickly and with warmth, the texts back and
forth increase in familiarity—and innuendo. "It is also a fairly nonthreat-
ening way to initiate communication with someone versus a phone call or
face-to-face methods, which demand greater bravery and often directness
of intention," Ellwood-Clayton noted.

As we catch up here in the United States, we are grappling with the 25
social implications that come along with texting.

As I learned, if emotions become involved, texting can quickly devolve 26
into a power play. Because people usually keep their cellphones within
reach, angry text forces the hand of the recipient: If you love me, you'll
respond right now! It's not the same interruption as a phone call. You can
work, watch television, sit in class or talk to a friend while texting.

My single friend Thomas says that "good morning" texts or short mes- 27
sages in the middle of the workday from a girlfriend are fine to let him
know she's thinking of him. But receiving a text at 7 p.m. asking "How are
you?" is a chicken way of saying "I want to talk to you without actually
calling." He says the woman is probably at home willing the phone to ring.
Her recourse? A text.

This deranged texting dance doesn't stop with singles. A married friend 28
rolled her eyes as she recounted how her husband, sitting in another room
in their house, sent her a sour text after an argument to cancel their night
out on the town. It was widely reported that Britney Spears ended her marriage to Kevin Federline via text.

But in text, nuances in tone, mood and intent go by the wayside. Just 29
like the pseudolives of millions of addicted MySpacers, too much texting
can create what media theorists call "parasocial" behavior. This term is applied to people who believe that constant virtual contact is more than just
pretend intimacy.

In an online and magazine ad campaign, mobile phone company Helio 30
put out guidelines on social etiquette and technology, filled with pop quizzes and diagrams. It includes a primer on emoticons and abbreviations (e.g.
YMMFS—you make my fingers sweat).

The company suggests several texting rules for dating: Don't flirt too 31
long virtually; if someone doesn't text you back in twenty-four hours, it's
not happening; only cowards settle arguments via text; and text breakups
don't count.

And the No. 1 text message rule: Keep it short.   32

The campaign is all tongue-in-cheek, but if you ask me, some people   33
need to pay attention.

I now believe that texting should be reserved for the following notifica-   34
tions: "I'm running late." "I'm outside." "Meet me at [insert location.]"
"It's noisy; I'll call you later." "What time are the reservations?"

And yes, "I love you" is fine—but only if you've already said those   35
words in person.

EXERCISING VOCABULARY

1. Record your own definition for each word below in your notebook.

   reeking (adj.) (5)   angst (n.) (20)
   soliloquy (n.) (5)   emote (v.) (21)
   giddy (adj.) (13)   innocuous (adj.) (24)
   articulate (v.) (19)   innuendo (n.) (24)

2. In paragraph 3, Moore states that she received "a logjam of text messages." What is the normal context of the word *logjam*? How does its
   use here enhance Moore's point?

3. In paragraph 13, Moore implies that her boyfriend is guilty of "passive
   aggression." What does this term mean? In what sense is it usually
   used? What does its use here tell you about the boyfriend?

4. Moore contends that MySpacers have "pseudolives" (para. 29). What
   does the prefix *pseudo* mean? Why would Moore believe that this is the
   experience of MySpace participants?

PROBING CONTENT

1. Why was Moore initially attracted to this boyfriend? When did the
   attraction begin to fade? What caused the final breakup?

2. Explain the difference that Barb Iverson sees between "digital immigrants" and "digital natives" (para. 21).

3. How is texting impacting dating and communication in countries other
   than the United Sates?

4. What is the "deranged texting dance" that Moore refers to in paragraph
   28? How does this affect relationships?

CONSIDERING CRAFT

1. What is the origin of the expression "rule of thumb"? What does this
   expression mean today? How does this title prepare the reader for
   Moore's essay?

2. What is the effect of Moore's first sentence on the reader? How does this brief introduction set the tone for her essay?

3. Moore uses irony to great effect in this selection. Select several instances and show how her use of irony furthers her purpose in the essay.

4. The core of Moore's essay is her own personal experience, but she expands the scope of her thoughts here to be much broader. Locate and briefly discuss several of the techniques she uses to accomplish this.

WRITING PROMPTS

Responding to the Topic   In your personal experience, is the rage for text messaging leading to less than desirable social interaction? Write an essay in which you examine what part text messaging plays in your life and the lives of your friends and acquaintances. Explore also what role you think it should play.

Responding to the Writer   Is Moore's assessment that "technology is slowly killing romance" (para. 6) accurate? In an essay, defend your position with relevant examples.

Responding to Multiple Viewpoints   Imagine a conversation between Geneva White ("Corporate Names and Products Creep into Everyday Language") and Natalie Moore ("Rule of Thumbs: Love in the Age of Texting") about changes they see in the ways we communicate. Create a dialogue between these two authors expressing their views, using material from their essays to support the position each of them voices in your paper.

For a quiz on this reading, go to bedfordstmartins.com/mirror.

How Do You Say *Extinct?*

JOHN J. MILLER

John J. Miller is a national political reporter for the *National Review*. He has also worked as a contributing editor for *Reason* and as vice president for the Center for Equal Opportunity. He is the author of *The Unmaking of Americans: How Multiculturalism Has Undermined America's Assimilation Ethic* (1998) and *A Gift of Freedom: How the John M. Olin Foundation Changed America* (2005). He is also the coauthor, with Mark Molesky, of *Our Oldest Enemy: A History of America's Disastrous Relationship with France* (2004). *The Wall Street Journal* published "How Do You Say *Extinct?*" in March 2002.

> **THINKING AHEAD** What is the relationship between language and culture? How important is it to all of us to protect languages spoken by very few people? Why? What is lost when a spoken language goes out of existence?

When Marie Smith-Jones passes away, she will take with her a small 1
but irreplaceable piece of human culture. That's because the octo-genarian[1] Anchorage resident is the last speaker of Eyak, the traditional language of her Alaskan tribe. "It's horrible to be alone," she has said.

Yet she isn't really alone, at least in the sense of being a last speaker. 2
There are many others like her. By one account, a last speaker of one of the world's six thousand languages dies every two weeks.

To UNESCO—the United Nations Educational, Scientific and Cultural 3
Organization—language extinction is a disaster of, well, unspeakable proportions. Its new report warns of a "catastrophic reduction in the number of languages spoken in the world" and estimates three thousand are "endangered, seriously endangered, or dying."

In other words, children have stopped learning half the world's 4
languages, and it's only a matter of time before their current speakers fall silent. UNESCO calls this an "irretrievable and tragic" development because "language diversity" is "one of humanity's most precious commodities."

But is it really? UNESCO's determined pessimism masks a trend that is 5
arguably worth celebrating: A growing number of people are speaking a smaller number of languages, meaning that age-old obstacles to communication are collapsing. Surely this is a good thing.

Except for those who believe that "diversity" trumps all else. We've heard 6
claims like this before, in debates over college admissions and snail darters,[2]

---

[1]**octogenarian:** A person in his or her eighties.
[2]**snail darters:** A threatened species of fish found only in the Tennessee River.

and they're often dubious. The chief problem with UNESCO's view—shared by many academic linguists—is its careless embrace of multiculturalism, or what it labels "egalitarian multilingualism." This outlook gives short shrift to the interests and choices of people in tiny language groups.

Languages disappear for all sorts of reasons, not least among them   7
their radical transformation over time. Consider English. It helps to have a gloss handy when reading Shakespeare's plays of four centuries ago. Chaucer's Middle English may be understood only with difficulty. And the Old English of the *Beowulf* poet is not only dead but unintelligible to modern speakers.

Because languages evolve, it should come as no surprise that some ex-   8
pire. Michael Krauss of the University of Alaska at Fairbanks—the leading expert on the Eyak of Ms. Smith-Jones—believes that ten thousand years ago there may have been as many as twenty thousand languages spoken by a total human population of perhaps ten million, roughly 0.17 percent of our current world census. Assuming this is true, it would suggest a connection between more people and fewer languages, and between language and the technology that lets people communicate over distance.

That makes sense, because geographic isolation is an incubator of   9
linguistic diversity. A language doesn't require more than a few hundred people to sustain it, assuming they keep to themselves. The forbidding terrain of Papua New Guinea is home to the highest concentration of languages anywhere—at least 820 different tongues in an area smaller than Utah and Wyoming combined. For UNESCO, this is a kind of Platonic[3] ideal. Its report describes Papua New Guinea as "a fitting example for other civilizations to follow."

That's an odd thing to say about a country where 99 percent of   10
the people don't own a phone, but it's typical of the attitude of the language preservationists, who apparently would like to see tribal members live in primitive bliss, preserving their exotic customs. A thread runs through the preservationist arguments suggesting that *we* can benefit from *them*—that is, we in the developed world have much to gain if they in the undeveloped world continue communicating in obscure languages we don't bother to learn ourselves.

David Crystal makes the point unwittingly in his book *Language Death*   11
when he describes an Australian aboriginal language "whose vocabulary provides different names for grubs (an important food source) according to the types of bush where they are found." He's trying to say that we may learn about biology if we preserve and study obscure languages—but he seems oblivious to the reality that most people would rather eat a Big Mac than a fistful of beetle larvae.

Many linguists are deadly serious about the biological connection;   12
they would like nothing better than to join forces with environmentalists.

---

[3]**Platonic:** Characteristic of the Greek philosopher Plato.

In *Vanishing Voices*, Daniel Nettle and Suzanne Romaine even write of "biolinguistic diversity," which they define as "the rich spectrum of life encompassing all the earth's species of plants and animals along with human cultures and their languages." This invention allows them to suggest that "the next great step in scientific development may lie locked up in some obscure language in a distant rainforest."

Then again, it may not—and the only way to find out requires that 13
some people continue living a premodern, close-to-nature existence. The UNESCO report and linguists everywhere say that governmental policies of forced assimilation have contributed mightily to language extinction, and they certainly have a point. But what they're endorsing now is a kind of forced dissimilation, in the hope, apparently, that a cure for cancer will one day find expression in an Amazonian dialect.

That's the fundamental mistake of the UNESCO report. "Linguistic 14
diversity is an invaluable asset and resource rather than an obstacle to progress," it claims. Yet the most important reason some languages are disappearing is precisely that their native speakers don't regard them as quite so precious. They view linguistic adaptation—especially for their kids—as a key to getting ahead. This is understandable when about half the world's population speaks one of only ten languages and when speaking English in particular is a profitable skill. Nowadays, the difference between knowing a lingua franca[4] and an obscure language is the difference between performing algorithms on a computer and counting with your fingers.

Linguists say that about half the world's population is already able to 15
speak at least two languages, and they insist that such bilingualism is a key to preserving "diversity." Perhaps, but it sounds better in theory than it works in practice. Simple verbal exchanges are one thing; communicating at high levels of proficiency is another. If bilingual education in the United States has revealed anything, it is that schools can teach a rudimentary knowledge of two languages to students while leaving them fluent in neither.

Each language captures something about a way of life, and when one 16
goes mute, it is hard not to feel a sense of loss. But languages are no less mortal than the men and women who speak them. Maybe linguists should try to learn as much as they can about "dying" languages before they vanish completely, rather than engage in a quixotic attempt to save them.

EXERCISING VOCABULARY

1. Record your own definition for each word below in your notebook.

irreplaceable (adj.) (1)   oblivious (adj.) (11)
trumps (v.) (6)   assimilation (n.) (13)
dubious (adj.) (6)   rudimentary (adj.) (15)
unwittingly (adv.) (11)

2. According to Miller, UNESCO considers language extinction "a disaster of, well, unspeakable proportions" (para. 3). What does *unspeakable* mean? Why does Miller choose this particular word to describe UNESCO's reaction?

3. What is "biolinguistic diversity" (para. 12)? Why and how may it unite linguists and environmentalists?

4. Miller conveys his viewpoint about the linguists' fight to preserve vanishing languages in the final sentence of his essay. Who is Don Quixote? How does Miller's use of the word *quixotic* reveal his viewpoint?

PROBING CONTENT

1. What trend defies UNESCO's pessimistic observations? According to Miller, why is this advantageous?

2. What are some of the reasons that languages expire? What role may native speakers play in their extinction or retention?

3. According to Miller, how effective has bilingual education proven to be in the United States? Why?

CONSIDERING CRAFT

1. What is ironic about the title of this essay? How does the use of irony in the title set the tone for this selection?

2. The author quotes UNESCO's report to note that three thousand languages are "endangered, seriously endangered, or dying" (para. 3). With what is the word *endangered* usually associated? What might this report have hoped to accomplish by linking the word *endangered* to languages?

3. Explain Miller's statement that "geographic isolation is an incubator of linguistic diversity" (para. 9).

WRITING PROMPTS

Responding to the Topic   How many of your friends and acquaintances speak more than one language? From your own experience, write an essay examining the benefits of personal linguistic diversity.

Responding to the Writer   Write an essay taking a position on whether the extinction of languages spoken by small populations should be a serious concern for all of us.

Responding to Multiple Viewpoints Would Patricia O'Conner, author of "Like," agree that languages undergo a "radical transformation over time" (para. 7, "How Do You Say *Extinct*?")? Would O'Conner see this as a threat? Support your answer with material from her essay.

For a quiz on this reading, go to bedfordstmartins.com/mirror.

In the Language of Our Ancestors

MINDY CAMERON

Mindy Cameron is a freelance writer based in Sandpoint, Idaho. She was formerly an editor for the *Seattle Times*, and she received that paper's Publisher's Circle Award for Executive of the Year. "In the Language of Our Ancestors" first appeared in *Northwest Education Magazine*. In it, she chronicles efforts to save dying Native American languages making important arguments about the ties between language and culture.

> **THINKING AHEAD** Should people who move to another country learn the language of that country's native residents? Why?

S tudents in Eva Boyd's class are typical teenagers. They fidget, wisecrack, 1 talk to friends, and only occasionally pay attention.

But when asked why they are in this class, they speak with one voice: 2 We are losing our language; we want to preserve our heritage. The presence of these Salish teens in this classroom, along with Eva Boyd, a tribal elder, is testimony to that singular desire to save a culture by saving the language.

Across Indian Country, many efforts to revive and revitalize Native 3 American languages are under way. And none too soon. Estimates vary, but of the hundreds of languages that existed here before the arrival of white settlers, as many as two-thirds may have disappeared. Of those that remain, many could die along with the elders, the dwindling brain trust of tribal language.

Boyd's story shows why so many of these languages disappeared, why 4 some survived, and how they might be saved.

The Toll of Assimilation

From the late-nineteenth century until the mid-twentieth century, the 5 national policy regarding American Indians and Alaska Natives was assimilation. After decades of removing indigenous people from their land to reservations, the federal government sought to mainstream them into American society.

Education was a critical aspect of the assimilation policy. It was be- 6 lieved that through education, Native Americans would learn the white man's language and culture and develop the skills to function effectively in white man's society. By 1887 the federal government had established more than two hundred Indian schools to carry out this mission.

Like many of her tribal contemporaries, Boyd was sent to an Indian 7
boarding school. At the typical boarding school, children were punished
for speaking their traditional language. Some were made to stand in the
corner, others had their knuckles rapped or rags tied around their mouths.
Many children eventually forgot their tribal language, and those who
remembered were often ashamed to use it.

Eva Boyd managed to escape that fate. She was a willful 10-year-old 8
when she went to boarding school. Decades later, she explains simply, "I
didn't like it, so I left." Three days after she arrived, Boyd walked out and
hitchhiked back home to the Camas Prairie area of the Flathead Reservation
in Western Montana. There, her grandmother raised her in the language of
their ancestors.

Boyd, a former foreign language instructor at Salish Kootenai College, 9
came out of retirement to teach three Salish language classes at Ronan
High School. For her, it's a simple matter of tribal survival. "If we don't
keep the language alive our tribe is going down. Without the language we
won't be Indians any more."

Students in her class understand that and struggle to learn the lan- 10
guage. A difficult task is made more difficult by a lack of resources. The
sole text is a Salish storybook, *The Story of a Mean Little Old Lady*, with
English translation.

"We have to do the best we can," says Boyd. Like her students, Boyd 11
wishes Native language instruction could start earlier, at an age when
learning a new language is not so difficult.

Julie Cajune agrees. She is Indian Education Coordinator for the 12
Ronan-Pablo School District. She admires and values what Eva Boyd is
doing. "A teacher such as Eva is one way to make the school more reflective of the community," she says, "but we are doing language at the
wrong end."

"Go to Nkwusm," Cajune insists. 13

Starting Early

Thirty miles down the road at Arlee, in a former bowling alley that also 14
houses a casino, is Nkwusm. It's a tribal-run language immersion school
for preschoolers.

Five little ones squirm on the floor at the feet of two elders, Pat Pierre 15
and Stephen Small Salmon. Like Boyd, the adults are fluent in Salish and
committed to keeping the language alive, even if it means coming out of
retirement, as Pierre has done.

On this damp and chilly day, he is reviewing the Salish names for 16
months, days of the week, and numbers. The children vigorously recite
the words. They follow Pierre to the window where he points to the sky,
the ground, and the distant hills. It is a short lesson in Salish about the
weather.

Pierre explains, "The power and wisdom of language is what has kept   17
our people together so that we can do meaningful things. If I can teach the
little ones the language, then we keep our identity."

The research is clear about learning languages. A second language is   18
more easily acquired early on as children develop their language skills,
rather than at a later stage. That has great importance for indigenous
people facing the extinction of their ancestral language. Language is
more than words and rules of usage. It is the repository of culture and
identity.

Using Language Nests

In Nkwusm, the Salish are replicating what has worked elsewhere to re-   19
vive indigenous languages; they are using what's called a "language nest."
As the name implies, a language nest is more than just another language
program. It is language immersion for the youngest members of a Native
population.

When the Maoris of New Zealand faced the extinction of their lan-   20
guage more than twenty years ago, they created language nests. Hawaiians
soon adopted the Maori model and, in the mid-1990s, a similar program
was established on the Blackfeet Reservation in Northwest Montana.

Language nests are seen by many as a key to reviving tribal lan-   21
guages. Last year Hawaii Senator Daniel Inouye proposed an amendment
to the Native American Languages Act of 1990. If passed, it would provide federal government support for Native American survival schools,
including language nests. The 1990 act establishes as national policy
the government's responsibility to "preserve, protect, and promote the
rights of Native Americans to use, practice, and develop" their Native
languages.

Last May, at a U.S. Senate hearing on the proposed amendment, a   22
delegation representing the Blackfeet Nation stressed the difference between Native American language survival schools and public schools. "The
academic outcomes of Native American language survival schools are as
strong as, or stronger than, public education systems and students become
speakers of their Native language," they said.

The Blackfeet Native language school in Browning, Montana—   23
Nizipuhwasin—has become a model for Nkwusm and for other communities that hope to develop programs for young speakers of tribal languages.

Few tribes, however, can sustain such schools indefinitely. Founders of   24
Nkwusm, which is now supported by grants and the Salish-Kootenai tribe,
hope eventually to be self-sustaining. They also seek to have an endow-
ment, run a K–12 school, and provide distance learning for the Flathead
Reservation.

As important as tribal programs such as Nizipuhwasin and Nkwusm   25
are, the current reality is that most Native youth are educated in public

schools, not tribal-run classrooms. Native educators say if traditional languages are to be saved, public schools will have to play a key role.

Integrating Language

In Washington's Marysville School District, Tulalip Elementary offers one example of how to develop an integrated curriculum of language, literature, and culture with Lushootseed—the language of the Tulalip tribe—at the center. 26

The program began several years ago at the school, which is about 70 percent American Indian. Tribal members and district staff worked together to develop a Tulalip-based classroom in the fourth grade. A non-Native teacher teamed with a tribal language teacher to create a new curriculum, which has now evolved into Lushootseed language and culture instruction at every grade level. 27

Any curriculum introduced in schools today must meet state standards and the requirements of the federal No Child Left Behind Act. The Tulalip-based curriculum in Marysville has managed to do that. 28

One of many challenges for schools that already have—or would like to start—Native language programs is finding qualified teachers. Some states have responded to that need by authorizing alternative certification for Native language teachers. In Montana, Washington, Oregon, and Idaho, the authority for granting certification to these teachers has been delegated to tribal authorities. (In Alaska, this authority is reserved for each school board or regional educational attendance area.) 29

Once a tribe has determined an applicant is fluent enough to qualify, he or she is recommended for certification to the State Board of Education. Upon certification, Native language teachers, usually tribal elders, get the same pay and benefits and must meet the same requirements for continuing education as other certified teachers. 30

There have been some issues involving classroom management. "[That's] no small matter in a room with more than a dozen teenagers," notes Julie Cajune. Even so, she thinks it's a good move. Without certification, Native language teachers, who were paid at the level of teacher aides, were devalued. 31

The Montana Board of Public Education adopted its policy for alternative certification, called Class 7 Specialist Certificate for Native American Languages, in 1995. At that time one tribe identified only five elders who were fluent in their Native language. Today, there are 112 Class 7 teachers in Montana. 32

Washington state adopted its alternative certification in 2003. It is a three-year pilot program with the purpose of contributing "to the recovery, revitalization, and promotion of First Peoples' languages." By the end of the first year, seven teachers had been certified under the program. 33

Indian English

Teaching Native American children, whether the subject is reading, math,   34
or their indigenous language, presents a unique set of circumstances.
While very few Native youngsters speak the language of their ancestors,
their first language is not necessarily the English of their white classmates, either. The first language of two-thirds of American Indian youth
today is Indian English, according to a research report by Washington
state's Office of the Superintendent of Public Instruction and the Evergreen Center for Educational Improvement at Evergreen State College in
Olympia.

Authors of the report, Magda Costantino and Joe St. Charles of   35
Evergreen, and Denny Hurtado of OSPI, describe Indian English as English
dialects used by American Indians that do not conform in certain ways
to standard English. Despite the differences, however, the dialects "are
nonetheless well-ordered and highly structured languages that reflect the
linguistic competencies that must underlie all languages."

In *American Indian English*, W. L. Leap provides important context for   36
the restoration of Native languages. He writes that distinctive characteristics of Indian English—what he calls "codes"—"derive, in large part, from
their close association with their speakers' ancestral language traditions.
In many cases, rules of grammar and discourse from that tradition provide
the basis for grammar and discourse in these English codes—even in instances where the speakers are not fluent in their ancestral language."

It can be argued, then, that Indian English serves as a language bridge   37
between the past and present. Understanding the role and importance of
Indian English, however, may not be as big a hurdle as the larger issues
and prevailing attitudes about language use and instruction. Many people
believe that because English is the dominant language, instruction should
be in English and all students should learn its proper usage. Disagreement
about the role and importance of bilingual education is a fact of life in
many school districts, tossing up one more barrier to public school efforts
to become involved in Native language revival.

What Research Shows

Advocates of Native language revival programs point to research that   38
shows academic advantages for children who speak two languages. Gina
Cantoni, a language pedagogy[1] professor at Northern Arizona University,
has written of "abundant evidence" that teaching the home language does
not interfere with the development of English skills. To the contrary, she
notes, instruction that "promotes proficiency in one's first language also
promotes proficiency in the second language."

[1]**pedagogy:** The art and science of teaching.

Cantoni contends that "mastery of more than one linguistic code re- 39
sults in a special kind of cognitive flexibility." Unfortunately, she notes, the
"special" abilities related to mastery of more than one language are not
covered by most tests used to measure academic achievement.

Research reinforces the argument for expanding Native language instruc- 40
tion. Even more compelling are the voices of Native American advocates, from
the students in Eva Boyd's class to the elders teaching youngsters at Nkwusm
and to longtime Montana educator Joyce Silverthorne.

Silverthorne, a member of the Salish tribe of the Flathead Reserva- 41
tion in Montana, has been a classroom teacher, college instructor, school
board member, program administrator on the reservation, and member of
the Montana Board of Public Education, where she worked for passage
of the Montana Class 7 certificate.

While language and culture are linked in all societies, "what is unique 42
to Native Americans is that this is our homeland," says Silverthorne. "There
is no 'old country' to return to. When language dies here, it dies forever."

Nkwusm founder and teacher Melanie Sandoval is committed to see- 43
ing that doesn't happen. Now 28, she says she has been trying to learn the
language of her tribe as long as she can remember. She now learns along
with the children, thanks to the two elders who come into the classroom
six hours a day, five days a week. After years of formal study, she is now
learning useful, everyday phrases like "blow your nose" and "jump down
off that."

What's happening at the school is more than preserving the language. 44
Sandoval observes that preservation "is like having a bottle on the shelf.
We want to breathe life into the language, to speak it, and pass it on to the
next generation."

EXERCISING VOCABULARY

1. Record your own definition for each word below in your notebook.

   singular (adj.) (2)   replicating (v.) (19)
   revitalize (v.) (3)   competencies (n.) (35)
   indigenous (adj.) (5)   discourse (n.) (36)
   immersion (adj.) (14)   advocates (n.) (40)
   repository (n.) (18)

2. Why does Cameron call tribal elders "the dwindling brain trust of tribal
   languages" (para. 3)? What is a brain trust? What does this imply about
   the status of the elders?

3. What is the denotative meaning of the word *assimilation*? How does
   one group of people become assimilated into another group? Is the
   connotative meaning of this word positive or negative as Cameron uses
   it in this essay?

4. Gina Cantoni believes that comprehending multiple languages results in "a special kind of cognitive flexibility" (para. 39). What does the term *cognitive* mean? What does "cognitive flexibility" imply?

PROBING CONTENT

1. What was the government's policy toward American Indians and Alaska Natives from the late nineteenth century until the mid-twentieth century? What was a primary tool in executing this policy?

2. What makes Eva Boyd's task more difficult? What might make language learning less difficult? What research supports this idea?

3. Explain the "language nest" concept. Name several ethnic groups that have used language nests successfully. Why may language nest instruction alone not be enough to save disappearing languages?

4. What is the first language of many American Indian youth? What are some characteristics of this language?

CONSIDERING CRAFT

1. What is the author's purpose in writing this essay? Defend your answer with text from the essay.

2. In this essay, Cameron uses quite a few Indian names, the pronunciation of which will not be familiar to most readers. What effect does their inclusion have on your reading of this essay? How does their use support Cameron's purpose?

3. Cameron does not specifically state her own opinion about preserving native languages, but her opinion is evident throughout the essay. Cite phrases and sentences from the text that reveal clearly her position on her topic. What does she accomplish by having the reader infer her position rather than stating it bluntly?

WRITING PROMPTS

Responding to the Topic   Cameron states that language "is the repository of culture and identity" (para. 18). Write an essay in which you examine the truth of this statement from your own experience.

Responding to the Writer   Eva Boyd says, "Without the language we won't be Indians any more" (para. 9). Cameron notes that we may "save a culture by saving the language" (para. 2). Write an essay in which you take a position on the necessity of preserving a language in order to preserve a culture.

Responding to Multiple Viewpoints   What do the young English teachers in Caitlin Miner-Le Grand's essay "More Than Language" have in common with Eva Boyd? Write an essay in which you examine how their situations, expectations, challenges, and goals are similar or different.

DRAWING CONNECTIONS

1. How would John Miller ("How Do You Say *Extinct*?") react to the concept and advisability of language nests as described by Cameron ("In the Language of Our Ancestors")? Support your answer with evidence from both selections.

2. How would Cameron regard the following statement by John Miller: "A growing number of people are speaking a smaller number of languages, meaning that age-old obstacles to communication are collapsing. Surely this is a good thing" (para. 5, "How Do You Say *Extinct*?"). Support your answer with evidence from both texts.

3. Why was the language preservation ideal in Papua New Guinea that John Miller discusses ("How Do You Say *Extinct*?") not possible for Native Americans?

For a quiz on this reading, go to bedfordstmartins.com/mirror.

Swoosh!

Read Mercer Schuchardt

Our culture lives by symbols. In fact, every day more and more of these symbols replace the words they represent. Read Mercer Schuchardt examines one of modern America's most successful icons, the Nike Swoosh, in this essay originally published in *Re:Generation Quarterly* and reprinted in the *Utne Reader* in 1997. He is currently Assistant Professor of Media Ecology, Film Studies, and Web Communication at Wheaton College and has published in the *Chicago Tribune* and the *Washington Times*. He is also the publisher of Metaphilm.com, a film criticism Web site. In 2008, he edited a collection of essays about the novel *Fight Club* titled *You Do Not Talk about Fight Club*.

> **THINKING AHEAD**   Think about some products whose symbols or icons are so well known that consumers recognize them without seeing the product's actual name. How did these symbols become so familiar to us? Why do we understand their meaning without the help of words? How do they work to unite us in a common understanding?

The early followers of Christ created a symbol to represent their beliefs and communicate with one another in times of persecution. The well-known Ichthus, or "Christian fish," consisted of two curved lines that transected each other to form the abstract outline of fish and tail. The word for *fish* also happened to be a Greek acronym wherein: 1

- Iota = Iesous = Jesus
- Chi = Christos = Christ
- Theta = Theos = God
- Upsilon = Huios = Son
- Sigma = Soter = Savior

Combining symbol and word, the fish provided believers with an integrated media package that could be easily explained and understood. When the threat of being fed to the lions forced Christians to be less explicit, they dropped the text. Without the acronym to define the symbol's significance, the fish could mean anything or nothing, an obvious advantage in a culture hostile to certain beliefs. But to Christians the textless symbol still signified silent rebellion against the ruling authorities. Within three centuries, the faith signified by the fish had transformed Rome into a Christian empire. 2

Today, in an electronically accelerated culture, a symbol can change the face of society in about one-sixteenth that time. Enter the Nike Swoosh, 3 the most ubiquitous icon in the country, and one that many other corporations have sought to emulate. In a world where technology, entertainment, and design are converging, the story of the Swoosh is by far the most fascinating case study of a systematic, integrated, and insanely successful formula for icon-driven marketing.

The simple version of the story is that a young Oregon design student   4
named Caroline Davidson got $35 in 1971 to create a logo for then-professor (now Nike CEO) Phil Knight's idea of importing and selling improved Japanese running shoes. Nike's innovative product line, combined with aggressive marketing and brand positioning, eventually created an unbreakable mental link between the Swoosh image and the company's name. As Nike put it, there was so much equity in the brand that they knew it wouldn't hurt to drop the word *Nike* and go with the Swoosh alone. Nike went to the textless format for U.S. advertising in March 1996 and expanded it globally later that year. While the Nike name and symbol appear together in ads today, the textless campaign set a new standard. In the modern global market, the truly successful icon must be able to stand by itself, evoking all the manufactured associations that form a corporation's public identity.

In the past, it would have been unthinkable to create an ad campaign   5
stripped of the company's name. Given what was at stake—Nike's advertising budget totals more than $100 million per year—what made them think they could pull it off?

First, consider the strength of the Swoosh as an icon. The Swoosh is a   6
simple shape that reproduces well at any size, in any color, and on almost any surface—three critical elements for a corporate logo that will be reproduced at sizes from a quarter of an inch to 500 feet. It most frequently appears in one of three arresting colors: black, red, or white. A textless icon, it nevertheless "reads" left to right, like most languages. Now consider the sound of the word *Swoosh*. According to various Nike ads, it's the last sound you hear before coming in second place, the sound of a basketball hitting nothing but net. It's also the onomatopoeic[1] analogue of the icon's visual stroke. Reading it left to right, the symbol itself actually seems to say "swoosh" as you look at it.

However it may read, the Swoosh transcends language, making it the   7
perfect corporate icon for the postliterate[2] global village.

With the invention of the printing press, according to Italian semi-   8
otician[3] Umberto Eco, the alphabet triumphed over the icon. But in an overstimulated electronic culture, the chief problem is what advertisers call "clutter" or "chatter"—too many words, too much redundancy, too many competing messages. Add the rise of illiteracy and an increasingly multicultural world and you have a real communications problem. A hyperlinked global economy requires a single global communications medium, and it's

[1]**onomatopoeic:** Relating to a term whose name imitates the sound that it makes.
[2]**postliterate:** Occurring after the advent of electronic media.
[3]**semiotician:** A person who studies signs and symbols and the way that they operate in everyday life.

simply easier to teach everyone a few common symbols than to teach the majority of non-English speakers a new language.

The unfortunate result is that language is being replaced by icons. From the rock star formerly known as Prince to e-mail "smileys" to the NAFTA[4]-induced symbolic laundry labels, the names and words we use to describe the world are being replaced by a set of universal hieroglyphs.[5] Leading the charge, as one would expect, are the organizations that stand to make the most money in a less text-dependent world: multinational corporations. With the decline of words, they now can fill in the blank of the consumer's associative mind with whatever images they deem appropriate.   9

After watching Nike do it, several companies have decided to go text-less themselves, including Mercedes-Benz, whose icon is easily confused with the peace sign (an association that can only help). According to one of their print ads, "right behind every powerful icon lies a powerful idea," which is precisely the definition of a global communications medium for an accelerated culture. Pepsi's new textless symbol does not need any verbal justification because it so clearly imitates the yin-yang[6] symbol. In fact, a close look reveals it to be almost identical to the Korean national flag, which is itself a stylized yin-yang symbol in red, white, and blue.   10

Never underestimate the power of symbols. Textless corporate symbols operate at a level beneath the radar of rational language, and the power they wield can be corrupting. Advertising that relies on propaganda methods can grab you and take you somewhere whether you want to go or not; and as history tells us, it matters where you're going.   11

Language is the mediator between our minds and the world, and the thing that defines us as rational creatures. By going textless, Nike and other corporations have succeeded in performing partial lobotomies[7] on our brains, conveying their messages without engaging our rational minds. Like Pavlov's[8] bell, the Swoosh has become a stimulus that elicits a conditioned response. The problem is not that we buy Nike shoes, but that we've been led to do so by the same methods used to train Pavlov's dogs. It's ironic, of course, that this reflex is triggered by a stylized check mark—the standard reward for academic achievement and ultimate symbol for the rational, linguistically agile mind.   12

If sport is the religion of the modern age, then Nike has successfully become the official church. It is a church whose icon is a window between this world and the other, between your existing self (you overweight slob) and your Nike self (you god of fitness), where salvation lies in achieving   13

[4]NAFTA: North American Free Trade Agreement, an agreement that in 1994 launched the world's largest free-trade area.
[5]hieroglyphs: Characters in a system of picture writing.
[6]yin-yang: A black and white Chinese symbol that represents completeness by combining both halves of the universe.
[7]lobotomies: Surgical procedures that sever nerves in the brain and once were used to control unruly psychiatric patients.
[8]Pavlov: Russian scientist Ivan Pavlov (1849–1936) who experimented with predicting behavior under certain circumstances; many of his experiments used dogs as subjects.

the athletic Nietzschean[9] ideal: no fear, no mercy, no second place. Like the Christian fish, the Swoosh is a true religious icon in that it both symbolizes the believer's reality and actually participates in it. After all, you do have to wear something to attain this special salvation, so why not something emblazoned with the Swoosh?

EXERCISING VOCABULARY

1. Record your own definition for each word below in your notebook.

transected (v.) (1)
emulate (v.) (3)
innovative (adj.) (4)
arresting (adj.) (6)
analogue (n.) (6)

transcends (v.) (7)
redundancy (n.) (8)
mediator (n.) (12)
stylized (adj.) (12)
emblazoned (v.) (13)

2. This essay begins with the history of an acronym. What is an acronym? Why are acronyms used? Give an example of an acronym that means something to you and explain what the letters stand for. *Scuba*, for example, stands for "self-contained underwater breathing apparatus," and *CEO* stands for "chief executive officer."

3. Schuchardt refers to the Nike Swoosh as "ubiquitous" in paragraph 3. How accurate is this word in describing the popularity of the Nike symbol? Name at least five different places where the Swoosh appears.

4. In paragraph 4, Schuchardt says that Nike was able to drop the word *Nike* from marketing campaigns because "there was so much equity in the brand." What does it mean to have equity in something? Give two or three examples. What does using the word *equity* here imply about the Nike corporation?

PROBING CONTENT

1. Why did the early Christians adopt the Ichthus symbol? What significance did it hold for them?

2. Why, according to Schuchardt, must a successful advertising icon not need supporting language to be clearly understood by a wide range of people? How do you determine whether an icon is successful as a marketing tool?

3. To what does Schuchardt attribute the success of the Nike symbol? Use specific references from the text to support your answer.

4. What does this essay describe as the conditioned or predictable response to the stimulus of the Nike Swoosh? How effective is the Swoosh in generating this response?

[9]**Nietzschean:** Referring to Friedrich Nietzsche (1844–1900), a German philosopher and author of *Man and Superman*.

CONSIDERING CRAFT

1. The writer chooses a complicated introduction. How well does the Christian fish symbol work as an introduction to this topic? Why do you think Schuchardt chose this symbol to introduce his essay?

2. This essay contains a number of unfamiliar references. If Schuchardt knew that some readers would not understand these references, why did he include them? How do they improve or weaken the essay?

3. What does the final paragraph have in common with the introduction? What does the author want to accomplish by using this strategy? To what extent is he successful?

WRITING PROMPTS

Responding to the Topic   Have you noticed a surge of "textless corporate symbols" (para. 11) around you? Develop an essay exploring the influence of such symbols on your everyday life. Support your essay with numerous specific examples.

Responding to the Writer   Do you agree with Schuchardt that "language is being replaced by icons" (para. 9)? Do you agree with him that if this has happened or were to happen, the result would be unfortunate? Write an essay in which you support your position on these questions with evidence from the text, as well as additional examples that you select.

Responding to Multiple Viewpoints   Caitlin Miner-Le Grand's essay ("More Than Language") is about the struggles of young teachers working with English-language learners. How would the three teachers in Miner-Le Grand's essay react to Schuchardt's idea about the takeover of language by icons? How might his ideas affect their teaching strategies?

For a quiz on this reading, go to bedfordstmartins.com/mirror.

Global Wording

ADAM JACOT DE BOINOD

Adam Jacot de Boinod was a researcher for the British Broadcasting Company when he noticed that the Albanian dictionary contained twenty-seven different words for eyebrows. Since then, he has obsessively researched foreign dictionaries and catalogued some the world's oddest and most precise terms. He has published two books from his findings, *The Meaning of Tingo: And Other Extraordinary Words from Around the World* (2006) and *Toujours Tingo* (2007). The following is an excerpt from *The Meaning of Tingo* that was republished in the March 2006 edition of *Smithsonian Magazine*.

> **THINKING AHEAD**   Name some words you use routinely that are not originally English words but were "borrowed" from other languages. When you use such words, are you aware that you are speaking Chinese, Arabic, or Spanish? Why or why not? How do words from languages other than English become so much a part of our everyday American speech?

One day while I was working as a researcher for the BBC quiz program *QI*, I picked up a weighty Albanian dictionary and discovered that the Albanians have no fewer than twenty-seven words for eyebrows and the same number for mustache, ranging from *mustaqe madh*, or brushy, to *mustaqe posht*, or drooping at both ends. Soon I was unable to go near a secondhand bookshop or library without seeking out the shelves where the foreign-language dictionaries were kept. I would scour books in friends' houses with a similar need to pan for gold. [1]

My curiosity became a passion, even an obsession. In time I combed through more than two million words in hundreds of dictionaries. I trawled the Internet, phoned embassies and tracked down foreign-language speakers who could confirm my findings. Who knew, for example, that Persian has a word for "a camel that won't give milk until her nostrils have been tickled" (*nakhur*)? Or that the Inuits[1] have a verb for "to exchange wives for a few days only" (*areodjarekput*)? Why does Pascuense, spoken on Easter Island,[2] offer *tingo*, which means "to borrow things from a friend's house, one by one, until there's nothing left"? [2]

The English language has a long-established and voracious tendency to naturalize foreign words: *ad hoc, feng shui, croissant, kindergarten*. We've been borrowing them from other cultures for centuries. But there are so many we've missed. [3]

---

[1]**Inuits:** Eskimos.
[2]**Easter Island:** An island in the southeast Pacific Ocean.

Our body-conscious culture might have some use for the Hawaiian *awawa*, for the gap between each finger or toe; the Afrikaans *waal*, for the area behind the knee; or the Ulwa (Nicaragua) *alang*, for the fold of skin under the chin. Surely we could use the Tulu (India) *karelu*, for the mark left on the skin by wearing anything tight. And how could we have passed up the German *Kummerspeck*, for the excess weight one gains from emotion-related overeating? (It translates literally as "grief bacon.") 4

Gras bilong fes, from the Papua New Guinea Tok Pisin, is more poetic than "beard"; it means "grass belonging to the face." And how about the German *Backpfeifengesicht*, or "face that cries out for a fist in it"? 5

In Wagiman (Australia), there's an infinitive—*murr-ma*—for "to walk along in the water searching for something with your feet." The Dutch have *uitwaaien*, for "to walk in windy weather for fun," but then Central American Spanish speakers may win a prize for articulating forms of motion with *achaplinarse*— "to hesitate and then run away in the manner of Charlie Chaplin."[3] 6

In Russian, they don't speak of crying over spilled milk; they say *kusat sebe lokti*, which means "to bite one's elbows." That may be better than breaking your heart in Japanese, because *harawata o tatsu* translates literally as "to sever one's intestines." To be hopelessly in love in Colombian Spanish is to be "swallowed like a postman's sock" (*tragado como media de cartero*). That happy state may lead to dancing closely, which in Central American Spanish is *pulir hebillas* ("to polish belt buckles"). 7

Malaysians recognize *kontal-kontil*, or "the swinging of long earrings or the swishing of a dress as one walks." Fuegian, in Chile, has a word for "that shared look of longing where both parties know the score yet neither is willing to make the first move" (*mamihlapinatapei*). But Italian has *biodegradabile*, for one "who falls in love easily and often." 8

Persian has *mahj*, for "looking beautiful after a disease"—which, deftly used, might well flatter (*vaseliner* in French, for "to apply Vaseline") some recovered patients. But you'd have to lay it on pretty thick for a *nedovtipa*, who in Czech is "someone who finds it difficult to take a hint." 9

On Easter Island, it may take two to *tingo*, but it takes only one to *hakamaru*, which means "to keep borrowed objects until the owner has to ask for them back." Of course, words once borrowed are seldom returned. But nobody is going *harawata o tatsu* over that. 10

EXERCISING VOCABULARY

1. Record your own definition for each word below in your notebook.

scour (v.) (1)	sever (v.) (7)
combed (v.) (2)	swishing (v.) (8)
voracious (adj.) (3)	longing (n.) (8)
naturalize (v.) (3)	deftly (adv.) (9)
articulating (v.) (6)	

[3]**Charlie Chaplin:** Famous star of silent movies known for his distinctive walk.

2. The expressive verb often used for searching the Internet is "to surf." Instead, de Boinod uses "trawled the Internet" (para. 2). In what ways are these two images alike? How are they different? Why does the author choose the verb *trawled*?

3. Throughout this essay, de Boinod uses a number of expressive verbs to highlight his actions as he pursues his new passion. Locate several of these descriptive verbs and explain why he chose them and how their use enhances the tone of his essay.

PROBING CONTENT

1. What started de Boinod on his quest for unusual words and phrases? How did he feed his growing hunger for new words?

2. Choose two of the foreign phrases that catch de Boinod's attention in this essay. Explain what language they come from and what they mean. To what extent would they be useful expressions for English-speakers to learn?

CONSIDERING CRAFT

1. Explain the play on words in the title. What is the word most often heard following *global* in magazines, on news programs, and in Congress? Why does de Boinod choose this association for his title?

2. Look at a number of examples of foreign phrases that de Boinod uses and translates in this essay. What do these expressions have in common? What characteristics seem to have been de Boinod's criteria for choosing his examples?

3. In an essay about foreign phrases and their meanings, the author uses quite a few idiomatic English expressions, which may be unfamiliar to some readers. For example, he explains a foreign phrase in paragraph 8 by saying that "both parties know the score," and in paragraph 9 he writes, "you'd have to lay it on pretty thick." What do these two idiomatic expressions mean? Why does he use idioms in English to explain idiomatic expressions in other languages?

WRITING PROMPTS

Responding to the Topic   Check the appendix of a collegiate dictionary to find a list of foreign words and phrases. Choose five or six that interest you and write an essay in which you explain their meanings and discuss their usefulness as additions to English vocabulary.

Responding to the Writer   De Boinod finds it intriguing that words and phrases from foreign tongues could be helpful if added to an American English vocabulary. Other people feel strongly that English should be kept pure, not infiltrated by non-English expressions. Write an essay in which you take a position on this issue. Be sure to use specific examples to reinforce your argument.

Responding to Multiple Viewpoints   How would the people who object to the infiltration of the word *like* into our everyday speech feel about the inclusion of foreign words and phrases? Write an essay in which you examine the similarities and differences between the frequent use of *like* and the use of these foreign expressions. Use text from this essay and from Patricia O'Conner's essay "Like" to support your position.

For a quiz on this reading, go to bedfordstmartins.com/mirror.

Caucasian Please! America's Cultural Double Standard for Misogyny and Racism

EDWARD RHYMES

You may be familiar with the common criticism that much of rap music contains lyrics that are violent, but do we have a double standard for lyrical content when it comes to rap versus genres of music more dominated by white artists (for example, heavy metal)? Edward Rhymes is the author of *When Racism Is Law and Prejudice Is Policy* (2007). He has a doctoral degree in sociology and has worked as a consultant on issues of race relations and diversity for the YWCA of Greater Pittsburgh as well as other organizations. This essay was published in June 2007 by *Alternet*.

> **THINKING AHEAD**   Do you listen to rap and hip-hop? Why or why not? If you do listen, how much attention do you pay to the words? What cultural associations do rap and hip-hop have for you?

Introduction

In this composition I will not be addressing the whole of hip-hop and rap, but rather hardcore and gangsta rap. It is my assertion that the mainstream media and political pundits[1] — right and left — have painted rap and hip-hop with a very broad brush. Let me be perfectly clear; hardcore and gangsta rap is not listened to, watched, consumed or supported in my home and never has been. I will not be an apologist for anything that chooses to frame the dialogue about Black women (and women in general) and Black life in morally bankrupt language and reprehensible symbols. 1

In the wake of MSNBC's and CBS's firing of Don Imus, the debate over misogyny, sexism and racism has now taken flight — or submerged, depending on your point of view. There are many, mostly white, people who believe that Imus was a fall guy and he is receiving blame and criticism for what many rap artists do continually in their lyrics and videos: debase and degrade Black women. A Black guest on an MSNBC news program even went as far as to say, "Where would a 66-year-old white guy even have heard the phrase nappy-headed ho" — alluding to hip-hop music's perceived powerful influence upon American culture and life (and apparently over the radio legend as well) — and by so doing gave a veneer of 2

---

[1]**pundits:** Those who offer authoritative opinions.

truth to the theory that rap music is the main culprit to be blamed for this contemporary brand of chauvinism.

However, I concur with bell hooks, the noted sociologist and black-feminist activist, who said that "to see gangsta rap as a reflection of dominant values in our culture rather than as an aberrant 'pathological' standpoint, does not mean that a rigorous feminist critique of the sexism and misogyny expressed in this music is not needed. Without a doubt black males, young and old, must be held politically accountable for their sexism.   3

"Yet this critique must always be contextualized or we risk making it appear that the behavior this thinking supports and condones—rape, male violence against women, etc.—is a black male thing. And this is what is happening. Young black males are forced to take the 'heat' for encouraging, via their music, the hatred of and violence against women that is a central core of patriarchy."   4

There are those in the media, mostly white males (but also some black pundits as well), who now want the Black community to take a look at hip-hop music and correct the diabolical "double-standard" that dwells therein. Before a real conversation can be had, we have to blow-up the myths, expose the lies and cast a powerful and discerning light on the "real" double-standards and duplicity. Kim Deterline and Art Jones in their essay, "Fear of a Rap Planet," points out that "the issue with media coverage of rap is not whether African Americans engaged in a campaign against what they see as violent, sexist or racist imagery in rap should be heard—they should. . . . [W]hy are community voices fighting racism and sexism in mainstream news media, films and advertisements not treated similarly?   5

"The answer may be found in white-owned corporate media's histori-cal role as facilitator of racial scapegoating.[2] Perhaps before advocating censorship of a music form with origins in a voiceless community, main-stream media pundits should look at the violence perpetuated by their own racism and sexism."   6

"Just as the mainstream media and the dominant culture-at-large treats all things "Black" in America as the "other" or as some sort of science exper-iment in a test tube in an isolated and controlled environment, so hardcore rap is treated as if it occurred in some kind of cultural vacuum; untouched, unbowed and uninformed by the larger, broader, dominant American culture. The conversation is always framed in the form of this question, "What is rap's influence on American society and culture?" Never do we ask, "What has been society's role in shaping and influencing hip-hop?"   7

Gangsta and hardcore rap is the product of a society that has histori-cally objectified and demeaned women, and commercialized sex. These dynamics are present in hip-hop to the extent that they are present in society. The rapper who grew up in the inner-city watched the same sex-ist television programs, commercials and movies; had access to the same   8

---

[2]scapegoating: Placing the blame on an individual or a group.

pornographic and misogynistic magazines and materials; and read the same textbooks that limited the presence and excluded the achievements of women (and people of color as well), as the All-American, Ivy-league bound, white kid in suburban America.

It is not sexism and misogyny that the dominant culture is opposed 9 to (history and commercialism has proven that). The dominant culture's opposition lies with hip-hop's cultural variation of the made-in-the-USA misogynistic themes and with the Black voices communicating the message. The debate and the dialogue must be understood in this context.

Popular Culture's Duplicitous Sexism and Violence in Black and White

In a piece I penned a couple of years ago, I endeavored to point out the 10 clear ethnic and racial double-standards of the media and society as it pertains to sex and violence. My assertion was, and remains, that the mainstream media and society-at-large appear to have not so much of a problem with the glorification of sex and violence, but rather with who is doing the glorifying. In it I stated that "if the brutality and violence in gangsta rap was truly the real issue, then shouldn't a series like *The Sopranos* be held to the same standard? If we are so concerned about bloodshed, then how did movies like *The Godfather*, *The Untouchables* and *Goodfellas* become classics?"

I then addressed the sexual aspect of this double-standard by pointing 11 out that *Sex and the City*, a series that focused, by and large, on the sexual relationships of four white women, was hailed as a powerful demonstration of female camaraderie[3] and empowerment.

"This show, during its run, was lavished with critical praise and 12 commercial success while hip-hop and rap artists are attacked by the morality police for their depiction of sex in their lyrics and videos. The don't-blink-or-you'll-miss-it appearance of Janet Jackson's right bosom during [a] Super Bowl halftime show . . . caused more of a furor than the countless commercials (also aired during the Super Bowl) that used sex to sell anything from beer to cars to gum. Not to mention the constant stream of commercials that rather openly talks about erectile dysfunction medication."

The exaltation of drugs, misogyny and violence in music lyrics has 13 a history that predates NWA, Ice Cube, Ice T and Snoop Dogg. Elton John's 1977 song "Tickin" was about a young man who goes into a bar and kills fourteen people; Bruce Springsteen's "Nebraska" featured a couple on a shooting spree, and his "Johnny 99" was about a gun-waving laid-off worker; and Stephen Sondheim's score for "Assassins" presented songs mostly in the first person about would-be and successful presidential assassins.

---

[3]**camaraderie:** Fellowship; friendship.

Eric Clapton's "Cocaine" and the Beatles' "Lucy in the Sky with Dia-   14
monds" (LSD) as well as almost anything by Jefferson Airplane or Spaceship.
Several songs from *Tommy* and Pink Floyd's *The Wall* are well known drug
songs. "Catholic Girls," "Centerfold," and "Sugar Walls" by Van Halen
were raunchy, misogynistic, lust-driven rock refrains.

Even the country music legend Kenny Rogers in his legendary bal-   15
lad, "Coward of the County," spoke of a violent gang-rape and then a
triple-homicide by the song's hero to avenge his assaulted lover. Marilyn
Manson declared that one of the aims of his provocative persona was to
see how much it would take to get the moralists as mad at white artists
as they got about 2LiveCrew. He said it took fake boobs, Satanism, simu-
lated sex on stage, death and angst,[4] along with semi-explicit lyrics, to
get the same screaming the 2LiveCrew got for one song. Manson thought
this reaction was hypocritical and hilarious.

In an article by Dana Williams titled "BEYOND RAP: Musical Mi-   16
sogyny," Ann Savage, associate professor of telecommunications at Butler
University, stated: "It's the repetitiveness of the messages, the repetitiveness
of the attitudes, and it builds on people. . . ." "People say rap is dangerous.
Yes, rap music does have misogyny, but there has always been an objectification and misogyny against women in music," said Savage. "Yet we focus
on the black artists, not the rockers and not even the white executives who
are making the big money from this kind of music."

Savage further asserts that the race-based double standard applies to   17
violent content in music as well. "There was the Eric Clapton remake of
Marley's 'I Shot the Sheriff,' and there was little to be said. But then you
have the 'Cop Killer' song by Ice-T and it's dangerous and threatening."

In this same article Cynthia Fuchs, an associate professor at George   18
Mason University, affirmed that "the public seems far more disturbed by
misogynistic lyrics in the music of rap and hip-hop artists who are largely black
than similar lyrics in rock music, perceived by most as a white genre."

"The flamboyance of rock is understood as performance, rather than   19
from the perspective of personal feelings," said Fuchs, who teaches courses
in film and media studies, African American studies and cultural studies.
"These guys are seen as innocuous. They appear to be players in the fence[5]
of accumulating women in skimpy costumes, but they aren't necessarily
seen as violent. The mainstream takes it (hip-hop and rap) to represent real-
life, so it's seen as more threatening than some of the angry, whiney white
boy rock, even though the same messages and images are portrayed."

Moreover, in a piece titled "C*ck Rock" from the October 21–November   20
3, 2003 edition of the online music magazine *Perfect Pitch*, it was revealed
that when the *Hustler* founder and entrepreneur Larry Flynt wanted to
combine the worlds of porn (the ultimate god of misogyny) and music he
did not turn to rap, but rather to rock.

---

[4]**angst:** Worry or insecurity.
[5]**fence:** Fraudulent or artificial action.

It was stated that since porn has been mainstreamed, they wanted a more   21
"contemporary" look—and when they looked for a contemporary look, did
they seek out the likes of Nelly, Chingy, 50 Cent or Ludacris? No. Rock
legend Nikki Sixx was chosen to "grace" the cover of *Hustler*'s new venture along with his adult-entertainment and former *Baywatch* star girlfriend
Donna D'Errico wearing nothing but a thong and Sixx's arms.

It is my belief that this paradigm,[6] this unjust paradox exists because   22
of the media stereotypes of black men as more violence-prone, and media's
disproportionate focus on black crime (which is confused with the personas that rappers adopt) contributes to the biased treatment of rap. The
double standard applied to rap music makes it easier to sell the idea that
"gangsta rap" is "more" misogynist, racist, violent and dangerous than
any other genre of music.

However, I believe that bell hooks conceptualized it best in her essay   23
"Sexism and Misogyny: Who Takes the Rap?": "To the white dominated
mass media, the controversy over gangsta rap makes great spectacle. Besides
the exploitation of these issues to attract audiences, a central motivation
for highlighting gangsta rap continues to be the sensationalist drama of
demonizing black youth culture in general and the contributions of young
black men in particular. It is a contemporary remake of *Birth of a Nation*[7]
only this time we are encouraged to believe it is not just vulnerable white
womanhood that risks destruction by black hands but everyone."

Part of the allure of gangsta or hardcore rap to the young person is its   24
(however deplorable) explicitness. The gangsta rapper says "bitches" and
"hos," defiantly and frankly (once again . . . deplorable) and that frankness
strikes a chord.

However, it is not the first time that a young man or woman has seen   25
society "treat" women like "bitches" and "hos." Like mother's milk, the
American male in this country has been "nourished" on a constant diet of
subtle messages and notions regarding female submission and inferiority
and when he is weaned, he begins to feed on the meat of more exploitative
mantras[8] and images of American misogyny long before he ever pops in his
first rap album into his CD player.

Young people, for better or worse, are looking for and craving authen-   26
ticity. Now, because this quality is in such rare-supply in today's society, they
gravitate towards those who appear to be "real" and "true to the game."
Tragically, they appreciate the explicitness without detesting or critically
deconstructing what the person is being explicit about.

There have been many who have said that even with Imus gone from   27
the airwaves, the American public in general and the Black community in
particular will still be inundated by the countless rap lyrics using derogatory

---

[6]**paradigm:** A way of thinking involving associated philosophies and theories.
[7]***Birth of a Nation:*** Director D. W. Griffiths's controversial silent film set during the Civil
   War, viewed through today's lens as portraying harmful racial stereotypes and glorifying
   white supremacy.
[8]**mantras:** Sayings repeated over and over.

and sexist language, as well as the endless videos displaying women in various stages of undress—and this is true.

However, by that same logic, if we were to rid the record stores, the 28
clubs and the iPods of all misogynistic hip-hop, we would still have amongst
us the corporately-controlled and predominantly white-owned entities of
Playboy, *Penthouse*, *Hustler* and Hooters. We would still have the reality
TV shows, whose casts are overwhelmingly white, reveling in excessive
intoxication and suspect sexual mores.

If misogynistic hip-hop was erased from American life and memory 29
today, tomorrow my e-mail box and the e-mail boxes of millions of others
would still be barraged with links to tens of thousands of adult entertainment
web sites. We would still have at our fingertips, courtesy of cable and satel-
lite television, porn-on-demand. We would still be awash in a society and
culture that rewards promiscuity and sexual explicitness with fame, fortune
and celebrity (reference Anna Nicole, Paris Hilton, Britney Spears).

And most hypocritically, if we were to purge the sexist and lewd lyrics 30
from hip-hop, there would still be a multitude of primarily white bands and
principally-white musical genres generating song after song glorifying sexism,
misogyny, violence and lionizing male sexuality and sexual conquest.

EXERCISING VOCABULARY

1. Record your own definition for each word below in your notebook.

apologist (n.) (1)	raunchy (adj.) (14)
reprehensible (adj.) (1)	provocative (adj.) (15)
misogyny (n.) (2)	innocuous (adj.) (19)
veneer (n.) (2)	disproportionate (adj.) (22)
chauvinism (n.) (2)	allure (n.) (24)
aberrant (adj.) (3)	inundated (v.) (27)
patriarchy (n.) (4)	mores (n.) (28)
duplicity (n.) (5)	barraged (v.) (29)

2. Rhymes distances himself from discussions that encompass women
   and black culture in "morally bankrupt language" (para. 1). What is the
   usual meaning of *bankrupt*? How could language be "morally bankrupt"?
   What would such language lack?

3. In paragraph 8, Rhymes states that our society "has historically objectified and demeaned women." What does it mean to objectify a person?
   What is frequently the effect of this behavior? Define *demean*.

4. Rhymes states that our culture offers "song after song glorifying sexism,
   misogyny, violence and lionizing male sexuality and sexual conquest"
   (para. 30). What does the term *lionizing* mean here? What is the source
   of this word? How effective is it in this context? Why?

PROBING CONTENT

1. On what basis do some people try to justify the language used by Don Imus? Where does this idea originate, according to Rhymes?

2. What is the double standard that critics see in rap and hip-hop? Why does it need to be explored? What does Rhymes identify as the "real" double standard?

3. According to Rhymes, it isn't sexism that society objects to, since it permeates our culture. To what does he believe the "dominant culture" actually objects?

4. In Cynthia Fuchs's opinion, why is hip-hop perceived as more dangerous than rock, even when the lyrics of the two cover the same subjects?

5. If hip-hop were eliminated from American life, what does Rhymes think the result would be? How does he support this opinion?

CONSIDERING CRAFT

1. Why does Rhymes immediately narrow the context for his essay in the first paragraph? How does this narrowed focus affect the reader?

2. Why does Rhymes include the names of numerous singers and songs in paragraphs 13 through 15. How does their inclusion work to prove Rhymes's point in these paragraphs?

3. Notice the sources that Rhymes quotes in paragraphs 16 through 19. Why does he choose these sources? What effect is he hoping to have on the reader by their inclusion?

WRITING PROMPTS

Responding to the Topic   How do you react to the violence portrayed in rap and hip-hop? Write an essay in which you examine your own response to the idea that this kind of music is more likely to promote violence.

Responding to the Writer   Rhymes asserts that modern culture has done more to shape rap and hip-hop than vice versa. Write an essay in which you agree or disagree with his viewpoint, offering examples to reinforce your ideas.

Responding to Multiple Viewpoints   In "In the Language of Our Ancestors," Mindy Cameron examines the loss of language as the loss of culture. Can her argument be applied to the effect of the loss of hip-hop expression on the black community? Why? Write an essay in which you decide whether Cameron's argument fits Rhymes's subject.

For a quiz on this reading, go to bedfordstmartins.com/mirror.

Wrapping Up Chapter 5

Focusing on Yesterday, Focusing on Today

In this still from the famous television show *My Favorite Martian*, actress Ann Marshall models typical 1960s teenage behavior. Look carefully at her clothes and hairstyle. Everything about this image says "ordinary teenager." Who is on the other end of that phone line?

Now look at the photo of the three young women together. Again, the photo says "ordinary teenagers." But times have certainly changed. To

"So He Said, and Then She Said. . . ."

whom do you think the three girls are sending text messages? Even without the cell phones, you would recognize this as a contemporary image. How?

- What do the two photos have in common? How are they clearly different?

- What does each photo say about the level of intimacy among friends?

- What do these two photos say about the art of communication and how that art has changed over the decades?

Text Someone Close to You

CONNECTING TO THE CULTURE

1. Choose a blog site and participate in its online conversations for at least a week. Write an essay in which you describe your experiences, including what kind of people you met online, what the topics of discussion were, what rules and etiquette seemed to govern the participants, and what you learned about online communication and language.

2. Choose a language other than English and research how new words become part of that language. Is there a governmental process, or do new words just appear when popular usage introduces them? Write an essay in which you explain the process and compare it with the way new words become part of American English.

3. Research the issue of bilingual education and then write an essay in which you take a position on its effectiveness for helping non-native speakers become fluent in English. Be sure to include specific examples to support your ideas.

4. Select one group of people who use their own jargon. This might be doctors, rappers, athletes, computer programmers, or some other group. Investigate the language they use to communicate within the group, including an interview with several group members, and then write an essay detailing how that specialized language functions within the select group. Be sure to support your writing with numerous specific examples.

5. Choose one significant textless symbol like the Nike Swoosh to research. How did it originate? How and where is it used? How widely is it recognized? Develop your information into an informative essay.

Analyzing the Image

 How prevalent have logos become in advertising here and abroad? To what extent have they replaced traditional written language? Has the advertising industry succeeded in taking America hostage and transforming its consumers into logo-obsessed shoppers?

This eye-catching version of a revered American icon, the Stars and Stripes, was created by Shi-Zhe Yung for the 2000 Creative Resistance Contest sponsored by *Adbusters*, a "watchdog" publication whose goal is to reveal the ways in which the advertising industry markets fantasy to consumers in the guise of truth.

- Describe your initial reaction to this image. Why did you react the way you did? Why do you think the artist chose to render the American flag in this way?

- How many of these logos do you or your classmates recognize?

- What does this logo recognition say about the impact of advertising in America today?

- What message is *Adbusters* sending to the viewer in this visual?

- What effect does the text appearing on the lower left corner have on you and your classmates? Compare it to the Pledge of Alligiance.

Research this topic with TopLinks at bedfordstmartins.com/toplinks.

GEARING UP   Make a list of all the brand-name products you have used, worn, or eaten since you got up this morning. Briefly describe commercials or advertisements for some of these products. How did this advertising influence your decision to buy or use them? Try to honestly evaluate why you made these choices. How much are your habits as a consumer influenced by advertising?

I remember the exact day. I was thirteen, and I saw this big billboard on Decatur Street, not far from my house, had this big, lean black guy, really good-looking, with his jeans rolled up, splashing water on a beach, cigarette in one hand and a slinky black chick on his back. All smiles. All perfect teeth. Salem menthols. What great fun. I thought to myself, Now there's the good life. I'd like to have some of that. So I went home, went to my drawer, got my money, walked down the street, and bought a pack of Salem menthols.

The speaker is Angel Weese, a young character in John Grisham's best-selling novel *The Runaway Jury*. Our own encounters with advertising may not cause such immediate and direct responses, but we do respond. Most of us want what Angel wants—some of the good life. And if those jeans, that flatscreen, that car, that iPod, or those sneakers help get us to the good life, we're there. Advertising is so much a part of our lives that we may not notice its pervasive, subtle effect. How are ads created? What messages are ads sending? Why do some ad mascots like the Geico gecko, the Energizer Bunny, and the AFLAC duck become our friends? Why do some jingles or famous ad phrases—like "Just do it," "For everything else, there's MasterCard," "Can you hear me now?" or "Easy, breezy, beautiful Cover Girl"—stay in our heads? How do ad agencies find the perfect pitch, the best "hook," the winning slogan?

What do the ads that get our attention and send us to the stores—whether real or virtual—say about us as consumers? We are advertising targets not just as individual consumers but also collectively. Of the groups you belong to—college students, men or women, particular racial or ethnic backgrounds—which ones seem to have been targeted by manufacturers' ad campaigns? One size never fits all in strategic advertising. When we move beyond asking what product an ad is selling and instead demand to know what the ad is really saying about ourselves and our culture, both here and abroad, we may be surprised by the insights we gain and the savvy consumers we become.

COLLABORATING   In groups of three or four students, list five phrases, symbols, jingles, or slogans associated with widely advertised products. Collect these lists and play an Advertising IQ game based on the *Jeopardy* model. Choose a host to read the clues aloud and to call on teams to guess the product. For example, if the clue read aloud is "I'm lovin' it," the correct response would be "What is an advertising slogan for McDonald's?"

After the game, discuss why you can easily supply questions for these advertising answers when it's so difficult to remember other things—like historical dates or the Periodic Table of the Elements.

Illusions Are Forever

JAY CHIAT

Do you think advertisements often show products that seem too good to be true? According to marketing executive Jay Chiat, ads are indeed full of lies—but not the lies you might expect. When Chiat died in 2002, he was remembered as a creative genius who revolutionized the advertising industry. In 1967, he founded the Chiat/Day ad agency, which quickly grew into one of the industry's most prestigious companies. Chiat was the mastermind behind many groundbreaking advertising campaigns, including the battery ads featuring the famous Energizer Bunny and the original Apple computer ads launched in 1984, featuring striking images from George Orwell's novel *1984*. He was also responsible for making the Super Bowl into the advertising showcase that it is today. In 1997, Chiat left the marketing industry to lead ScreamingMedia, a provider of information management services. "Illusions Are Forever" was first published in the October 2, 2000, issue of *Forbes* magazine.

> **THINKING AHEAD** What image of the world does advertising present to us as consumers? How can this image affect us? How attainable is this world for most of us?

I know what you're thinking: That's rich,[1] asking an adman to define truth. 1
Advertising people aren't known either for their wisdom or their morals, so it's hard to see why an adman is the right person for this assignment. Well, it's just common sense—like asking an alcoholic about sobriety, or a sinner about piety. Who is likely to be more obsessively attentive to a subject than the transgressor?

Everyone thinks that advertising is full of lies, but it's not what you 2
think. The facts presented in advertising are almost always accurate, not because advertising people are sticklers[2] but because their ads are very closely regulated. If you make a false claim in a commercial on network television, the FTC[3] will catch it. Someone always blows the whistle.[4]

The real lie in advertising—some would call it the "art" of advertising—is 3
harder to detect. What's false in advertising lies in the presentation of situations, values, beliefs, and cultural norms that form a backdrop for the selling message.

---

[1]**That's rich:** Sarcastic expression meaning amusing and ironic.
[2]**sticklers:** People who enforce discipline and order.
[3]**FTC:** The Federal Trade Commission, an organization that regulates trade between the United States and other countries.
[4]**blows the whistle:** Reports unfavorable information or alerts authorities to illegal or dangerous practices.

Advertising—including movies, TV, and music videos—presents to us 4
a world that is not our world but rather a collection of images and ideas
created for the purpose of selling. These images paint a picture of the ideal
family life, the perfect home. What a beautiful woman is, and is not. A
prescription for being a good parent and a good citizen.

The power of these messages lies in their unrelenting pervasiveness, 5
the twenty-four-hour-a-day drumbeat that leaves no room for an alternative view. We've become acculturated to the way advertisers and other
media-makers look at things, so much so that we have trouble seeing things
in our own natural way. Advertising robs us of the most intimate moments in
our lives because it substitutes an advertiser's idea of what ought to be—
What should a romantic moment be like?

You know the De Beers diamond advertising campaign? A clever strat- 6
egy, persuading insecure young men that two months' salary is the appropriate sum to pay for an engagement ring. The arbitrary algorithm[5] is
preposterous, of course, but imagine the fiancée who receives a ring costing
only half a month's salary? The advertising-induced insult is grounds for
calling off the engagement, I imagine. That's marketing telling the fiancée
what to feel and what's real.

Unmediated is a great word: It means "without media," without the 7
in-between layer that makes direct experience almost impossible. Media
interferes with our capacity to experience naturally, spontaneously, and
genuinely, and thereby spoils our capacity for some important kinds of
personal "truth." Although media opens our horizons infinitely, it costs us.
We have very little direct personal knowledge of anything in the world that
is not filtered by media.

Truth seems to be in a particular state of crisis now. When what we 8
watch is patently fictional, like most movies and commercials, it's worri-
some enough. But it's absolutely pernicious when it's packaged as reality.
Nothing represents a bigger threat to truth than reality-based television,
in both its lowbrow and highbrow versions—from *Survivor*[6] to A&E's
Biography.[7] The lies are sometimes intentional, sometimes errors, often innocent, but in all cases they are the "truth" of a media-maker who claims
to be representing reality.

The Internet is also a culprit, obscuring the author, the figure behind 9
the curtain, even more completely. Chat rooms, which sponsor intimate
conversation, also allow the participants to misrepresent themselves in
every way possible. The creation of authoritative-looking Web sites is within
the grasp of any reasonably talented twelve-year-old, creating the appearance of professionalism and expertise where no expert is present. And any

[5]**algorithm:** A procedure for solving a mathematical problem in a finite number of steps,
often involving repetition of the same basic operation.
[6]***Survivor:*** A television program that shows participants using survival skills to compete for
a one-million-dollar prize.
[7]**A&E's** *Biography:* A television program on the Arts and Entertainment channel that profiles
celebrities and historical figures.

mischief-maker can write a totally plausible-looking, totally fake stock analyst's report and post it on the Internet. When the traditional signals of authority are so misleading, how can we know what's for real?

But I believe technology, for all its weaknesses, will be our savior. The Internet is our only hope for true democratization,[8] a truly populist[9] publishing form, a mass communication tool completely accessible to individuals. The Internet puts CNN on the same plane with the freelance journalist and the lady down the street with a conspiracy theory,[10] allowing cultural and ideological pluralism[11] that never previously existed.

This is good for the cause of truth, because it underscores what is otherwise often forgotten—truth's instability. Truth is not absolute: It is presented, represented, and re-presented by the individuals who have the floor,[12] whether they're powerful or powerless. The more we hear from powerless ones, the less we are in the grasp of powerful ones—and the less we believe that "truth" is inviolable, given, and closed to interpretation. We also come closer to seeking our own truth.

That's the choice we're given every day. We can accept the very compelling, very seductive version of "truth" offered to us daily by media-makers, or we can tune out its influence for a shot at finding our own individual, confusing, messy version of it. After all, isn't personal truth the ultimate truth?

EXERCISING VOCABULARY

1. Record your own definition for each word below in your notebook.

sobriety (n.) (1)	infinitely (adv.) (7)
piety (n.) (1)	patently (adv.) (8)
transgressor (n.) (1)	pernicious (adj.) (8)
unrelenting (adj.) (5)	culprit (n.) (9)
pervasiveness (n.) (5)	obscuring (v.) (9)
acculturated (adj.) (5)	plausible (adj.) (9)
arbitrary (adj.) (6)	inviolable (adj.) (11)
preposterous (adj.) (6)	

2. Chiat states that advertising gives us "a prescription for being a good parent and a good citizen" (para. 4). Who usually gives us a prescription? For what reason? Explain how and why advertising's prescriptions may be different.

---

[8]**democratization:** The process of placing a country under the control of its citizens by allowing them to participate in government or decision-making processes in a free and equal way.

[9]**populist:** Advocating the rights and interests of ordinary people in politics or the arts.

[10]**conspiracy theory:** A belief that a particular event is the result of a secret plot and not the result of chance or the actions of an individual.

[11]**pluralism:** The existence of groups with different ethnic, religious, or political backgrounds within one society.

[12]**have the floor:** Have permission to speak.

3. The author tells us that most of our knowledge of the world is "filtered by media" (para. 7). What does it mean to filter something? What can you think of that is filtered? How can the media filter our knowledge of the world? Why do the media do this?

4. In paragraph 8, Chiat speaks of "lowbrow and highbrow versions" of reality-based television. Examine his examples and think of some of your own. What is the difference between lowbrow and highbrow?

PROBING CONTENT

1. What did Jay Chiat do for a living? Why is this important to know when you read this essay?

2. In Chiat's opinion, what is "the real lie in advertising"? What truth does advertising represent? Explain your response.

3. Why is advertising so effective, according to this author? In what ways is this either beneficial or harmful for consumers?

4. According to Chiat, what will be "our savior" (para. 10)? From what will it save us? How will this be accomplished?

CONSIDERING CRAFT

1. In the first sentence of this essay, the author addresses the reader directly. Why does he do this? How do you respond to his introduction? Is this an effective opening strategy? Why or why not?

2. Chiat uses an extended example in paragraph 6. Describe this example. Why did the author choose this particular example to support his argument? How effective is his choice? Defend your response.

3. The author ends his essay with a rhetorical question. Explain what a rhetorical question is and how one might be used. Find one of the other rhetorical questions Chiat uses. How effective is his use of this writing strategy throughout the essay, including in the conclusion?

WRITING PROMPTS

Responding to the Topic   Have you ever taken a job or done something that you had mixed feelings about? Why? What were the circumstances surrounding your decision? Write an essay in which you detail your experiences.

Responding to the Writer   In his concluding paragraph, Chiat suggests that we "tune out" the influence of the media to find our own version of "truth." To what extent is this possible? Explain your conclusion.

Responding to Multiple Viewpoints   The impact of the Internet on the advertising industry is enormous (see *The Economist*'s "The Ultimate Marketing Machine" and Michael Specter's "Damn Spam"). Chiat writes about the ultimate "lie" in advertising in his essay "Illusions Are Forever." What do you see as the future of the advertising industry? Are the illusions that advertisers sell to consumers around the world really "forever"? To what extent will the Internet strengthen advertising?

For a quiz on this reading, go to bedfordstmartins.com/mirror.

Champagne Taste, Beer Budget

DELIA CLEVELAND

Have you ever bought something you couldn't afford and regretted it later? In "Champagne Taste, Beer Budget," Delia Cleveland recounts her own experiences as a victim of the advertising machine. The following essay first appeared in the March 2001 issue of *Essence* magazine. Cleveland wrote this essay while attending New York University as a media studies major and has had her work published in *Black Elegance* and *Spice* magazines.

> **THINKING AHEAD**   Have you ever been obsessed with owning something, going somewhere, or doing some particular thing? How did this obsession affect you? How did you achieve the object of your desire? To what extent did reaching your goal satisfy you?

My name is Dee, and I'm a recovering junkie. Yeah, I was hooked on   1
the strong stuff. Stuff that emptied my wallet and maxed out my credit card during a single trip to the mall. I was a fashion addict. I wore a designer emblem on my chest like a badge of honor and respect. But the unnatural high of sporting a pricey label distorted my understanding of what it really meant to have "arrived."

At first I just took pride in being the best-dressed female at my high   2
school. Fellows adored my jiggy style; girls were insanely jealous. I became a fiend for the attention. In my mind, clothes made the woman and everything else was secondary. Who cared about geometry? Every Friday I spent all my paltry paycheck from my part-time job on designer clothes. Life as I knew it revolved around a classy façade. Then slowly my money started getting tight, so tight I even resorted to borrowing from my mother. Me, go out looking average? Hell no! I'd cut a class or wouldn't bother going to school at all, unable to bear the thought of friends saying that I had fallen off and was no longer in vogue.

Out of concern, my mother started snooping around my bedroom to   3
see where my paycheck was going. She found a telltale receipt I'd carelessly left in a shopping bag. Worse, she had set up a savings account for me, and I secretly withdrew most of the money—$1,000—to satisfy my jones.[1] Then I feverishly charged $600 for yet another quick fashion fix.

"Delia, you're turning into a lunatic, giving all your hard-earned money   4
to multimillionaires!" she screamed.

"Mama," I shrugged, "you're behind the times." I was looking fly,[2] and   5
that was all that mattered.

---

[1]**jones:** A craving for something.
[2]**fly:** Cool; fabulous.

Until I got left back in the tenth grade.   6

The fact that I was an A student before I discovered labels put fire under   7
my mother's feet. In her eyes, I was letting brand names control my life,
and I needed help. Feeling she had no other choice, she got me transferred
to another school. I had screwed up so badly that a change did seem to be
in order. Besides, I wanted to show her that labels couldn't control me. So
even though everyone, including me, knew I was "smart" and an excellent
student, I found myself at an alternative high school.

Meanwhile, I began looking at how other well-dressed addicts lived   8
to see where they were headed. The sobering reality: They weren't going
anywhere. In fact, the farthest they'd venture was the neighborhood
corner or a party—all dressed up, nowhere to go. I watched them bop
around[3] in $150 hiking boots—they'd never been hiking. They sported
$300 ski jackets—never went near a slope. I saw parents take three-hour
bus trips to buy their kids discount-price designer labels, yet these parents
wouldn't take a trip to make a bank deposit in their child's name. Watching
them, I was forced to look at myself, at my own financial and intellectual
stagnation, at the soaring interest on my overused credit card.

That's when it all became clear. At my new high school I attended   9
classes with adults—less emphasis on clothes, more emphasis on work.
Although the alternative school gave me invaluable work experience, I
never received the kind of high-school education I should have had—no
sports, no prom, no fun. I realized I had sacrificed an important part of my
life for material stuff that wasn't benefiting me at all.

That was twelve years ago. Today I'm enjoying a clean-and-sober life-   10
style. Armed with a new awareness, I've vowed to leave designer labels to
people who can truly afford them. I refuse to tote a $500 baguette[4] until I
can fill it with an equal amount of cash. I'm not swaggering around in over-
priced Italian shoes till I can book a trip to Italy. On my road to recovery, I
have continued to purchase clothing—sensibly priced. And every now and
then, the money I save goes toward a Broadway play or a vacation in the
sun. I'm determined to seek the culture my designer clothes once implied I
had. I no longer look the part—because I'm too busy living it.

EXERCISING VOCABULARY

1. Record your own definition for each word below in your notebook.

paltry (adj.) (2)	tote (v.) (10)
façade (n.) (2)	swaggering (v.) (10)
stagnation (n.) (8)	

---

[3]**bop around:** To go freely from place to place.
[4]**baguette:** A handbag shaped like a loaf of French bread.

2. Examine the title. What does the phrase "champagne taste" imply? How would such taste be in conflict with a "beer budget"? How well does this title work for this essay?

3. Cleveland comments that in high school she couldn't bear the thought of not being "in vogue" (para. 2). What does it mean to be in vogue? How could being in vogue in one area of the United States mean being hopelessly out of fashion in another area? Give several examples to illustrate your answer.

PROBING CONTENT

1. What was the author's obsession in high school? What effect did this have on her life?

2. How did Cleveland's mother find out about her daughter's problem? How did her mother's reaction to this discovery change Cleveland?

3. What event finally caught Cleveland's attention? What action did her mother take? Why was this an unexpected decision?

4. What important realizations did the author reach? How did she arrive at these conclusions?

5. What evidence does Cleveland offer to confirm that she has recovered from her addiction?

CONSIDERING CRAFT

1. When you begin reading this essay, you might think that Cleveland's obsession is going to be with drugs. What language does she use to encourage this misdirection? Cite several specific examples. Why does the author deliberately allow the reader to be misled in this way? How does her use of such language affect the way you read the essay?

2. Throughout her essay, Cleveland sprinkles slang that may be unfamiliar to you. Cite several examples of such language. Why would the author include these expressions if many readers might not be familiar with them and most dictionaries do not include them? What would be lost if they were to be omitted or replaced by standard English?

WRITING PROMPTS

Responding to the Topic   To what extent do you identify with Cleveland's willingness to invest most of her money in clothes? Does the fact that her decisions caused her to miss much of the fun of high school make you sympathize with her? Did you know people like Delia Cleveland in high school, or do you know them now in college? What advice would you offer them?

Responding to the Writer   Cleveland admits to being a recovering "fashion addict" who once "wore a designer emblem on [her] chest like a badge of honor and respect" (para. 1). To what extent should consumers blame the advertising industry for their own harmful shopping habits? What steps should consumers take to make sure that they do not become victims of misleading advertising?

Responding to Multiple Viewpoints   Based on your reading of the essays in this chapter, write an essay in which you identify the most effective advertising strategies used by marketers today. Consider the role of the Internet, celebrity endorsements, and the green movement.

DRAWING CONNECTIONS

1. Pretend that you are Cleveland, author of "Champagne Taste, Beer Budget." Write a letter in response to the following quotation from Jay Chiat's "Illusions Are Forever": "We can accept the very compelling, very seductive version of 'truth' offered to us daily by media-makers, or we can tune out its influence for a shot at finding our own individual, confusing, messy version of it" (para. 12).

2. Imagine a conversation between the late advertising executive Jay Chiat ("Illusions Are Forever") and recovering fashion addict Cleveland. Write a dialogue in which Cleveland confronts Chiat and asks him to explain to her the morality of his profession.

For a quiz on this reading, go to bedfordstmartins.com/mirror.

The Croc Epidemic

MEGHAN O'ROURKE

Looking back at trends like bell-bottoms and big shoulder pads, you might feel that some hot styles of the past look quite silly, but in this essay Meghan O'Rourke is puzzled by the very recent trend of Crocs and tries to understand their appeal. O'Rourke is poetry coeditor for the *Paris Review* and culture editor for the webzine *Slate*. Her essays and reviews have also appeared in the *New York Times*, the *Los Angeles Book Review*, and the *Yale Review*. Her first poetry collection, *Halflife*, was published in 2007. "The Croc Epidemic" first appeared on *Slate* in July 2007.

> **THINKING AHEAD**   Think about fashions that many people consider unattractive. List several of them. Do you or would you consider wearing them? Why or why not? How do generally unattractive styles still become popular?

I n the demi-monde[1] of footwear, the term *croc* was once synonymous with elegance — the reptile skin covering a pair of stiletto sling-backs. Today, it's synonymous with an entirely different — and altogether vegetarian — phenomenon. In just a few years, the exquisitely ugly shoes known as "Crocs" have spread around the world like a Paris Hilton sex tape, giving rise to an epidemic of croc babies and their more egregious counterparts, croc parents. The shoe looks adorable on sun-kissed toddlers, but, alas, the fad did not stop there. For such a modest item (a typical edition sells for $29.99), the Croc has traveled in high places, disgracing the extremities of such celebrities as Mario Batali[2] (who prefers the bright orange variety) and George W. Bush (who paired them with shorts and dark socks). 1

As fans will tell you, Crocs aren't just footwear; they're the closest thing to religion that the foot has experienced. The company's stock has skyrocketed in value over the past year, and Crocs is now poised to launch a new product line this fall. Yet Crocs are heinous in appearance. A Croc is not a shoe; it is a Tinkertoy on steroids. How did this peculiar shoe-manqué[3] achieve ubiquity — and can it possibly stick around? 2

In the interest of science and as a defender of fashion, I went to Paragon Sports in New York to buy my first pair of Crocs — the shoes were a bright patch in a sea of sportswear. A woman with petite feet may discover that the 3

---

[1]**demi-monde:** A distinct world that is often an isolated part of a larger world; especially one having low reputation or prestige.
[2]**Mario Batali:** A celebrity chef.
[3]**manqué:** Falling short of or frustrated in the fulfillment of one's aspirations or talents; from the French word meaning "lacking."

smallest size in a popular edition, such as "Cayman" (the Crocs aesthetic is eco-beach), will not fit her; instead, she will have to head to the kids' section—piling ignominy upon ignominy. The Crocs palette tends toward the bold: orange, primary green, bright blue, periwinkle.[4] Having selected a periwinkle pair, I was approached by a young salesclerk, who had noticed my skeptical look. "These styles are *very* popular," he said reassuringly. "Can I help you with anything?" Yes. Would he be kind enough to reveal if *he* would ever wear a shoe like this? "Me?" he said, stepping backward. "Nah, they're too ugly. The flip-flop, maybe—but *these* go too far for me."

A first-time Crocs wearer will indeed find that the shoes are springy and light, as their fans aver,[5] and cushion the feet with what some have called a "marshmallow fluffiness." On a muggy New York day, the holes punched in the toe box allow for a soothing breeze to cool the sweating foot. Even so, the ratio of shame to comfort was extreme. When everyone else on the avenue is garbed in proper footwear—even something as unpretentious as flat sandals or ballet flats—an adult, it seemed to me, must blush at the sight of her bulbous feet. But those who wear Crocs all day long swear that the springy material holds up like nothing else; one painter reported that his chronic shin splints[6] disappeared after he began wearing Crocs. Thus was born what one blogger has labeled the "Croc conundrum[7]": Crocs make you look absurd, but they can change your life. 4

Comfort and function were always the main Crocs pitch. The shoes' original home was Boulder, Colorado. The early Crocs customer was probably a Pacific Northwesterner who liked to boat or garden—this was a niche shoe, after all. He or she was drawn in by the "no slip" grip on the sole, by the aerating holes, and by the featherweight heft of the thing (a pair weighs a mere six ounces). The clunky look was not a drawback (this is the region, after all, that brought us grunge), and many customers were pleased that the shoe was made of a proprietary[8] nonplastic resin formula (known as Croslite)—it was, as one testified, "vegan." Because the material is soft, bacteria-resistant and has a strangely "natural" feel, the Croc fits in with the Northwest's typically green and mildly counterculture ethos.[9] Soon nurses, doctors, cooks, painters and other workers who stand on their feet all day had discovered Crocs and found them to be life-changing. The company is careful to play up its shoes' supposed orthotic[10] benefits, to the distress of some skeptical podiatrists; a new line for diabetics is in the works. 5

In the meantime, the company cleverly positioned itself as an eco-conscious, no-frills-attached corporation. Crocs was conceived by three friends—Scott Seamans, George Boedecker and Lyndon Hanson—on a 6

---

[4] **periwinkle:** A light purplish blue.
[5] **aver:** Claim.
[6] **shin splints:** A painful leg condition.
[7] **conundrum:** An intricate and difficult problem.
[8] **proprietary:** Indicating exclusive ownership.
[9] **ethos:** The dominant assumptions of a people or period.
[10] **orthotic:** Supportive.

trip in the Caribbean, when Seamans showed his friends the extraordinary slip-resistant clog he was wearing; learning that it was made by a Canadian company called "Foam Creations," the friends spotted an opportunity. Soon they had licensed and were trying to "develop" the shoe (by adding a strap to the back); the name was the first thing that had to go. They realized the tops looked like crocodile snouts from the side. Presto! Crocs was born. In 2002, the company earned a gross profit of $1,000 from sales in America. By 2006, following a series of strategic licensing deals (you can now get NASCAR and Disney Crocs, for example), it was earning more than $200 million a year from sales in forty countries. (I even spotted knockoffs called Rockies in Jerusalem's Muslim quarter.) Nor have consumers' appetites yet been whetted:[11] During the first quarter of 2007, the company's sales had increased 217 percent from the same period the previous year.

In moving from a niche shoe to widespread wear, Crocs capitalized on its several strengths. The first is that the shoes are ideal for kids, who like their brightness, their lightness, their squishiness, and the strange holes in the front, in which charms can be placed. (Perhaps the only thing uglier than a Cayman Croc is a Croc adorned with "Jibbitz," as the charms are called.) Meanwhile, their parents like that they are dishwasher-safe, waterproof and odor-free. Their amorphous shape may be an aesthetic crime, but it lends the shoes a jovial quality that appeals to the knee-high and the anti-bourgeois everywhere. (One *Slate* contributor and early Croc-adopter reports that when she went to her daughter's school dressed in Crocs, the kids all wanted to know why she wore "clown shoes.") And the Croc fad, like the Ugg fad, benefits from the shoe's appropriation of an ethnic look (in this case, the Dutch clog) that one could deem "authentic." Ugly is OK, it would seem, as long as it's imported; then it's considered "practical" and earthy. In a classic cultural inversion, Ugly becomes Good: It represents an authentic critique of the marketing and branding that surround us every day. (Think of Ugly Dolls.) And so Crocs even ran ads in *Rolling Stone* proclaiming "Ugly can be beautiful." Finally, whereas Uggs were embraced by the fashion world, and became a status symbol, Crocs are a bottom-up brand, embraced by ordinary Americans everywhere. It is a democratic purchase. It looks painful to wear — like something you might find in the rock-bottom bins at Kmart — but is actually soft and high-tech, defeating class-based assumptions.

Footwear has always been particularly susceptible to fads, as the fashion authority Colin McDowell observes in *Shoes: Fashion and Fantasy*. Shoe fashion tends to swing dramatically on the pendulum from practical to beautiful, largely because shoes are even more utilitarian than clothes — and stylish clothes are rarely as uncomfortable as stylish shoes. Since everyone needs shoes, they are particularly susceptible to the tipping point phenomenon: When enough people are wearing ugly but comfortable shoes, others jump eagerly on the bandwagon, thrilled to be released

[11] **whetted:** Sharpened.

from the bondage of straps and buckles. And so Crocs represent a kind of rebellion—a vanguard[12] of the comfort movement. As footwear retailers reported this spring, shoe sales are unpredictable this year, with one exception: what retailers call "fashion comfort" styles—including ballet flats, shoes like Geox (which are popular among businessmen), and, of course, Crocs. One retailer called them "a category of their own."

The popularity of Crocs has also led to the inevitable backlash. Croc-mocking is rampant. The Web site Ihatecrocs.com chronicles its proprietors' attempts to destroy Crocs (using fireworks, scissors and lighter fluid). According to *Maclean's*, some hospitals have decided to ban Crocs, citing the fact that they do not protect against infection (the toe box has open holes). Meanwhile, there are reports of mysterious "Crocs shocks" shorting out crucial medical equipment; allegedly, the resin formula doesn't just keep out bacteria; it stores electricity. This sounds like urban legend, but one nurse who was skeptical of such accounts did tell *Maclean's* that when she started wearing Crocs she began giving her patients small electric shocks. Tales have come in from Crocs-haters in Sweden about children whose Crocs melt on escalators or get otherwise stuck in the cracks between steps; the most horrific of these involves a little boy whose toe got "pulled off" when his Crocs got stuck. A crock? Probably.   9

What is more certain is that some podiatrists are alarmed by their patients' fanatical embrace of Crocs; most Crocs, doctors point out, provide only moderate support. "I'll get people with strained arches because they've been running around in Crocs for five days," said Arnold Ravick, a doctor of podiatric medicine in Washington, D.C., and a spokesman for the American Podiatric Medical Association. "When it comes to shoes, people mistake comfort for support. Comfort is fool's gold—a soft gushy shoe that makes your arches collapse," he told me. "Crocs are popular because they're inexpensive and interchangeable. For people with certain problems, they can be a good shoe. Are they good for your foot, in general? No."   10

Crocs may be popular, but it's the rare Croc lover who considers them fashionable. As Kim France, the editor in chief of *Lucky*, the shopping magazine, told me, "Uggs I can make an argument for. Jellies also had their moment of being cute and cool. Crocs are just a pox.[13]" The first time she saw a male friend in them, she recalls, she asked him, "Are you really going to make me walk down the street with you?" And so today, the company is at a crossroads. The public's affection for shoe styles is notoriously fickle. (Remember earth shoes?) In June, 50 percent of Croc's shares were sold short by short-seller investors[14] who think that the company's stock will plummet soon. Though the company has made a series of strategic licensing deals and partnerships with subsidiaries, it is still largely dependent on its signature clogs and now flip-flops. Striving to position itself for a fall-off in demand,   11

---

[12] **vanguard:** The forefront of an action or movement; leader.
[13] **pox:** A contagious disease.
[14] **short-seller investors:** Those who make money by investing in and quickly selling products that they expect to fail.

Crocs plans to launch new clothing and shoe lines this fall that will depart from its signature resin formula and will feature pieces costing between $70 and $100. Who knows whether this strategy will succeed, but at Paragon, one employee was waiting eagerly for the shipment of new flip-flop styles. "I hate the way the old Crocs look," he said. "But they *are* comfortable."

History suggests that Crocs are more likely to be a passing fad, like   12
Dr. Scholl's, than a true innovation, like the sneaker. The very thing that has made them such a huge hit, after all—their ugly duckling distinctiveness—is also likely to make it hard for the company to go mainstream in any enduring sense. On the other hand, the trademarked Croslite material is an ace in the hole: If the traditional Croc clogs I tried on felt too confining on a summer day, the Croc flip-flops were delightfully springy. The company's sporty Sassari wedge suggests that when it comes to summerwear its designers may be developing at least some aesthetic sense. But for now, my old platform flip-flops will do.

EXERCISING VOCABULARY

1. Record your own definition for each word below in your notebook.

synonymous (adj.) (1)	aerating (adj.) (5)
exquisitely (adv.) (1)	amorphous (adj.) (7)
egregious (adj.) (1)	jovial (adj.) (7)
ubiquity (n.) (2)	utilitarian (adj.) (8)
aesthetic (n.) (3)	backlash (n.) (9)
ignominy (n.) (3)	rampant (adj.) (9)
palette (n.) (3)	fickle (adj.) (11)
bulbous (adj.) (4)	plummet (v.) (11)
chronic (adj.) (4)	subsidiaries (n.) (11)

2. O'Rourke refers to early Crocs as "a niche shoe" (para. 5). What is a niche? What do you usually find or place in a niche? What then is a niche shoe?

3. In paragraph 5, the author refers to Crocs as "vegan." When people call themselves vegans, what do they mean? How can a shoe be "vegan"?

4. O'Rourke quotes Dr. Arnold Ravick, who says that "Comfort is fool's gold" (para. 10). What is fool's gold? What then does this quotation mean in reference to Crocs?

PROBING CONTENT

1. How did Crocs come into being? How did the name originate?

2. Which factors were responsible for Crocs' move from being a "niche shoe" to a larger market? What have continued to be Crocs' main selling points?

3. What kind of backlash has developed against Crocs? What do podiatrists think of the shoe?

4. What plans has Crocs made for the future? How does O'Rourke envision the future of the brand?

CONSIDERING CRAFT

1. Paragraph 9 concludes with a play on words. Explain the author's intent here. How effective is her word choice? Why?

2. Crocs are personified in several places in the essay. Locate three such instances. How does the author's use of personification of the product affect your reading?

3. Why does O'Rourke include an anecdote about her first experience shopping for Crocs? How does its inclusion further her purpose for writing this essay?

4. Examine the beginning and ending paragraphs of the essay. With what time period is each concerned? Why do you think O'Rourke made this choice? How effective is this strategy?

WRITING PROMPTS

Responding to the Topic   From your own experience, identify a fashion fad that you have found totally unattractive. Write an essay like this one in which you examine the origin of the fad, its appeal to the masses, and its fate.

Responding to the Writer   Write an essay in which you respond to Kim France's claim that "Crocs are just a pox" (para. 11). Does this fashion trend deserve such a strong reaction? Why or why not?

Responding to Multiple Viewpoints   What would the reformed fashion addict Delia Cleveland, author of "Champagne Taste, Beer Budget," think of Crocs? Would she agree with O'Rourke's personal opinion of them? Why or why not? To what extent would Cleveland approve of a very recognizable, yet affordable fashion trend like Crocs or Sarah Jessica Parker's clothing line, Bitten? How would such a fashion fit into Cleveland's new lifestyle? Write an essay in which you respond to these questions.

For a quiz on this reading go, to bedfordstmartins.com/mirror.

On Covers of Many Magazines, a Full Racial Palette Is Still Rare

DAVID CARR

Think of all the magazine covers you've observed over the years. Are you aware of how few nonwhite faces have stared back at you from them? In a November 18, 2002, article in the *New York Times*, David Carr considers this problem. Carr has worked as editor of the *Washington City Paper*, an alternative newspaper owned by the *Chicago Reader*. His articles have appeared in *Salon.com* and the *Atlantic Monthly*. He is currently the media critic for the *New York Times*.

> **THINKING AHEAD** What are you looking for when you look at a magazine's cover? How much does the cover influence your decision about whether to buy that magazine? How do you feel about nonwhite faces appearing on magazine covers?

H alle Berry, in her role as the sexy superspy Jinx in *Die Another Day*, helps James Bond save the world from certain doom. But Ms. Berry may be performing an even more improbable feat as the cover model of the December issue of *Cosmopolitan* magazine. [1]

Ms. Berry became only the fifth black to appear on the cover of *Cosmopolitan* since the magazine began using cover photographs in 1964, and she is the first since Naomi Campbell in 1990. Ms. Berry is evidently one of a tiny cadre of nonwhite celebrities who are deemed to have enough crossover appeal to appear on the cover of mass consumer magazines. [2]

There are signs that the freeze-out may be beginning to thaw, as the continuing explosion of hip-hop has pushed many black artists into prominence, and as teenagers' magazines that are less anxious about race are bringing more diversity. But in many broad-circulation magazines, the unspoken but routinely observed practice of not using nonwhite cover subjects—for fear they will depress newsstand sales—remains largely in effect. [3]

A survey of 471 covers from 31 magazines published in 2002—an array of men's and women's magazines, entertainment publications and teenagers' magazines—conducted two weeks ago by the *New York Times* found that about one in five depicted minority members. Five years ago, according to the survey, which examined all the covers of those 31 magazines back through 1998, the figure was only 12.7 percent. And fashion magazines have more than doubled their use of nonwhite cover subjects. [See p. 231.] [4]

But in a country with a nonwhite population of almost 30 percent, the incremental progress leaves some people unimpressed. [5]

"The magazine industry has been slow and reluctant to embrace the change in our culture," said Roy S. Johnson, editorial director of Vanguarde Media and editor in chief of *Savoy*, a magazine aimed at black men. "The change is broad and profound, and in many ways is now the mainstream." 6

The absence of cover-model diversity could reflect the industry's racial homogeneity. Four years ago, the trade publication *Mediaweek* found that only 6.1 percent of the magazine industry's professional staff was nonwhite. 7

"We do not see ourselves in magazines," said Diane Weathers, editor in chief of *Essence*, a monthly magazine for black women. "Considering what the country we live in looks like today, I think it's appalling." 8

The women's category has seen the most profound changes, largely as a result of O, the Oprah magazine, whose cover repeatedly hosts Oprah Winfrey and has a large white readership. 9

Both *Cosmo* and O are published by Hearst magazines. As a newsstand giant, selling two million copies a month, *Cosmo* uses a near scientific blend of sex and Middle American beauty on its covers—a formula that does not seem to include black women. O magazine, in contrast, transcends race with a new, spiritually based female empowerment. 10

Publishing is a conservative industry, one that has been known to define risk as using a cover model with dark hair instead of blond. But a wave of Latina superstars like Jennifer Lopez, along with genre-breaking athletes like Tiger Woods[1] and the Williams sisters,[2] have redefined what a celebrity looks like. And the audience is changing as well. In the last five years, the nonwhite audience for magazines has increased to 17 percent from 15 percent, according to Mediamark Research Inc. 11

Yet, even as black and Hispanic women slowly make their way onto the covers of magazines of various genres, black males still find themselves mainly confined to a ghetto of music and sports magazines. 12

"When it comes to magazine covers, my client, who is one of the busiest guys in Hollywood, can't get arrested," said an agent for an A-list[3] Hollywood actor who declined to give her name or the name of her client for fear of making a bad situation even worse. "Magazines are in trouble and they are fearful of offending their audience of Middle Americans," she said. "But those same people are buying tickets to his movies." 13

Daniel Peres, editor of *Details*, a men's magazine owned by Fairchild Publications, said there was pressure to stick with outdated conventions because newsstands now display so many more titles competing for the consumer's attention. 14

"Everyone is terrified of a misstep," he said. "While most people in the business would prefer it go unspoken because they are horrified at being perceived as racist, it is a well-known legend that blacks, especially black males, do not help generate newsstand sales." 15

[1]**Tiger Woods:** One of the top golfers in America today.
[2]**the Williams sisters:** Serena and Venus Williams; American star tennis players.
[3]**A-list:** The most sought-after and hence most highly paid celebrities.

Christina Kelly, now editor in chief of *YM*, a teenagers' magazine owned   16
by Gruner & Jahr USA, recalls a struggle with the circulation people when
she worked as an editor in 1993 at the now-closed *Sassy* magazine.

"We wanted to put Mecca from the band Digable Planets on the cover   17
because she was huge at the time and gorgeous," she recalled. "The circulation guys hated the idea, but we just went ahead and did it. The magazine
was bagged with a separate beauty booklet, which was usually placed in
the back, but this time, it was bagged in front. It just happened to have a
picture of a blond, blue-eyed woman on it."

Today, magazines like *Teen People* and *YM* feature cover subjects of a va-   18
riety of hues. In the last year, *YM* has had covers that included nonwhite artists
like Ashanti and Enrique Iglesias. And in August, *Teen People* chose Usher, a
black R&B singer, as its No. 1 "hot guy" and featured him on the cover.

"Race is a much more fluid concept among teens," said Barbara O'Dair,   19
managing editor of *Teen People*.

Magazines for teenagers, because of their reliance on the heavily inte-   20
grated music industry, use 25 percent nonwhite subjects on their covers. If
white teenagers are crossing over to embrace minority artists, many artists
are meeting them halfway in terms of style.

Fashion, previously a very segregated world, has become transracial, with   21
young white women adopting street fashion while black artists wear long,
flowing tresses. Certain totems[4] of beauty—blond hair, among other things—
can now be seamlessly situated on almost anyone regardless of race. The
singers Shakira, Beyoncé Knowles, and Christina Aguilera, all nonwhite, have
at times worn blond hair that is indiscernible from that of Britney Spears.

"There is virtually no stigma attached to black celebrities changing   22
their hair as there has been in the past," said Leon E. Wynter, author of
American Skin: Pop Culture, Big Business, and the End of White America
(Crown Publishers, 2002). "The hair thing is completely over."

And race itself has become more complicated and less definable, said   23
Mr. Wynter. He suggests that many of the Latin superstars like Jennifer
Lopez are often seen not as minorities by young white teenagers, but as a
different kind of white person. Very few of the breakout artists[5] featured
on covers are dark skinned.

The growing acceptance of nonwhite cover subjects is not restricted to   24
teenaged girls. Men's magazines, for example, are not as racially monolithic[6]
as they once were. *GQ*, which has a nonwhite readership of 18 percent, has
always had more diverse images by featuring minority athletes and actors.

But a newer generation of men's magazines seems to find ethnicity sexy.   25
In the last year, five of the twelve women featured on the cover of *Maxim*, the
spectacularly successful young men's magazine owned by Dennis Publishing
USA, were other than white.

---

[4]**totems:** Things treated with the kind of respect normally reserved for religious icons.
[5]**breakout artists:** People who become stars quickly and sometimes unexpectedly.
[6]**monolithic:** Uniform in character and slow to change.

"It doesn't stem from any political motivation," said Keith Blanchard,   26
editor in chief of *Maxim*. His readers, mostly white young men, "are listening to Shakira and Beyoncé. They are cheering for Lucy Liu kicking butt in
Charlie's Angels. And I think there is a certain attraction to exotic women."

But there are those who would argue that equal opportunity objec-   27
tification of women does not represent progress. "What is attractive is
socially constructed," said Robin D. G. Kelley, a professor of history at
New York University who has written extensively about race and black
culture. "I think that race still matters, and many times what is happening
is that these poly-racial figures are used to fulfill fantasies. It's the Jezebel[7]
phenomenon."

As for the December *Cosmopolitan*, Kate White, the magazine's editor in   28
chief, said Ms. Berry was on her cover simply because she meets all the criteria
of a typical *Cosmo* girl. "She is beautiful, powerful, successful, and she can
open a movie," Ms. White said, suggesting that Ms. Berry has the kind of
wattage[8] that can draw people into a movie, or to buy a magazine. Ms. White
said the absence of nonwhite women on the cover of *Cosmo* reflected the
celebrities that Hollywood produces, not the magazine's preferences.

Still, when the magazine uses a model instead of a celebrity, it almost   29
invariably chooses a white person. "We choose models who have already
started to gain critical mass,[9] regardless of hair or eye color," said a Hearst
spokeswoman in response. "We want the reader to have a sense of having seen
them before."

It probably helps, in terms of both newsstand and advertising, that   30
Ms. Berry's face is everywhere now that she has been selected as a spokeswoman for the cosmetics company Revlon. There are important business,
as well as cultural, reasons why after so many years that black, at least in
some magazines, may be beautiful.

"Part of what is going on is that the beauty industry woke up and re-   31
alized there was a big market there," said Roberta Myers, editor in chief
of *Elle*, a women's fashion magazine that is uncommonly diverse in cover
selections. "The old assumptions that there was only one kind of beauty,
the typical blond, blue-eyed Christie Brinkley[10] type, are gone."

While editors sweat over the consequences of diversifying their cover   32
mix, they may fall behind a coming generation of young consumers who have
decided that race is much less important than how hot a given celebrity's latest
record or film is.

"The list of who is acceptable or hot is slowly expanding," said   33
Mr. Wynter. "In the current generation, there is an underlying urge, an aspi-
ration, to assert one's common humanity. You can't see it in the magazines
that are on the shelves now, but it is coming to the fore."

---

[7]**Jezebel:** In the Hebrew scriptures, a ninth-century B.C. queen who married Ahab and promoted
    idol worship; in general, an immoral woman.
[8]**wattage:** Star power.
[9]**critical mass:** The amount necessary to have a significant effect.
[10]**Christie Brinkley:** American supermodel during the 1970s and 1980s.

Cover Census

According to the United States Census Bureau, almost 30 percent of America's population belongs to minority groups. Over the last five years, however, the images on the covers of mass-market consumer magazines featured members of a minority less than 25 percent of the time in most categories.

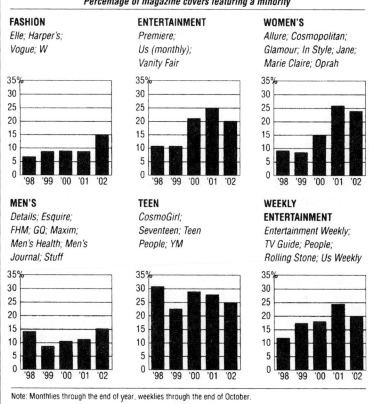

Percentage of magazine covers featuring a minority

FASHION
Elle; Harper's;
Vogue; W

ENTERTAINMENT
Premiere;
Us (monthly);
Vanity Fair

WOMEN'S
Allure; Cosmopolitan;
Glamour; In Style; Jane;
Marie Claire; Oprah

MEN'S
Details; Esquire;
FHM; GQ; Maxim;
Men's Health; Men's
Journal; Stuff

TEEN
CosmoGirl;
Seventeen; Teen
People; YM

**WEEKLY
ENTERTAINMENT**
Entertainment Weekly;
TV Guide; People;
Rolling Stone; Us Weekly

Note: Monthlies through the end of year, weeklies through the end of October.

EXERCISING VOCABULARY

1. Record your own definition for each word below in your notebook.

palette (n.) (title)
feat (n.) (1)
cadre (n.) (2)
deemed (v.) (2)
incremental (adj.) (5)
mainstream (n.) (6)
homogeneity (n.) (7)
transcends (v.) (10)

empowerment (n.) (10)
genre (n.) (11)
misstep (n.) (15)
indiscernible (adj.) (21)
stigma (n.) (22)
invariably (adv.) (29)
fore (n.) (33)

2. In paragraph 12, Carr writes that "black males still find themselves mainly confined to a ghetto of music and sports magazines." What is a ghetto? Why have people been confined to a ghetto in the past? What does the author imply by his word choice here?

3. What does Carr mean by the phrase "equal opportunity objectification of women" (para. 27)? Is this expression positive or negative? Why? What does equal opportunity usually mean in the working world? Is it normally regarded as positive or negative? Explain your answer.

PROBING CONTENT

1. How has fashion become "transracial"? Give an example that illustrates this change.

2. What effect has the music world had on magazine covers? What target audience has most directly influenced a change in magazine covers?

3. Why has the magazine industry been slow to reflect the growing numbers of nonwhite celebrities and readers? What kinds of magazines have been most likely to feature minorities on their covers? What evidence is there of change?

CONSIDERING CRAFT

1. This article originally appeared in the business section of the *New York Times*. What audience would have read this essay in its original form? How would the article differ if it had been written for the fashion section?

2. What role do the bar graphs play? How do they enhance your reading of the essay?

3. Halle Berry is mentioned at the beginning and near the end of the essay. Why does Carr use this strategy? How effective a choice is Berry for the writer's purpose? Why?

WRITING PROMPTS

Responding to the Topic   Explain your magazine reading experience and the effect it has on you. What kinds of magazines or e-zines do you read? How much attention do you pay to the covers? Why? How much consideration do you give to the ethnicity of the people pictured or written about in the magazines?

Responding to the Writer   How important is it to increase the appearance of nonwhite celebrities on popular magazine covers? Why? Explain your response.

Responding to Multiple Viewpoints   How do you think the advertising executives at Modernista (see Bob Garfield's "Taking Cadillac from Stodgy to Sexy: Kate Walsh") and those responsible for the Crocs ad campaigns (see Meghan O'Rourke's "The Croc Epidemic") would react to the idea of including a "full racial palette" in their advertisements? Write an essay in which you answer this question.

For a quiz on this reading, go to bedfordstmartins.com/mirror.

Custom-Made

Tara Parker-Pope

Tara Parker-Pope is a health columnist for the *New York Times*, where she maintains a blog on health entitled *Well*. Before that, she wrote a weekly health column for the *Wall Street Journal*. She is the author of *Cigarettes: Anatomy of an Industry from Seed to Smoke* (2001). "Custom-Made" was first published in the *Wall Street Journal Europe* on September 30, 1996. In this essay, Parker-Pope takes us on a fascinating trip around the world and behind the scenes where marketing decisions are made to see what's hot and what's not about American favorites.

> **THINKING AHEAD** What is the strangest food or combi-
> nation of foods you have ever tasted? Why did you eat this? Where
> were you? What did you learn from the experience? What foods
> would you like to try that you have never tasted? Why?

Pity the poor Domino's Pizza Inc. delivery man. 1

In Britain, customers don't like the idea of him knocking on their 2 doors — they think it's rude. In Japan, houses aren't numbered sequentially — finding an address means searching among rows of houses numbered willy-nilly.[1] And in Kuwait, pizza is more likely to be delivered to a waiting limousine than to someone's front door.

"We honestly believe we have the best pizza delivery system in the 3 world," says Gary McCausland, managing director of Domino's international division. "But delivering pizza isn't the same all over the world."

And neither is making cars, selling soap, or packaging toilet paper. 4 International marketers have found that just because a product plays in Peoria, that doesn't mean it will be a hit in Helsinki.

To satisfy local tastes, products ranging from Heinz ketchup to Cheetos 5 chips are tweaked, reformulated, and reflavored. Fast-food companies such as McDonald's Corp., popular for the "sameness" they offer all over the world, have discovered that to succeed, they also need to offer some local appeal — selling beer in Germany and adding British Cadbury chocolate sticks to their ice-cream cones in England.

The result is a delicate balancing act for international marketers: 6 How does a company exploit the economies of scale that can be gained by global marketing while at the same time making its products appeal to local tastes?

---

[1]**willy-nilly:** In random order.

The answer: Be flexible, even when it means changing a tried-and-true recipe, even when consumer preferences, like Häagen-Dazs green tea ice cream, sound awful to the Western palate. 7

"It's a dilemma we all live with every day," says Nick Harding, H. J. Heinz Co.'s managing director for Northern Europe. Heinz varies the recipe of its famous ketchup in different markets, selling a less-sweet version in Belgium and Holland, for instance, because consumers there use ketchup as a pasta sauce (and mayonnaise on french fries). "We're looking for the economies from globalizing our ideas, but we want to maintain the differences necessary for local markets," says Mr. Harding. 8

For those who don't heed such advice, the costs are high. U.S. auto makers, for instance, have done poorly in Japan, at least in part because they failed to adapt. Until recently, most didn't bother even to put steering wheels on the right, as is the standard in Japan. While some American makers are beginning to conform, European companies such as Volkswagen AG, Daimler-Benz AG, and Bayerische Motoren Werke AG did it much sooner, and have done far better in the Japanese market as a result. 9

For Domino's, the balancing act has meant maintaining the same basic pizza delivery system world-wide—and then teaming up with local franchisers[2] to tailor the system to each country's needs. In Japan, detailed wall maps, three times larger than those used in its stores elsewhere, help delivery people find the proper address despite the odd street numbering system. 10

In Iceland, where much of the population doesn't have phone service, Domino's has teamed with a Reykjavik drive-in movie theater to gain access to consumers. Customers craving a reindeer-sausage pizza (a popular flavor there) flash their turn signal, and a theater employee brings them a cellular phone to order a pizza, which is then delivered to the car. 11

Local Domino's managers have developed new pizza flavors, including mayo jaga (mayonnaise and potato) in Tokyo and pickled ginger in India. The company, which now has 1,160 stores in 46 countries, is currently trying to develop a nonbeef pepperoni topping for its stores in India. 12

When Pillsbury Co., a unit of Britain's Grand Metropolitan PLC, wanted to begin marketing its Green Giant brand vegetables outside the United States, it decided to start with canned sweet corn, a basic product unlikely to require any flavor changes across international markets. But to Pillsbury's surprise, the product still was subject to local influences. Instead of being eaten as a hot side dish, the French add it to salad and eat it cold. In Britain, corn is used as a sandwich and pizza topping. In Japan, school children gobble down canned corn as an after-school treat. And in Korea, the sweet corn is sprinkled over ice cream. 13

So Green Giant tailored its advertising to different markets. Spots show corn kernels falling off a cob into salads and pastas, or topping an ice-cream sundae. 14

[2]**franchisers:** People who pay for the right to use a company's name and to market its products.

"Initially we thought it would be used the same as in the United States,"   15
says Stephen Moss, vice president, strategy and development, for Green Giant.
"But we've found there are very different uses for corn all over the world."

And Green Giant has faced some cultural hurdles in its race to foreign   16
markets. Although vegetables are a significant part of the Asian diet, Green
Giant discovered that Japanese mothers, in particular, take pride in the
time they take to prepare a family meal and saw frozen vegetables as an
unwelcome shortcut. "Along with the convenience comes a little bit of
guilt," says Mr. Moss.

The solution? Convince moms that using frozen vegetables gives them   17
the opportunity to prepare their families' favorite foods more often. To
that end, Green Giant focused on a frozen mixture of julienned[3] carrots
and burdock root, a traditional favorite root vegetable that requires several
hours of tedious preparation.

The company also has introduced individual seasoned vegetable serv-   18
ings for school lunch boxes, with such flavors as sesame-seasoned lotus
root. Although fresh vegetables still dominate the market, Green Giant says
its strategy is starting to show results, and frozen varieties now account for
half the vegetable company's sales in Japan.

The drive for localization has been taken to extremes in some cases: 19
Cheetos, the bright orange and cheesy-tasting chip brand of PepsiCo Inc.'s
Frito-Lay unit, are cheeseless in China. The reason? Chinese consumers
generally don't like cheese, in part because many of them are lactose-
intolerant.[4] So Cheetos tested such flavors as Peking duck, fried egg, and
even dog to tempt the palates of Chinese.

Ultimately, says Tom Kuthy, vice president of marketing for PepsiCo   20
Foods International's Asia-Pacific operations, the company picked a but-
ter flavor, called American cream, and an Asianized barbecue flavor called
Japanese steak. Last year, Frito rolled out its third flavor, seafood.

In addition to changing the taste, the company also packaged Cheetos   21
in a 15-gram size priced at one yuan, about 12 cents, so that even kids with
little spending money can afford them.

The bottom line: These efforts to adapt to the local market have paid   22
off. Mr. Kuthy estimates that close to 300 million packages of Cheetos
have been sold since they were introduced two years ago in Guangzhou.
Cheetos are now available in Shanghai and Beijing as well.

Frito isn't through trying to adapt. Now the company is introducing   23
a 33-gram pack for two yuan. Mr. Kuthy also is considering more flavors,
but dog won't be one of them. "Yes, we tested the concept, but it was never
made into a product," he says. "Its performance was mediocre."

Other PepsiCo units have followed with their own flavor variations. In   24
Thailand, Pizza Hut has a tom yam-flavored pizza based on the spices of

---

[3]**julienned:** Sliced into thin strips.
[4]**lactose-intolerant:** Unable to properly digest lactose, the sugar in milk and certain other
dairy products.

the traditional Thai soup. In Singapore, you can get a KFC Zinger chicken burger that is hot and spicy with Asia's ubiquitous chili. The Singaporean pizza at Pizza Hut comes with ground beef, green peppers, and chili. Elsewhere in Asia, pizzas come in flavors such as Mongolian, with pork, chili, and garlic; salmon, with a creamy lobster sauce; and Satay, with grilled chicken and beef.

Coming up with the right flavor combinations for international con-   25
sumers isn't easy. Part of the challenge is building relationships with customers in far-flung markets. For years, the founders of Ben & Jerry's Homemade Inc. had relied on friends, co-workers, and their own taste buds to concoct such unusual ice-cream flavors as Chunky Monkey and Cherry Garcia.

But introducing their ice cream abroad, by definition, meant losing that   26
close connection with their customers that made them successful. "For Ben and me, since we've grown up in the United States, our customers were people like us, and the flavors we made appealed to us," says co-founder Jerry Greenfield, scooping ice cream at a media event in the Royal Albert Hall in London. "I don't think we have the same seat-of-the-pants feel for places like England. It's a different culture."

As a result, one of the company's most popular flavors in the United   27
States, Chocolate Chip Cookie Dough, flopped in Britain. The nostalgia quotient of the ice cream, vanilla-flavored with chunks of raw cookie dough, was simply lost on the Brits, who historically haven't eaten chocolate-chip cookies. "People didn't grow up in this country sneaking raw cookie-dough batter from Mom," says Mr. Greenfield.

The solution? Hold a contest to concoct a quintessential British ice   28
cream. After reviewing hundreds of entries, including Choc Ness Monster and Cream Victoria, the company in July introduced Cool Britannia, a combination of vanilla ice cream, strawberries, and chocolate-covered Scottish shortbread. (The company plans to sell Cool Britannia in the United States eventually.)

And in a stab at building a quirky relationship with Brits, the duo   29
opted for a publicity stunt when Britain's beef crisis meant farmers were left with herds of cattle that couldn't be sold at market. Ben & Jerry's creative solution: Use the cows to advertise. The company's logo was draped across the backs of grazing cattle, and the stunt made the front page of major London newspapers.

The company has just begun selling ice cream in France but isn't sure   30
whether the company will try contests for a French flavor in that market. One reason: It's unclear whether Ben & Jerry's wry humor, amusing to the Brits, will be understood by the laconic French. "We're going to try to get more in touch, more comfortable with the feel of the French market first," says Mr. Greenfield.

But for every success story, there have been a slew of global marketing   31
mistakes. In Japan, consumer-products marketer Procter & Gamble Co. made several stumbles when it first entered the market in the early 1970s.

The company thought its thicker, more-absorbent Pampers diapers in   32
big packs like those favored in America would be big sellers in Japan. But
Japanese women change their babies twice as often as Americans and prefer thin diapers. Moreover, they often have tiny apartments and no room
to store huge diaper packs.

The company adapted by making thinner diapers packaged in smaller   33
bags. Because the company shifted gears quickly, Procter & Gamble is now
one of the largest and most successful consumer-goods companies in Japan,
with more than $1 billion in annual sales and market leadership in several
categories.

EXERCISING VOCABULARY

1. Record your own definition for each word below in your notebook.

   sequentially (adv.) (2)   quintessential (adj.) (28)
   tweaked (v.) (5)   quirky (adj.) (29)
   globalizing (v.) (8)   laconic (adj.) (30)
   ubiquitous (adj.) (24)   slew (n.) (31)
   concoct (v.) (28)

2. According to the article, Ben & Jerry's Chocolate Chip Cookie Dough
   ice cream failed to appeal to the British because in England that flavor
   has no "nostalgia quotient" (para. 27). What does the word *nostalgia*
   mean? What other foods have a high nostalgia value for Americans?
   Why is this true?

3. What does the verb *opted* mean in paragraph 29? In answering, consider
   what the noun *option* means.

PROBING CONTENT

1. According to Parker-Pope, why must companies custom-market American
   products to suit the tastes of international consumers?

2. Choose one of the author's examples and discuss the changes made to
   the product to market it in another country. Explain why the effort failed
   or succeeded.

3. Not only are the ingredients in American products often varied for international markets, but sometimes whole products are put to entirely
   different uses outside the United States. What examples does Parker-Pope
   give of such products?

4. What kind of pizza topping is Domino's trying to develop for its Indian
   market? Why would such a product sell in India?

CONSIDERING CRAFT

1. This essay first appeared in the World Business section of the *Wall Street Journal Europe.* Knowing this, how might you characterize Parker-Pope's audience? Why would this essay also appeal to readers outside that audience?

2. Why does this author need to provide specific examples of marketing campaigns or custom-made products? How do you think Parker-Pope determined how many examples to use?

3. How does the writer use the example in the final paragraph to create a satisfying conclusion? How else might the author have ended this essay?

WRITING PROMPTS

Responding to the Topic   Write an essay in which you consider your food choices. How open are you to including foods from other countries in your diet? Would you Americanize certain dishes, or would you eat them in the same way they are prepared in their native countries?

Responding to the Writer   To what extent should foods and food packaging and services be adapted for foreign consumers? What are the advantages? What are the disadvantages?

Responding to Multiple Viewpoints   In her essay "Custom-Made," Parker-Pope writes, "Part of the challenge [of global marketing] is building relationships with customers in far-flung markets" (para. 25). Do some research on a highly successful global advertising campaign, such as the one conducted by McDonald's. Then using what you have learned from that research and from the readings in this chapter, write an essay in which you detail one such successful worldwide campaign and the reasons for its success.

For a quiz on this reading, go to bedfordstmartins.com/mirror.

Cleaning Up

Rob Walker

Rob Walker writes a column on marketing for the *New York Times.* He also
started the Web site murketing.com, dedicated to investigating consumer
behavior, and in 2008 he published *Buying In: The Secret Dialogue between
What We Buy and Who We Are.* In "Cleaning Up," originally published in
the *New York Times* in 2006, Walker discusses ethical questions surrounding a company's need for profit and its initiatives to promote well-being.

> **THINKING AHEAD** How much thought have you given to
> the ways in which companies market products, either in the United
> States or abroad? What are the moral implications of advertising agen-
> cies' attempts to make poverty-stricken people brand-conscious?

"Corporate social responsibility" often means leveraging the concern   1
(or guilt) of the affluent on behalf of those less fortunate: Sell to first-
world consumers and redistribute some of the profits to address third-world
problems. But a case has been made for a different strategy that involves
selling to the poor themselves. In a speech last month, for instance, Harish
Manwani, the chairman of Hindustan Lever Limited, pointed to his firm's
marketing Lifebuoy soap to India's sprawling underclass as an example of
its efforts to bring "social responsibility to the heart of our business."

Hindustan Lever is a subsidiary of Unilever, the packaged-goods giant (it   2
owns brands including Dove and Ben & Jerry's) that was formed in 1929 by the
merger of the British soap maker Lever Brothers and the Dutch food company
Margarine Unie. Global brands seem like a recent phenomenon, but Lever was
already operating around the world when Lifebuoy entered the Indian market
more than a hundred years ago. Another thing that existed a hundred years
ago and is still around today is a large number of preventable deaths.

In his speech, Manwani focused on deaths caused by diarrhea-related   3
diseases (the World Health Organization estimates such illnesses kill
1.8 million people a year) and noted that better hand-washing habits—
using soap—is one way to prevent their spread. For several years, the
World Bank has been involved in initiatives with multinationals, including
Unilever, to address the issue.

Hindustan Lever's Lifebuoy campaign, however, is not philanthropy; it's   4
business. Throughout its long life, the antibacterial soap has been positioned
as a health-and-wellness product: a 1902 ad in Harper's promised "this wonderful cleanser and purifier" was "the enemy of dirt and disease." That "core
proposition" remains, says Punit Misra, the marketing manager who oversees
Lifebuoy and other skin-cleansing brands for Hindustan Lever. Perhaps the

most significant change to the product itself in recent years has been the introduction of smaller, and thus cheaper, bars: a half-size, fifty-gram bar, for five rupees (about two ounces, for roughly twelve cents), was introduced in the early 1990s. (The small-package approach is now used by many companies in developing markets.) More recently, the packaging was made "more contemporary" by replacing the "strapping young man" on the package with an image of a couple and their children, Misra says.

And five years ago, the company introduced a campaign called Swasthya 5
Chetna or "Glowing Health," which, boiled down, argues that even clean-looking hands may carry dangerous germs, so use more soap. It began a concentrated effort to take this message into the tens of thousands of villages where the rural poor reside, often with little access to media. "Lifebuoy teams visit each village several times," Manwani said in his speech, using "a glo-germ kit[1] to show schoolchildren" that soap-washed hands are cleaner. Manwani says this program has reached "around eighty million rural folk" and added that "sales of Lifebuoy have risen sharply." The small bar has become the brand's top seller.

C. K. Prahalad, a University of Michigan professor (and Hindustan Lever 6
board member), uses the India Lifebuoy story as a case study in his 2004 book *The Fortune at the Bottom of the Pyramid*, which argues that the profit motive can be a powerful force in addressing global poverty issues. Building a campaign around a well-known product like Lifebuoy can be effective precisely because even the world's poorest citizens can be "brand-conscious." (Hindustan Lever's Misra agrees, saying that such consumers will stick with a brand they trust, because "money means that much more to them.")

Still, is this really the right place for the profit motive? Hindustan Lever's 7
position is that profitable responsibility is the point. "If it's not really self-sustaining," Misra says, "somewhere along the line it will drop off." Prahalad makes similar points. "The question that comes up all the time is: These companies are pushing consumption, but what we need is livelihood improvement," he told me in an interview. But preventing illness also means a family might avoid a potentially devastating loss of several days' work. And ultimately, he says, campaigns like Lifebuoy's Swasthya Chetna should be evaluated not ideologically but by their impact on the global poor. "The alternative," he said, "is needless death."

EXERCISING VOCABULARY

1. Record your own definition for each word below in your notebook.

affluent (adj.) (1)	core (adj.) (4)
sprawling (adj.) (1)	strapping (adj.) (4)
subsidiary (n.) (2)	reside (v.) (5)
initiatives (n.) (3)	devastating (adj.) (7)
philanthropy (n.) (4)	

[1] **glo-germ kit:** A kit containing a powder or oil that, when applied to skin, causes areas that are not germ-free to glow under ultraviolet light.

2. In the opening paragraph of his essay, Walker speaks of "leveraging the concern (or guilt) of the affluent." What is a lever? How is it used? What then does the word *leveraging* mean in the quotation?

3. In paragraph 7, the author quotes C. K. Prahalad, who says that "campaigns like Lifebuoy's Swasthya Chetna should be evaluated not ideologically but by their impact on the global poor." What does *ideologically* mean? How does this definition relate to the root word *idea*?

4. In paragraph 5, Walker says, " 'Glowing Health,' . . . boiled down, argues that even clean-looking hands may carry dangerous germs." Which kinds of things do you normally boil? What is the effect of boiling something down? What does the expression *boiled down* mean?

PROBING CONTENT

1. What is the history of Hindustan Lever's marketing campaign for Lifebuoy soap in India?

2. What was the most important change to Hindustan Lever's Lifebuoy soap? What was the reason for this change?

3. What is Swasthya Chetna? How successful was it? Why?

4. Who are Punit Misra and C. K. Prahalad? What do they think of Hindustan Lever's Lifebuoy campaign?

CONSIDERING CRAFT

1. What is the play on words in the essay's title? How does it announce the subject of the essay?

2. Walker quotes or paraphrases several other people in his essay. Find three places where he does this. How does the author's inclusion of their ideas affect your reading of the essay?

3. Why does Walker begin the concluding paragraph with a question? What does he hope to accomplish? How effective is this strategy?

WRITING PROMPTS

Responding to the Topic   In what ways do you believe that marketing firms should consider the economic status of their potential consumers in third world countries? Where does one draw the line between "moral" marketing and exploitation? Write an essay in which you discuss these questions. Make sure to provide specific examples.

Responding to the Writer   Walker quotes C. K. Prahalad, who argues that "the profit motive can be a powerful force in addressing global poverty issues" (para. 6). How do you respond to this statement? To what extent do companies have a moral responsibility to consumers, especially those in poverty-ridden areas? Can you think of specific situations in which the profit motive should not be the first priority? Write an essay in which you take a position on this issue and defend it with sufficient support to make your point.

Responding to Multiple Viewpoints   What advice might Tara Parker-Pope, author of "Custom-Made," offer to Hindustan Lever advertising executives concerning marketing American soap to an Indian population? How might Parker-Pope's knowledge of worldwide marketing successes and failures prove beneficial?

For a quiz on this reading, go to bedfordstmartins.com/mirror.

Damn Spam

Michael Specter

Michael Specter is a staff writer for *The New Yorker*, where he focuses on science and technology. He previously worked as Moscow bureau chief for the *New York Times* and as national science reporter for the *Washington Post*. In 2002, Specter won a Science Journalism Award from the American Association for the Advancement of Science. Published in *The New Yorker* in August 2007, "Damn Spam" chronicles the history of and efforts to combat electronic junk mail.

> **THINKING AHEAD**   How often do you use e-mail? How much of your e-mail is spam? What kinds of spam do you receive? How much effort do you invest in eliminating the spam you receive? Should sending spam be illegal? Why?

I n the spring of 1978, an energetic marketing man named Gary Thuerk   1
wanted to let people in the technology world know that his company, the Digital Equipment Corporation, was about to introduce a powerful new computer system. DEC operated out of an old wool mill in Maynard, Massachusetts, and was well known on the East Coast, but Thuerk hoped to reach the technological community in California as well. He decided that the best way to do it was through the network of government and university computers then known as the Arpanet. Only a few thousand people used it regularly, but their names were conveniently printed in a single directory. After selecting six hundred West Coast addresses, Thuerk realized that he would never have time to call each one of them, or even to send out hundreds of individual messages. Then another idea occurred to him: what if he simply used the network to dispatch a single e-mail to *all* of them? "We invite you to come see the 2020 and hear about the DECSystem-20 family," the message read. As historic lines go, it didn't have quite the ring of "One small step for a man," yet Gary Thuerk's impact cannot be disputed. When he pushed the send button, he became the father of spam.

The reaction was immediate and almost completely hostile. "This was   2
a flagrant violation of the Arpanet," one recipient wrote. Another noted that "advertising of particular products" should be strongly discouraged on the network. The system administrator promised to respond at once, and Thuerk was harshly reprimanded. Nevertheless, his company sold more than twenty of the computer systems, for a million dollars apiece. Thuerk saw no harm in his actions; he and others viewed the network as an emerging symbol of intellectual freedom. Even if unsolicited e-mail became a nuisance, a greater danger would be posed by placing limits on

how this powerful new tool could be deployed. "The amount of harm done by any of the cited 'unfair' things the net has been used for is clearly very small," the Internet pioneer Richard Stallman wrote a few days after the DEC e-mail. Stallman opposed any action that would interfere with the aggressive openness that came to define the Web. And he still does. In his message about the DEC spam, Stallman pointed out—three decades before the appearance of Craigslist and Monster.com—that the network provided a unique opportunity to advertise jobs and an entirely new way to sell products. He went even further: "Would a dating service on the net be 'frowned upon' . . . ? I hope not. But even if it is, don't let that stop you from notifying me via net mail if you start one."

I have no idea whether anyone on the Arpanet tried to help Stallman   3
find a date, but thousands of people have tried to help me. In the past few weeks, I have received several e-mails from the Dating Adult Friend line, and several dozen from a site called Adult Friend Finder. In addition, there were fourteen messages from someone calling himself Damian Dominques, who offered, repeatedly, to help me meet "delicious babes." I also received fairly unambiguous invitations for personal interaction from people named Antonia, Heather, Helen, Joyce, Olivia, Kelly, Sally, Sophie and Sue, among dozens of others.

Wading through dating-service spam is a minor inconvenience compared   4
to dealing with advertisements for products designed to help those dates succeed. I received 317 pieces of mail offering, through surgical, mechanical and above all, pharmaceutical means, to help "fatten" my "love muscle," as one of them put it. There were also several hundred solicitations for low- and no-interest car loans, automatic mortgage approvals, sleeping pills, dubious heart medicines, diet aids, gastric bypass surgery, contact lenses, air-conditioning systems, watches, online casinos, laptops, high-definition television sets, bootleg[1] software and jobs that promised to let me work at home, do practically nothing, and earn millions of dollars. In all, last month my three principal e-mail addresses pulled in 4,321 messages that went straight into various spam folders. Another hundred or so made it to my inbox.

As the Web evolves into an increasingly essential part of American life, the   5
sheer volume of spam grows exponentially every year, and so, it would appear, do the sophisticated methods used to send it. Nearly two million e-mails are dispatched every second, 171 billion messages a day. Most of those messages have something to sell. Even the most foolish and unsavory advertisements can earn money—in part because the economic bar for success is so low. If somebody wants to send you junk mail the old-fashioned way, through the United States Postal Service, he has to pay for it; the more he sends, the greater the expense. With electronic junk mail, the opposite is true: it costs a pittance[2] to send a million messages—or

[1] **bootleg:** Manufactured or distributed without legal permission.
[2] **pittance:** A very small amount.

even a billion—and recipients almost always spend more than the sender. (Assume that someone can unleash a hundred million spams from a twenty-dollar broadband account each month; at those rates, a penny would pay for fifty thousand pieces of mail.)

Spam's growth has been metastatic, both in raw numbers and as a per-   6 centage of all mail. In 2001, spam accounted for about five percent of the traffic on the Internet; by 2004, that figure had risen to more than seventy percent. This year, in some regions, it has edged above ninety percent— more than a hundred billion unsolicited messages clogging the arterial passages of the world's computer networks every day. The flow of spam is often seasonal. It slows in the spring, and then, in the month that technology specialists call "black September"—when hundreds of thousands of students return to college, many armed with new computers and access to fast Internet connections—the levels rise sharply.

Attempts to police the Internet have met with only partial success.   7 On May 23rd, the federal government indicted Robert Alan Soloway on thirty-five counts, including mail fraud, wire fraud, money laundering and aggravated identity theft. (He has pleaded not guilty.) In its indictment, the government contended that Soloway had sent out tens of millions of illegal e-mails in the past four years, seeking to drum up business for his Internet marketing firm. Federal agents described Soloway, a twenty-seven-year-old Seattle "entrepreneur," as the nation's spam king, and said that the arrest would have a major effect on the flow of unwanted e-mail. "Taking Soloway off the streets is terrific," I was told not long ago by Matt Sergeant, the chief anti-spam technologist at MessageLabs, one of the leaders in the growing industry dedicated to ridding the Internet of junk mail. "But turn on your computer tomorrow and see if you notice a difference. These guys are sophisticated and they are everywhere. Each time we think we have them, they respond with something new."

Spam seemed to vanish after the DEC incident of 1978. Throughout the   8 1980s, the Internet remained largely the province of academics, few of whom had any desire to see their network turned into a platform for virtual garage sales and dating services. But, driven by the rise of eBay, in the nineties, and other commercial applications, the Internet soon became more powerful than the people who had created it. The World Wide Web was conceived in an environment where trust was assumed and identity never doubted, and that openness has been among its greatest assets and its biggest flaws. The Internet permits individuals to act without supervision, permission or control. If you have the e-mail address, you can write directly to whomever you want; protocols and rules that have governed written communication for hundreds of years no longer apply. That absolute freedom makes cyberspace an ideal place to agitate for democracy in China, sell seventeenth-century carpets or blog about early music. Blending these new freedoms with any sense of order or discipline has proved nearly impossible, however, and so has virtually every attempt to contain the explosion of spam.

All e-mail includes simple information about where it is going and who   9
sent it. The mail is sorted along the way by routers—electronic devices that
connect networks—which have no way of verifying that you are who you
say you are. Most solutions for controlling spam would alter that practice,
placing significant limits on the free exchange of information. Even many
of those who fear that weak security is destroying the Internet are reluctant
to support measures that appear to limit free speech. The Electronic Frontier Foundation's chairman, Brad Templeton, has written frequently on the
history of spam. As his group put it in a recent white paper,[3] "One person's
spam is another's critical political update."

Under those circumstances, the emergence of spam in its modern   10
form—mass, anonymous, and often fraudulent—was inevitable. The on-
slaught apparently began on April 12, 1994, when two lawyers—Laurence
Canter and his wife, Martha Siegel—bombarded the Internet with e-mail
offering their services to immigrants seeking to remain permanently in
the United States. ("Green Card Lottery 1994 May Be The Last One!
THE DEADLINE HAS BEEN ANNOUNCED.") Millions of messages went out
within a few hours. The two were denounced, and their Internet-service
provider immediately revoked their accounts. The sanctions didn't much
matter. Canter and Siegel got what they wanted—more than a thousand
clients—and were soon back online, planning their next mailing. The two
later claimed that they made a hundred thousand dollars from the e-mail
campaign—a compelling demonstration of the peculiar economics of the
Internet. The couple embraced their notoriety and went on to write a book,
How to Make a Fortune on the Information Superhighway. It didn't take
long for thousands of others to try.

The original Spam (a contraction of "spiced ham") is made by the   11
Hormel Corporation, which sent enough cans of it overseas during the
Second World War to feed every G.I. In a celebrated 1970 Monty Python
skit, a diner tries repeatedly and in vain to order a dish, any dish, without Spam. She is drowned out by a group of Vikings in horned helmets,
who chant the word dozens of times—"Spam! Spam! Spam! Spam! Spam!
Spam! Spam! Spam!"—eliminating any possibility of rational thought. The
word was rapidly adopted by computer programmers as a verb meaning to
flood a chat room or a bulletin board with so much data that it crashes.

Definitions vary, as does the line between spam and annoying but legal   12
ads. (Like pornography, however, which has profited greatly from the ease
and privacy of electronic junk mail, you know it when you see it.) Few
companies could function without attempting to stop spam from invading their employees' in-boxes. The costs are not always easy to assess, but
several studies have found that in the United States more than ten billion
dollars is spent each year trying to contain spam. The success rate of such
anti-spam efforts usually exceeds ninety-five percent, but spam behaves on

[3] **white paper:** An authoritative report.

the Internet in much the same way that viruses do when they infect humans: it might take a million of them to attack an immune system before one gets through, but one is enough. The same is true of e-mail. The more spam that is blocked, the greater the volume spammers will need to send in order to make money. "If you used to have to send fifty thousand pieces of spam to get a response, now you have to send a million," John Scarrow, the general manager of anti-spam technologies at Microsoft, told me. (Spammers usually need to send a million e-mails to get fifteen positive responses; for the average direct-mail campaign, the response rate is three thousand per million.) "Spammers just shrug it off and send a million." That amount of e-mail can overwhelm servers and waste time, particularly for those who check their mail several times a day. (It takes at least five seconds to recognize and delete an e-mail. If a billion spam messages elude detection every day—which means that ninety-nine percent do not—that adds up to 159 years of collective time lost hitting the delete button every day.) Scarrow told me that of the four billion e-mails processed by Hotmail every day, they deliver only six hundred million. The rest are spam.

Hotmail is one of the world's largest providers of e-mail service, with 285   13 million registered accounts in more than two hundred countries. "We filter them all, and that takes huge amounts of computer processing power and Internet bandwidth, and it requires us to work constantly to keep the numbers from getting worse," Scarrow said. "We do this to minimize the impact on our customers, but it's a hell of a job." Microsoft maintains 130 thousand special Hotmail accounts specifically for the purpose of trapping and examining suspicious e-mail. Many function as "honeypots"—decoys that spammers think have been infected but will actually record the source's Internet address. Honeypots have no filters. "It is the raw Internet, 24/7," Scarrow said. "They will try absolutely everything. And it is often pretty raw."

In 2003, the federal government passed the Controlling the Assault of   14 Non-Solicited Pornography and Marketing Act, which is widely referred to as the CAN-SPAM Act. The law requires people who send e-mail advertisements to offer recipients the opportunity to decline future messages. It also mandates prison terms for violators. Early in 2004, motivated in part by the excitement of the new legislation—but also by the technology achievements of researchers and engineers—Bill Gates told a group of people attending the World Economic Forum, in Davos, Switzerland, "Two years from now, spam will be solved." The comment received a lot of attention, and, for a while at least, Gates's optimism seemed justified: the deluge seemed to slow. The new law established clear guidelines about what was legal, and several companies made aggressive attempts to catch and prosecute the most significant criminals. It began to cost spammers money to evade the law, and that made them wary—for a while. The act was not meant to stop spam—simply to regulate it. Even so, it has been widely seen as a disappointment. The law permits spammers to continue sending e-mails unless specifically asked to stop, and it allows them largely to dictate the steps necessary to avoid the messages.

In the year after the law was enacted, less than seven percent of spam   15
complied with the requirements of the legislation, according to MX Logic,
an Internet-security firm. Last year, compliance with the law never even
reached one percent. Corporate technology administrators watched, often
dumbfounded, as spam volumes jumped noticeably in October, and then
again in November. Postini, a prominent Internet-security firm, stopped
twenty-two billion messages from reaching the mailboxes of its thirty-six
thousand clients in November alone. The company now intercepts twelve
spam messages for every e-mail delivered. During 2006, the year by which
Gates predicted that spam would be "solved," it more than doubled in
volume compared with the previous year.

We now know why. Even as Congress was passing the CAN-SPAM Act,   16
spammers were changing their tactics. Until 2003, bulk e-mail had largely
followed the approach taken by conventional mass-market mail, offering
products like printing supplies and magazine subscriptions. It wasn't hard
to find out who the e-mail came from, and almost nobody lied about his
identity. Viruses were hardly unknown, but "it used to be all kiddies writing scripts in their bedrooms," Matt Sergeant, of MessageLabs, told me.
"In 2003, spammers started paying people to write viruses to take control
of home computers. The easy days were over." Viruses are actually tiny
software programs that exploit weaknesses in networks or computer operating systems like Windows. They find a way to burrow into a computer's
hard drive. That summer, a virus called Sobig infected millions of computers throughout the world. In a single day, MessageLabs intercepted a
million copies, and AOL stopped more than twenty-five million.

Sobig was the first commercial virus created by spammers designed spe-   17
cifically to infect machines, embed its code, and then turn those machines
into networks that could send millions of e-mails. Because the e-mails were
sent by innocent people who never knew that their computers were infected, the criminals were almost impossible to trace. Suddenly, spam had
created an industry: a netherworld[4] of hijacked PCs (called zombies or
slaves), linked together in rogue robot networks (or botnets) controlled by
underground bot herders, who operate from anywhere in the world. These
networks can unleash millions of pieces of mail in a few minutes; when
the botnets disband, the herders regroup and seize tens of thousands of
other computers. Even the cheapest machines now have enough processing
power to churn randomly through millions of address combinations until
they stumble on a few that are correct.

The increase in spam levels—nearly tenfold in the past three years—is   18
almost solely a result of botnets. Messages routinely carried viruses, many
of which were designed to evade traditional filters. It's not hard to do:
Many people use common, easily guessed passwords to protect their
wireless networks—and a surprising number don't use passwords at all.

[4] **netherworld:** Underworld.

Clicking on the wrong link at a Web address can also permit malicious software to install itself on a computer and force it to manufacture spam. This is called a "drive-by download." Once a computer virus invades, it will seek out any address book, sending copies of itself to every e-mail address it can find. Spammers today almost never use their own computers or Internet connections. It is rarely necessary, since they can seize control remotely from computers all around the world. "By the end of last year, spammers had taken over enough PCs that they could really do whatever they wanted with them," Sergeant said. "Half of the time, they are doing it on your computer and you wouldn't even have a clue."

Thomas Bayes was an eighteenth-century British clergyman and avid mathematician who became interested in probability. At the time, people had just begun to focus on the risks and rewards associated with the new field of insurance and actuarial statistics; Bayes developed a theorem that helped determine the probabilities behind the statistics. Bayesian reasoning, it turns out, can also be used to gauge the likelihood that an e-mail message is spam. Almost all defenses against spam rely on filters, which inspect words, phrases, the history of mail exchanges between the sender and the recipient, Internet-protocol (I.P.) addresses—unique numbers that are supposed to identify every computer—and other aspects of e-mail. The filters employ a series of complicated statistical methods to determine whether the message seems like spam. If an e-mail contains the words "free," "Viagra," and "herbal," for example, then the filter is likely to conclude that the message is spam. Naturally, filters make mistakes, and legitimate mail can end up in spam folders. False positives can pose a bigger problem than spam itself. "The one thing people do not want to see is genuinely important e-mail that doesn't make it to their inbox," Keith Coleman, the product manager for Google's Gmail, told me. "When that happens with any regularity, they lose their faith in e-mail completely." [19]

A spammer's job is to confound the filters. The spellings "V1agra" or "Vi-agr@" mean nothing to a machine, but almost any human reader gets the point. In 2002, the programmer Paul Graham wrote an essay called "A Plan for Spam," which became an intellectual manifesto[5] for the thousands of researchers trying to find a way to clean up the Internet. "I think it's possible to stop spam, and that content-based filters are the way to do it," he wrote. "The Achilles' heel[6] of the spammers is their message. They can circumvent any other barrier you set up. But they have to deliver their message, whatever it is. There is no way they can get around that." [20]

Graham compared every character—dashes, apostrophes, numbers, symbols—in thousands of genuine e-mails with those in thousands of pieces of spam. He was able to train his software to use the context of a [21]

---

[5] **manifesto:** A public, written statement of one's views.
[6] **Achilles' heel:** A spot at which a person is vulnerable; Achilles was a Greek hero who could be wounded only in his heel.

message to guess how likely it was that an e-mail containing certain words in relation to each other was spam. The words "republic" and "madam" seem innocent enough, but when they appear together in an e-mail they are often from a Nigerian huckster who has addressed his e-mail "Dear Sir or Madam." Mail like that is invariably spam.

As filters become more sophisticated, spam becomes more elusive. 22 There are millions of ways to write a word using punctuation, numbers and other symbols. One mathematically minded blogger who looked into it found that there are 600,426,974,379,824,381,952 ways to spell Viagra. "If I thought that I could keep up current rates of spam filtering, I would consider this problem solved," Graham wrote. "But it doesn't mean much to be able to filter out most present-day spam, because spam evolves." Indeed, most anti-spam techniques so far have been like pesticides that do nothing other than create a more resistant strain of bugs.

It has never been easy to devise a way to sort the mail we want from the 23 mail we don't want. Some software attempts to analyze the reputation of the sender. Has its domain sent spam before? Is its I.P. address legitimate? The most common approach is to create a fingerprint for spam, using software that assigns numeric values to different words and patterns it sees in an e-mail. These methods worked for a while, and then the arms race kicked in. The battle has moved this way for years: spam eludes filters, engineers improve the software. Each parry has been met by a new thrust. There are now blacklists, gray lists and white lists, which permit people to choose whom they want to receive mail from, rather than whose mail to delete.

Stopping spam this way is a bit like trying to stop the rain by catching 24 every drop before it hits the ground. The Internet itself is always available to help an aspiring spammer. There are many sites, and they are neither concealed nor subtle. There are spam supermarkets, online forums, often hosted in China or Russia, with names like specialham.com and spamforum .biz. When one is shut down, another pops up instantly. One site, send-safe .com, advertises an entire range of software packages. There is, for instance, "send-safe honeypot hunter," which is designed to help people determine whether a fake computer is on the other end of their message. The most basic program is called "send-safe mailer," software that promises to "make it impossible for anyone to trace the e-mail back to your ISP. . . . This gives you a safe haven in which to send your mail." The program, which you can buy on the Internet after a free trial, costs about seventy dollars. (One Russian Web site sells a kit called Web-attacker, which contains scripts that simplify the task of infecting computers. It can be downloaded for about twenty dollars.) "You can get into the business without being technical at all," Brad Taylor, the spam czar[7] at Google, told me. "You buy your spamming program and your spamming network. You obtain a list of mailing addresses. Anyone can do this in an hour. Then you put them all together and set up a Web site or go to a service provider. You can buy a server for

[7] **czar**: A leader; from the Russian word for *emperor*.

a few hundred dollars and spam from that. Usually, the provider will shut you down quickly and you will be blacklisted. But then you move on to the next." Among the systems that have been infected by networks of remote computers in the past two years were computers at the weapons division of the United States Naval Air Warfare Center and many machines operated by the Department of Defense.

Spam is one of globalization's true success stories. Servers can operate   25 from anywhere, and spam gangs sell lists of "fresh proxies" (newly infected PCs), offer "bullet-proof hosting" (spam service Web sites, often based in China), and advise each other on new spam techniques and on which networks are "spam-friendly" (those which will host spammers in exchange for the spammers' paying for high-priced services they don't need). These days, many of the world's most prodigious and talented spammers are hidden in Eastern Europe and Russia, where, despite increasingly vigorous efforts, the F.B.I. and other international law-enforcement agencies have little genuine authority. Half the time, nobody even knows their real names. Spamhaus, an organization that tracks spammers and protects networks, keeps a list of the world's biggest spam operators, and many of the best of them go by obvious pseudonyms, like the Ukrainian spammer who calls himself, variously, Alex Blood, Alexander Mosh, AlekseyB and Alex Polyakov. For a while, people thought that his actual name might have been Polyakov and that he was in Moscow, where they hunted him aggressively. But the name seemed familiar, and one day somebody remembered why: Alex Polyakov was the name of a Soviet operative in *Tinker, Tailor, Soldier, Spy*.

Last year, spammers began to take advantage of the fact that computers   26 can't see and buried their messages in images. Most filters look for words and phrases or Internet address information. A picture contains so much more data that it is hard for the computer to find the message embedded in all the noise. Humans who click on the message have no trouble seeing it, though. Image spam consumes far more bandwidth than written messages, and that means it will devour even more space on computer servers throughout the world, costing more money and wasting more time. But spammers aren't stopping there. They are learning to send out polymorphic spam, thousands of variations of the same message, which makes each message unique and therefore hard to categorize.

In May, death-threat spam began to appear. The message comes from a   27 "hit man" hired to kill the recipient. "I have been hired to assassinate you," the mail typically begins. "I do not know why they want you dead, but you are now being watched." Any user scared or gullible enough to respond will be asked to wire money to save his life. The amount varies.

When I asked Brad Taylor why he had gone into this line of work, he   28 said, "I remember my first spam. I don't remember what they were selling. It was 1994, I think, and I was so annoyed that I found out who that person's Internet provider was and reported him. I began spending the first hour of every day tracking these people down. And I felt so good about doing that.

But soon it got to the point where I was getting twenty of these e-mails a day. Then thirty. At one point, I just gave up.

"But I wanted to fix the problem and return to the bliss that existed   29
before spam," he said. "Often the fight is fun, like a game. But last year there were some low points. We started getting these image spams, and the spammer would adapt to anything we did. He would write software that cut the image into little pieces that reassembled by the time you opened your mail. When we figured out how to deal with that, he started making text that waved around and curved in odd ways. So we figured that out. Then he started with random images." Taylor laughed. "This went on for a while. But, finally, he just gave up. And that's our hope. It's kind of like war. One side eventually gets tired. And we just can't let it be us."

EXERCISING VOCABULARY

1. Record your own definition for each word below in your notebook.

flagrant (adj.) (2)	notoriety (n.) (10)
deployed (v.) (2)	elude (v.) (12)
dubious (adj.) (4)	decoys (n.) (13)
exponentially (adv.) (5)	deluge (n.) (14)
unsavory (adj.) (5)	malicious (adj.) (18)
fraudulent (adj.) (10)	circumvent (v.) (20)
denounced (v.) (10)	prodigious (adj.) (25)

2. In paragraph 6, Specter writes that "spam's growth has been metastatic" and that spam is "clogging the arterial passages of the world's computer networks." Explain these references. How does this use of figurative language contribute to the author's purpose in this essay?

3. Explain the origin of the word *spam*. What is its historical significance? What does the word mean to computer programmers?

4. In paragraph 18, Specter explains a "drive-by download." What does this term mean? With what activity is the term *drive-by* usually associated? What does Specter accomplish by associating spam with drive-bys?

PROBING CONTENT

1. Discuss how and by whom spam was created. What was the purpose of spam? How effective was this method?

2. How many e-mails are sent each second? How many are sent per day? What is the purpose of most of these spam e-mails?

3. What factors have made it difficult to control the proliferation of spam? Why is the flow of spam somewhat seasonal?

4. What is the CAN-SPAM Act? What are its primary provisions and limitations?

CONSIDERING CRAFT

1. Who originally said, "One small step for a man"? What was the occasion? What point is the author making by including this quotation in the first paragraph?

2. Specter begins paragraph 24 with figurative language. What type of figurative language does he employ? How does this language express his feelings about spam?

3. In this essay, what is Specter's own position with regard to spam? Cite specific lines of text to support your response. What does the author achieve by maintaining this stance toward his subject?

4. In describing the exchanges between spam and spam-filtering software, Specter writes, "Each parry has been met by a new thrust" (para. 23). With what activity are the nouns *parry* and *thrust* usually associated? How does using them here affect how the reader views the interaction between spammers and those who develop software to control spam?

WRITING PROMPTS

Responding to the Topic   How much of a nuisance is spam to you personally? What steps are you willing to take to eliminate it? Interview five friends and ask them their opinions on these questions. Then write an essay summarizing your attitude and theirs about spam.

Responding to the Writer   Just how free should the Internet be? Write an essay in which you take and defend a position about Internet restrictions—including restrictions on content, frequency of transmissions, spam, blocked sites, and other areas of potential limitations.

Responding to Multiple Viewpoints   How would Jay Chiat ("Illusions Are Forever") have felt about Specter's concerns about spam? How would Chiat have responded to Specter's suggestions about how to deal with spam? Cite text from both essays to support your response.

For a quiz on this reading, go to bedfordstmartins.com/mirror.

You've Got Spam

ANALYZING THE IMAGE

Are you deluged daily with junk mail of both the snail mail and "damn spam" varieties? What would you like to do with all that mail? In the original digital illustration by Ned Shaw, the bright blue mailbox with its red "In" flag is set against a blue sky with a white cloud. The artist's vision adds some humor to what many consider a not-so-funny situation.

1. What is unique about this mailbox?

2. Describe in detail the kind of mail that is pouring out of the box.

3. What do the little creatures symbolize? What is significant about their positions and the looks on their faces?

4. What is the message of this visual? Why did red, white, and blue figure so prominently in the original?

The Ultimate Marketing Machine

From *The Economist*

Founded in 1843, *The Economist* is a weekly magazine of news and international affairs, based in London. Unlike other selections in this book, you will notice that this one does not have a credited author. *The Economist* is written anonymously, according to its editor, "because it is a paper whose collective voice and personality matter more than the identities of individual journalists." What do you think about this approach? The following essay, "The Ultimate Marketing Machine," appeared in 2006. It chronicles the impact of the Internet on the ways in which advertisers sell their products.

> **THINKING AHEAD** Think about all the different ways advertising is used on the Internet. How much influence does the Web have on your buying habits? What items have you bought online? Why did you choose to buy these items online?

In terms of efficiency, if not size, the advertising industry is only now start- 1
ing to grow out of its century-long infancy, which might be called "the Wanamaker era." It was John Wanamaker, a devoutly Christian merchant from Philadelphia, who in the 1870s not only invented department stores and price tags (to eliminate haggling, since everybody should be equal before God and price), but also became the first modern advertiser when he bought space in newspapers to promote his stores. He went about it in a Christian way, neither advertising on Sundays nor fibbing (thus minting the concept of "truth in advertising"). And, with his precise business mind, he expounded a witticism that has ever since seemed like an economic law: "Half the money I spend on advertising is wasted," he said. "The trouble is, I don't know which half."

Wanamaker's wasted half is not entirely proverbial. The worldwide 2
advertising industry is likely to be worth $428 billion in revenues this year, according to ZenithOptimedia, a market-research firm. Greg Stuart, the author of a forthcoming book on the industry and the boss of the Interactive Advertising Bureau, a trade association, estimates that advertisers waste — that is, they send messages that reach the wrong audience or none at all — $112 billion a year in America and $220 billion worldwide, or just over half of their total spending. Wanamaker was remarkably accurate.

What Wanamaker could not have foreseen, however, was the Internet. 3
A bevy[1] of entrepreneurial firms — from Google, the world's most valuable

---

[1]**bevy:** A large grouping.

online advertising agency disguised as a Web-search engine, to tiny Silicon Valley upstarts, many of them only months old—are now selling advertisers new tools to reduce waste. These come in many exotic forms, but they have one thing in common: a desire to replace the old approach to advertising, in which advertisers pay for the privilege of "exposing" a theoretical audience to their message, with one in which advertisers pay only for real and measurable actions by consumers, such as clicking on a Web link, sharing a video, placing a call, printing a coupon or buying something.

Rishad Tobaccowala, the "chief innovation officer" of Publicis, one of   4
the world's biggest advertising groups, and boss of Denuo, a Chicago-based unit within Publicis with the job of probing the limits of new advertising models, likens traditional Wanamaker-era advertising to "an atom bomb dropped on a big city." The best example is the thirty-second spot on broadcast television. An independent firm (such as Nielsen, in America) estimates how many television sets are tuned to a given channel at a given time. Advertisers then pay a rate, called CPM (cost per thousand), for the right to expose the implied audience to their spot. If Nielsen estimates that, say, one million people ("the city") are watching a show, an advertiser paying a CPM of $20 would fork out $20,000 for his commercial ("the atom bomb").

Gone for a Brew

The problem is obvious. The television room may be empty. Its owners may   5
have gone to the kitchen to make a cup of tea or to the toilet. They may have switched channels during the commercial break, be napping or talking on the telephone. The viewer may be a teenaged girl, even though the advertisement promotes Viagra. It might even be a TiVo or other such device that records the show so that the owner can watch it later and skip through the commercials. Parks Associates, a consumer-technology consultancy, estimates that ten million American households already have a digital video recorder.

"Segmentation," an advertising trend during the past two decades tied   6
to fragmentation in the media, represents only a cosmetic change, thinks Mr. Tobaccowala. Advertisers airing a spot on a niche channel on cable television, for example, might be able to make more educated guesses about the audience (in their thirties, gay and affluent, say), but they are still paying a CPM rate in order blindly to cast a message in a general direction. Instead of atom bombs on cities, says Mr. Tobaccowala, segmentation is at best "dropping conventional bombs on villages." The collateral damage is still considerable.

By contrast, the new advertising models based on Internet technologies   7
amount to innovation. Instead of bombs, says Mr. Tobaccowala, advertisers now "make lots of spearheads and then get people to impale themselves." The idea is based on consumers themselves taking the initiative by showing up voluntarily and interacting with what they find online.

In its simplest form, this involves querying a search engine with keywords   8
("used cars," say), then scanning the search results, as well as the sponsored

links from advertisers, and then clicking on one such link. In effect, the consumer has expressed an intention twice (first with his query, then with his click). The average cost to an advertiser from one such combination is 50 cents, which corresponds to a CPM of $500; by contrast, the average CPM in traditional ("exposure") media is $20. A consumer's action, in other words, is twenty-five times as valuable as his exposure.

The person who deserves more credit than anybody else for this insight is Bill Gross, an Internet entrepreneur with a kinetic mind and frenetic speech who in 1996 started Idealab, a sort of factory for inventions. One of the companies to come out of his factory was GoTo.com, later renamed Overture, which pioneered the market for "paid search" or "pay-per-click" advertising. In 2001 Mr. Gross ran into Sergey Brin and Larry Page, the young co-founders of Google, a search engine that was just then becoming popular, but still had no way of making money. He offered them a partnership or merger, but Messrs[2] Brin and Page were purists at the time about not diluting the integrity of their search results with commercialism and they turned him down.

Within a year, however, Messrs Brin and Page changed their minds and came up with AdWords, a system based on Overture's idea of putting advertising links next to relevant search results and charging only for clicks (but with the added twist that advertisers could bid for keywords in an online auction). Google soon added AdSense, a system that goes beyond search-results pages and places "sponsored" (i.e., advertising) links on the Web pages of newspapers and other publishers that sign up to be part of Google's network. Like AdWords, these AdSense advertisements are "contextual"—relevant to the Web page's content—and the advertiser pays for them only when a Web surfer clicks. Together, AdWords and AdSense produced $6.1 billion in revenues for Google last year.

Because this advertising model is so lucrative, all Internet portals want to catch up with Google. In 2003 Yahoo!, the largest media property on the Web, bought Overture from Mr. Gross for $1.6 billion. Yahoo! then dropped the technology it had been licensing from Google. Then Microsoft, which owns MSN, another large Internet portal, built adCenter, its version of a "monetization engine," which has now replaced Yahoo! as the advertising system for searches on MSN. In addition, eBay, the largest auction site on the Web, has a version called AdContext. Pay-per-click advertising is not without its problems—especially "click fraud," the practice of generating bogus clicks for devious reasons, such as making a rival advertiser pay for nothing. Nonetheless, pay-per-click remains much more efficient than traditional marketing for many advertisers. It is the fastest-growing segment of the online advertising market.

Some companies are already exploring other methods of charging advertisers for consumers' actions. Mike Hogan, the boss of ZiXXo, a

[2]**Messrs:** The plural form of *Mr.*; from the French *messieurs*.

start-up near San Francisco, says that he is "disrupting the existing coupon system," dominated by companies such as Valpak and Valassis in America. Some 335 billion coupons were distributed in America last year—priced, like other traditional media, in CPM—but only 4.5 billion were redeemed, which amounts to a "Wanamaker waste" of almost 99 percent. ZiXXo, by contrast, lets advertisers issue coupons online and places them on search results, online maps and other such places, but charges advertisers only when a consumer prints one out (50 cents per coupon from next year), thus expressing an intent to redeem it.

As ZiXXo is pioneering "pay-per-print" advertising, Ingenio, another 13
San Francisco firm, is betting on "pay-per-call." Instead of coupons, it places toll-free telephone numbers on local-search pages—its biggest partner is AOL—and charges advertisers only when they receive a live call from a consumer. This is especially popular among accountants, lawyers, plumbers and other service providers who find it easier to close a deal on the telephone. EBay is planning to sell pay-per-call advertising on a larger scale, by placing little buttons from Skype, an Internet-telephony firm it bought last year, on its own Web pages and perhaps those of others, so that consumers can talk with a seller after just a single click.

Meanwhile, Mr. Gross, almost famous from his first innovation (and not 14
at all bitter that Google got most of the credit), is once again busy pursuing what he considers the "Holy Grail" of advertising—the complete elimination of Wanamaker waste. He calls this cost-per-action, or CPA, although he means cost-per-sale, and says that it "just makes too much sense" not to catch on. His start-up this time is called Snap.com, a small search engine. An airline, say, that advertises on Snap's search results would pay not when a consumer clicks on its link but only when he buys a ticket. Google, which is researching almost all conceivable advertising methods, also has plans for CPA. Its new Google Checkout, an online payments system set up to rival eBay's PayPal, will allow Google to know more about how many users who click on one of its advertisements subsequently go on to complete a purchase.

Branded

If the Internet enables such snazzy performance-based advertising methods, it 15
is also sparking a renaissance[3] in branded advertising. Some products—such as mortgages—might conceivably be sold entirely through performance-based marketing one day, says Mr. Stuart at the Interactive Advertising Bureau, but many other products—such as cars, cosmetics and alcohol—will probably always require branding as well. Even when consumers start their shopping research on a search engine, they still see several competing sponsored links,

[3]**renaissance:** A rebirth; a new beginning.

and may be swayed by their previous brand exposure in deciding which one of these links to click on. And in the "offline" world, brands are still "the ultimate navigation device," says Mr. Tobaccowala at Denuo, and often determine which door a tired traveler far away from home walks through.

Brand advertising is inherently about leaving an impression on a con- 16 sumer, and thus about some sort of exposure. On the Internet, however, an exposure can also be tied to an action by a consumer, and these actions can be counted, tracked and analyzed in ways that exposure in the established mass media cannot. Consumers also tend to be more alert on the Internet. Whereas people might watch a television show in a semi-comatose state of mind and at obtuse angles on their couches, consumers typically surf the Web leaning forward while "paying attention to the screen," says Mr. Stuart.

A good example is video games, which increasingly take place online 17 and involve thousands or millions of other players. Companies such as Massive and Double Fusion are already placing two-dimensional brand advertisements into games. A player moving through the streets of New York to kill something or other might see a DHL truck or a billboard. "But the future is intelligent three-dimensional ads" and "ads with be-havior," says Jonathan Epstein, Double Fusion's boss. For instance, his technology will soon allow Coca-Cola to place a Coke can into a game, where it fizzes when a player walks by and might give him certain pow-ers if he picks it up. If a character uses a mobile phone inside a game, the technology can swap the brand and model of the phone depending on which country the player is in. But the most important aspect of the tech-nology, says Mr. Epstein, is that it will track exactly how long the player uses the phone, thus leaving no doubt about whether an "impression" had indeed been made.

Propagating the Message

That same transparency is now coming to "viral" marketing. Kontraband, 18 a firm in London, takes funny, bizarre, conspiratorial or otherwise interest-ing video clips from its clients and places them on its own site and on popu-lar video-sharing sites such as YouTube.com or Google Video. The hope in viral marketing is to create something that is so much fun that it will propagate by itself, as people e-mail it to each other or put the Web link on their blogs. This means that a pure "cost-per-feed" system is out of the question, says Richard Spalding, Kontraband's co-founder, since a success-ful viral campaign "that gets out of hand and is watched by millions would run the client out of business." So Kontraband charges a flat fee based on a hoped-for audience, leaving the client with the economic upside if the real audience turns out to be larger. The important point, says Mr. Spalding, is once again that the "sprites" (i.e., bits of software) inside the video let Kontraband track exactly how many times a video is viewed and where, so that clients can see neat pie charts that summarize their success.

Understandably, this strange and thrilling online world can be unsettling 19 to the old hands of the advertising industry, whether they are marketing bosses for advertisers or intermediaries at the agencies. "All of us have been classically trained, and now we're in a jazz age," says Mr. Tobaccowala. Advertisers and their agents, he recalls, have already changed their minds about the Internet twice. During the technology boom of the late 1990s, he says, the general outcry was, "Oh my God, I need a dotcom[4] unit." When the boom turned to bust at the beginning of this decade, he says, there was a sigh of relief ("See, the Internet is not for real."), and it suddenly seemed as though only those who did not "get it" still had jobs.

This was a mistake, says Mr. Tobaccowala, since the skeptics confused 20 the performance of the NASDAQ and the fate of individual dotcoms with genuine changes in consumer behavior. In the consumer-driven market for classified advertising, for instance, ordinary people instinctively grasped the efficiencies of online sites such as Craigslist, thus causing a drop in classified revenues at newspapers. The large advertisers stayed more conservative, however, which may explain why the Internet-advertising market is still disproportionately small. The Online Publishers Association, a trade group, estimates that all Web advertising in America came to about 6 percent of total advertising expenditures last year, even though consumers spent 23 percent of their media time online.

Now, however, chief executives are taking trips to Silicon Valley, often 21 without their "chief marketing officers," to educate themselves. And what they hear impresses them. Tim Armstrong, Google's advertising boss in North America, preaches to his clients a "notion of asset management" for their products that "shocks" them. Traditionally, he says, most firms would advertise only 5 percent to 10 percent of their wares—the blockbusters—in the mass media to publicize their brand, hoping that it shines a halo on the remainder of their products. Now, however, "companies market each individual product in that big digital stream," says Mr. Armstrong, from the best seller to the tiniest toothbrush. This is called exploiting the economics of the "long tail."

They do this, first, because the Internet, in effect, eliminates scarcity 22 in the medium. There are as many Web pages for advertisers as there are keywords that can be typed into a search engine, situations that game players might find themselves in, and so forth. Each one comes with its own context, and almost every context suits some product. The second reason is that if you can track the success of advertising, especially if you can follow sales leads, then marketing ceases to be just a cost-center, with an arbitrary budget allocated to it. Instead, advertising becomes a variable cost of production that measurably results in making more profit.

This often leads to more subtle changes in the way that advertisers think 23 about their craft, says Mr. Armstrong. In the traditional media, he says,

---

[4] **dotcom:** Companies whose business focuses on the Internet.

advertisers are always "trying to block the stream of information to the user" in order to "blast their message" to him. That quickly gets annoying and turns consumers off. In American prime-time television, advertising interruptions added up to eighteen minutes an hour last year, up from thirteen minutes an hour in 1992, according to Parks Associates. On the Internet, by contrast, advertisers have no choice but to "go with the user," says Mr. Armstrong, and "the information coming back from the users is more important than the messages going out."

For consumers this may turn out to be the biggest change. The kids in 24
"Generation Y," "echo-boomers" and "millennials"—young people who tend to be adept at using media, constantly online and skeptical—are increasingly immune to the clichés of prime-time television and radio and mentally tune out these nuisances. Online, however, they may accept advertising if it is unobtrusive, relevant and fun. Insofar as they took some action to invite the advertisement, they may even find it useful. And this, aptly enough, is a consumer reaction that John Wanamaker would have expected all along.

EXERCISING VOCABULARY

1. Record your own definition for each word below in your notebook.

fibbing (v.) (1)	frenetic (adj.) (9)
witticism (n.) (1)	purist (adj.) (9)
proverbial (adj.) (2)	diluting (v.) (9)
entrepreneurial (adj.) (3)	lucrative (adj.) (11)
affluent (adj.) (6)	propagating (v.) (header between 17 and 18)
niche (adj.) (6)	intermediaries (n.) (19)
querying (v.) (8)	adept (adj.) (24)
kinetic (adj.) (9)	

2. In paragraph 14, the essay mentions what Bill Gross considers to be "the 'Holy Grail' of advertising." What is the Holy Grail? Who sought it? Why was it considered so valuable?

3. The essay tells us that the "viral" marketing firm Kontraband "takes funny, bizarre, conspiratorial or otherwise interesting video clips from its clients and places them on its own site and on popular video-sharing sites such as YouTube.com or Google Video" (para. 18). What is a conspiracy? With what sorts of people or groups do you associate the word *conspiracy*? What does it mean to be conspiratorial? How can a video clip be conspiratorial?

4. In the final paragraph, the essay states that "Generation Y" young people are "increasingly immune to the clichés of prime-time television and radio." What does it mean to be immune to a disease? How can one be immune to a cliché?

PROBING CONTENT

1. Who was John Wanamaker? What does the essay call "the Wanamaker era" of advertising?

2. Who is Bill Gross? For what idea is he responsible? How has his idea changed advertising?

3. What is viral marketing? How does it work? Why is it important?

4. According to the essay, what is the essential difference between television and radio advertising and online advertising? Why is this difference important to the members of "Generation Y"?

CONSIDERING CRAFT

1. This essay contains many facts and figures. How does their inclusion affect your reading?

2. In paragraphs 6 and 7, the essay quotes Rishad Tobaccowala, who uses militaristic metaphors to compare traditional television and radio advertising with online advertising. Explain the figures of speech and how these metaphors affect your reading?

3. In paragraph 1 Tim Armstrong says, "most firms would advertise only 5 percent to 10 percent of their wares—the blockbusters— in the mass media to publicize their brand, hoping that it shines a halo on the remainder of their products." With whom do we associate halos? What then does the metaphor "shines a halo" mean?

WRITING PROMPTS

Responding to the Topic   Write an essay in which you detail your online shopping activity. Consider the following questions: How often do you shop online? Why or why not do you shop online? Is security an issue for you? How aware of on line advertising are you? Use specific examples in your paper.

Responding to the Writer   Write an essay in which you agree or disagree with the article's argument that members of "Generation Y" will increasingly use Internet advertising and "may even find it useful." Provide numerous examples to prove your thesis.

Responding to Multiple Viewpoints   "The Ultimate Marketing Machine" claims that advertising can be "fun" (para. 24). Would authors such as Delia Cleveland, Jay Chiat, or Meghan O'Rourke agree? Consider their varying opinions on this subject as you consider this claim. Then write an essay in which you comment on the role that "fun" plays in advertising. Provide specific examples.

For a quiz on this reading, go to bedfordstmartins.com/mirror.

Taking Cadillac from Stodgy to Sexy: Kate Walsh

Bob Garfield

Bob Garfield is a media critic who writes a regular column about TV commercials for the magazine *Advertising Age*. He also hosts the Peabody Award–winning show *On the Media*, which is produced and broadcast by National Public Radio. He has published two books of his writing, *Waking Up Screaming from the American Dream* (Scribner, 1997) and his manifesto on advertising, *And Now a Few Words from Me* (McGraw-Hill, 2003). His writing has also appeared in *Wired*, *Sports Illustrated*, and the *New York Times*. He is currently writing his third book, *Listenomics*, on his blog at AdAge.com. In the following article, which was first posted in 2007, Garfield discusses the efforts to rebrand Cadillac as young and sexy.

> **THINKING AHEAD** Think about the role advertising has played in your own car-buying experience or that of a friend or family member. To what extent have print, television, or online ads influenced you or someone close to you?

adillac . . . sexy? 1

That should be a laugh line. For most of the past forty years, Cadil- 2 lac has more or less been synonymous with white-belted retirees driving at thirty-nine mph to get their prostates checked. By the 1970s, the once-proud luxury brand, the erstwhile[1] mark of wealth and achievement, had devolved into a sofa on wheels.

Then it became a Chevy with fancy trim. Then it became a non-factor 3 in the luxury car market, holding cachet[2] only for extremely aggressive Mary Kay distributors and the near dead.

But then GM set about designing a stylish car worthy of the already 4 impressive Northstar engine and in 2003 introduced a boldly faceted CTS, a midsize sedan trapped in a stealth fighter's[3] body. It turned heads appropriately, showed up in *Matrix Reloaded* and benefited from a fair amount of buzz.

It did not, however, turn the brand around. 5

This had something to do with Leo Burnett's unexceptional advertising 6 and something to do with accrued bad will. Since then, in classic GM fashion,

---

[1]**erstwhile:** Former; previous.
[2]**cachet:** Superior status; prestige.
[3]**stealth fighter:** A sleek fighter plane that is difficult to detect on radar.

the glacial product cycle killed off whatever buzz momentum Cadillac briefly enjoyed and, as the 2008 model year commences, it's back at square one.

But wait. The CTS has been thoroughly redesigned. It's a gorgeous little   7
rocket that could have exactly the halo effect GM is looking for, provided anybody ever notices the introduction. And, count on one thing: They will. New TV spots from Modernista, Boston, are eye-catching, ear-catching, informative, cerebral and—dare we say?—pretty freakin' sexy.

This owes partly to the celebrity talent—notably Kate Walsh from   8
Grey's Anatomy. We want her to have our children. No, really. We have three children, and she can have all of them if she'll just read copy for us—any copy: cat food, industrial boilers, HeadOn, anything—the way she reads her Cadillac lines:

"In today's luxury game, the question isn't whether or not your car   9
has available features like a forty-gig hard drive. It isn't about sun roofs or Sapelli wood accents, popup nav screens or any of that. No, the real question is: When you turn your car on, *does it return the favor*?" The italics are mine, because the printed word falls here. You need to hear her voice. Walsh sounds a little bored, her words slightly slurred, as if she were two pomegranate martinis into the evening but with her wits totally about her.

For instance, though she first dismisses the significance of luxury-car   10
features per se, she still manages to list the highlights. And they're duly registered—right up to where she mentions erotic stimulation and floors the gas pedal in her high-heeled sandal.

Sure enough, suddenly the GPS system doesn't seem to matter. And pros-   11
tate patients everywhere feel hope. (And so will women, who are sure to see this brazen foxiness as empowering—and maybe more than that. . . .)

Another spot, featuring Martin Henderson from *Smokin' Aces*, is one of   12
two that dares BMW and Lexus prospects to get out of lockstep: "You can practice risk avoidance. You can aspire to blend in quietly. You can live in, drive and wear social camouflage. And you can believe in the philosophy that the nail that sticks out gets hammered down. Or you can be the hammer."

Iconoclasm,[4] of course, is often the last refuge of a marginal brand.   13
But this is a three hundred-horsepower variant, not merely challenging conformists but enticing them and playing to their vanity. It doesn't hurt, either, that the car looks just plain . . . sexy.

EXERCISING VOCABULARY

1. Record your own definition for each word below in your notebook.

stodgy (adj.) (title)	faceted (adj.) (4)
synonymous (adj.) (2)	accrued (adj.) (6)
devolved (v.) (2)	cerebral (adj.) (7)

---

[4]**iconoclasm:** The destruction of cherished beliefs or traditional institutions.

2. What is the literal translation of the Latin phrase *per se*? What does it mean in paragraph 10?

3. Garfield writes that the new CTS ads dare "BMW and Lexus prospects to get out of lockstep" (para. 12). What is a lockstep? What does the author mean here?

4. In paragraph 12, Garfield quotes the CTS ads: "you can believe in the philosophy that the nail that sticks out gets hammered down. Or you can be the hammer." What does the expression "the nail that sticks out gets hammered down" mean? What then is the ad implying about the new Cadillac CTS?

PROBING CONTENT

1. For the past four decades, what has been the image of the Cadillac? Why?

2. How has that image changed with the introduction of the 2008 CTS model?

3. Why has the new advertising campaign for the CTS been so successful? Which two celebrities have been featured in this campaign?

CONSIDERING CRAFT

1. Examine Garfield's use of humor in his essay. Find two examples and comment on their effectiveness.

2. The author makes extensive use of figurative language throughout the essay. Locate three examples and explain their effect.

3. In paragraph 9, Garfield quotes from the ad copy. How does this quotation affect your reading?

4. Reread the opening and closing paragraphs of the essay. Which word does the author repeat? Why?

WRITING PROMPTS

Responding to the Topic   To what extent are celebrity endorsers responsible for your personal buying habits? Think about advertisements (print, radio, television, or online advertisements, or even product placement in films) that feature celebrities. Using specific examples, write an essay in which you consider the effect of celebrity endorsement on your own buying decisions.

Responding to the Writer   We all know the saying "Sex sells." But can advertising be too sexy? Write an essay in which you take a stand on this issue. Make sure that you use specific examples.

Responding to Multiple Viewpoints   What might the marketers of Crocs learn from the advertising executives at Modernista, the Boston agency whose new television spots have breathed new life and sex appeal into the Cadillac? Write an essay in which you speculate whether the "ugly duckling distinctiveness" ("The Croc Epidemic," para. 12) of Crocs could—or should—make a transition similar to the one Cadillac has made, from a stodgy "sofa on wheels" ("Taking Cadillac from Stodgy to Sexy," para. 2) to a sexy "little rocket" (para. 7).

For a quiz on this reading, go to bedfordstmartins.com/mirror.

Wrapping Up Chapter 6

Focusing on Yesterday, Focusing on Today

"Let's see. . . . Gossip magazines, dark chocolate, Italian shoes, definitely a Kansas City ribeye, and pulling up to the boys' club in one of these. These are just a few of my favorite things."

These lines are delivered by Kate Walsh, beautiful star of *Grey's Anatomy* and *Private Practice*, in one of her sexy television ads for the Cadillac CTS. Walsh smiles coyly as she pulls her $40,000 red sports car alongside a shiny black car driven by two attractive young men wearing suits. As the light turns green, she floors it and leaves them in the dust. As the advertisement comes to a close, we see the red, blue, and gold Cadillac symbol and slogan, which reads, "Life, Liberty, and the Pursuit."

You Could Guess What Car She Came In!

The pursuit of what? Where have you heard those words before? What is the star of this TV ad pursuing? Even though Walsh hasn't reached her destination, it's obvious she's arrived.

And so have the two women in these magazine advertisements, one from a 1958 American magazine ad for Cadillac, and the other from a recent British ad for Rover. The 1950s advertisement, like the TV spot, also features a red car and a woman in white. Even though they are not the only people in the ads, the spotlight is focused squarely on them. They know where they're going, they know what they want, and no one will get in their way.

- Describe the women in each ad. How are they similar? How are they different? Note their expressions, body language, clothing, accessories, and surroundings.

- How does the setting affect your reading of each advertisement? What message does it convey?

- What other people or animals appear in the ads? What is their purpose?

- How does the text—or lack thereof—affect the effectiveness of these ads?

- What message is each advertiser trying to send? What are the ads selling besides automobiles?

- Who makes up the target audiences for the ads? Consider demographics such as age, gender, socioeconomic level, and ethnicity.

She's Arrived!

CONNECTING TO THE CULTURE

1. Locate at least five different ads that try to sell products or fashions by using the same hook. Consider sex, celebrities, unusual art, shock value, children, or animals as possible hooks. Analyze each ad and explain how the same advertising angle is used differently to sell each product or brand. Explore the real message each ad sends to consumers. Review Chapter 2, "Deconstructing Media: Analyzing an Image", to help you organize your essay.

2. Choose one group of people (for example, Latinos, the elderly, teenagers, women, parents, gay people, or African Americans) and develop a hypothesis about how they are portrayed in advertising. Then go to magazines, television, or the Internet to locate ads featuring that group. If the evidence you find supports your hypothesis, you have a thesis. If the evidence contradicts your hypothesis, develop a new thesis based on the evidence. Write an essay using your examples to fully support your thesis.

3. Watch a movie or several television shows and make notes about all the product and fashion brands that are featured or mentioned. Are these brands essential to the plot or to character development? Why are they used? What message does their use convey to viewers?

4. Invent a product or a fashion brand and create an advertising campaign for it. Include details such as how the print and Web ads will look, where the print ads will be placed, how a short script for a television ad will read, who will star in the commercials, what background music will play in the ads, and who the target audience will be.

5. Think about what kind of fashion consumer you are. What do you spend your money on and why? Do you feel pressured to buy—or to avoid—certain brands? Write an essay in which you examine your consumer habits and what they say about you and the culture in which you live.

Seeing the Big Picture
Reflecting Culture in Film

Analyzing the Image

This photograph was taken on February 23, 2008, outside the Kodak Theater in Hollywood, California, where preparations were under way for the eightieth annual Academy Awards ceremony. The next day, hundreds of millions of eager fans from around the world would tune in to see their favorite stars glittering in their designer fashions on the red carpet.

In this photo, partially screened from view, stands a larger-than-life replica of the coveted statuette that represents excellence in the film industry. Although the golden icon's official name is the Academy Award of Merit, film lovers all over the world know him as Oscar and agree that he is the biggest star of all.

- What first captures your attention when you look at this photograph?

- Why do you think the Oscar statue in the photo is so large?

- Who do you think the three men in the photograph are? What are they trying to do?

- The signs behind the Oscar statue are red with gold lettering. How are the color and design of the signs significant? Why are they pictured on a slant?

- Why are so many of us so interested in the Academy Awards?

GEARING UP If you could assume the life of any character in a film, whose life would you choose? What would be the advantages and disadvantages of being this character?

The Oscars. Hollywood. Bollywood. Blockbusters. Big stars. Independent films. YouTube. Popcorn. Chick flicks. Horror films. Documentaries. Superheroes. DVDs. CGI. IMAX. Megaplexes.

What do all these words and phrases have in common? They all refer to the wonderful world of film. From the silent "flicks" of a hundred years ago through the studio classics of the Golden Age of Hollywood in the 1930s and 1940s to the computer-generated films of today, moving pictures, or "movies," have played a central role in popular culture. Whether they are viewed in a theater, on a computer, or on an iPhone, whether they are created by a famous director or an unknown Web auteur, films tell the story of our lives past, present, and future. They reflect our wishes and dreams and also our nightmares. They show us at our noblest and at our most monstrous. They make us laugh, cry, and scream. According to famed writer and director,

Stephen King, they provide an outlet for our emotions and help us tame the beast within. Film provides a unique bond among people. Movies provide us with a shared experience and a shared discourse. Not just Americans, but people from around the world will recognize lines like these: "May the force be with you." "Bond. James Bond." "Go ahead. Make my day." "Life is like a box of chocolates. You never know what you're going to get." "Make him an offer he can't refuse." These expressions speak to people who otherwise might not speak to each other or even speak the same language. Although we may argue about individual films — What do they mean? Should they win an Oscar? Are they too violent? Do they demean the members of a certain group, such as black or gay people? Are they too politically controversial? Have special effects had a negative impact on acting and story lines? What limits should be placed on videos posted on the Web? — most of us agree that film is one of the most important and enjoyable forms of media today. In fact, many of us associate the milestones of our lives with the movies we saw, where we saw them, and with whom we shared that experience.

In a world that seems to get smaller every day, perhaps film's most important role is to show us people's other lives. Whether it is a Bollywood epic about a royal marriage in the sixteenth century, a documentary about the underground beauty salons in Iraq, or a film based on a Japanese novel or an iconic American superhero, the world of film reflects who we are and who we may become, for better or worse. It's a magic mirror in which we see our successes and our failures. Perhaps there is no better example of the global impact of film than former vice president Al Gore's documentary about global warming, *An Inconvenient Truth*. Can a movie save the world?

What does film mean to you? What role has it played in your life? Would you rather watch a film than read a book? To what extent are you influenced by film? What part have the movies that you've watched played in who you are and how you view the world around you?

> **COLLABORATING**   Working in small groups of three or four, brainstorm a list of fads or trends that you can trace back to a film you have seen. Be sure you recall the specific movie. Consider such things as hairstyles, clothing, jewelry, automobiles, home furnishings, words or expressions, food fads, and habits or mannerisms.

Why We Crave Horror Movies

S T E P H E N K I N G

An old English prayer—"From ghoulies and ghosties, long-leggedy beasties, and things that go bump in the night, Lord God protect us"—suggests that people have worried about "things that go bump in the night" for a long time. If ghouls and ghosts frighten us so, why do so many of us love scary movies? The famous author of this essay provides us with the answer to this question. Horror master Stephen King needs no introduction to either readers or film buffs around the world. He is the creator of such frightening tales as *Carrie* (1973), *The Shining* (1977), *Misery* (1987), *The Eyes of the Dragon* (1987), *Bag of Bones* (1998), *Hearts in Atlantis* (1999), and *Riding the Bullet* (2000), an e-book available only on the Internet. King repopularized the serial novel with *The Green Mile*, published in six installments from March through August 1996. He has also authored many short stories and screenplays and has played cameo roles in several films based on his works. The king of horror's prolific writing career nearly came to an end in 1999, when he was struck by a van and critically injured while walking near his summer home in western Maine. The author chronicles this painful period of both his personal and professional life in *On Writing: A Memoir of the Craft* (2000). His most recent books are *Duma Key* (2008) and *Just after Sunset* (2008), a collection of short stories. "Why We Crave Horror Movies" is King's attempt to explain why we love it when he scares us to nightmares. The essay was first published in *Playboy* in December 1981.

> **THINKING AHEAD** Do you like horror movies? Which ones terrify you? Why? If they frighten you, why do you watch them?

I think that we're all mentally ill; those of us outside the asylums only hide it a little better—and maybe not all that much better, after all. We've all known people who talk to themselves, people who sometimes squinch their faces into horrible grimaces when they believe no one is watching, people who have some hysterical fear—of snakes, the dark, the tight place, the long drop . . . and, of course, those final worms and grubs that are waiting so patiently underground.

When we pay our four or five bucks and seat ourselves at tenth-row center in a theater showing a horror movie, we are daring the nightmare.

Why? Some of the reasons are simple and obvious. To show that we can, that we are not afraid, that we can ride this roller coaster. Which is not to say that a really good horror movie may not surprise a scream out of us at some point, the way we may scream when the roller coaster twists through a complete 360 or plows through a lake at the bottom of the drop. And horror movies, like roller coasters, have always been the special province of the young; by the time one turns forty or fifty, one's appetite for double twists or 360-degree loops may be considerably depleted.

We also go to reestablish our feelings of essential normality; the horror movie is innately conservative, even reactionary. Freda Jackson as the horrible melting woman in *Die, Monster, Die!* confirms for us that no matter how far we may be removed from the beauty of a Robert Redford or a Diana Ross, we are still light-years from true ugliness.

And we go to have fun.

Ah, but this is where the ground starts to slope away, isn't it? Because this is a very peculiar sort of fun indeed. The fun comes from seeing others menaced—sometimes killed. One critic suggested that if pro football has become the voyeur's version of combat, then the horror film has become the modern version of the public lynching.

It is true that the mythic, "fairy-tale" horror film intends to take away the shades of gray. . . . It urges us to put away our more civilized and adult penchant for analysis and to become children again, seeing things in pure blacks and whites. It may be that horror movies provide psychic relief on this level because this invitation to lapse into simplicity, irrationality, and even outright madness is extended so rarely. We are told we may allow our emotions a free rein . . . or no rein at all.

If we are all insane, then sanity becomes a matter of degree. If your insanity leads you to carve up women like Jack the Ripper or the Cleveland Torso Murderer, we clap you away in the funny farm (but neither of those two amateur-night surgeons was ever caught, heh-heh-heh); if, on the other hand, your insanity leads you only to talk to yourself when you're under stress or to pick your nose on your morning bus, then you are left alone to go about your business . . . though it is doubtful that you will ever be invited to the best parties.

The potential lyncher is in almost all of us (excluding saints, past and present; but then, most saints have been crazy in their own ways), and every now and then, he has to be let loose to scream and roll around in the grass. Our emotions and our fears form their own body, and we recognize that it demands its own exercise to maintain proper muscle tone. Certain of these emotional muscles are accepted—even exalted—in civilized society; they are, of course, the emotions that tend to maintain the status quo of civilization itself. Love, friendship, loyalty, kindness—these are all the emotions that we applaud, emotions that have been immortalized in the couplets of Hallmark cards and in the verses (I don't dare call it poetry) of Leonard Nimoy.[1]

When we exhibit these emotions, society showers us with positive reinforcement; we learn this even before we get out of diapers. When, as children, we hug our rotten little puke of a sister and give her a kiss, all the aunts and uncles smile and twit and cry, "Isn't he the sweetest little

[1] **Leonard Nimoy:** An actor who played Commander Spock in television's original *Star Trek* series.

thing?" Such coveted treats as chocolate-covered graham crackers often follow. But if we deliberately slam the rotten little puke of a sister's fingers in the door, sanctions follow—angry remonstrance from parents, aunts, and uncles; instead of a chocolate-covered graham cracker, a spanking.

But anticivilization emotions don't go away, and they demand periodic   11 exercise. We have such "sick" jokes as "What's the difference between a truckload of bowling balls and a truckload of dead babies?" (You can't unload the truckload of bowling balls with a pitchfork . . . a joke, by the way, that I heard originally from a ten-year-old.) Such a joke may surprise a laugh or a grin out of us even as we recoil, a possibility that confirms the thesis: If we share a brotherhood of man, then we also share an insanity of man. None of which is intended as a defense of either the sick joke or insanity but merely as an explanation of why the best horror films, like the best fairy tales, manage to be reactionary, anarchistic, and revolutionary all at the same time.

The mythic horror movie, like the sick joke, has a dirty job to do. It   12 deliberately appeals to all that is worst in us. It is morbidity unchained, our most base instincts let free, our nastiest fantasies realized . . . and it all happens, fittingly enough in the dark. For those reasons, good liberals often shy away from horror films. For myself, I like to see the most aggressive of them—*Dawn of the Dead*, for instance—as lifting a trapdoor in the civilized forebrain and throwing a basket of raw meat to the hungry alligators swimming around in that subterranean river beneath.

Why bother? Because it keeps them from getting out, man, it keeps   13 them down there and me up here. It was Lennon and McCartney who said that all you need is love, and I would agree with that.

As long as you keep the gators fed.   14

EXERCISING VOCABULARY

1. Record your own definition for each word below in your notebook.

   grimaces (n.) (1)   status quo (n.) (9)
   depleted (v.) (3)   sanctions (n.) (10)
   innately (adv.) (4)   remonstrance (n.) (10)
   voyeur (n.) (6)   recoil (v.) (11)
   penchant (n.) (7)

2. At the end of paragraph 11, King asserts that really good horror movies "manage to be reactionary, anarchistic, and revolutionary all at the same time." Define these three adjectives. Usually these words have a political meaning and are used to refer to governments. Explain their meaning when King applies them to horror movies.

3. In paragraph 12, King describes the "mythic horror movie" as "morbidity unchained." Define *morbidity* and explain King's use of it here.

PROBING CONTENT

1. To what is King referring when he mentions "those final worms and grubs that are waiting so patiently underground" (para. 1)? How does this reference contribute to the main point of this essay? How does it establish the author's tone?

2. How is watching a horror movie "daring the nightmare" (para. 2)? Why, according to King, do we do this?

3. In what sense, according to the essay, do horror movies encourage us to think like children? Why might adults want an opportunity to think like children again?

4. Which emotions does King say "tend to maintain the status quo of civilization itself" (para. 9)? Why are these emotions so important to society?

5. What "dirty job" does King think horror movies perform for us? Why is it important that something assume this job?

6. What do "the hungry alligators" in paragraph 12 represent? How do horror movies feed these alligators?

CONSIDERING CRAFT

1. Does King literally "think that we're all mentally ill," as he says in paragraph 1? Why does he write this? What does such a statement add to King's essay?

2. Locate two single-sentence paragraphs in the essay. Describe the effect of these paragraphs. How does this effect aid the overall impact of each point? How does it aid the essay's main idea?

3. Some of the language and references deliberately chosen by King are not polite — "to pick your nose" (para. 8), "rotten little puke of a sister" (para. 10), and the joke about dead babies in paragraph 11. What do you expect audience reaction to these references to be? What is your own reaction? Why does King include these?

WRITING PROMPTS

Responding to the Topic From your own experience, evaluate King's explanation of why we like horror movies. How accurate is it to assume that a dark side is lurking in each of us just beneath our civilized skins? What difference does it make in your relationships with other people if you accept or reject this notion?

Responding to the Writer   Write an essay in which you agree or disagree with King's argument that horror films allow a safe release for what would otherwise be expressed as insane or even criminal behavior. You may extend your argument to include other forms of "dangerous" leisure-time activities, such as playing violent video or computer games, watching violent television shows, reading violent novels, or listening to violent music.

Responding to Multiple Viewpoints   In "Shrinking the Big Screen," Wesley Morris poses the following question as his subtitle: "Are the movies being taken over by TV?" In the final paragraph of the essay, the author writes, "Maybe in an age of TiVo and first-run movies that we can watch on a portable 3½-inch screen, the line between a television set and movie theater has dissolved." Based on the reading you have done in this chapter, how might film directors and screenwriters like Stephen King, George Romero, or Tyler Perry answer this question? Pick one of these directors or another one discussed in one of the chapter's essays. Write an interview complete with questions you would pose to your subject and his or her answers.

For a quiz on this reading, go to bedfordstmartins.com/mirror.

Horror Auteur Is Unfinished
with the Undead

KATRINA ONSTAD

Katrina Onstad is a journalist and a columnist for the Canadian magazine *Chatelaine* and for CBCNews.ca. Her essays and film criticism have appeared in the *National Post, Toronto Life*, and *Elle*. In 2006, she published a novel, *How Happy to Be*. The following essay about horror pioneer George A. Romero appeared in the *New York Times* in February 2008. In it, Onstad chronicles the return of the legendary director to the zombie movie genre he helped define.

> **THINKING AHEAD**   What do you think of the zombie film genre? With what films and directors are you familiar? To what extent do you think this kind of film can comment on contemporary society?

We get the zombies we deserve. 1

Over five films and four decades the director George A. Romero's 2 slack-jawed undead have been our tour guides through a brainless, barbaric America that seems barely hospitable to the living. They lurch across a bigoted civil-rights-era countryside (*Night of the Living Dead*, 1968), claw at a suburban shopping mall (*Dawn of the Dead*, 1978) and wander dazed in an anxious post-9/11 world (*Land of the Dead*, 2005).

Mr. Romero is now 68, and his influence has long saturated the cultural 3 mainstream, but he's exhumed his living dead yet again for *Diary of the Dead*, opening Friday. The zombies'—and Mr. Romero's—current bugaboo?[1] The blogging, uploading, navel-gazing infotainment age.

"It's scary out there, man," Mr. Romero said, gesturing at a laptop as 4 he sat in his apartment here, chain-smoking Marlboros. "There's just so much information, and it's absolutely uncontrolled. Half of it isn't even information. It's entertainment or opinion. I wanted to do something that would get at this octopus. It may be the darkest film I've done since *Night of the Living Dead*."

The only sign that Mr. Romero, the world's foremost zombie auteur, 5 lives in the small, cat-toy-filled apartment was a framed photo by the front door showing him in a group hug with some cheerful ghouls. "My little friends," he said.

Since Mr. Romero's head-eating friends made their debut four decades 6 ago in the cult classic *Night of the Living Dead*—now in the National Film Registry—zombie variations have kept coming. Last year alone brought

[1] **bugaboo:** Something that causes fear or worry.

279

I Am Legend; Robert Rodriguez's *Planet Terror* in *Grindhouse*; *Resident Evil: Extinction*; and *28 Weeks Later*.

Mr. Romero's latest offering seems modest in comparison. *Diary of the Dead* is about a group of Pittsburgh college students shooting a cheapo mummy movie in the woods when the zombies start swarming. These kids will go down filming, and the result is metazombie; a film within the film is called *The Death of Death*.

Shot for under $4 million in Toronto (Mr. Romero's hometown for three years or so, since he decamped from Pittsburgh) and starring a largely unknown Canadian cast, *Diary of the Dead* also marks a return to Mr. Romero's signature filmmaking style: cheap, local and studio free. After the $16 million Universal production *Land of the Dead*, starring Dennis Hopper, Mr. Romero decided to scale back. (The movie made about $21 million domestically.)

"It was a grueling shoot, and it was all getting too big, too *Thunderdome*," Mr. Romero said. "I wanted to make something with some film students, find a dentist that would put up a quarter of a million and do it way under the radar for DVD release."

Instead Mr. Romero's producing partner, Peter Grunwald, showed the script to the Los Angeles company Artfire Films, which put up the money. "But we had absolute control," Mr. Romero said, emphatically. The Weinstein Company bought North American distribution rights.

Diary of the Dead enters a horror market dominated by all-gore-all-the-time franchises like *Saw* and *Hostel*. "I don't get the torture porn films," Mr. Romero said. "They're lacking metaphor. For me the gore is always a slap in the face saying, 'Wait a minute. Look at this other thing.'"

The man who made entrails-chomping a horror staple shows restraint in *Diary of the Dead*. Sure, a daughter catches her mom devouring her dad's heart, but Mr. Romero doesn't linger on it. The moderation was partly a function of the plot: The film is supposedly shot by a film student running for his life, with no time for close-ups. But Mr. Romero said he also felt little need to add to the landslide of violent images in the news.

"I was glad to back off the gore in the current political climate," Mr. Romero said. "I thought that because we were using the subjective camera, it would be spookier to stay away, not to get too close. Being removed from the horror is what's scary, like watching an accident."

Using stock footage from recent disasters like Hurricane Katrina, Mr. Romero makes a dark joke out of a zombified, politically inert populace. The video gamer kids in the movie are either watching horror or recording it, forever at a distance.

"I always thought of the zombies as being about revolution, one generation consuming the next," said Mr. Romero, who has a gentle hippie quality about him (gray ponytail, propensity to use the word *man*). "But I wasn't trying to come down hard on these kids particularly. This blogosphere thing is our time. All my films are snapshots of North America at a particular moment. I have an ability within the genre to be able to do that."

Among the masters of horror, Mr. Romero joked, he has the "the Michael Moore slot."

Mr. Romero was raised in the Bronx, a horror-comic fan and self-described "film freak" who would ride the subway into Manhattan to rent the reels of *The Tales of Hoffmann* (1951), an outsized Moira Shearer musical based on the Jacques Offenbach opera. On those rare occasions when the movie wasn't available, he was told that the only other person who took it out was around his age. "And that kid was Martin Scorsese," Mr. Romero said, grinning.   16

He briefly studied film and drama at Carnegie Mellon University in Pittsburgh (then Carnegie Institute of Technology), landing his first paid directing gig shooting documentary segments for the public television children's show *Mr. Rogers' Neighborhood.* "Mr. Rogers Gets a Tonsillectomy" may have been his first experiment with gore.   17

In 1967 Mr. Romero and a group of friends pulled together $114,000 and ventured into the woods south of Pittsburgh to shoot *Night of the Living Dead*, a black-and-white horror film inspired by the Richard Matheson novel *I Am Legend.* (Mr. Romero said he hasn't seen the recent Will Smith version.) The book, about the last man alive in Los Angeles, was more vampire than zombie; Mr. Romero drafted his own mythology of the undead.   18

"Before George zombies in movies were voodoo," said Max Brooks, author of *The Zombie Survival Guide.* "He redefined the zombie as a flesh eater created from science, not magic. He took the zombie from fringe horror to apocalyptic horror. Suddenly they could be anywhere."   19

Mr. Romero also tacked social commentary to the genre's escapism, initially by accident. Because he gave the best audition, a black actor, Duane Jones, was cast as the heroic lead, a role never intended for an African American. Mr. Jones plays a good man protecting (mostly) odious white people; for his selfless actions he's rewarded with a fatal gunshot from a lynchlike mob.   20

"We started to realize the casting had changed the meaning of the film while we were making it," Mr. Romero said. "The night we finished, we're driving to New York, with the print in the trunk of the car, and heard on the radio that Martin Luther King had been shot. We went, 'Oh, no, this is good for us.'"   21

A decade later, after *Night of the Living Dead* had been championed in the pages of *Cahiers du Cinema*[2] and established a following, Mr. Romero set the sequel in a shopping mall. *Dawn of the Dead* is poppy[3] and cartoonish, with zombie escalator gags and canned-music-theme slayings.   22

"Other zombie movies don't match George's eye for satire or wit," the actor Simon Pegg wrote in an e-mail message. Mr. Pegg was a writer and star of the 2004 zombie sendup[4] *Shaun of the Dead.* "Even films such as *28 Days*   23

---

[2]*Cahiers du Cinema*: A famous and critically influential French film magazine.
[3]**poppy**: Light and loosely structured, like pop music.
[4]**sendup**: A parody.

Later, which I really enjoyed, delivered the allegory but with a very straight face. George seems able to scare, disgust, challenge and amuse, simultaneously."

Mr. Pegg's voice can be heard in *Diary of the Dead* as a Cronkite-   24
esque[5] announcer booming doom across the airwaves. Mr. Romero also got Wes Craven, Quentin Tarantino, Guillermo del Toro and Stephen King to contribute their voices — a *Who's Who* of nerd-boy film.

"He's the kind of director other directors really admire, the last baby boomer   25
who has yet to sell out," Mr. Brooks said of Mr. Romero. "He appeals to the rest of us who would love to be that pure but who still like to pay our bills."

Mr. Romero said he's never seen much money from his films. He's had   26
many failures too, like the Reagan-era *Day of the Dead* and most of his nonzombie films, including *Monkey Shines* (1988) and *The Dark Half* (1993). (An exception is the 1982 film *Creepshow.*)

Sealing his indie[6] credibility, or his financial fate, he left Pittsburgh for   27
Toronto. Mr. Romero filmed a straight-to-DVD movie called *Bruiser* there in 2000 and liked the crews so much that he eventually moved there. He is separated from his wife and former collaborator, the actress Christine Forrest, and now lives with his girlfriend.

In Toronto and everywhere he goes in the iMovie age he satirizes,   28
people slip Mr. Romero homemade zombie movies. "There's enough of them out there already," he said with a sigh, though he admitted that he's working on a sequel to *Diary of the Dead*. "It always comes down to 'Well, what's your idea? What's the film about?' Because zombies alone. . . ." He laughed. "Like, get off it, man."

EXERCISING VOCABULARY

1. Record your own definition for each word below in your notebook.

barbaric (adj.) (2)	propensity (n.) (15)
genre (n.) (15)	drafted (v.) (18)
lurch (v.) (2)	mythology (n.) (18)
bigoted (adj.) (2)	apocalyptic (adj.) (19)
exhumed (v.) (3)	odious (adj.) (20)
ghouls (n.) (5)	selfless (adj.) (20)
decamped (v.) (8)	credibility (n.) (27)
grueling (adj.) (9)	
emphatically (adv.) (10)	
inert (adj.) (14)	

2. In paragraph 5, Onstad calls George A. Romero "the world's foremost zombie auteur." Look up the word *auteur* in a dictionary. From which language does it derive? What does it mean? What is a film auteur?

---

[5] **Cronkite-esque:** Recalling Walter Cronkite, famous journalist and twentieth-century nighttime news anchor.
[6] **indie:** Independent; with little or no studio support.

3. Onstad says that Romero's "influence has long saturated the cultural mainstream" (para. 3). What does the word *saturated* mean? What happens when a stream is saturated? What does Onstad mean by "cultural mainstream"? How is her statement a play on words?

4. In paragraph 9, the author quotes Romero as saying that he wanted to release *Diary of the Dead* "under the radar." What does the phrase "under the radar" mean? What then does it mean to release a film "under the radar"?

PROBING CONTENT

1. Why is George A. Romero an important name in film? What frightens him about contemporary culture?

2. What is the title of his latest film? How does it differ from other recent horror films?

3. Onstad writes, "Among the masters of horror, Mr. Romero joked, he has 'the Michael Moore slot'" (para. 15). Who is Michael Moore? What does Romero mean in this quotation? What message do Romero's films send about America?

4. Who is Duane Jones? What role did he play in Romero's development as a director?

5. Who is Simon Pegg? What does he think of Romero?

CONSIDERING CRAFT

1. Examine the essay's title. What is unique about it?

2. How does Onstad give us a complete picture of her subject George A. Romero? Name the different writing strategies she uses. Discuss why she uses each one.

3. Onstad uses descriptive language in a unique way in her essay. Examine phrases like "The blogging, uploading, navel-gazing infotainment age" (para. 3), "a *Who's Who* of nerd-boy film" (para. 24), and "the iMovie age" (para. 28). How do these descriptions function in the essay?

4. Explain the verbal irony Onstad uses in the beginning of paragraph 12. How does her use of irony here fit her tone in the remainder of the essay?

WRITING PROMPTS

Responding to the Topic   What do you think of horror film? Are you a fan? Why? In an essay, detail your reaction to this particular genre of movies. Use specific details to support your position.

Responding to the Writer   George A. Romero claims that his films are "snapshots of North America at a particular moment" (para. 15) and calls himself the Michael Moore of the zombie genre. To what extent do you believe that films reflect the culture of their time? How important is it that films fulfill this role? Write an essay in which you answer these questions. Make sure that you use specific examples to prove your position.

Responding to Multiple Viewpoints   Onstad begins her essay "Horror Auteur Is Unfinished with the Undead" with the following claim: "We get the zombies we deserve. Over five films and four decades the director George A. Romero's slack-jawed undead have been our tour guides through a brainless, barbaric America that seems barely hospitable to the living. They lurch across a bigoted civil-rights-era countryside (*Night of the Living Dead*, 1968), claw at a suburban shopping mall (*Dawn of the Dead*, 1978) and wander dazed in an anxious post-9/11 world (*Land of the Dead*, 2005)." Pick one or more of the directors mentioned in your readings from this chapter. Then write an essay in which you discuss how they would respond to Onstad.

For a quiz on this reading, go to bedfordstmartins.com/mirror.

DRAWING CONNECTIONS

1. In "Why We Crave Horror Movies," Stephen King writes, "I like to see the most aggressive of them [horror films]—*Dawn of the Dead*, for instance—as lifting a trapdoor in the civilized forebrain and throwing a basket of raw meat to the hungry alligators swimming around in that subterranean river beneath" (para. 12). How would George A. Romero respond to King? Write an essay in which you answer this question. Provide adequate textual evidence to support your position.

2. According to Stephen King ("Why We Crave Horror Movies"), "It is true that the mythic, 'fairy-tale' horror film intends to take away the shades of gray. . . . It urges us to put away our more civilized and adult penchant for analysis and to become children again, seeing things in pure blacks and whites" (para. 7). Write an essay in which you answer the following question: Would George A. Romero agree with King's statement? Why?

3. The essays "Why We Crave Horror Movies" by Stephen King and "Horror Auteur Is Unfinished with the Undead" by Onstad both refer to "sick" (King, para. 11) or "dark" (Onstad, para. 14) jokes. Reread both essays, focusing on these paragraphs. Then write an essay in which you compare the black humor of these two filmmakers and how it is reflected in their visions of the horror genre.

Bollywood Princess, Hollywood Hopeful: Aishwarya's Quest for Global Stardom

ANUPAMA CHOPRA

Anupama Chopra is a book and film critic for *India Today*, India's largest English-language magazine, and for NDTV, New Delhi Television Limited. In 2007, she published *King of Bollywood: Shah Rukh Khan and the Seductive World of Indian Cinema.* "Bollywood Princess, Hollywood Hopeful" was published in the *New York Times* in 2008. In it, she takes a look at what it takes for an actor in India's Bollywood film industry to make the leap to international stardom in Hollywood.

THINKING AHEAD   Think about any foreign films that you have seen. Where were the films made? What was your reaction to these films and to the actors in them?

Last October Aishwarya Bachchan grappled with a tough choice. The Bollywood star could either stay in Los Angeles to pursue a lead role in Will Smith's new film, *Seven Pounds*, or she could return home to Mumbai to celebrate Karva Chauth, a daylong ceremonial fast that some married Hindu women observe as a prayer for their husband's health and long life. (The observance is a new one for Ms. Bachchan; in April she married Abhishek Bachchan, an actor and the son of the Indian film star Amitabh Bachchan, a union that prompted *Time* magazine to describe the three as "Bollywood's Father, Son and Holy Babe.")   1

Ultimately Ms. Bachchan chose to return to Mumbai and starve with a smile. National television channels covered her first Karva Chauth as headline news. Two months later she shrugged off her loss in an interview. "You do what you have to do," she said. "Feeling torn and thereby unhappy, confused or guilty is not something I want to feel. So you make your choices and go with it. You get some and some you don't."   2

This month Ms. Bachchan brings some of that clarity and traditionalism to a role she was born to play: that of Queen Jodhaa in the sumptuous-looking historical drama *Jodhaa Akbar*. The $10 million film is one of Bollywood's biggest productions this year. It will be released worldwide on Friday, in more than 115 theaters in the United States alone, making it the biggest American release ever for a Hindi[1] film.   3

Jodhaa Akbar focuses on that quintessentially Indian subject: arranged marriage. Set in the sixteenth century, it explores the marriage between the great Mughal Emperor Akbar, a Muslim, and his Hindu wife Jodhaa.   4

---

[1] **Hindi:** The most widely spoken language in India, spoken mostly in the north; along with English, it is the official language of India.

Historians have described the union as a political alliance, but in the   5
hands of Ashutosh Gowariker, the film's director, the story has become "an
epic romance with its share of battles, harem politics and intrigue," he said
in a telephone interview. Mr. Gowariker, whose 2001 period film,[2] *Lagaan:
Once Upon a Time in India*, was nominated for an Oscar for best foreign
film, isn't claiming factual accuracy but insists that the film is "embedded
in historical truth."

He cast Ms. Bachchan as the queen (a figure some Indian historians   6
dispute ever existed) because, he said, "Aishwarya is a comic book princess
with a certain dignity, elegance and sense of purity." For the role of Akbar,
Mr. Gowariker wanted someone with "the physique of a warrior and the face
of a romantic," and selected another Bollywood superstar, Hrithik Roshan.

Mr. Gowariker described it as a dream cast, which, at least as far as   7
box office appeal goes, seems accurate. Both actors, to steal the phrase
Pauline Kael invented to describe Michelle Pfeiffer, are "paradisically beautiful," and are consummate superstars. With their ethnically indeterminate
looks and impeccable English, Ms. Bachchan and Mr. Roshan could be
India's first international movie stars.

Ms. Bachchan has already made considerable progress in that direc-   8
tion. She is the international face of L'Oréal[3] and Longines,[4] as well as a
consistently glamorous presence at the Cannes Film Festival; in 2003 she
became the first Bollywood actress to serve on the jury. In 2004 she made
Time magazine's list of the 100 most influential people in the world.

So far Ms. Bachchan's international projects — *Bride & Prejudice, The   9
Mistress of Spices* and *The Last Legion* — have sputtered commercially and
critically, but with her high-profile marriage, A-list brand endorsements
and plum Hindi film projects, she continues to generate global attention.

Mr. Smith, who wanted to cast her in *Hitch*, but couldn't, because of   10
scheduling conflicts, remains an ardent admirer. "She has this powerful
energy where she doesn't have to say anything; do anything; she can just
stand there," he said in a February 2006 interview with BBC News. "Anything
she's making, I'll be there."

Next February Ms. Bachchan will be seen in *Pink Panther 2*, in which   11
Inspector Clouseau, played by Steve Martin, teams up with a squad of international detectives to catch a thief with a penchant for historical artifacts.

As it happens, her *Jodhaa Akbar* co-star, Mr. Roshan, thirty-three, rejected   12
a role in the same film because it wasn't important enough.

In an interview in Mumbai, Mr. Roshan made it clear that while he is   13
"actively pursuing Hollywood" he would not "do a film just because it's
Hollywood."

Hollywood and Mr. Roshan have been flirting with each other since   14
he burst into Bollywood with a film called *Kaho Na Pyar Hai* (*Say You*

---

[2] **period film:** A film set in a specific historical period.
[3] **L'Oréal:** Company that produces beauty products and perfumes.
[4] **Longines:** Swiss manufacturer of luxury watches.

Love Me) in 2000. The film, directed and produced by his father, Rakesh Roshan, was a blockbuster and catapulted the newcomer to superstar status in India.

In 2002 the American edition of GQ ran a profile headlined "The most famous person you've never heard of," and rumors of a project with Tarsem Singh, the Indian-born director of *The Cell*, and Jennifer Lopez swirled in the Indian press. It didn't happen, nor did a series of other proposed projects that for various reasons Mr. Roshan declined. But last October he took his first concrete step toward a Hollywood career by signing with Brillstein Entertainment Partners in Los Angeles.

Despite their global stardom—Bollywood has an estimated annual worldwide audience of 3.6 billion—Ms. Bachchan and Mr. Roshan will not find it easy to break into Hollywood. The two film industries are forging closer ties (last year Sony Pictures Entertainment released its first Hindi production, *Saawariya*), and a few Indian names like Mira Nair, Kal Penn and Shekhar Kapur diversify the Hollywood landscape. Still, for a variety of reasons, no actor has successfully made the transition from Bollywood to Hollywood.

Schedules and expectations are difficult to match. Bollywood superstars are generally unwilling to play supporting roles in American movies, and there just aren't many movies coming out of Los Angeles that feature Indians as leads.

"You don't want to sacrifice your own kingdom to set up somewhere else," Mr. Gowariker said. "But an international star can only be in the English language."

If Ms. Bachchan and Mr. Roshan do cross over, they could be Hollywood's most old-fashioned stars. Until she married at thirty-three, Ms. Bachchan (now thirty-four), lived with her parents, which both Oprah Winfrey and David Letterman noted when she appeared on their shows in 2005. ("We don't need to take appointments with our parents to meet for dinner," she replied cheekily to Mr. Letterman.) Now that she is married, Ms. Bachchan lives with her husband at his parents' house in Mumbai.

As for Mr. Roshan, he is married to his childhood sweetheart. They are expecting their second child this year, and they also continue to live with the senior Roshans.

Unlike Ms. Bachchan, Mr. Roshan has yet to find a Hollywood film that fits his taste and schedule. Currently he is "breaking the ice," which means reading two scripts a week and giving feedback so that he and his Hollywood managers can "get to know each other."

He said he is hopeful that *Jodhaa Akbar* will be a first step in expanding the traditional fan base, and UTV Motion Pictures, the co-producer and worldwide distributor of the film, is pushing hard to make sure that it does. Theatrical trailers were released globally as early as September.

"Of course we are relying on South Asian viewers," said Siddharth Roy Kapur, the director of UTV, in a telephone interview. "But this is the perfect film for anyone who is curious about Bollywood. It has scale, stars, drama, song and dance."

EXERCISING VOCABULARY

1. Record your own definition for each word below in your notebook.

   grappled (v.) (1)

   sumptuous (adj.) (3)

   quintessentially (adv.) (4)

   epic (adj.) (5)

   harem (adj.) (5)

   consummate (adj.) (7)

   indeterminate (adj.) (7)

   impeccable (adj.) (7)

   plum (adj.) (9)

   penchant (n.) (11)

   artifacts (n.) (11)

   swirled (v.) (15)

   forging (v.) (16)

   cheekily (adv.) (19)

   scale (n.) (23)

2. Chopra writes, "So far Ms. Bachchan's international projects— *Bride & Prejudice*, *The Mistress of Spices* and *The Last Legion*—have sputtered commercially and critically" (para. 9). What does it mean when we say something "sputtered" in a literal sense? What kinds of things sputter? What does Chopra's figurative use of the term "sputter" reveal here about Bachchan's films?

3. In paragraph 22, Chopra writes that "theatrical trailers were released globally." What are theatrical trailers? To what are they attached? In what other contexts is the word *trailers* used? What do these other trailers and film trailers have in common?

4. Hrithik Roshan's film *Kaho Na Pyar Hai* "catapulted the newcomer to superstar status" (para. 14). What is a catapult? What does Chopra's use of this verb indicate about the actor?

PROBING CONTENT

1. Why did Aishwarya Bachchan turn down a role in Will Smith's new film? What did she do instead?

2. What role is Aishwarya Bachchan playing in the film *Jodhaa Akbar*? Does the author believe that this is a fitting role for the actor? Why?

3. Who may be the next two international film stars from India, according to Chopra? Why?

4. According to the writer, what is the current relationship between Bollywood and Hollywood? What are some of the problems that Indian actors face if they attempt to cross over from one system to the other?

CONSIDERING CRAFT

1. Look at the title and subtitle of the essay. Then read the title aloud. Why do you think Chopra chose this particular title?

2. Chopra quotes actor Will Smith and director Ashutosh Gowariker in the essay. Why does the author choose these two people?

3. In paragraph 14, Chopra notes that "Hollywood and Mr. Roshan have been flirting with each other" for some time. By choosing this expression, what does the author reveal about the relationship between Hollywood and the actor?

WRITING PROMPTS

Responding to the Topic   Write an essay in which you discuss your experience with foreign film. Detail which foreign films, if any, you have seen. If you have not seen any films produced in another country, explain why you have not chosen to see any. What have you learned—or do you think you could learn—about another culture by watching the films of that culture?

Responding to the Writer   Do you agree with Aishwarya Bachchan's decision to place her personal moral code above her career? How could this affect her professional opportunities? In an essay, explain why you agree or disagree with her position and the impact that you think her moral code will have on her career.

Responding to Multiple Viewpoints   Read Eugene Robinson's essay "Tyler Perry's Money Machine." What advice might Tyler Perry give Aishwarya Bachchan about her attempt to cross over into mainstream Hollywood? Write an essay in the form of a letter from Perry to Bachchan.

For a quiz on this reading, go to bedfordstmartins.com/mirror.

The Bollywood Princess Waiting for Her Prince to Come

ANALYZING THE IMAGE

In this film image, called a movie still, from the epic romance *Jodhaa Akbar*, some would say we see Bollywood Princess Aishwarya Rai Bachchan dreaming of her Prince Charming, played by Bollywood superstar Hrithik Roshan. The film was released worldwide in 2008 and in 115 theaters in the United States, thus making history as the largest Hindi release in this country. This lush historical epic from director Ashutosh Gowariker traces the complicated relationship between the great Mughal emperor Akbar, a Muslim, and Jodhaa, a Hindu beauty who becomes his wife. Although the historical basis of the epic is disputed, it is clear that these two Indian actors have a chance of becoming the first truly global Bollywood superstars.

1. What do you first notice about this movie still?

2. What do you think Jodhaa and Akbar are thinking about?

3. Why are the two figures different sizes?

4. How do the stars' clothing and positioning indicate the sixteenth-century Indian setting of this film?

5. In the original visual, the colors gold, red, and white predominate. What significance might these three colors have in an epic romance?

6. Does this visual make you want to see the film *Jodhaa Akbar*? Why?

Tyler Perry's Money Machine

EUGENE ROBINSON

Eugene Robinson is an assistant managing editor for the *Washington Post* and writes a twice-weekly column. In his career at the paper, he has also worked as a city hall reporter, city editor, and foreign correspondent. He is the author of *Coal to Cream: A Black Man's Journey beyond Color to an Affirmation of Race* (1999) and *Last Dance in Havana: The Final Days of Fidel and the Start of the New Cuban Revolution* (2004). "Tyler Perry's Money Machine," which appeared in the *Washington Post* on October 16, 2007, discusses the phenomenal success of African American writer, actor, and filmmaker Tyler Perry.

> **THINKING AHEAD** Think about African Americans that you have see on-screen, either on television or in the movies. What roles do you remember African Americans portraying? In which films or shows? Which African American directors, actors, films, and television shows do you like? Why?

G eorge Clooney is a big-time movie star. Cate Blanchett is a big-time movie star. But Tyler Perry's new movie did more box-office on its opening weekend than Clooney's and Blanchett's new movies combined, which makes Perry a big-time movie star, too, and also a phenomenon. 1

Perry's *Why Did I Get Married?*—which features singers Janet Jackson and Jill Scott—ruled the weekend with $21.5 million in sales. Clooney's thriller *Michael Clayton* struggled to earn half that much, while Blanchett's costume drama[1] *Elizabeth: The Golden Age* barely broke $6 million. 2

What makes this worth noting? According to Perry's distributor, Lions Gate Films, around 90 percent of the audience for *Why Did I Get Married?* was African American. The ensemble cast is African American, too. 3

A playwright, actor and filmmaker—based not in Hollywood but in somewhat less glamorous Atlanta—Perry is making a habit of pulling this kind of stunt. Last year his *Madea's Family Reunion* opened with a $30 million weekend. Critics find Perry's films formulaic, but clearly he has found a formula that works. And he has found an untapped audience that literally can't wait to see itself on the big screen. 4

In his plays and movies, Perry shows African Americans as they . . . well, I was about to say he shows us as we really are, but that's not true. Reality is for documentaries; Perry's characters are unsubtle, his humor is broad, and his plots are soaked with melodrama. Among his big themes 5

---

[1] **costume drama:** A film set in a historical period and employing authentic costumes of the period.

are love, fidelity and the importance of family, and his movies usually have religious overtones.

What Perry does is depict black Americans as people relating to other people—not as mere plot devices and not as characters defined solely by how they relate to the white world. The rest of the movie industry would do well to take note.   6

In depicting African Americans, mainstream Hollywood still struggles to leave behind the "magic Negro" paradigm[2]—the idea, epitomized by *Driving Miss Daisy*, that black characters exist solely to teach valuable lessons to white characters. We still don't get a lot of films in which black characters bestow their moral wisdom on one another. Even in *The Pursuit of Happyness*, Will Smith's character was only secondarily a lesson-giver to his son; mostly, his role was to teach and uplift the audience.   7

There's nothing wrong with a little inspiration. But African American moviegoers who want to see their own concerns and struggles—their own lives, even if rendered in broad outline—projected at the cineplex still aren't getting much love from Hollywood.   8

The same is true on the small screen. A new Nielsen report says that there has been a remarkable convergence of white and black television viewing habits; for the first time in years, lists of the top twenty shows among whites and blacks are largely the same. But that is at least partly due to the fact that UPN and WB, which used to carry a lot of black-oriented programming, were merged into one network, which meant jettisoning a number of shows popular with black viewers. And it's at least partly due to the dominance of *American Idol*, *Dancing With the Stars* and other reality shows that choose their contestants with diversity in mind.   9

Nielsen calls African Americans a "high-growth, high-potential audience." African Americans are "embracing and using the newest technologies at rates that exceed the national average," including high-definition television and movies-on-demand, Nielsen reports.   10

But black viewers still won't watch *Desperate Housewives*. They'd rather watch *Girlfriends* instead.   11

Perry's movies are based on his stage plays, which play to packed audiences around the country. *Why Did I Get Married?* is about the black middle class. It's about relationships, the universal subject of date movies. Perry's movies aren't great art-house films,[3] but neither are Adam Sandler's; they succeed at what counts, which is speaking to their audience.   12

Tom Ortenberg, president of Lions Gate Films, told the *Los Angeles Times* that Perry's "message of family values and personal redemption speaks very strongly to people who are not frequent moviegoers." He added, "My strong hunch is that this is the last time anybody will underestimate Tyler Perry."   13

---

[2] **paradigm:** A set of assumptions, concepts, values, and practices that constitutes a way of viewing reality for the community that shares them.

[3] **art-house films:** Movies intended to be primarily artistic works rather than commercial films of mass appeal.

"African Americans have learned to flex their market muscle," Nielsen   14
said in its report, noting that African American buying power will top
$900 billion within a few years.

If the pattern from his earlier films holds true, *Why Did I Get Married?*   15
will probably drop off next weekend—black audiences anticipate his films
and rush out to see them as soon as they open. That eagerness suggests
a hunger that others might want to try to satisfy. That is, if they want to
make money.

EXERCISING VOCABULARY

1. Record your own definition for each word below in your notebook.

phenomenon (n.) (1)	rendered (v.) (8)
formulaic (adj.) (4)	convergence (n.) (9)
melodrama (n.) (5)	jettisoning (v.) (9)
overtones (n.) (5)	universal (adj.) (12)
epitomized (adj.) (7)	hunch (n.) (13)
bestow (v.) (7)	

2. In paragraph 14, Robinson quotes the Nielsen report, which says that "African Americans have learned to flex their market muscle." What does it mean to flex a muscle? How does a group develop "market muscle"? What would result from flexing that market muscle?

3. The author writes that Tyler Perry "has found an untapped audience that literally can't wait to see itself on the big screen" (para. 4). What does it mean to tap someone or something? Give some examples of people or things that can be tapped. What does Robinson's description of the audience for Perry's films indicate?

PROBING CONTENT

1. According to Robinson, how are African Americans depicted in Tyler Perry's plays and films? What are his major themes?

2. How does mainstream Hollywood depict African Americans? What is the "'magic Negro' paradigm" (para. 7)? How does Hollywood handle it?

3. Who is Tom Ortenberg? What is his opinion of Tyler Perry's work? Why does he hold this opinion? Why is his opinion significant?

4. What has recently become notable about "white and black television viewing habits" (para. 9)? To what does Robinson attribute this change?

CONSIDERING CRAFT

1. Why does Robinson begin his essay with statistics about movies? Why did he pick the films that he did? How does this opening introduce his purpose in this essay?

2. The author uses informal conversational language in his essay on several occasions. Find two such examples and explain how they affect the tone of the essay.

3. What does the Nielsen report measure? Why does Robinson cite the Nielsen report in his essay? Is this an effective strategy? Why?

WRITING PROMPTS

Responding to the Topic   Why do you go to the movies? According to Robinson, many people go to see themselves on the big screen. Is this the reason you and your friends attend movies? In an essay, detail your personal reasons for choosing the films you do. Support your ideas with numerous specific examples.

Responding to the Writer   Robinson believes that one reason for the success of Perry's films is that they move beyond showing African Americans only as "they relate to the white world" (para. 6). What will it take for any film that depicts a minority group to have broad appeal outside that population? Write an essay in which you take a position on this issue and provide examples of films that support your thesis.

Responding to Multiple Viewpoints   In "Tyler Perry's Money Machine," Robinson argues that Perry's movies are especially popular with African American audiences. Stephen King, in "Why We Crave Horror Movies," writes, "And horror movies, like roller coasters, have always been the special province of the young" (para. 3). Finally, Andrew O'Hehir, in "Oscar and Hollywood in Splitsville!" claims that recent Academy Award–winning films are "more tightly focused on an educated, upper-middle-class audience" (para. 11) than were those of the past. Based on your reading of these essays and others in this chapter, write an essay in which you consider the advantanges and disadvantages of producing movies that target specific audiences. Provide numerous examples to support your position.

For a quiz on this reading, go to bedfordstmartins.com/mirror.

Drag Hags

JENNIE YABROFF

Jennie Yabroff writes movie and book reviews, as well as features on women in pop culture, for publications such as *Newsweek*, the *New York Times*, the *San Francisco Chronicle*, and *Salon*. The following essay, "Drag Hags," was first published in *Newsweek* in July 2007. In it, Yabroff examines some recent comedies in which male actors have portrayed women and raises an interesting point: In an America that is so attuned to being sensitive to others' identities, is gender still a blind spot?

> **THINKING AHEAD** Which movies, plays, or television shows have you seen in which men dress as women? Why did the men dress this way? How did this affect your entertainment experience?

Edna Turnblad has a weakness for pink-sequined dresses, a passion for 1 her husband and a triple-E bra. Edna also has a secret. Edna is a man. To be precise, her character in *Hairspray* has always been played by a man: drag queen Divine in the original John Waters film, gruff-voiced Harvey Fierstein in the Broadway musical and, starting this week, John Travolta in the movie musical. Just as Peter Pan is almost always played by a woman, it's impossible to imagine a *Hairspray* in which Edna isn't hiding a stubble under her pancake makeup. The obvious reason is that more-is-more is part of the *Hairspray* ethos, from the hairstyles to the musical numbers. Having a man play the plus-size Edna makes her funnier and adds a wink-wink knowingness to the depiction of an archetype[1] of maternity.

But what is that wink all about? Edna is hardly the only iconic female 2 character who's really a he. Tyler Perry has made a career of playing the overweight, overbearing grandmother Madea, while both Eddie Murphy and Martin Lawrence strapped on fat suits and wigs in recent films. Despite decades-long careers, Dustin Hoffman's and Robin Williams's most beloved alter egos[2] are arguably Tootsie and Mrs. Doubtfire. "Jack Lemmon doing the tango with Joe E. Brown in *Some Like It Hot* was hilarious, but you can't tell me there wasn't the further charge of what it was representing," says Richard Barrios, a film historian and author of *Screened Out: Playing Gay in Hollywood from Edison to Stonewall*. "It's a blurring of differences between masculinity and femininity." But lots of conventions of drama don't fly anymore. A white actor wouldn't dare put on dark makeup

---

[1] **archetype:** An original model; a prototype or ideal example.
[2] **alter egos:** Personas; second selves.

to appear black today—Angelina Jolie took a lot of heat for slightly darkening her complexion to play Mariane Pearl in *A Mighty Heart*. A non-Asian actor would never get away with taping his eyes and assuming a silly accent to sound Chinese, as Mickey Rooney did in *Breakfast at Tiffany's* (1961). Even fat activists complain when actors don fat suits for laughs, as Gwyneth Paltrow found out when she artificially bulked up for *Shallow Hal*. So it would seem logical that drag today, especially when the man playing the part is straight, is both misogynistic (notice how the "women" in these movies are always awkward and ugly) and homophobic (notice how they also flutter and flounce like a stereotypical gay man). So why is it still OK for male actors to wear dresses?

The convention of men playing women dates back to ancient Greece and also has roots in Japanese Kabuki theater. Men played all the roles in Shakespeare's day, heightening the gender confusion in plays such as *As You Like It*, where Rosalind, originally played by a male actor, disguises herself as a man to win her lover's heart. Men wearing dresses have been a comedy staple in both Britain and America since the 1892 play *Charley's Aunt*, which was first made into a film in 1915. Bugs Bunny has even dolled himself up to outwit (and mock-seduce) Elmer Fudd. As long as women have worn dresses, male actors have been borrowing them to get a laugh. "There have been surveys of movies in which men play women, and they were all successes," says Craig Zadan, executive producer of *Hairspray*. "The public loves the idea of men playing women in film, especially in a comedy." 3

Take Martin Lawrence. In the *Big Momma* movies, Lawrence follows a time-honored tradition of male characters who are forced to go "undercover" as women, either to elude the bad guys or to win the heart of a real, yet surprisingly clueless woman. This wolf-in-sheep's-clothing ruse powers *Some Like It Hot*, *Tootsie* and countless fraternity films in which the brothers depilate[3] and rouge themselves (ineptly, of course) to pass as women. In the more thoughtful movies, drag can be a vehicle for personal growth for the men, who, after initial outrage at the way they are treated as women, remain sensitized even after they wipe off their lipstick. However, the women in these films never experience the same fulfilling character arc. It's the men who emancipate them from their second-class status; in *Tootsie*, Michael's alter ego, Dorothy, lobbies for gender equality in the workplace. Though much of the visual comedy comes from the man's struggle to adopt "feminine" ways, the female love interest never seems to question the gender of her new best friend, and accepts the switch unquestioningly once the "gal pal" unmasks himself as a potential suitor. In *Some Like It Hot*, when Josephine reveals that he is really Joe, Sugar (Marilyn Monroe) shrugs off his concerns that she'll feel betrayed, saying, "I told you. I'm not very bright." Though some critics laud *Some Like It Hot* for lampooning[4] 4

---

[3]**depilate:** To remove hair by shaving or waxing.
[4]**lampooning:** Satirizing; ridiculing.

gender stereotypes, the message of the film could also be that a woman isn't nearly as bright as a man in a dress.

Tyler Perry's Madea, Eddie Murphy's Rasputia and Travolta's Edna, on the other hand, never appear on screen as men. So why not just cast a woman in the roles in the first place—Rosie O'Donnell would have made a great Edna. "It seems not only are we to be made fun of and demeaned in films, but we are also being put out of work," says writer Jill Nelson. "If Martin and Eddie can dress up and be us, why do the studios need to make an effort to hire black women? It's like they're killing us two ways." Travolta has been called out by gay activists who claim Edna is an iconic gay role (Waters and Fierstein are gay, as was Divine), and therefore should be played by a gay man. While blackface[5] is universally reviled, drag is trickier: some gays embrace it as an important aspect of alternative culture, while others believe it perpetuates tired stereotypes of gay men as secretly wanting to be women. Most agree, though, that drag's charge, negative or positive, is neutralized when a straight man does it. When Waters cast Divine, a flamboyant gay man and real-life drag queen, as a traditional loving mother, it underscored the film's message of acceptance. But that nuance is lost when Edna is played simply for laughs. And Travolta's Edna is as straight as they come.

Yet Zadan says he never considered any women for Edna, choosing to honor the tradition begun by Waters when he created the role for Divine. "Why would you put up boundaries for what an actor's capable of accomplishing in film?" asks Zadan. "With visual effects, makeup, so many things at our disposal, there's no limit to what you can accomplish." Prosthetically enhanced gender swapping, Travolta style, may be the drag of the future. His Edna has more in common with Mike Myers's Fat Bastard, Jim Carrey's Grinch or Paltrow's Rosemary Shanahan than Divine. When actors such as Travolta, Murphy or Lawrence take on these roles, they actually downplay any gender confusion; Travolta has said he didn't want to portray Edna as a "drag joke." Instead, these macho actors brag about the physical discomfort required to transform themselves into wig-topped Jabba the Huttettes.[6] "Good drag is used knowingly for its transgressive[7] qualities," says Barrios. "But films like *Big Momma* and *Hairspray* don't want to be attuned to whatever transgressiveness they may contain. Drag is just an easy way to get laughs without extending themselves beyond putting on some latex." And when drag becomes more about latex than subtext, it's not funny at all.

5

6

---

[5]**blackface:** The practice of white actors playing black roles while wearing dark makeup; a conventionalized comic travesty of black people, especially in a minstrel show.

[6]**Jabba the Huttettes:** Refers to the film character Jabba the Hutt, a grotesquely overweight alien who was a criminal overlord in George Lucas's *Star Wars* saga.

[7]**transgressive:** Exceeding or overstepping a limit.

EXERCISING VOCABULARY

1. Record your own definition for each word below in your notebook.

ethos (n.) (1)
iconic (adj.) (2)
overbearing (adj.) (2)
misogynistic (adj.) (2)
staple (n.) (3)
elude (v.) (4)
ruse (n.) (4)
ineptly (adv.) (4)
lobbies (v.) (4)

shrugs (v.) (4)
laud (v.) (4)
demeaned (v.) (5)
reviled (v.) (5)
nuance (n.) (5)
prosthetically (adv.) (6)
downplay (v.) (6)
attuned (v.) (6)

2. Yabroff writes that drag seems "homophobic" (para. 2). What does it mean to be phobic? Name some common phobias and the words that describe them. Look up the prefix *homo* in the dictionary. What does it mean when used in a term like *homo sapiens*? What then does it mean to be homophobic?

3. In the final sentence of her essay, Yabroff states, "And when drag becomes more about latex than subtext, it's not funny at all." What does the prefix *sub* mean? What are some words of which it is a part? What then is a subtext?

4. Yabroff describes Divine as "a flamboyant gay man" (para. 5). Look up the word *flamboyant*. From what language does it derive? How is it related to the word *flame*? What does the author mean when she calls Divine a "flamboyant" gay man? How does knowing the origin of the word add to your understanding and to the word's descriptive quality?

PROBING CONTENT

1. How long have men played women's roles? Why have men dressed in women's clothing to play these roles?

2. How does Yabroff feel about men dressing as women? Does she approve? Why?

3. In which other situations is it unacceptable for one person to pretend to be another? What reasons does Yabroff give?

4. What effect does male actors' dressing in drag have on women? On female actors? On gay men?

CONSIDERING CRAFT

1. Examine the title of the essay. What is unique about it? How effective is this title?

2. Yabroff includes several questions in her essay. Find four examples where she does so. Why does Yabroff use this writing strategy?

3. The author provides a multitude of examples in her essay. Why does she include examples other than men playing women's roles? Locate three of these and comment on why Yabroff includes them.

4. The essay begins and ends with mentions of John Travolta's role in *Hairspray*. Why does Yabroff use this strategy? How effective is it?

WRITING PROMPTS

Responding to the Topic What films have you seen in which men dress as women or women dress as men? In an essay, detail how these "drag" roles affected your opinion of the film. To what extent do you believe there was a subtext or larger message in these roles? Make sure that you provide specific examples from the films.

Responding to the Writer In the final line of her essay, Yabroff states, "And when drag becomes more about latex than subtext, it's not funny at all." Write an essay in which you take a position on this statement. Provide adequate examples to support your stance.

Responding to Multiple Viewpoints Yabroff claims that "Tyler Perry's Madea, Eddie Murphy's Rasputia and Travolta's Edna, on the other hand, never appear on screen as men. So why not just cast a woman in the roles in the first place—Rosie O'Donnell would have made a great Edna" (para. 5). Would Eugene Robinson, author of "Tyler Perry's Money Machine," agree with Yabroff that it would be advantageous to cast women in roles like Madea's, Rasputia's, and Edna's instead of casting men? Write an essay in which you answer this question. Provide adequate detail and examples to prove your position.

For a quiz on this reading, go to bedfordstmartins.com/mirror.

Shrinking the Big Screen: Are the Movies Being Taken Over by TV?

WESLEY MORRIS

In the past, many successful television series were inspired by films. However, according to film critic Wesley Morris, that relationship may be reversing itself today. Morris is a film critic for the *Boston Globe*, where "Shrinking the Big Screen" appeared in August 2007. He has also written for the *San Francisco Examiner*, the *San Francisco Chronicle*, and *Slate*.

> **THINKING AHEAD**   Which movies have you seen or heard of that are based on a television series? Is this a good idea? Why? What is lost or gained when a television show moves to a full-length film?

There's a point in Judd Apatow's *Knocked Up* when the movie's two childish men, played by Seth Rogen and Paul Rudd, visit a pool hall and bemoan their respective romantic relationships. Rudd's character, Pete, sums up marriage with an allusion. It's "like *Everybody Loves Raymond*, except nobody laughs." Well, we do—at his marriage. We laugh because it's almost as advertised. Pete is Ray Barone, and his exasperated, hypersensitive wife, Debbie (Leslie Mann), is Ray's exasperated, hypersensitive wife, Debra. It's been observed that *Knocked Up* represents some unknown new frontier for the romantic comedy. But that frontier is actually pretty familiar: the sitcom.

This is a summer in which television comes naturally to the movies. *The Simpsons* arrived at megaplexes virtually indistinguishable from its formidable prime-time self. *Hairspray* is a musical about a bunch of teenagers desperate to integrate a television dance show. What is *I Now Pronounce You Chuck and Larry* if not a *Bosom Buddies* overhaul? And *Superbad*, which opened Friday, was produced by Apatow—it could have been one of his canceled shows.

Each of these pictures is a hit. Either we wanted more familiar movies or we miss new network television.

After decades of demonizing television as a threat to everything from the sanctity of the American family to the sanity of the national psyche, Hollywood movies have finally and perhaps fully fallen under the influence of television, which has been expanding its cultural grip since its arrival in American homes more than six decades ago. For years, the movies tended to treat television like a younger sibling, striking out against it defensively and enviously. Then it became more toxic. In Douglas Sirk's *All That Heaven Allows* (1955),

300

the television set is Jane Wyman's terrifying consolation for having lost her strapping younger boyfriend—it's a gift from her kids and her unhappy face reflected in the screen is one of the saddest images in the history of the movies. Two years later, Elia Kazan's *A Face in the Crowd* gave us television as a star-making medium that could turn a simpleton[1] into a megalomaniacal[2] monster. By 1976, we were getting the pitch-black farce of *Network*, a violent allergic reaction to television's infantilization of its audience.

In 1982, little Heather O'Rourke was sucked into the television set in *Poltergeist*, a movie whose final shot of Craig T. Nelson pushing a little set out of the family's motel room is its punch line. In Barry Levinson's *Avalon* (1990), television is subtly blamed for the demise of one large American family and by extension all of them—there it is lurking in the background of some early shots but growing more cancerously prominent as the film goes on.

The movies could act with great moral and artistic superiority toward television, and going to the movies was still an event. The line between the mediums was distinct. Initially, this made business sense. The corporations that owned the movie studios were competing with the corporations that owned the television stations and the networks. A raft of mergers took the edge off that rivalry. And the wild success of 1992's *Wayne's World*, taken from a *Saturday Night Live* sketch about two suburban kids and their public-access television show, marked a sea change.[3] Television was coming to the movies, and it was staying. *SNL* sketches (*Coneheads*, *It's Pat*, *A Night at the Roxbury*, *Superstar*, *The Ladies Man*) and old shows (*The Beverly Hillbillies*, *The Addams Family*, *The Brady Bunch*, *Car 54, Where Are You? Charlie's Angels*, *The Mod Squad*, *Starsky and Hutch*) were being expanded into movies.

As O'Rourke might have put it, her hands pressed against that snowy glass screen like a psychic with her crystal ball: They're here.

The multiplex was being repurposed as a repository for kitsch.[4] Maybe it was good for mocking the good old days. Maybe it was a synergistic[5] way to generate interest in future box-set DVDs of the old shows. Whatever the explanation, the line between the two mediums had become porous. While the movies started looking more like television, television started looking more like the movies. One premium cable channel even had a catchy diagnosis for the upgrade: It wasn't television; it was HBO. It's been noted that several seasons of HBO's *The Sopranos* were better than any Hollywood movie made during the years the show was on the air.

Other earlier crime dramas, like *Miami Vice* and *The Equalizer*, were clearly inspired by the movies, but the ones that hung around played by

[1]**simpleton:** A foolish person.
[2]**megalomaniacal:** Referring to a psychopathological condition characterized by delusional fantasies of wealth, power, or omnipotence; an obsession with grandiose or extravagant things or actions.
[3]**sea change:** A striking alteration.
[4]**kitsch:** Something of tawdry or low-quality design, appearance, or content created to appeal to popular or undiscriminating taste.
[5]**synergistic:** Working together.

the old rules of television. Even more than *Twin Peaks,* another deeply cinematic reworking of a genre[6] idea, *The Sopranos* made a cogent case for elevating television's standards. *The Sopranos* had a Hollywood polish, a great movie's depth, and almost European art-house ideas of closure. In the mob doings, there was Kurosawa and Scorsese. In Tony and Carmela's marriage, there was Bergman and Rohmer. In the show's dreaminess, there was Fellini. This was an amalgam[7] that had gotten away from the movies, where even the great Scorsese isn't really completely himself anymore. Kids, *do* try this at home.

In a less grand sense, television started doing another movie staple   10 better than the movies, too: the screwball romantic comedy.[8] As the *New Yorker* film critic David Denby observed recently, the genre hasn't been as magnificent since Woody Allen's *Annie Hall* (1977) and *Manhattan* (1979). *Sex and the City,* on HBO, restored the glamour and zaniness and the candor that had gone missing at the movies. And when it was at its best, *Will & Grace,* on NBC, concocted the kind of slyly subversive, lightning-fast comedy that the movies' two greatest romantic comedy directors of the screwball era, Preston Sturges and Ernst Lubitsch, might have made.

Of course, the tipping point in the transfer of the classical Hollywood   11 screwball comedy from big screen to small came in 1982 with a film about a struggling actor who disguises himself as a woman and becomes a surprise television star. Sydney Pollack's *Tootsie* was a true screwball comedy, but it knowingly killed the fantasy of the romantic comedy. The play between Katharine Hepburn and Spencer Tracy, Rosalind Russell and Cary Grant, or even Doris Day and Rock Hudson was no longer possible. *Tootsie* was a romantic comedy about sexual politics, and it changed how we expect men and women to talk to each other.

Never mind that the woman doing most of the talking was really a   12 man. The genre received a slow, increasingly depressing cultural makeover. The visual sparkle vanished. The wit dissolved. And a defensive, cynical, post-feminist sensibility materialized. The successful woman needed a new fluff. The fantasy of the screwball comedy became the lie of the chick flick. In the chick flick, women searched and searched and searched for Mr. Right, meaning Mr. Mature, Mr. Sane, Mr. Responsible. Realism had ruined romance. That ruin is secretly what *Knocked Up* is about. Its being expressed in the idiom of the television sitcom means the classical Hollywood romantic comedy as we've known it is gone.

On the other hand, the sitcom might be dead on television—increasingly   13 replaced by reality television and cable dramas (starring great Oscar-winning women) and network serials, like *24, Lost,* and *Heroes,* that look

---

[6]**genre:** A type or class of something; a class or category of artistic endeavor having a particular form, content, or technique.

[7]**amalgam:** A mixture or combination.

[8]**screwball romantic comedy:** A 1930s–1940s film that focuses on the twists and turns of a comic love relationship between a man and a woman; named for the screwball throw in baseball.

and feel a lot like films. But it's alive at the movies, where Apatow is making a mark. Apatow is a veteran writer and producer in both mediums who's tried and failed to keep a number of very good television series on the air. Now he just appears to be turning them into movies. That they happen to be more sensitive, more humanely insightful, and more entertaining than most other American movies today is both a testament to the resonance and generosity of his vision and a sign that, with all respect to whoever brought us *Transformers*, too many writers, directors and studio heads are robots.

Apatow proudly puts a lot of television in his movies. For one thing,   14 *Knocked Up* is visually basic at best. Part of what gives the movie such a plain network television feel is that it often looks like a show. Apatow's previous movie, *The 40-Year-Old Virgin*, had a more surrealist[9] gusto in both premise and style. But he's not a natural-born filmmaker. For no particular reason, the camera, in one shot, peeks out from behind a case of restaurant wine shelves. Elsewhere, the margins of *Knocked Up* are studded with current *SNL* cast members; Joanna Kerns, the *Growing Pains* matriarch, plays Katherine Heigl's mom; and Rogen's housemates have appeared on other Apatow shows. The very idea that Pete thinks marriage most approximates *Everybody Loves Raymond* and not, say, *The War of the Roses*, works as a criticism of American movies' stunted ideas of marriage. Lately, television has done it more truly and deeply.

The movie also merges at least three classic sitcom paradigms—newly   15 married couple, dudes in a house and baby on the way. Even the ancient trope[10] of schlubby[11] guy-sexy woman is applied here. But Apatow invests them all with degrees of feeling that only lasting television comedies ever do.

At this point, seeing a difference between the mediums might be fruitless.   16 Maybe in an age of TiVo and first-run movies that we can watch on a portable 3½-inch screen, the line between a television set and movie theater has dissolved. So if you're a Hollywood movie executive, your limitations seem like strengths. Thinking inside the box might not be such a crime after all.

EXERCISING VOCABULARY

1. Record your own definition for each word below in your notebook.

bemoan (v.) (1)	subtly (adv.) (5)
allusion (n.) (1)	demise (n.) (5)
exasperated (adj.) (1)	raft (n.) (6)
formidable (adj.) (2)	repository (n.) (8)
sanctity (n.) (4)	cogent (adj.) (9)
toxic (adj.) (4)	zaniness (n.) (10)

[9]**surrealist:** Characterized by the irrational and by unexpected juxtapositions.
[10]**trope:** Any literary or rhetorical device, such as metaphor and irony, that consists of the use of words in other than their literal sense.
[11]**schlubby:** Slang term for clumsy, stupid, or unattractive.

candor (n.) (10)
concocted (v.) (10)
subversive (adj.) (10)
idiom (n.) (12)
resonance (n.) (13)
gusto (n.) (14)

premise (n.) (14)
matriarch (n.) (14)
stunted (adj.) (14)
paradigms (n.) (15)
fruitless (adj.) (16)

2. In paragraph 4, Morris writes, "After decades of demonizing television as a threat to everything from the sanctity of the American family to the sanity of the national psyche, Hollywood movies have finally and perhaps fully fallen under the influence of TV, which has been expanding its cultural grip since its arrival in American homes more than six decades ago." What is a demon? What does it mean to demonize something or someone? What do you normally grip? What does Morris mean by TV's cultural grip?

3. The author claims that the film *Network* was "a violent allergic reaction to television's infantilization of its audience" (para. 4). What familiar word forms the root of *infantilization*? How is it related to the meaning of *infantilization* in this context?

4. In paragraph 8, Morris writes that "the line between the two mediums [film and television] had become porous." What does it mean if something is porous? What does the author mean when he says that the boundary between the two mediums is porous?

PROBING CONTENT

1. How has television been portrayed in film in the past? Give an example of this treatment.

2. When did film begin to embrace television? Why did this make sense from a business point of view?

3. According to Morris, what role did the film *Tootsie* play in film history? What effect did it have on the classic Hollywood screwball romantic comedy? Which television shows continued the tradition of the romantic comedy?

4. What connection do Judd Apatow's films have to television? Give specific examples.

CONSIDERING CRAFT

1. Examine the title of the essay. How does it announce the topic of the essay? How effective is it in capturing your attention?

2. Morris uses numerous examples of specific films and television shows in his essay. How does this affect your reading?

3. Locate two very short paragraphs in the essay. Examine them carefully. What effect does Morris achieve by making these two paragraphs much shorter than the others?

4. Explain the play on words in the final sentence of the essay. What does the author mean when he writes, "Thinking inside the box might not be such a crime after all"?

WRITING PROMPTS

Responding to the Topic   In your opinion, how successful are films based on television series? Write an essay in which you respond to this question. Make sure that you base your essay on one or more specific examples of a film or films that take their inspiration from television.

Responding to the Writer   Do you believe that television is a positive or a negative influence on film? Write an essay in which you take a position on this question. Provide specific examples from both television shows and movies to support your thesis.

Responding to Multiple Viewpoints   Authors Morris ("Shrinking the Big Screen"), Andrew O'Hehir ("Oscar and Hollywood in Splitsville!"), John Clark ("Hollywood Clicks on the Work of Web Auteurs"), Stephen King ("Why We Crave Horror Movies"), and Katrina Onstad ("Horror Auteur Is Unfinished with the Undead") all write about the reasons certain films appeal to the public. Based on your reading of these essays, write an essay in which you explore the reasons that a particular film genre such as romantic comedy, horror, action, mystery, or science fiction appeals to a certain audience. You may model your essay on one of the readings. Provide specific examples of films to support your thesis.

For a quiz on this reading, go to bedfordstmartins.com/mirror.

Oscar and Hollywood in Splitsville!

ANDREW O'HEHIR

Andrew O'Hehir is a senior arts and entertainment writer for *Salon.com*. His blog "Beyond the Multiplex" focuses on independent cinema. He has also published book reviews in the *New York Times* and on Powells.com. This essay appeared on *Salon.com* in February 2008. As you read it, think about all the films you've seen lately that have been nominated for Oscars and how closely they resemble your idea of what the standard Hollywood film looks like.

> **THINKING AHEAD** Do you watch the Academy Awards show on television? What about the show attracts your attention or causes you to watch? What is your opinion of those films that have recently won Oscars? How do the Academy Award results affect your personal film-viewing choices?

E very year without fail, some journalist comes wandering out of 1 hibernation and notices, with the force of revelation, that the Academy Awards are *not* based on popularity or, on the other hand, on some sober and considered judgment of cinematic quality. By God, it's just a big party where the film industry congratulates itself! I'm thunderstruck![1]

In years gone by, this generally took the form of disdainful cinephiles 2 bemoaning the Academy's atrocious taste. (*Ordinary People* wins over *Raging Bull*! *Dances With Wolves* wins over *GoodFellas*! Yul Brynner wins over Olivier! And so on.) More recently, we've heard the inverse of that criticism, in which the Oscars have become an inward-looking, bicoastal-elite, anti-populist celebration of arty niche movies that no regular folks out there in cud-munching Middle America have actually seen. You know, weird obscurities like *The Departed, Chicago, The Lord of the Rings: The Return of the King, A Beautiful Mind* and *Gladiator*—all of them twenty-first-century best-picture winners, with a cumulative $1 billion-plus in domestic ticket sales.

Right-wing movie critic Michael Medved is the acknowledged kung-fu[2] 3 master of this complaint, but he's stayed quiet this year, even with an indie-rich[3] roster of Oscar nominees to rail[4] against. (Maybe he's still exhausted from all the righteous indignation he worked up against *Brokeback Mountain*

---

[1]**thunderstruck:** Amazed; surprised.
[2]**kung-fu:** Refers to any of various Chinese martial arts, especially those forms in which sharp blows and kicks are applied to pressure points on the body of an opponent.
[3]**indie:** Short for "independent"; refers to a film produced with little or no major studio support.
[4]**rail:** To complain bitterly.

in 2006.) Still, the Oscars-vs.-ordinary-moviegoers meme[5] comes up every winter like a hothouse orchid: *Time* magazine's Richard Corliss took it out for a spin in December (in an essay with the self-recriminating title "Do Film Critics Know Anything?"), and freelancer Michael Ordoña just cranked out a noncommittal reported piece on the subject for the *Los Angeles Times*. His conclusion: There are movies that pile up awards and movies that pile up money. They aren't usually the same, except when they are.

There's a reason why this idea that the Oscars have become a snobbed-up, limousine-liberal affair, out of touch with ordinary Americans, never goes away: It has a grain of truth, however teensy and elusive, at its core. At first glance, mind you, it seems pretty silly, and maybe at second glance too. OK, so *Spider-Man 3* and *Shrek the Third* (this year's box-office champs) didn't exactly rack up the nominations. Those were summer movies for tweens and teens, destined to melt into sludge long before awards season, like a double-pistachio cone dropped on the beach boardwalk on Labor Day. As the list of recent winners given above suggests, Academy voters' tastes seem every bit as middlebrow[6] and mainstream-friendly as they ever were. 4

Oscar's perceived divorce from public opinion nonetheless reflects something real. It reflects how closely the Academy Awards are now identified with a specific grade of Indiewood product, meaning movies distributed and marketed by the studios' specialty divisions (Fox Searchlight, Warner Independent, Picturehouse, Miramax, et al.) but not generally produced by them. Overwhelmingly, this means mid-budget, independently produced dramas and comedies with A-minus casts, name directors, adult themes, faintly literary origins and a slightly eccentric style. You know: Little Miss Juno Crashes Sideways Into Brokeback Mountain, Where There Will Be Blood. 5

Beyond that, it reflects anxiety over a real and recent shift in the Hollywood economy—which has abruptly split itself into a relatively low-budget prestige wing and a deranged, 'roided-out[7] industrial production line—whose overall effect on the art and business of film is not yet clear (but is unlikely to be salubrious). More broadly still, the widening gulf between Indiewood's Oscar-targeted fare and the media conglomerates' lumbering blockbusters speaks to Hollywood's growing internal unease in an era of global expansion and consolidation that depends on ever bigger, ever dumber and ever more standardized productions. 6

Looking beyond that list of recent hits that went home with statuettes, things have changed rapidly in Oscarville over the last few years. Most obviously, there's the much-discussed indie takeover. As recently as 2003, four of the five best-picture nominees were wide-release studio films that grossed at least $90 million apiece, with one unconventional outsider thrown in to spice the pot. (That year it was *Lost in Translation*.) But in the last three Oscar seasons, ten of the fifteen nominees have been 7

[5]**meme:** A unit of cultural information, such as a cultural practice or idea, that is transmitted verbally or by repeated action from one mind to another.
[6]**middlebrow:** Neither highbrow nor lowbrow; referring to the middle class.
[7]**'roided-out:** Relating to the effect of steroid use; big; powerful.

independent or quasi-independent productions. Moreover, at least three of the five exceptions were indie-flavored, mid-budget pictures made at studios thanks to the clout of a star producer (George Clooney, in the case of *Michael Clayton* and *Good Night, and Good Luck,* and Clint Eastwood, in the case of *Letters from Iwo Jima*).

At least on the surface, that's a startling transformation. As always in Hollywood, it's wise to view the terminology and statistics with a skeptical eye. We've had several waves of "independent film" since the early '80s, but the phrase remains a slippery term of art, at best, that means different things to different people. Within the industry, it generally refers to the mechanics of how a film is financed and produced; it has nothing to do with daring or unconventionality or artistic ambition or amount of drugs consumed on-set or any other such intangibles.   8

It's not like the Academy fell out of its collective tree one day in 2005, removed the scales from its eyes and began handing out awards to five-hour Hungarian films or $5,000 "mumblecore"[8] productions or whatever. *Juno* and *Crash* and *Sideways* and *Brokeback Mountain* and *No Country for Old Men,* along with most of the other recent indie-esque Oscar candidates, are exactly the kinds of prestige movies the Hollywood studios could and probably would have made under different circumstances or in other eras.   9

Conversely, as you drill backward into Oscar history you keep finding things — Hollywood classics, in some cases — that could only be made now as independent films. I'm pretty confident that nobody in Hollywood would see much sex or sizzle potential in *Hope and Glory* (a 1987 best-picture nominee) or *Gandhi* (1982) or *Deliverance* (1972). (And they'd be right; none of those movies made much money.) For that matter, try to imagine pitching such vintage Oscar fodder as *Annie Hall* or *The Graduate* or *To Kill a Mockingbird* to a contemporary Hollywood executive. (Well, OK, maybe *The Graduate* — if you made it wackier and made Mrs. Robinson, like, twenty-nine and insanely hot.)   10

Allowing for shifts in taste and sensibility, I think it's clear that the classic middlebrow "Academy film" (as historian David Thomson has observed, it's pretty much a genre unto itself) is still with us. Much as I admire this year's list of best-picture nominees, all five of them fit the description. Only the nomenclature,[9] the financial details and the circumstances of production have changed. Indiewood's new breed of Academy films aren't necessarily worse or better than the ones produced under the old system, but they're cheaper and leaner and more tightly focused on an educated, upper-middle-class audience. They don't usually cost as much money, or make as much back. What has suddenly and almost completely vanished from the Oscar ecosystem is the major Hollywood blockbuster, or even the midsize one.   11

In 2007, there were at least eleven studio films released that earned more than $200 million apiece in domestic box office. That's a lot of success   12

---

[8]**mumblecore:** A genre of low-budget movie using nonprofessionals to depict mundane postcollege or early-adult existence.
[9]**nomenclature:** Name.

for a business that's constantly whining about its financial predicament. Of those movies, only the animated *Ratatouille* was nominated in any major Academy Award categories. (*The Bourne Ultimatum* and *Transformers* got several technical nominations.) Conversely, there have been only two films among the last fifteen best-picture nominees that grossed even $80 million (*Juno* this year and *The Departed* last year).

This year's best-picture list has *collectively* earned less than $300 million, with almost half of that total coming from the unexpected success of *Juno*. While I haven't tried to do the math, in constant-dollar terms that's got to be at or near an all-time low. And it's not a fluke.[10] If you exclude the *Lord of the Rings* trilogy, which strikes me as a special case in recent movie history, no film that earned $200 million or more has been nominated as best picture since *The Sixth Sense* in 1999.

It's not that the Oscar voters have suddenly embraced finely honed yupscale tastes and left multiplex America behind. At least, it isn't *just* that. It's more that Hollywood, in the corporate oligopoly[11] sense of the word, has left the older, affluent, movieland-insider demographic[12] of the Academy behind. Today the major Hollywood studios are run as industrial production arms of multinational entertainment conglomerates. They have outsourced the production of adult-oriented, Oscar-plausible films to independent producers so they can focus on their core product lines: action franchises for teenage boys, romantic comedies for young women, animated spectacles for kids and a handful of other generic options. While the abrupt indie-fication of Oscar night was presumably an unintended consequence, it was a logical and even predictable outcome.

It decidedly wasn't always this way. While the very biggest blockbusters weren't always Oscar fare, the Hollywood studios specialized, across many decades, in crafting large-scale entertainments that drew large and diverse audiences and Academy voters alike. Step into the way-back machine and you'll see what I mean. In 1997, which in retrospect looks like the end of a long era in Oscar history, the best-picture winner was *Titanic*, one of that decade's biggest hits. There were two other nominees that year—*As Good as It Gets* and *Good Will Hunting*—that topped $100 million.

Five years earlier, the nominees included *A Few Good Men*, one of the year's biggest hits, along with *Scent of a Woman* and the eventual winner, *Unforgiven*, smaller Hollywood films that did exceptional business by the standards of the time. Five years before that, in 1987, best-picture nods went to *Fatal Attraction* and *Moonstruck*, two highly popular, adult-oriented films, and the Oscar went to *The Last Emperor*, a three-hour historical spectacle from a European director that was partly financed by Columbia Pictures. (Try to make that deal happen today!)

---

[10]**fluke:** A chance occurrence; an accident.
[11]**oligopoly:** The market condition that exists when there are just a few sellers, as a result of which they can greatly influence price and other market factors.
[12]**demographic:** A portion of a population, especially consumers.

In 1982, the nominees included Steven Spielberg's *E.T.*, one of the   17
biggest box-office films in Hollywood history, along with *Tootsie*, which
grossed $177 million (perhaps twice that much in present-day dollars).
Five years earlier, we find the movie that changed everything in Hollywood,
George Lucas's *Star Wars*, nominated alongside *The Goodbye Girl*, which
also topped $100 million. (Best picture went to *Annie Hall*, which decidedly
did not.) Another half-decade earlier, in 1972, we find one of the legendary
years in Oscar history, when the nominees included *The Godfather* and
Cabaret, two big hits, alongside the critical fave *Deliverance*.

I think you get the point: More often than not, there was a crowd-   18
pleasing Hollywood smash, or several of them, on Oscar's short list. In
1965, *Doctor Zhivago* and *The Sound of Music* were both nominated. A
year earlier, *Mary Poppins* and *My Fair Lady* got nods alongside *Dr. Strange-
love*, *Becket* and *Zorba the Greek*. In 1962, *Lawrence of Arabia*, that era's
defining big-screen spectacle film, was nominated and won. In 1958, the
roster included *Cat on a Hot Tin Roof*, *Auntie Mame*, *The Defiant Ones*
and *Gigi* (the winner), all of them box-office hits; infamously, neither Alfred
Hitchcock's *Vertigo* nor Orson Welles' *Touch of Evil* was even nominated.

Sure, the big studios still crank out productions aimed at adult audiences   19
and awards voters (see *American Gangster* or *Dreamgirls*), but they do it
less and less frequently with less and less aptitude (see *American Gangster*
and *Dreamgirls*). We're only five years removed from seeing a major-studio
musical that grossed $170 million take home the big prize, and it's not like
that could never happen again. But we've reached the culmination of a long
historical process whereby the production of Hollywood blockbusters aimed
at undifferentiated masses of young people and the production of smaller
and more purportedly serious movies aimed at grownups have become distinct and mutually irrelevant operations.

Does this have dire consequences for art and/or the future of democ-   20
racy? Are Indiewood's Oscar films somehow less significant because they
generally cost less to make and reach fewer viewers? Most important of
all, will network viewers still tune in, in vast numbers, to see Jon Stewart's
quips, the fabulous and horrifying gowns and the abysmal production numbers, even if they haven't seen the movies? Right now I would answer those
questions probably not, probably not and maybe. But on that "maybe"
hangs the future of a tottering cultural empire.

EXERCISING VOCABULARY

1. Record your own definition for each word below in your notebook.

disdainful (adj.) (2)   self-recriminating (adj.) (3)
bemoaning (v.) (2)   noncommittal (adj.) (3)
inverse (n.) (2)   salubrious (adj.) (6)
anti-populist (adj.) (2)   lumbering (adj.) (6)
niche (adj.) (2)   clout (n.) (7)

intangibles (n.) (8)

fodder (n.) (10)

honed (adj.) (14)

infamously (adv.) (18)

culmination (n.) (19)

undifferentiated (adj.) (19)

purportedly (adv.) (19)

irrelevant (adj.) (19)

dire (adj.) (20)

abysmal (adj.) (20)

tottering (adj.) (20)

2. Examine the two parts of the word *cinephiles* (para. 2). What does the prefix *cine* mean? What does the suffix *phile* mean? What other words do you know that include either *cine* or *phile*? What then is a cinephile?

3. In paragraph 5, O'Hehir writes of "Oscar's perceived divorce from public opinion." What happens when two people divorce each other? How does this relate to the essay's title? What effect does the addition of the word *perceived* have here?

4. The author mentions "finely honed yupscale tastes" in paragraph 14. *Yupscale* is a combination of which two words? What does each word mean? If a knife is finely honed, what does that mean? What then are "finely honed yupscale tastes"?

PROBING CONTENT

1. According to O'Hehir, what two kinds of complaints are made about the Academy Awards every year? What accounts for these opposing complaints?

2. What kind of movie has won Academy Awards since 2005? What does "Indiewood" (para. 5) mean? How is it related to Hollywood?

3. How do Indiewood's Academy Award–winning films compare to older Hollywood films? What kind of film has disappeared from what O'Hehir calls "Oscarville" (para. 7)?

4. How has the business of Hollywood changed in the past few years? On which film genres does Hollywood now concentrate?

CONSIDERING CRAFT

1. The original subtitle of the essay read, "The Academy has turned its back on the multiplex moneymakers and wrapped smaller indie films in its warm, glittery embrace. But Hollywood isn't crying (yet)." What is personification? How is it used in this subtitle? How does the subtitle frame the content of this essay?

2. Reread the first paragraph. Describe the author's tone. How does this tone affect your reading of the rest of the essay? Where else in the essay does the author employ this tone?

3. In paragraph 5, O'Hehir describes a certain kind of independent film as "Little Miss Juno Crashes Sideways Into Brokeback Mountain, Where There Will Be Blood." To which specific films is the author referring? How effective is his writing strategy here?

4. Examine the metaphor and simile used in the fourth sentence of paragraph 4. Explain what these figures of speech convey about summer movies for "tweens and teens." Then explain O'Hehir's use of figurative language in the first sentences of paragraphs 9 and 10.

5. The author includes numerous statistics in his essay. Find three examples and comment on how effectively they further his purpose in this essay.

WRITING PROMPTS

Responding to the Topic   Design your own Academy Awards show and then describe it in detail in an essay. Reflect on questions such as the following: Who would be the host? What would that person wear? How big a role would the presenter play? How would he or she enter? What kind of opening film montage would there be? What would the production numbers be like? How long would the show last? What rules would you give to the Oscar recipients about their speeches?

Responding to the Writer   Consult IMDb.com (Internet Movie Database) for a list of Oscar winners for Best Picture in the last five years. Pick one film and watch or rewatch it. Then write an essay in which you argue that the film should or should not have won the Oscar for Best Picture based on your personal criteria.

Responding to Multiple Viewpoints   In the final paragraph of his essay "Oscar and Hollywood in Splitsville!" O'Hehir asks, "will network viewers still tune in, in vast numbers, to see Jon Stewart's quips, the fabulous and horrifying gowns and the abysmal production numbers, even if they haven't seen the movies?" He then says that the future of "a tottering cultural empire" hangs on the answer to that question. Based on your reading of his essay and others in this chapter, write an essay in which you discuss what you believe is in store for the Oscars over the next ten years.

For a quiz on this reading, go to bedfordstmartins.com/mirror.

Hollywood Clicks on the Work
of Web Auteurs[1]

JOHN CLARK

With the rise in popularity of sites like YouTube and College Humor, it is easier than ever for aspiring filmmakers to find an audience. But to what extent will video on the Web influence the way Hollywood makes movies? John Clark published "Hollywood Clicks on the Work of Web Auteurs" in the *New York Times* in July 2006. He has also written entertainment stories for the *Los Angeles Times*.

> **THINKING AHEAD**   How much time do you spend watching video on the Web? What sites do you visit? Why do you like those sites? Have you or anyone you know ever posted a video online? What was the subject?

1   Even as David Lehre's *MySpace: The Movie*, an eleven-minute parody of the social-networking Web site, spawned a high-profile feeding frenzy, some of the Hollywood agents, managers and lawyers who were clamoring to represent him didn't know much about who he was, what he did or what they would do if they got him. But they wanted him anyway.

2   "It's their fear of not being a part of it," said Scott Vener, Mr. Lehre's manager, who first discovered him on the video-sharing Web site YouTube, where *MySpace* became an Internet phenomenon.

3   Their fears were justified in at least one respect. Calls about Mr. Lehre didn't start really rolling in to Mr. Vener's office at the Schiff Company in Beverly Hills until reports about *MySpace: The Movie* appeared in the old media, and talent agents aren't going to get rich chasing artists who are already being widely celebrated. If Mr. Lehre proves to be a harbinger[2] of things to come, talent agents will have to become Internet literate, or hire people who are.

4   Some people say that the film industry has more to fear than just being late to the party. If the Net begins spawning films—and not simply helping to market or deliver them, as has happened to date—studios' grip on the business of putting pictures on screens may be challenged.

5   "Their nightmare is a direct feed from moviemaker to audience," said Walter Kirn, a frequent contributor to the *New York Times* who has been serializing his novel *The Unbinding* on www.slate.com and saw one of his other novels, *Thumbsucker*, adapted to the big screen. "Their only trump

---

[1]auteurs: French word meaning "authors"; film directors known for a particular style.
[2]harbinger: Someone who initiates a major change or foreshadows what is to come.

cards are that they are pools of capital for making expensive things. Otherwise they are cut out of the action."

Geoffrey Gilmore, director of the Sundance Film Festival, said, "We are probably at a period of greater change than we have had in the past fifty years. The industry is scared about what they should make and how they should deliver it. What's the next step? Where's the development coming from?"   6

MySpace: The Movie first appeared on YouTube on January 31, and since then has had millions of hits, enough viewers to rival big-budget films or TV shows. Mr. Lehre, who is twenty-one and lived at his parents' home in Washington, Michigan, when he created the video, shot it there with friends. He scored the music himself so he wouldn't have to deal with copyright issues, designed the graphics and Googled any technical questions he had. This development and distribution process makes even independent films, with their retinue of maxed-out credit cards and frenzied film festivals, look positively mainstream in comparison.   7

The Net is particularly conducive to short-form comedy—skits, parodies, satires, even stand-up acts—because surfers tend to look at video in small increments. But so far television, especially cable, has been more receptive than the feature film world to these possibilities. Mr. Lehre signed with Fox and will produce a sketch-oriented television show that is set in his hometown and features his friends.   8

Recently, Carson Daly Productions signed Brooke Brodack, a twenty-year-old receptionist who lives in Massachusetts, to a production deal after her video diaries, comic shorts and music parodies attracted a wide following on YouTube. Andy Milonakis, star of his own show on MTV2, got his start on the Net, as did Tim Heidecker and Eric Wareheim, whose *Tom Goes to the Mayor* is on the Cartoon Network. Mike Rizzo, an agent at International Creative Management, which represents Mr. Lehre, said that established comedians are taking a hard look at what's available on the Net.   9

And despite their youth and inexperience, some of these video bloggers, or vloggers, have already made the jump from TV to film. In addition to his television contract, Mr. Lehre has a film deal with Fox in the works, Mr. Vener said. Andy Samberg, a former member of the Net comedy troupe the Lonely Island, is a regular on *Saturday Night Live* and has signed to appear in Paramount's film *Hot Rod*.   10

Whether the Internet will ever become a seed bed for full-length movies remains to be seen. The independent filmmaker Joe Swanberg (*Kissing on the Mouth*, *LOL*), who was hired by Nervevideo.com to create what he describes as an "indie[3] soap opera for the Web" called *Young American Bodies*, said the Net is the wrong place to watch a conventional narrative of conventional length.   11

"I have a hard time focusing on the computer screen for 90 minutes," Mr. Swanberg, 25, said. "A feature film isn't interactive. I think a theater is still the best venue for that."   12

---

[3]indie: Independent; refers to film production not associated with a big studio.

Yet Web users have already shown that they can bend a movie to their   13
tastes. The most obvious instance has been New Line Cinema's coming
film *Snakes on a Plane*, which was the subject of endless Internet interest,
mostly spoofing the title and its self-evident premise. New Line decided to
play to this audience by incorporating some of its ideas, requiring a week
of reshoots and a change in ratings from PG-13 to R.

"We really got to service the fans," said *Snakes* director David Ellis.   14
"Decisions are usually made by guys 50, 60 years old. They only know during
test screenings. If you can get it out early, you can deliver what they want."

Still, to let the audience feel genuinely in charge of the phenomenon,   15
Mr. Ellis and New Line had to sacrifice prerogatives that directors and
movie companies normally hold dear. "The worst thing we can do is take
it over," New Line's marketing chief, Russell Schwartz, said of trying to
control the *Snakes* Web boom.

These new horizons are not to everyone's liking. Pointing to the prece-   16
dent of *American Idol*, Mr. Gilmore said, "If you were told a decade ago that
a TV show would determine the next major pop star, would you believe it? I
have a fear of the tyranny of mass taste." Mr. Gilmore also wondered what
sort of "filtering mechanisms" would evolve on the Internet, if any. Of course
what makes the Web attractive is that there are no gatekeepers[4]—managers,
agents, studio executives or film-festival programmers—to get past. But
that's also what makes finding truly satisfying entertainment difficult. On
YouTube alone tens of thousands of videos are posted every day.

Another basic question is how many of the new Web-based talents will   17
stay on the Internet exclusively. Mr. Swanberg, for one, said he doesn't care
where his work is shown. But he noted that his two feature films, which
were screened at the South by Southwest[5] festival, were seen by far fewer
people than his *Young American Bodies*.

Mr. Kirn predicted that "all of the zoo animals are going to get out."   18
He continued, "The question is whether they will be paid," because the Net
so far has offered virtually unlimited freedom but very limited rewards.

As Hollywood scrambles to tap the Web's creative energy, one obvious—   19
and to some people ominous—possibility is that the film industry will find
a way to co-opt its major outposts. The entertainment business tried to do
that once before, toward the end of the dot-com[6] boom, when Hollywood
executives and talent tried to start Web sites like the ill-fated Pop.com,
which found little success in its attempt to distribute short films over the
Internet.

Rupert Murdoch's News Corporation has already purchased MySpace   20
in order to get in on the action, and other media entities are aligning
themselves with popular Web sites. Mr. Rizzo said that these giants would

[4]**gatekeepers:** Guardians or monitors.
[5]**South by Southwest:** One of the nation's premier film festivals, held each spring in Austin,
   Texas, and focused on locating talented new directors.
[6]**dot-com:** Part of a Web address originally intended to designate commercial entities; in
   popular usage, a company whose business focus is the Internet.

dominate the Internet in much the same way they've taken over the cable business, though it isn't clear that owning Web sites would position them to make blockbusters.

"Is buying MySpace the answer to that?" asked John Cooper, director   21
of programming at Sundance. "Culture is content driven, not medium driven."

Yet Mr. Kirn insisted that the medium would leave a deep imprint on   22
any entertainment that it generates. "The Net is a self-consciously anti-authoritarian audience," he said. "They are spit-ballers, defacers, vandals, skeptics. It's a class without a teacher. The movies that will succeed on it will have those properties."

"The Net is going to unleash a hybrid talent and a hybrid sensibility,"   23
he said. "What it needs is an Orson Welles,[7] an unclassifiable polymath.[8] It will reward someone with that kind of talent. Whether Hollywood can contain and absorb and dominate those energies will decide its fate."

EXERCISING VOCABULARY

1. Record your own definition for each word below in your notebook.

parody (n.) (1)	spoofing (v.) (13)
spawned (v.) (1)	prerogatives (n.) (15)
clamoring (v.) (1)	scrambles (v.) (19)
graphics (n.) (7)	ominous (adj.) (19)
retinue (n.) (7)	entities (n.) (20)
frenzied (adj.) (7)	aligning (v.) (20)
mainstream (adj.) (7)	unleash (v.) (23)
conducive (adj.) (8)	hybrid (adj.) (23)
increments (n.) (8)	sensibility (n.) (23)
venue (n.) (12)	

2. Clark writes that Walter Kirn "has been serializing his novel *The Unbinding* on www.slate.com" (para. 5). What is a serial? What does it mean to serialize something? Give several examples of a serial.

3. In paragraph 5, the author quotes Walter Kirn, who says that the studios' "only trump cards are that they are pools of capital for making expensive things." What are trump cards? What role do they play in card games? What trump cards do the studios hold? What advantage does this give them?

4. Clark writes that Geoffrey Gilmore has "a fear of the tyranny of mass taste" (para. 16). Define tyranny. In what context is the word normally used? What is *mass taste*? What is the connotative meaning implied by the term *mass taste*? How can mass taste be equated with tyranny?

---

[7]**Orson Welles:** Twentieth-century American film director whose masterpiece was *Citizen Kane*.
[8]**polymath:** A person of great learning in several fields of study.

5. In paragraph 19, Clark writes of the possibility "that the film industry will find a way to co-opt [the Web's] major outposts." What does it mean to co-opt something? What is an outpost? What are the Web's major outposts?

PROBING CONTENT

1. Who is David Lehre? Why did he become important?

2. What kind of film works best on the Web? Why?

3. What does the film industry have to fear from the Web? What does director Geoffrey Gilmore see as the major concern?

4. What does John Cooper mean when he says that "Culture is content driven, not medium driven" (para. 21)? Why does Walter Kirn disagree with him?

5. How did New Line Cinema use the Web with *Snakes on a Plane*? What did this require the movie studio to do?

CONSIDERING CRAFT

1. Examine the title of the essay. Describe the play on words here. How does the title forecast the topic of the essay?

2. John Clark devotes a large part of his essay to one Web auteur: David Lehre. Why do you think he chose this particular person? How effective is Clark's writing strategy?

3. Reread paragraph 4. Explain how personification is used in this paragraph. How does the connotative meaning of the language here convey an opinion about the subject?

4. This essay has numerous quotations from other people. Why does Clark devote so much space in his essay to the words of others? To what extent does this add to or take away from his own authority as a writer?

WRITING PROMPTS

Responding to the Topic   In an essay, describe your experiences watching videos on the Web. If you have never watched a Web video, use a computer at a library to watch one or two. How does this experience compare to seeing movies in a theater?

Responding to the Writer   In paragraph 22, Clark quotes Walter Kirn as saying, "The Net is a self-consciously anti-authoritarian audience. . . . They are spit-ballers, defacers, vandals, skeptics. It's a class without a teacher. The movies that will succeed on it will have those properties." Write an essay in which you take a position on Kirn's statement and defend your opinion.

Responding to Multiple Viewpoints   Wesley Morris, in "Shrinking the Big Screen," claims that "the line between the two mediums had become porous. While the movies started looking more like television, TV started looking more like the movies" (para. 8). Based on your reading of Clark's "Hollywood Clicks on the Work of Web Auteurs," write an essay addressing how Morris would view the Web's effect on both television and film.

For a quiz on this reading, go to bedfordstmartins.com/mirror.

Virtual Humans

KELLY TYLER-LEWIS

Kelly Tyler-Lewis is a producer for PBS's *Nova*. She coproduced the program "Special Effects of *Titanic* and Beyond" and is also an associate producer for the large-format film unit, working on projects such as *Stormchasers* (1995), *Special Effects* (1996), *Island of the Sharks* (1999), and *The Endurance: Shackleton's Epic Journey* (2001), which won an Emmy for Best Historical Documentary. Tyler-Lewis is also the author of *The Lost Men: The Harrowing Saga of Shackelton's Ross Sea Party* (2006). In "Virtual Humans," written for Nova Online, she discusses the realistic computer-generated characters made possible by new advances in technology.

> **THINKING AHEAD**   Which films that use virtual actors are you familiar with? What do you think of these computer-generated actors? What are the benefits of using them? What are the disadvantages? How do computer-generated actors compare to human ones?

After millions of years of natural selection, human beings have some serious competition for their lofty perch on the evolutionary ladder—and the challenger has only been evolving for less than a decade. Some computer artists contend that anything we can do, "virtual humans" can do better, and they're poised to revolutionize moviemaking with a new species that doesn't require an astronomical salary, works around the clock without complaint, and lives quietly on a hard drive between death-defying stunts.

A generation of computer-generated (CG) characters, called "synthespians" or "vactors," is attracting notice in Hollywood. Some insiders envision a future when digital stars compete for roles with the flesh-and-blood variety. While a photoreal digital actor has yet to carry a major motion picture, synthespians have captured supporting roles for some time now, whenever the going gets too tough or too expensive. Synthespians serve as doubles for breathtaking stunts too dangerous for mortal stars: a girl leaping from a skyscraper in *The Fifth Element*, Sylvester Stallone chasing through the skies on an airborne motorcycle in *Judge Dredd*, and a luckless attorney becoming tyrannosaur fodder in *Jurassic Park*. And producers cut costs on the "cast of thousands" by using digital extras to stand in for the legions of troops in *Hamlet*, mobs of Washington demonstrators in *Forrest Gump*, and passengers aboard the doomed *Titanic*.

Fooling the Eye

The leap from extra to starring role for synthespians is a big one, since   3
it invites heightened scrutiny from the viewer. Human beings have a finely tuned ability to recognize their kind, an ability that is thought to be both innate and learned, and that ups the ante for filmmakers seeking to fool them with a synthetic stand-in. Creating convincing movement is particularly difficult. Animators can take the perceptual challenge head-on and painstakingly create movement for their characters frame by frame from scratch, or they can use the real thing. A technique called motion capture allows actual movement to be recorded and applied to digital characters. An actor wears reflective markers at key body joints, and surrounding cameras record the motion of reflected infrared light in the computer. Later, this motion data is transferred to the digital character.

The human face presents an even more daunting challenge. Ed Catmull,   4
a computer graphics pioneer since the late 1970s and a founder of Pixar (*Toy Story*, *A Bug's Life*), regards it as a central issue in character animation.

"The human face is a unique problem," he says. "We are genetically pro-   5
grammed to recognize human faces. We're so good that most people aren't even aware of it while they think about it. It turns out, for instance, that if we make a perfectly symmetrical face, we see it as being wrong. So we want things to be not quite perfect, have a lot of subtlety, but if they're too imper-fect, then we think that they're strange."

For Scott Ross, President of Digital Domain, the problem is more intan-   6
gible: "One of the things that I'm mostly concerned about in terms of virtual actors is that there's been millions of years of experience in our genetic code. And I'm concerned that when you create a close-up of a virtual actor and look into its eyes, that it will take real skill to be able to give that virtual actor soul. And I've not yet seen that."

The Silicon Rush

The quest to create virtual actors is comparatively recent; the first interactive   7
computer graphics program was only developed in 1961. Designed by Ivan Sutherland at the Massachusetts Institute of Technology, Sketchpad genera-ted simple geometrical line drawings for design and engineering applications. These simple operations required a state-of-the-art TX-2 defense computer to run.

The silicon[1] rush in Hollywood began in 1985, when a knight sprang   8
from a stained glass window and handily dispatched a human opponent
in *Young Sherlock Holmes*, courtesy of computer animation. A virtual
stampede of digital characters followed: the water creature of *The Abyss*,
the quicksilver[2] T-1000 of *Terminator 2: Judgment Day*, the menagerie of
Jumanji, and the dinosaurs of *Jurassic Park*. In 1995, *Toy Story* was released, the first CG film in history, populated entirely by digital characters
in a world made of bits and bytes.

The reason for this explosion? Jim Blinn, an early computer graphics   9
innovator who created the well-known *Voyager* fly-by animations for the
Jet Propulsion Laboratory, credits the decreasing cost of computer memory.
"In my lifetime, the cost of the basic tools of my trade—of making images
with a computer—has gone from about $500,000 to about $2,000," he
says. "It's a factor of two hundred or three hundred to one." A corre-
sponding inverse growth in computer power and memory has equipped
CG Pygmalions[3] to cope with the high degree of complexity and detail
inherent in living creatures. Today's microcomputers have roughly four
hundred times more memory and operate about five thousand times faster
than the TX-2 used by Sutherland.

Scott Ross projects continuing growth in hardware capability, spurring   10
increasingly sophisticated animation. "The concept of Moore's law states
that the processing power of computing doubles every year," he says. "We're
seeing that in terms of what we're doing today in the film industry."

Building a Better Human

With this enhanced technology, animators have turned from fantasy charac-   11
ters and extinct animals to a new digital grail: a photorealistic *Homo sapiens*.
Ellen Poon, a visual effects supervisor for Industrial Light and Magic who
has been involved with such films as *Jumanji* and *Men in Black*, is optimistic,
but sees technical challenges ahead.

"I think we are very close to creating a realistic-looking virtual person,"   12
she says. "There are a few things that have to be right, and we're still in
the process of researching them. And those elements are hair, skin, clothing,
movement, and facial expressions."

The problem of hair has bedeviled animators for years. There are thou-   13
sands of hairs on the human head, which vary in color, light reflectance,

---

[1]**silicon:** The material used as the base for most integrated circuits; hardware, especially
    integrated circuits or microprocessor-based computer systems.
[2]**quicksilver:** Liquid silver; mercury.
[3]**Pygmalions:** Creators; refers to Pygmalion, who, according to Greek legend, sculpted a
    woman named Galatea out of ivory, fell in love with her, and convinced Venus to bring
    her to life.

and texture and can move either singly or together. The lion in *Jumanji* required the modeling of one million individual hairs for the mane alone. Nadia Mangenat Thalmann of Miralab, a computer research center at the University of Geneva, tackled similar complexity as she developed clothing for digital characters.

"Fabric is very difficult," says Thalmann. "The computer has to know   14 every moment where the wrinkles are that are created by the movement of the fabric. We used two or three hours of calculation for one single frame of animation to get it right—and there are twenty-four frames in one second of film."

Questioning the Digital Grail

Hurdles notwithstanding, the advantages of a virtual actor are appealing.   15 A child synthespian won't have temper tantrums or work hours mandated by labor laws. A vactor will never be busy when it's time for re-shoots after a film has wrapped. A virtual human never grows old. And, to the delight of producers, a digital superstar won't require a $20 million salary, a deluxe trailer and a coterie of bodyguards, masseuses and aromatherapists to get the job done.

For the animators at Miralab, it's only a matter of time and comput-   16 ing power before icons of the past take the limelight again. Thalmann has developed a virtual Marilyn Monroe. She is uncannily realistic, but the illusion loses its photorealistic quality in close-up. Continuing technical advances raise the possibility that there may someday be stars who truly will live forever.

Even so, many in the special effects industry question whether silicon ac-   17 tors will ever pose a real threat to the carbon-based variety. Dennis Muren, visual effects supervisor for Industrial Light and Magic and nine-time Oscar winner, is skeptical of the creative benefits.

"What's the point?" he wonders. "If you want to put Marilyn Monroe   18 in a movie, you could get a terrific actress, give her a great make-up artist, six months of studying and voice training, and she could do a better Marilyn Monroe than we could ever do."

Jim Blinn questions whether synthespians make economic sense: "A   19 dinosaur doesn't exist, so it's practical to simulate it. With human beings, however, having a staff of twenty people all working on the lighting, the modeling, and the motion might not be a great trade-off, because you can replace that whole team with one human actor who can do what the director wants."

To the Future . . . and Beyond

Thalmann contemplates taking virtual humans to a new level. "I'm not so   20 much interested to see pictures, which you watch passively," she says. "My ultimate goal is to be able to live in the virtual worlds, and to meet virtual humans that are collaborators," says Thalmann.

Thalmann is not alone. Computer game developers have begun ex-   21
perimenting with artificial intelligence[4] (AI), endowing game characters
with the capacity to learn and interact with their environment and the
game player.

John Lasseter, director of *Toy Story*, is charting a different course. "I'm   22
interested in creating a film with characters that people obviously know don't
exist," he says. "But then they look at it and say, 'It seems so real. I know it
doesn't—but wait. I know those toys aren't alive, but it looks so real. No,
they can't be alive, no. Are they?' So I think that's one of the really exciting
things that computer animation can give you: a combination of fantasy and
the photorealistic which has never been seen before."

With the latest generation of talent and tools at their disposal, visual   23
effects filmmakers see a wide range of possibilities in the future, with or
without virtual humans. "I think we can do just about anything right now
if we had the time and money," says Dennis Muren. "It's really like your
imagination has no boundaries at the moment. . . . I'd rather put the work
into something that's unique and new, and you haven't seen anywhere before,
and there's no way a person could do it."

EXERCISING VOCABULARY

1. Record your own definition for each word below in your notebook.

fodder (n.) (2)	innovator (n.) (9)
legions (n.) (2)	inverse (adj.) (9)
scrutiny (n.) (3)	inherent (adj.) (9)
innate (adj.) (3)	spurring (v.) (10)
synthetic (adj.) (3)	bedeviled (v.) (13)
perceptual (adj.) (3)	tackled (v.) (13)
daunting (adj.) (4)	hurdles (n). (15)
genetically (adv.) (5)	mandated (v.) (15)
symmetrical (adj.) (5)	coterie (n.) (15)
intangible (adj.) (6)	uncannily (adv.) (16)
handily (adv.) (8)	passively (adv.) (20)
dispatched (v.) (8)	collaborators (n.) (20)
menagerie (n.) (8)	

2. In paragraph 3, Tyler-Lewis writes that our human ability to instinctively
recognize other humans "ups the ante for filmmakers" who would de-
ceive us. What is the source of the expression "ups the ante?" How
does the author use the expression here?

---

[4]**artificial intelligence:** The ability of a computer or other machine to perform those activities
that are normally thought to require human intelligence; the branch of computer science
concerned with the development of machines having this ability.

3. In paragraph 11, Tyler-Lewis calls "a photorealistic *Homo sapiens*" "a new digital grail." From which language does the term *Homo sapiens* originate? What do the two parts of the term mean? What is the Holy Grail? Who sought it? Why was it so sought after? Why is "a photorealistic *Homo sapiens*" the "new digital grail" for computer animators?

4. The author writes, "It's only a matter of time and computing power before icons of the past take the limelight again" (para. 16). What is an icon? How can an actor be an icon? What is a limelight? In the theater, what does it mean to take the limelight? How does this meaning relate to Tyler-Lewis's use of the phrase?

5. In paragraph 22, Tyler-Lewis writes that John Lasseter, the director of *Toy Story,* "is charting a different course." With what context is the phrase "charting a different course normally" associated? What does the author mean here?

PROBING CONTENT

1. What are some reasons that directors choose to cast synthespians over real actors in their films?

2. What is motion capture? How does it work?

3. Who are Ed Catmull and Scott Ross? According to them, why is portraying the human face digitally so difficult?

4. When did the surge in CG films begin? What was responsible for the "silicon rush"?

5. What strategies must a production team use to achieve box-office success, given the obviously fictitious storylines and cast of CG films?

CONSIDERING CRAFT

1. In the opening paragraph, Tyler-Lewis writes, "After millions of years of natural selection, human beings have some serious competition for their lofty perch on the evolutionary ladder." Describe how the figurative language used here works in this sentence to introduce the topic.

2. Tyler-Lewis uses several headings in her essay. Examine each one and then comment on the ways in which they affect your reading and understanding. Would you substitute another title for any of the author's headings? How would this make the essay more effective?

3. Find five places in the essay in which the author uses examples from specific films. Not every reader will have seen the movies she cites as examples. Why then does she do this?

4. In her essay, Tyler-Lewis quotes several different people. Locate four such examples. Which kinds of people does she cite? Why did she choose these individuals?

WRITING PROMPTS

Responding to the Topic   Describe your experience viewing a film containing one or more synthespians. If you have not seen a movie with vactors, rent or borrow one from the library. How would the experience differ if the director had cast live actors? Did the film contain any specific scenes or stunts that would have to be cut from the shooting script had they not been performed by vactors?

Responding to the Writer   Should digital actors be cast in roles previously envisioned for flesh-and-blood actors? How far will this technological "evolution" go? Will vactors ever replace human actors? Why? To what extent are the benefits of synthespians worth exploring and developing? After considering the positions of others like Dennis Muren, Nadia Thalmann, and Jim Blinn, write an essay in which you detail your own position. Provide specific examples from films to support your argument.

Responding to Multiple Viewpoints   What would Stephen King ("Why We Crave Horror Movies") and George A. Romero ("Horror Auteur Is Unfinished with the Undead") think of virtual actors? How might vactors be especially useful in the horror genre of film? What kinds of parts could they play? What would be the benefits and drawbacks of using synthespians instead of human actors?

For a quiz on this reading, go to bedfordstmartins.com/mirror.

An Unlikely Commuter

ANALYZING THE IMAGE

Who is that strange little creature sitting next to two ordinary commuters on a New York City subway train? It's Gollum, the computer-generated character from Peter Jackson's *The Lord of the Rings* film trilogy, based on the fantasy novels of British writer J. R. R. Tolkien. Gollum's presence in this photograph is part of an inspired publicity campaign for the second film, *The Lord of the Rings: The Two Towers* (2002). This campaign transformed the subway into the "Middle-Earth Shuttle" by decorating the trains with Middle-Earth creatures, vines, moss, and stones to celebrate the November 18, 2003, DVD and VHS release of the Special Extended Edition of *The Lord of the Rings: The Two Towers*.

1. Where is your eye drawn first when you look at this visual? Why?

2. How would you describe the expressions on the faces of the two human commuters?

3. How would you react to seeing a life-size replica of the virtual actor Gollum as you go about your daily activities?

4. What else in the visual forms part of the publicity campaign? Why is it there?

5. How successful do you think this publicity campaign was and why?

Wrapping Up Chapter 7

CONNECTING TO THE CULTURE

1. Go to your university library or to a video store and rent a movie that is based on a television show and a DVD collection of episodes for that television show. Watch both the movie and the television show episodes and take notes while you're watching them. Then write an essay in which you compare the film with the relevant episode(s) of the TV series on which it is based. You may want to refer to Wesley Morris's "Shrinking the Big Screen" before writing your paper.

2. Using the essays in this chapter, as well as your own observations and experiences, write an essay in which you discuss how the self-image of men or women is handled or mishandled in movies. Include several specific examples from films you have seen. You may also refer to other essays in this book, such as those in Chapters 3, 4, and 6.

3. Write an essay in which you argue for the iconic status of one particular film. You may wish to refer to "Oscar and Hollywood in Splitsville!" in this chapter or "*Harry Potter* and Magical Realism" in Chapter 8. First consider what qualifies as an iconic movie. Then make a list of at least five films, past or present, that could be the subject of your essay. Make your final choice, watch the movie, and take notes as you watch it. You may also wish to consult Internet sources such as IMDb.com (Internet Movie Database) or the Web site for the film you have chosen.

4. Go to a Web site like YouTube and watch a film by one of the filmmakers mentioned in "Hollywood Clicks on the Work of Web Auteurs" or by a director of your choice. Take notes as you watch the film. Then write a review of it. Consult IMDb.com (Internet Movie Database) for examples of reviews by trusted reviewers such as Roger Ebert, James Berardinelli, or Peter Travers.

5. Choose a film whose story line deals with an ethnic group other than your own. You might choose a film like *Crash* that focuses on the interactions among characters from several different groups or a film like *Madea* that focuses on a single group. Watch the film and take notes on it. Then write an essay in which you examine the ways in which ethnicity is presented in the film. You may wish to refer to "Tyler Perry's Money Machine" in this chapter as you write your paper.

Focusing on Yesterday, Focusing on Today

"They're here!" Carol Anne, the little girl in the iconic 1982 horror movie *Poltergeist*, utters these words as she reaches up to touch the screen of the family TV. At that moment in the film, a chill runs through us as we realize that Carol Anne sees something or someone we don't. After all, the only thing we see on the TV screen is static. But soon thereafter, the seemingly harmless poltergeists, or ghosts, that Carol Anne has been communicating with through the television set abduct the little girl.

The *Ring* films and the Japanese horror film *Ringu*, on which they are based, also feature a vengeful ghost and a mysterious television set. In these films, the victims view a disturbing videotape and then hear the phone ring.

"They're Here!"

The voice on the other end warns them that they will die in seven days. This movie still from 2000 shows the gruesome murderer Sadako, her long hair dripping wet from the well water in which she drowned, crawling out of the TV set to claim her victim.

What role does the television set play in each visual? What role does each girl play? Based on what you know about *Poltergeist* and *Ringu*, how effectively do these two visuals convey a sense of horror? Which image do you find more frightening? Why? Who is the real villain in these two films? Is it a ghostly presence, or is it something more sinister? If the medium really is the message, as famed media theorist Marshall McLuhan said, what is it telling us? In what ways can technological advances threaten our culture's very existence?

"Ring, Ring. You're Dead."

8 American Idols
Representations of American Culture

Analyzing the Image

This arresting photograph, which at first glance appears to be New York City, is actually the New York–New York Hotel and Casino in Las Vegas, Nevada. The photograph ingeniously merges two well-recognized American icons. Very few citizens of any country would fail to recognize this intrinsically American skyline.

- What about this photograph makes it unmistakably New York City? What makes it distinctly *not* a photograph of the real New York City?

- Why have Las Vegas and New York City endured through generations as iconic American locations?

- What about these two cities makes them international travel destinations?

- Which foreign cities do Americans recognize as iconic? Why? For what are these cities noted?

Research this topic with TopLinks at bedfordstmartins.com/toplinks.

GEARING UP   Think about people, places, or things that are solidly part of American culture. Perhaps John Wayne, McDonald's, the Energizer Bunny, blue jeans, jazz, or baseball comes to mind. When something or someone is of significance to an entire culture, it achieves a special status. We have a shared idea about its importance. What elevates something or someone to this iconic status? What American icons can you name? How do these typically American people, places, events and things translate into other cultures? When they are exported, what do they say about America and Americans?

Even with the extended reign of *American Idol* as one of television's most popular shows, most of us spend very little time thinking about those things that we idolize. If we stop to think about the word *idol* at all, we probably think of the word's religious connotation. Actually, however, an idol, also called an icon, is anything to which people show exceptional devotion. What aspects of American culture are so clearly significant to most of us that they might be considered icons? Is the television show *American Idol* an icon to the millions who watch it devotedly?

How does someone or something become important to an entire culture? Perhaps such recognition happens because of sheer numbers, as in the case of Starbucks. Perhaps it's a unique idea that bursts onto the cultural scene at just the right moment, like the concept of a shopping mall. Maybe it represents a suppressed urge in each of us to act out our fantasies of who we might be if we weren't so busy being real and living our everyday, mundane lives; think about Madonna's shifts in persona. To achieve iconic status, something or someone must hold our collective attention over a long span of time. Consider Dolly Parton or Billy Joel. What happens when these typically American icons are exported abroad? How does a Hooters restaurant look in China? And what happens when icons from across an ocean, such as Volvos, sushi, and Harry Potter, become a fixed part of American culture?

In this chapter, we examine notable cultural icons. We look not only at what achieves iconic status in America, but also at what those icons project about our national image and what happens when their relevance is called into question by a dissenting minority.

COLLABORATING   Working in small groups, determine which criteria something or someone should meet to become an American icon. Then make a list of twenty people, places, events or objects that meet those criteria. Be prepared to justify your contributions to the list. Swap lists with another group to look for similarities and differences.

Hooters Translates in China

CRAIG SIMONS

American businesses are highly visible throughout the world, but some-times, as this essay shows, particularly iconic businesses can be reinter-preted by different world cultures. Craig Simons covers the region from India to Japan for Cox News Service. His particular focus is China, where he first lived as a Peace Corps volunteer from 1996 to 1998. Since then, he has been a regular contributor to *Newsweek* and an editor and a re-porter in the Singapore bureau of Reuters news service. His writing has also appeared in the *New York Times* and the *International Herald Tribune*. "Hooters Translates in China" was published through the Cox syndicate in February 2006.

> **THINKING AHEAD**   What do you know about the Hooters restaurant chain? Have you ever been to a Hooters restaurant? What was your primary reason for choosing that restaurant? If you've never been, would you go if given an opportunity? Why?

Zhou Shouya is a textbook example of how a simple idea can appeal 1 across cultures.

Dressed in a tight tank top and hip-hugging orange shorts—the uni- 2 form worn by Hooters Girls around the world—the twenty-three-year-old law student paused from delivering sandwiches and plates of buffalo wings at China's first Hooters franchise to say that many of her customers are regulars.

"Some people come every day. It's like a home to them," she said. "I 3 guess they feel relaxed here."

That's one way to explain the Shanghai restaurant's success. Since open- 4 ing in October 2004, "business has been consistently profitable," market-ing director Xu Fan said, adding that between 250 and 300 customers visit daily.

The owners paid Atlanta-based Hooters of America an undisclosed 5 amount of money to franchise the brand and expect to open a second Shanghai location in April. Plans are in the works to open one or two Beijing branches by the end of the year.

"We think there's a good growth potential in China," Xu said. 6

If Hooters does develop from its small beginnings behind a Shanghai 7 mall into a Chinese food and beverage force, it would take a page from the company's U.S. history.

"Hooters was appropriately incorporated on April Fool's Day, 1983, 8 when six businessmen with absolutely no previous restaurant experience got together and decided to open a place they couldn't get kicked out of," a Web site set up by the original founders said.

The owners—a painting contractor, a liquor salesman, a retired service   9
station proprietor, a real estate executive, a mason and the co-manager of a painting business—"found a little dive in Clearwater," Florida, and devised a "creative menu" that "combined nicely with the most important element, the beautiful and vivacious Hooters Girls," the site said.

The founders soon found partners that helped the company grow far be-   10
yond that original restaurant. It now has more than four hundred restaurants including thirty-six foreign franchises in cities such as Lima, Peru; Interlaken, Switzerland; and Singapore.

"It's a pretty steep learning curve to take an all-American concept like   11
Hooters and take it international," Hooters of America marketing vice president Mike McNeil said. "But we see the future as very, very bright internationally."

Shanghai marketing director Xu agreed.   12

While most of the customers at the Shanghai franchise are Westerners,   13
increasing numbers of Chinese are patronizing the eatery.

"Hooters isn't just a restaurant," she said. "It's also American culture,   14
and that appeals to many Chinese."

Chinese acceptance of the brand owes as much to a loosening of   15
Chinese views on sexuality over the past decades as it does to the market savvy of the "Hooters Six."

During the Cultural Revolution[1] in the 1960s and '70s, Chinese women   16
who wore revealing clothing or grew their hair long were often punished for failing to uphold the socialist[2] state's image of a model worker. Even in the 1990s, shorts and miniskirts were rarely worn in many parts of China.

"The younger generation is very different from our parents," Xu said.   17
"There has been a big change in Chinese values."

While the use of female sexuality as a marketing tool has provoked   18
anger among some Americans, McNeil said, Chinese businesses routinely hire attractive young women to sell products. Many Chinese companies require applicants to submit recent photographs when applying for jobs.

"It's natural for employers to hire good-looking people to deal with the   19
public," Xu said, adding that the Shanghai franchise had never received a complaint about the waitresses' uniforms.

"Hooters is a very fun and clean environment," Xu said. "Hooters   20
Girls are like cheerleaders."

Zhou, who uses the English name Lucky and was named "China Hooters   21
Girl of the Year" last year, actually is a cheerleader. Besides studying at

[1]Cultural Revolution: Attempt by Chairman Mao Zedong to reassert his influence on China's people.
[2]socialist: Advocating community or government ownership of means of production and all goods.

Shanghai's Fudan University and working twenty hours a week at Hooters, she cheers for the Shanghai Sharks, the basketball team that Houston Rockets center Yao Ming once played for.

Zhou likes the job because she can improve her English, make new friends, and earn several hundred dollars a month.   22

"And working at Hooters has taught me a lot about American culture," she said, before delivering another plate of buffalo wings.   23

EXERCISING VOCABULARY

1. Record your own definition for each word below in your notebook.

   franchise (n.) (2)
   consistently (adv.) (4)
   undisclosed (adj.) (5)
   proprietor (n.) (9)
   mason (n.) (9)

   vivacious (adj.) (9)
   patronizing (v.) (13)
   uphold (v.) (16)
   provoked (v.) (18)

2. Simons opens his essay with this statement: "Zhou Shouya is a textbook example of how a simple idea can appeal across cultures." You know what a textbook is. How can a person serve as a textbook example? What qualities would such a person have?

3. According to Simons, the success of Hooters didn't depend solely on "the market savvy" of the men who started Hooters (para. 15). What does the noun *savvy* mean? Which market is being referred to here? What is "market savvy"?

PROBING CONTENT

1. When and how was the Hooters restaurant chain created? What is significant about the date?

2. Who are the "Hooters Six"? Why are they unlikely restaurant owners?

3. Why does visiting Hooters appeal to many Chinese? What attitudes in China had to shift for Hooters to be successful there?

4. Describe Zhou Shouya. Why does she work at Hooters? How suited is Zhou to her job?

CONSIDERING CRAFT

1. Why does Simons select this title for his essay? In what sense is the word *translates* a play on words?

2. What does Simons accomplish by focusing on just one Hooters server instead of interviewing several? Why does he select Zhou Shouya? To what extent is his strategy successful?

3. Simons writes, "If Hooters does develop from its small beginnings behind a Shanghai mall into a Chinese food and beverage force, it would take a page from the company's U.S. history" (para. 7). Explain the figure of speech Simons uses here and comment on its effectiveness.

WRITING PROMPTS

Responding to the Topic   Mike McNeil, marketing vice president for Hooters of America, argues that "it's a pretty steep learning curve to take an all-American concept like Hooters and take it international" (para. 11). Which other "all-American" concepts have been successful internationally? Write an essay in which you review the American businesses that you're aware of that have been successful internationally. Describe what you believe accounts for their success.

Responding to the Writer   Xu Fan, marketing director of Hooters, notes that "Hooters isn't just a restaurant. It's also American culture, and that appeals to many Chinese" (para. 14). Zhou Shouya feels that working at Hooters "has taught [her] a lot about American culture" (para. 23). To what extent does Hooters represent American culture? Write an essay in which you take a position on this question and support it with evidence from this essay and from other sources that you incorporate.

Responding to Multiple Viewpoints   In "*Harry Potter* and Magical Realism," Daniel Nexon references some of the difficulties that the British-based books and movies had to overcome to be accepted in America. Compare those obstacles with those faced by Hooters in its bid for widespread acceptance in China.

For a quiz on this reading, go to bedfordstmartins.com/mirror.

Signs of Our Times

VIRGINIA POSTREL

From diners to car dealerships, neon signs used to be common beacons on roadsides and in busy commercial areas. But, as this essay explains, changes in attitudes and technology are turning neon signs into an iconic, but disappearing American art form. Virginia Postrel is a contributing editor to the *Atlantic*. She is the author of *The Future and Its Enemies: The Growing Conflict over Creativity, Enterprise, and Progress* (1999) and *The Substance of Style: How the Rise of Aesthetic Value Is Remaking Commerce, Culture, and Consciousness* (2004). She has also worked as an editor for *Reason* and as an economics columnist for the *New York Times*. She wrote "Signs of Our Times" for the *Atlantic* in 2006.

> **THINKING AHEAD**   Describe any neon signs that you have seen. What did they advertise or represent? Where have you seen them? Would you describe them as art? Why?

Like the skyscraper, the automobile, and the motion-picture palace, neon signs once symbolized popular hopes for a new era of technological achievement and commercial abundance. From the 1920s to the 1950s, neon-lit streets pulsed with visual excitement from Vancouver to Miami. Large-scale spectaculars—tropical fish up to forty-three feet long hypnotically swimming past the Wrigley Spearman, or acrobatic Little Lulu lighting up each letter of a giant Kleenex box as she tumbled across it—provided free entertainment, while the humblest shop signs turned the urban night into well-lighted public space.

Neon's glowing colors and sinuous shapes haven't changed significantly since the 1920s, but the medium's meanings, and its fortunes, have shifted dramatically over the decades. The history of neon signs suggests how thoroughly entangled memory, identity, and hope are with even the purest sensory pleasures—and how truly subjective are the clashing tastes that shape aesthetic regulations.

In their heyday,[1] neon signs "were very much a symbol of modernism," says Adolfo Nodal, the former general manager of the Los Angeles Cultural Affairs Department. "They became a symbol of the new age, the Jazz Age, the new era that was sweeping the country." Nodal spearheaded a campaign that over the past decade has restored about 130 of the city's historic signs, mostly the long-neglected rooftop markers of apartment buildings

---

[1]**heyday:** Period of greatest popularity or strength.

and hotels. "They're beautiful objects in their own right," says Nodal, "and lighting them brings back . . . a more beautiful time."

Neon inspires passion. It still exists today largely because of the efforts of enthusiasts, mostly older baby boomers with fond memories of roadside America. They nurtured the craft back to life and preserved the "garish" signs that zealous civic beautifiers had tried to wipe out. In the late 1970s, neon "was a little bit like the last buffalo tied up outside the Indian gift store somewhere—almost extinct, certainly thirsty and hungry," recalls the artist Rudi Stern, whom many neon lovers credit with saving the medium. In 1972, Stern founded Let There Be Neon, a gallery and workshop in New York, which trained artists to use neon and promoted it as an artistic medium. "I wanted to turn people on to the beauty of it, to the creative, expressive possibilities of it." 4

Today, neon signs are treasured by collectors, displayed in museums, and encouraged, even subsidized, by towns hoping to add zip to districts that go dark at 5 p.m. When the automotive specialist RM Auctions held a memorabilia sale this past June, a Thunderbird Motel neon sign fetched $27,600, one for the Cloud 9 Motel went for $21,275, and just the star from atop an old Holiday Inn neon sign brought $3,220. "These things that formerly had no value are now seen as folk art," says Len Davidson, a sign maker and the author of *Vintage Neon*. 5

In 1983, Davidson gave up an academic career in sociology to pursue his love of neon. He has turned his vintage-sign collection into the Neon Museum of Philadelphia, which displays signs in businesses around the city. Elsewhere, neon has found permanent quarters, notably in the American Sign Museum in Cincinnati, founded in 1999, and Los Angeles's Museum of Neon Art, founded in 1981 to preserve old signs and exhibit fine art that incorporates neon. All this neon appreciation represents a major change in attitudes. Beginning in the 1960s, neon signs were persecuted throughout the United States and Canada—torn down and outlawed by city officials determined to avoid the "carnival atmosphere" and "visual clutter" of such blatant commercialism. "The signs and the billboards are bullying you thousands of times a day," Alderman Warnett Kennedy told the residents of Vancouver, calling on "the more thoughtful citizens" to "become nuisances on the subject of ugliness." Soon enough, Vancouver's streets, formerly awash in color, started to go dark. The anti-neon movement reflected both elite taste and consensus ideology. The bright colors and pulsing animation of the signs defied the formal geometry of aristocratic modernism and the tidied-up corporatism of the Galbraithian[2] "New Industrial State." 6

Dan Holzschuh, a Dallas-area sign maker and collector, remembers a trade-magazine article from the early 1970s documenting the trend with photos of a crane "cleaning up" a downtown street by removing all the 7

[2]**Galbraithian:** Based on the principles of John Kenneth Galbraith, a famous economist.

neon signs. Then "it shows trailers going to the landfill and dumping, dumping all these neon signs."

By the 1970s, neon was almost dead. The skilled craftsmen who could   8
wire signs and bend glass were retiring without successors. "They were hardly even training anyone anymore," says Tama Starr, an old friend of mine and the president of Artkraft Strauss in New York, the company that for three generations built the neon spectaculars of Times Square. In the 1970s, the main demand for her family's wares[3] came from porn merchants—like the red neon curtains of the Pussycat Theater façade—a relationship that made neon seem even less reputable. The signs also fell victim to the symbolic politics of the energy crisis. With Americans turning down thermostats and sitting in gas lines, big blinking signs seemed wasteful—even though they weren't. Neon signs don't consume much power, but they *look* like they do. A cousin of fluorescent lighting, neon is actually quite energy efficient. A neon tube glows coolly when high-voltage, low-amperage electrical power excites the gas within it. The color depends on which inert gas the tube contains—neon for red, argon for blue—and whether additives like mercury are present. For more variety, the glass itself can be colored or a fluorescent coating added.

The low point for neon came in 1982, when Holiday Inn did away with   9
its signature "Great Sign," replacing the neon extravaganza with a forgettable green plastic box. Of the thousands of Holiday Inn signs that once shone on America's highways, only one remains to be seen, in the Henry Ford Museum, in Dearborn, Michigan. What good taste and aggressive regulation couldn't squelch, corporate image making did. Out went lighted tubes, and in came bright plastic signs or, a bit later, individual plastic letters discreetly illuminated by internal neon tubes.

Neon had a resurgence in the 1980s. Cities including Vancouver and   10
San Diego reversed their anti-neon ordinances, and the Times Square spectaculars reclaimed their dignity when Japanese electronics companies re-imported the medium from Tokyo. But today neon is threatened by a new technology: low-maintenance, easily programmed light-emitting diodes, or LEDs, which often use even less power than neon and glow more sharply. A year ago, one of the country's most famous neon signs, the pulsing Citgo logo near Boston's Fenway Park, was replaced with an LED copy—not quite as elegant, perhaps, but able to survive a Boston winter without repairs. Advertisers prefer LEDs and video screens, which are visible even in the daytime. Instead of wooing customers with mesmerizing signs of identity and presence, these new media display constantly changing information, from brand announcements to recycled television commercials. With neon, "you were looking at a piece of art, and now you're looking at a manufactured object," says Starr. Most of those artworks are long

---

[3]**wares:** Merchandise for sale.

gone, carted to the dump to be crushed into compact cubes of glass and steel. Storage problems make neon signs the most ephemeral of commercial arts.

Bob Jackowitz, the vice president of Artkraft Strauss, recalls one of his   11
favorite creations—four nine-foot-high vertical sine waves,[4] each a different color, that danced in and out of one another, perfectly synchronized so
they never collided. "If it was at MOMA,[5] it would be a piece of sculpture,"
he says. "If it was in front of an office building, it would be functional art.
But it was in a disco, so it was a lighting fixture." When the disco was torn
down, Jackowitz was asked if he wanted to reclaim the piece. "I did want
it," he says, "but where was I going to put it?"

Artkraft Strauss itself preserved largely what the workers in its fac-   12
tory happened to find amusing and portable enough to hang on the wall.
These remnants—mostly individual letters or small pieces from bakeries
and bandstands—went on the auction block in May of this year after Starr
sold Artkraft's sign-construction and -maintenance operation to Clear
Channel (which hired the workers but won't be building new neon signs).
As bidders were paying $8,365 for the nearly six-foot-high *i* from the A&E
Biography sign that hung high over Columbus Circle from 1998 to 2005,
and $1,793 for a restaurant's neon caricature[6] of Bob Hope, a crew was
dismantling the glass-bending room at the Artkraft factory.

Starr believes that neon had a good run but has no future in the sign   13
business. "There's no way neon is going to come back," she says. "It's
very high voltage. It's dangerous. It involves gases. You've got mercury. To
dispose of it is a big pain in the neck. It's expensive. It's all handmade."
Artkraft Strauss's business now consists only of designing signs, making deals, and maintaining a huge archive of photos and other historic
materials. Of neon, she says: "I like it a lot, but I just can't see it."

But a medium as beloved as neon doesn't disappear—it becomes an   14
art form, justifying special materials and high prices. "We're up 30 percent
for the year, and 90 percent of what we do has neon in it," says Jay Blazek,
owner of Western Neon in Seattle. Blazek grew up in the business—his
father ran a neon school in Wisconsin—but, unlike the traditional sign
maker, he takes a decidedly contemporary, upscale approach. Western
Neon not only makes signs but also designs subtle interior lighting, using
neon in curved ceiling recesses, for restaurants and other businesses. Two
of Blazek's fifteen employees are full-time designers, and the shop includes
gallery space. "The only way that I can forge my destiny in this business is
by creating really interesting things," says Blazek. "If we just make square
boxes and channel letters, other things will come along that are new and
improved."

[4]**sine waves:** A wave-shaped pattern with periodic fluctuations.
[5]**MOMA:** The Museum of Modern Art.
[6]**caricature:** A drawing that distorts characteristics or features for comic effect.

EXERCISING VOCABULARY

1. Record your own definition for each word below in your notebook.

   pulsed (v.) (1)
   sinuous (adj.) (2)
   aesthetic (adj.) (2)
   garish (adj.) (4)
   zealous (adj.) (4)
   subsidized (v.) (5)
   zip (n.) (5)
   memorabilia (n.) (5)
   vintage (adj.) (6)
   persecuted (v.) (6)
   blatant (adj.) (6)

   façade (n.) (8)
   squelch (v.) (9)
   resurgence (n.) (10)
   ordinances (n.) (10)
   mesmerizing (adj.) (10)
   ephemeral (adj.) (10)
   synchronized (v.) (11)
   portable (adj.) (12)
   remnants (n.) (12)
   dismantling (v.) (12)
   archive (n.) (13)

2. Postrel reports that "enthusiasts . . . nurtured the [neon] craft back to life" (para. 4). In what context does nurturing usually take place? What does the word *nurtured* mean in this sense?

3. Sign maker Len Davidson defines neon signs as "folk art" (para. 5). What exactly is folk art? How do neon signs fit this definition?

4. According to Postrel, "The anti-neon movement reflected both elite taste and consensus ideology" (para. 6). What characteristics mark something as elite? Study the meaning of both *consensus* and *ideology* and then explain the phrase "consensus ideology."

PROBING CONTENT

1. Why do neon signs still exist today? Who is responsible?

2. What is the purpose of Let There Be Neon? How is the title a play on words?

3. Name and locate two museums dedicated to preserving neon art. Why is it significant that such museums exist?

4. Why did neon signs fall "victim to the symbolic politics of the energy crisis" (para. 8)? Was it legitimate to target neon signs, based on energy consumption?

5. What country was responsible for the comeback of neon lighting? What new technology puts neon at risk today? Why?

CONSIDERING CRAFT

1. What is the play on words in the title? To what extent is this title effective?

2. The thesis of this essay is clearly stated in the first two paragraphs. Write out the thesis sentence. Why does Postrel choose to state rather than imply her thesis? Why does she choose to do this early in the selection?

3. How does Postrel herself feel about neon signs? Cite text to support your answer.

4. Explain Postrel's use of irony in the juxtaposition of facts presented in the last sentence of paragraph 12. How does this irony further her purpose for writing this essay?

WRITING PROMPTS

Responding to the Topic   How do you define art? What makes something worthy of being considered art? In an essay, describe several works that merit the distinction of being recognized as art. What makes them worthy of this distinction?

Responding to the Writer   In the 1960s, when much else was being liberated from traditional constraints, some city officials condemned neon signs as representative of a "'carnival atmosphere' and 'visual clutter'" (para. 6). Write an essay in which you either agree with this assertion or defend neon signs as meaningful art. You will need to cite specific examples of neon signs to support your position. If you haven't seen many neon signs, use the Web to locate images.

Responding to Multiple Viewpoints   In a historical sense, what do neon signs have in common with the Native American mascots of some sports teams (see Phyllis Raybin Emert's "Native American Mascots: Racial Slur or Cherished Tradition")? Are both misunderstood, or have both simply outlived their time? Write an essay in which you take a position on this issue in order to answer these questions.

For a quiz on this reading, go to bedfordstmartins.com/mirror.

The Worst Op-Ed Ever Written?

RON ROSENBAUM

The popularity of the coffee chain Starbucks introduced a new lingo and system for ordering coffee, with much grumbling from some about the overly complex method for obtaining a simple cup of joe. In this satirical essay, Rob Rosenbaum pokes fun at an op-ed article by the noted academic Stanley Fish that was critical of the Starbucks ordering system. Rosenbaum is an acclaimed journalist who has written for the *Village Voice*, the *New York Observer*, and the *New York Times Magazine*, among other publications. Some of his work is collected in *The Secret Parts of Fortune: Three Decades of Intense Investigations and Edgy Enthusiasms* (2001). He is also the author of five nonfiction books, including *Travels with Doctor Death* (1991), *Explaining Hitler* (1998), and most recently *The Shakespeare Wars* (2006). "The Worst Op-Ed Ever Written?" was published by *Slate* in August 2007.

> **THINKING AHEAD** Have you ever purchased coffee or anything else in Starbucks? Why? How many Starbucks stores are in your neighborhood, either at school or at home? Are their products worth the purchase price? Why? To what extent is Starbucks an icon representative of American culture?

It was August 5, and Professor Stanley Fish, the famous postmodernist[1] and "guest columnist" for the *New York Times*, had some breaking news to expound upon in an op-ed piece. He had discovered a new development in American culture that deserved the kind of exegesis[2] only he could deliver: the appearance of a new kind of coffee place. 1

Have you heard about these new coffee places? Professor Fish's column made it seem as though they had never been noticed or discussed before. 2

"Getting Coffee Is Hard to Do" was the title of his essay, which in its self-satisfied cluelessness may just qualify as the worst op-ed[3] ever written. (I'm not sure if "Worst Ever" will become a recurrent feature in this space, but my column on "The Worst Celebrity Profile Ever Written" [*Esquire*'s pretentiously fawning profile of "the best woman in the world," Angelina Jolie] stirred up some useful controversy.) 3

---

[1]**postmodernist:** One who believes in traditional values as opposed to modern ones; may take traditional values to absurd extremes.
[2]**exegesis:** An explanation.
[3]**op-ed:** Short for "opposite editorial," a page often opposite the editorial page in a newspaper with special features.

At the very least, Fish's column showcases what happens when certain   4
academics descend from the ivory tower to offer us their special insights on
popular culture.

Not that Fish would cop to living in a tower. The professor took great   5
pains to demonstrate that he is not one of those academics who mingle
among the commoners for a mere twenty minutes or so before pronouncing
on their baffling customs.

It seems that Professor Fish is a real man of the people who has been   6
getting his coffee served to him amidst the regular folk for years, at the
kind of place where you could order your coffee and cheese Danish, and
"twenty seconds later, tops, they arrived, just as you were settling into the
sports page."

You can tell he's a down-to-the-earth guy, not some pointy-headed in-   7
tellectual, because he uses phrases like "twenty seconds later, tops" and
reads "the sports page."

But our professor seems to think he has encountered a brand-new cul-   8
tural phenomenon: coffee places that are disturbingly different from the
lunch counters of yesteryear.

Well, I did a little Googling, and it turns out he's right! There are   9
hosts of these coffee chain stores, including one with the improbable name
Starbucks, infiltrating our cities. I don't understand why the *Times'* cutting-
edge "Styles" section hasn't done something on this before. Wake up and
smell the coffee, "Styles" section editors!

It turns out these new coffee places are incredibly difficult to navigate,   10
even for a brilliant academic like Professor Fish.

Here's how he describes his harrowing experience: "As you walk in,   11
everything is saying, 'This is very sophisticated and you'd better be up
to it.'"

Of course, we know that Professor Fish is being *ironic* here. Some   12
might say condescendingly so. From his tone, we know that the elements
of what he mockingly describes as "sophistication"—"wood or concrete
floors, lots of earth tones, soft, high-style lighting, open barrels of coffee
beans, folk-rock and indie[4] music, photographs of urban landscapes and
copies of *The Onion*"[5]—aren't true sophistication to a man of Professor
Fish's discernment. They're kitsch,[6] faux[7]-sophistication—and you can't
fool him. He can see right through it!

Although at this point you begin to wonder if his op-ed wasn't meant   13
to be a feature in *The Onion* ("Area professor befuddled by coffee place"),
Fish is apparently serious about the profound difficulty this new cultural
phenomenon presents.

---

[4]**indie:** Short for "independent."
[5]***The Onion:*** A fake news publication that features satirical articles.
[6]**kitsch:** Something that appeals to popular taste but is often of low quality.
[7]**faux:** French word meaning "false."

In any case, Professor Fish's description of his terrifying encounter with 14
this coffee store is enough to make a grown man weep:

First, unlike his previous coffee shop, which evidently was never 15
crowded, you have to get in line [!] and wait to be served for more than
twenty seconds, tops. In fact, "You may have one or two people in front of
you who are ordering a drink with more parts than an internal combustion
engine." Oh the humanity!

What's worse, these, these PEOPLE, whoever they are, use unfamiliar 16
terms: "something about 'double shot,' 'skinny,' 'breve,' 'grande,' 'au lait'
and a lot of other words that never pass my lips."

Not only are they unfamiliar, practically indecipherable, these terms (what 17
could *au lait*[8] possibly mean? It doesn't even sound like English!), you virtually
have to sound them out to read them. They are, furthermore, literally, unspeak-
ably vulgar to a man of educated taste. (They "never pass my lips" — imagine
if a man of his intellectual distinction had to say *au lait*!)

And by the way, you satirists and improv comics out there. Why haven't 18
you picked up on this elaborate coffee-name trend and made fun of it?
That new show I've heard of, *Seinfeld*, could really get some mileage out
of those funny names for coffee sizes. Tall is small! Comedy gold! (I myself
have tangled with Starbucks, though mostly back in the day when *Seinfeld*
was still on the air. But my tiffs[9] were with its management, not with the
twenty-second-plus wait or the beleaguered baristas.[10])

But Professor Fish's ordeal does not end with the profoundly con- 19
fusing names, confusing even for someone who specializes in language.
(And I should say here I am an admirer of his early, pre-postmodern work
Surprised by Sin, a controversial study of Milton's *Paradise Lost.*)

No, the ordeal continues even after you master the ordering process: 20
"[Y]ou get to put in your order, but then you have to find a place to stand
while you wait for it."

Professor Fish is particularly good on the inhuman stress positions this 21
requires of him. "[Y]ou shift your body, first here and then there, trying to
get out of the way of those you can't help get in the way of."

How he maintains his priceless sense of humor in this Abu Ghraib–like[11] 22
environment of torment is hard to imagine. But it gets worse. You can
bump into people and spill coffee, and it's hard to find a seat. I'm not
kidding. (Well, he isn't.)

But there's more! "[T]hen your real problems begin," he says with stoic 23
grit. Some readers, the faint of heart, may want to skip this next part,
because things really get ugly: the "accessories" difficulty. (Note to self:
Tell agent about plans for thriller to rival *The Bourne Ultimatum* — *The
Accessories Difficulty.*)

---

[8]**au lait:** French for "with milk."
[9]**tiffs:** Petty arguments.
[10]**baristas:** People who serve coffee.
[11]**Abu Ghraib:** Former Iraqi prison used by the U.S. military for detainees.

You must face "a staggering array" of "things you put in, on and   24
around your coffee. . . ." Here, he's referring to such highly fraught
choices as sugar or Splenda,[12] whole milk or skim. High stakes choices,
with so little time to tease out the implications and consequences. What's
more, there's no service person to help him make these terrible decisions.
"[S]o you lunge after one thing and then after another with awkward
reaches."

At this point, one can sympathize not so much with Professor Fish   25
as with the *Times* op-ed editors who had to come up with a "pull quote"
for the hard-copy edition. You know, the pithy phrase that billboards the
column's essence. Here's what they came up with:

"Cream? Sugar? Get it yourself."   26

I think that about captures the unbearable excitement of these revela-   27
tions. Oh, the exquisite, um, awkwardness of those "awkward reaches"! But
he "got it himself" despite the indignity. And he lived to tell about it. And
make it relevant! In fact, one can see a hint of Professor Fish's signature moral
relativism—known in the lit-crit[13] trade as *anti-foundationalism*—creep
into his prose as he attempts to grapple with the accessories difficulty.

"There is no 'right' place to start," he notes, no solid philosophical   28
foundation upon which to base difficult sweetener decisions. As with the
most difficult questions of philosophy, politics and literature, there are only
subjective perspectives.

He is once again face to face with the tragedy of the human situation.   29

But he's got a much larger point to make. The dread "New Coffee Ex-   30
perience" turns out to be emblematic of one of the key ills of modern times,
the servant problem:

It is "just one instance of the growing practice of shifting the burden of   31
labor to the consumer—gas stations, grocery and drug stores, bagel shops
(why should I put on my own cream cheese?), airline check-ins, parking
lots."

Imagine, a man of his distinction, forced to "put on my own cream   32
cheese." Why is there no one to do it for him?

He might have mentioned ATMs. Used to be you could walk into a   33
bank and ask a teller to give you a couple hundred bucks, and they'd hand
it over, "twenty seconds, tops." No troubling paperwork, remember? And
what about credit card machines? Now, it's "insert this, swipe that, choose
credit or debit, enter your PIN, push the red button, error, start again."

One wants to feel sympathy for Professor Fish in his distress. But   34
although most of the unintentional humor in Professor Fish's column
comes from his comic cluelessness about things he thinks are "new" in the
culture, this note of entitlement gives it a kind of nasty edge.

---

[12]**Splenda:** A popular sugar substitute.
[13]**lit-crit:** Abbreviation for "literary criticism."

He concedes toward the close of his column: "[N]one of us has chosen   35
to take over the jobs of those we pay to serve us."

Is it just me, or is there something grating in that phrase: "those we pay   36
to serve us"? So distasteful, the life of the servant class, compared with the
life of the mind.

But at least in the old days the servant class hopped to it and got Professor   37
Fish his coffee and Danish in "twenty seconds, tops" and worked themselves to the point of exhaustion all day for less than a minimum wage to
make sure he would have something to consume with his "sports page."

As multidegreed as he is, I have a feeling that it would be an invalu-   38
able addition to his education if Professor Fish spent a week "serving" as a
barista. You know: For someone who believes in perspectives rather than
foundations (except when it comes to grants), it would seem like a useful
additional perspective on the whole coffee-servant question.

He also might want to consider that, while in some ways we do more   39
ourselves these days, some of us might just prefer that to having servants.
Just another perspective.

Still, the column makes clear why his kind of deep thinking has earned   40
him academic stardom and university deanships. Such a man deserves to be
served. Not to have to serve himself.

In any case, the op-ed may not have been a total loss; it might suggest   41
the subject for his next magnum opus:[14] *Surprised by Starbucks*.

EXERCISING VOCABULARY

1. Record your own definition for each word below in your notebook.

expound (v.) (1)	beleaguered (adj.) (18)
pretentiously (adv.) (3)	stoic (adj.) (23)
fawning (adj.) (3)	staggering (adj.) (24)
baffling (adj.) (5)	fraught (adj.) (24)
infiltrating (v.) (9)	pithy (adj.) (25)
harrowing (adj.) (11)	grapple (v.) (27)
discernment (n.) (12)	emblematic (adj.) (30)
indecipherable (adj.) (17)	grating (adj.) (36)

2. In paragraph 24, Rosenbaum writes about Professor Fish's having "so
   little time to tease out the implications and consequences" of the decisions Starbucks requires. What does it mean to "tease out" something?
   With what do we usually associate teasing? How does the use of this
   image here fit Rosenbaum's purpose?

3. Rosenbaum believes that Professor Fish's writing has a "note of entitlement [that] gives it a kind of nasty edge" (para. 34). What is entitlement?

---

[14]**magnum opus:** Latin for "great work"; an author's or artist's best work.

Who generally feels entitled to have life correspond to his or her own terms? How can this sense of entitlement take on a "nasty edge"?

4. What are "improv comics" (para. 18)? For what is the word *improv* an abbreviation? How is this entire essay like an improv comic's routine?

PROBING CONTENT

1. Why does Rosenbaum feel that Professor Fish's essay's title reflects "self-satisfied cluelessness" (para. 3)? About what is the professor clueless?

2. According to Professor Fish, what are the problems with Starbucks?

3. What is a "pull quote" (para. 25)? According to Rosenbaum, how effective is the one selected for Professor Fish's essay?

4. Why is it so difficult for Professor Fish to select a form of sweetener for his coffee?

5. According to Professor Fish, what is "the servant problem" (para. 30)?

CONSIDERING CRAFT

1. At several points in this essay, Rosenbaum uses slang. For example, look at paragraph 5: "Not that Fish would cop to living in [an ivory] tower." What does *cop to* mean here? How does this use of slang help Rosenbaum make his point? What is an ivory tower?

2. The use of irony is evident throughout this essay. Select two examples of verbal irony and explain how Rosenbaum uses them to reinforce his intention for the essay.

3. Rosenbaum's attitude toward his subject—Professor Fish and his essay—is clearly evident throughout this selection. Using specific text references, document Rosenbaum's attitude.

4. Rosenbaum repeats the phrase "twenty seconds later, tops" at numerous points throughout the essay. Where and why is the phrase introduced? What does this repetition accomplish?

WRITING PROMPTS

Responding to the Topic   In your own opinion and that of your friends and colleagues, how significant is Starbucks to American culture? Write an essay in which you explore the history of Starbucks and the company's rise to power and iconic status. Then evaluate the impact of this economic success story on our culture.

Responding to the Writer   Some writers argue that American culture is now so firmly identified with icons like Starbucks and McDonald's that their removal from the American landscape would shift others' view of American culture in unexpected directions. Write an essay in which you agree or disagree, explaining which cultural icons would alter America's cultural, as well as geographic, landscape. Be certain to use specific examples.

Responding to Multiple Viewpoints   How would Daniel Alarcon, author of "Grand Mall Seizure," react to Rosenbaum's account of Professor Fish's experience with Starbucks? Compose an essay in which you examine what Alarcon might write. Support your analysis with evidence from both essays.

For a quiz on this reading, go to bedfordstmartins.com/mirror.

iPod Nation

Steven Levy

In "iPod Nation," Steven Levy explores the omnipresence of the stylish little digital music machine that put Apple CEO Steve Jobs back on top and led to the iTunes Music Store, a second blockbuster hit for his computer company. Levy has been writing about digital technology and its effects on our society for more than twenty years. From 1995 to 2008, he was a senior editor and award-winning author of "The Technologist" column for *Newsweek* magazine. In 2008, he joined the staff of *Wired* magazine as a full-time writer. He is the author of six books, including *Hackers* (1984), *Artificial Life* (1992), *Crypto* (2001), and *The Perfect Thing: How the iPod Shuffles Commerce, Culture, and Coolness* (2006). His writing has appeared in *The New Yorker,* the *New York Times Magazine, Harper's, Premiere,* and *Wired.* "iPod Nation" first appeared as the cover story for the July 26, 2004, issue of *Newsweek.*

> **THINKING AHEAD**   Do you own an iPod? Would you like to own one? Why? How do or would you use it? What is your opinion about how iPods influence the way we buy, listen to, and appreciate music?

S teve Jobs noticed something earlier this year in New York City. "I was 1 on Madison," says Apple's CEO, "and it was, like, on every block, there was someone with white headphones, and I thought, 'Oh, my God, it's starting to happen.'" Jonathan Ive, the company's design guru, had a similar experience in London: "On the streets and coming out of the tubes, you'd see people fiddling with it." And Victor Katch, a 59-year-old professor of kinesiology[1] at the University of Michigan, saw it in Ann Arbor. "When you walk across campus, the ratio seems as high as 2 out of 3 people," he says.

They're talking about the sudden ubiquity of the iPod, the cigarette- 2 box-size digital music player (and its colorful credit-card-size little sister, the Mini) that's smacked right into the sweet spot where a consumer product becomes something much, much more: an icon, a pet, a status indicator and an indispensable part of one's life. To 3 million-plus owners, iPods not only give constant access to their entire collection of songs and CDs, but membership into an implicit society that's transforming the way music will be consumed in the future. "When my students see me on campus with my iPod, they smile," says Professor Katch, whose unit stores everything from Mozart to Dean Martin. "It's sort of a bonding."

[1]kinesiology: The study of how parts of the body move.

The glue for the bond is a tiny, limited-function computer with a capacious disk drive, decked in white plastic and loaded with something that until very recently was the province of ultrageeks and music pirates:[2] digital files that play back as songs. Apple wasn't the first company to come out with a player, but the earlier ones were either low-capacity toys that played the same few songs, or brick-size beasts with impenetrable controls. Apple's device is not only powerful and easy to use, but has an incandescent style that makes people go nuts about it. Or, in the case of 16-year-old Brittany Vendryes of Miami, to dub it "Bob the Music Machine." ("I wanted to keep it close to my heart and give it a name," she explains.)

Adding to the appeal is the cachet of A-list approbation. "I love it!" says songwriter Denise Rich. "I have my whole catalog on it and I take it everywhere." She is only one voice in a chorus of celebrity Podsters who sing the same praises voiced by ordinary iPod users, but add a dollop[3] of coolness to the device, as if it needed it. Will Smith has burbled[4] to Jay Leno and *Wired* magazine about his infatuation with "the gadget of the century." Gwyneth Paltrow confided her Pod-love to *Vogue* (her new baby is named Apple—coincidence?). It's been seen on innumerable TV shows, movies and music videos, so much so that Fox TV recently informed Josh Schwartz, producer of its hit series *The O.C.*, that future depictions of music players would have to forgo the telltale white ear buds. Schwartz, himself a 27-year-old who still hasn't recovered from the shock of having his unit stolen from his BMW, was outraged. "It's what our audience uses and what our characters would use," he says.

People who actually create music are among the biggest fans: "The layout reminds the musician of music," says tunester John Mayer. And couture maven[5] Karl Lagerfeld's iPod collection is up to 60, coded in the back by laser etching so he can tell what's on them. "It's *the* way to store music," he says. Lagerfeld's tribute to the iPod is a $1,500 Fendi pink copper rectangular purse that holds 12 iPods. It is one of more than 200 third-party accessories ranging from external speakers, microphones and—fasten your seat belt—a special connector that lets you control your iPod from the steering wheel of a BMW.

Music hits people's emotions, and the purchase of something that opens up one's entire music collection—up to 10,000 songs in your pocket—makes for an intense relationship. When people buy iPods, they often obsess, talking incessantly about playlists and segues,[6] grumbling about glitches, fixating on battery life and panicking at the very thought of losing their new digital friend. "I'd be devastated if I lost it," says Krystyn Lynch, a Boston investment marketer.

[2]**music pirates:** People who download music illegally.
[3]**dollop:** A small amount.
[4]**burbled:** Talked excitedly.
[5]**couture maven:** An expert or knowledgeable enthusiast in designer fashions.
[6]**segues:** Smooth transitions.

Fans of the devices use it for more than music. "It's the limousine for   7
the spoken word," says Audible CEO Don Katz, whose struggling digital
audiobook company has been revitalized by having its products on Apple's
iTunes store. (Podsters downloaded thousands of copies of Bill Clinton's
autobiography within minutes of its 3 a.m. release last month.) And computer users have discovered that its vast storage space makes it a useful
vault for huge digital files—the makers of the *Lord of the Rings* movies
used iPods to shuttle dailies[7] from the set to the studio. Thousands of less-
accomplished shutterbugs store digital photos on them.

iPods aren't conspicuous everywhere—their popularity seems centered on   8
big cities and college towns—but sometimes it seems that way. "I notice that
when I'm in the gym, as I look down the treadmills, that just about everybody
in the row has one," says Scott Piro, a New York City book publicist. And the
capper came earlier this year during the *Apple vs. Apple* case—wherein the
Beatles' record company is suing the computer firm on a trademark issue.
The judge wondered if he should recuse[8] himself—because he is an avid iPod
user. (The litigants[9] had no objection to his staying on.)

In 1997, when Steve Jobs returned to the then struggling company he   9
had cofounded, he says, there were no plans for a music initiative. In fact,
he says, there wasn't a plan for anything. "Our goal was to revitalize and
get organized, and if there were opportunities we'd see them," he says.
"We just had to be ready to catch the ball when it's thrown by life." After
some painful pink-slipping[10] and some joyous innovating, the company
was solvent.

But in the flurry, Jobs & Co. initially failed to notice the impending rev-   10
olution in digital music. Once that omission was understood, Apple com-
pensated by developing a slick "jukebox" application known as iTunes. It
was then that Apple's brain trust noticed that digital music players weren't
selling. Why not? "The products stank," says Apple VP Greg Joswiak.

Life had tossed Jobs a softball, and early in 2001 he ordered his engi-   11
neers to catch it. That February, Apple's hardware czar,[11] Jon Rubinstein,
picked a team leader from outside the company—an engineer named
Tony Fadell. "I was on the ski slopes in Vail when I got the call," says
Fadell, who was told that the idea was to create a ground-breaking music
player—and have it on sale for Christmas season that year. The requirements:
A very fast connection to one's computer (via Apple's high-speed Firewire
standard) so songs could be quickly uploaded. A close synchronization
with the iTunes software to make it easy to organize music. An interface
that would be simple to use. And gorgeous.

---

[7]**dailies:** Rough, unedited clips of film that are reviewed on the same day they are shot.
[8]**recuse:** To remove from participation because of bias.
[9]**litigants:** People involved in a lawsuit.
[10]**pink-slipping:** Firing from a job.
[11]**czar:** An absolute ruler; one with great authority and power to control.

Fadell was able to draw on all of Apple's talents from Jobs on down. VP   12
Phil Schiller came up with the idea of a scroll wheel that made the menus
accelerate as your finger spun on it. Meanwhile, Apple's industrial designer
Ive embarked on a search for the obvious. "From early on we wanted a
product that would seem so natural and so inevitable and so simple you
almost wouldn't think of it as having been designed," he says. This auster-
ity extended to the whiteness of the iPod, a double-crystal polymer Antarc-
tica, a blankness that screams in brilliant colors across a crowded subway.
"It's neutral, but it is a bold neutral, just shockingly neutral," says Ive.

Assessing the final product, Jobs bestows, for him, the ultimate acco-   13
lade: "It's as Apple as anything Apple has ever done."

The October 2001 launch was barely a month after 9/11, with the   14
country on edge and the tech industry in the toilet.[12] Skeptics scoffed at the
$399 price and the fact that only Macintosh users, less than a twentieth
of the marketplace, could use it. But savvy Mac-heads saw the value, and
the iPod was a hit, if not yet a sensation. What pushed it to the next level
was a number of Apple initiatives beginning with a quick upgrade cycle
that increased the number of songs (while actually lowering the price).
Then Apple released a version that would run on Windows and Mac, dramatically increasing the potential market. Finally, after intense negotiations
with the record labels, Apple licensed hundreds of thousands of songs for
its iTunes Music Store, which blended seamlessly with the iPod. As with the
iPod itself, the legal-download store was not the first of its kind but was so
felicitous and efficient that it leapt to a 70 percent market share.

Then sales began to spike. No one was surprised that Apple sold an   15
impressive 733,000 iPods during the Christmas season last year, but the
normally quiet quarter after that saw an increase to 807,000. And last
week Apple announced that sales in the just-completed third quarter, traditionally another dead one—hit 860,000, up from 249,000 a year ago.

That total would have been higher had Apple not had problems get-   16
ting parts for the latest iteration,[13] the iPod Mini. Though critics praised its
compactness and its panache[14]—a burnished metallic surface made it look
like a futuristic Zippo[15]—they sniffed at its relatively low capacity (only
1,000 songs!). But apparently there were lots of people like Los Angeles
chiropractor Pat Dengler, who saw the Mini as a must. "At first I thought,
I already have an iPod, I don't need it," she says. "But after I played with
it, I thought, I really dig it. Now I use them both." Dengler was lucky, as
many had to suffer through a month-long waiting list. To the delight of
Apple (and the chagrin of Sony), the no-brainer description of the iPod is
"the Walkman of the 21st century." And just as the Walkman changed the

[12]**in the toilet:** In serious danger of failing.
[13]**iteration:** Version.
[14]**panache:** Style.
[15]**Zippo:** A brand of cigarette lighter.

landscape of music and the soundscape of our lives, the iPod and the iTunes store are making their mark on the way we handle our music, and even the way we listen to it.

The store has proved that many people will pay for digital music (though certainly many millions of gigabytes of iPod space are loaded with tunes plucked from the dark side of the Internet). "The iPod and iTunes store are a shining light at a very bleak time in the industry," says Cary Sherman, president of the Record Industry Association of America. Since just about everybody feels that within a decade almost everybody will get their music from such places, this is very big. 17

An equally big deal is the way the iPod is changing our listening style. Michael Bull, a lecturer at the University of Sussex, has interviewed thousands of iPod users, finding that the ability to take your whole music collection with you changes everything. "People define their own narrative through their music collection," says Bull. 18

The primary way to exploit this ability is the iPod's "shuffle" feature. This takes your entire music collection, reorders it with the thoroughness of a Las Vegas blackjack dealer and then plays back the crazy-quilt mélange.[16] "Shuffle throws up almost anything—you don't know it's coming but you know you like it," says Bull. "Because of this people often say, 'It's almost as if my iPod understands me.'" 19

Shuffle winds up helping people make connections between different genres of music. "People feel they're walking through musicology,"[17] says rocker John Mayer. These abilities have a predictable effect: people who use iPods wind up listening to more music, and with more passion. 20

And since the iTunes store encourages customers to eschew buying entire CDs, instead buying the best song or two for a buck a pop, it's easy to see why some think that the era of the CD is playing its final tracks, a circumstance many will lament. "The one cool thing about a CD is really getting to know an album," says iPod fan Wil-Dog Abers, bassist for the hip-hop collective Ozomatli. "I don't know what we're gonna do about that." 21

In Silicon Valley, the question is what Apple can do to maintain its dominant position in the field. While Apple execs say that they are surprised at how lame[18] the competition has been to date, it's reasonable to think that rivals might eventually close the gap. Almost all the hounds chasing Apple use technology from its longtime rival Microsoft. And Sony, whose initial efforts in the field were constrained by the copy-protection demands of its music unit, is introducing a new line of digital players this summer. "We feel that the experience is as good as Apple's, and we have the Walkman brand, which has sold 200 million units. We're in the game," says Sony America's CEO Howard Stringer. Meanwhile, the ultimate 22

---

[16] **crazy-quilt mélange:** A mixture in random order.
[17] **musicology:** The scholarly study of music.
[18] **lame:** Ineffective; weak.

competition may come from services that stream unlimited music for a monthly fee, like Real Networks' Rhapsody. "The fat lady isn't even on the stage yet," says Chris Gorog, CEO of Napster.

But at the moment, the iPod *is* the category. And everything points to a 23 humongous Christmas season for the iPod. The introduction of the new iPods this week extends the company's technology lead. If Apple, as promised, manages to get enough drives to satisfy the demand, the Mini iPod may achieve the ubiquity of its wide-bodied companion. And later this summer, when computer giant HP begins selling a cobranded version of the iPod, consumers will be able to get iPods in thousands of additional retail stores.

All this is infinitely gratifying for Steve Jobs, the computer pioneer and 24 studio CEO who turns 50 next February. "I have a very simple life," he says, without a trace of irony. "I have my family and I have Apple and Pixar. And I don't do much else." But the night before our interview, Jobs and his kids sat down for their first family screening of Pixar's 2004 release *The Incredibles*. After that, he tracked the countdown to the 100 millionth song sold on the iTunes store. Apple had promised a prize to the person who moved the odometer to 10 figures, and as the big number approached, fortune seekers snapped up files at a furious rate. At around 10:15, 20-year-old Kevin Britten of Hays, Kansas, bought a song by the electronica band Zero 7, and Jobs himself got on the phone to tell him that he'd won. Then Jobs asked a potentially embarrassing question: "Do you have a Mac or PC?"

"I have a Macintosh . . . *duh*!" said Britten. 25

Jobs laughs while recounting this. Even though Macintosh sales have 26 gone up recently, he knows that the odds are small of anyone's owning a Mac as opposed to the competition. He doesn't want that to happen with his company's music player. "There are lots of examples where not the best product wins," he says. "Windows would be one of those, but there are examples where the best product wins. And the iPod is a great example of that." As anyone can see from all those white cords dangling from people's ears.

EXERCISING VOCABULARY

1. Record your own definition for each word below in your notebook.

guru (n.) (1)	solvent (adj.) (9)
ubiquity (n.) (2)	flurry (n.) (10)
implicit (adj.) (2)	synchronization (n.) (11)
capacious (adj.) (3)	austerity (n.) (12)
impenetrable (adj.) (3)	accolade (n.) (13)
incandescent (adj.) (3)	savvy (adj.) (14)
telltale (adj.) (4)	felicitous (adj.) (14)
glitches (n.) (6)	chagrin (n.) (16)
revitalized (v.) (7)	eschew (v.) (21)
conspicuous (adj.) (8)	lament (v.) (21)

2. In Levy's original article, a line of text across the title reads "In just three years, Apple's adorable Mini music player has gone from gizmo to life-changing cultural icon." What is a gizmo? What is a cultural icon? How are the two different?

3. Levy states that iPods have "the cachet of A-list approbation" (para. 4). Define *cachet*. What does *approbation* mean? Who is on an A-list? What does having A-list approbation signify about iPods?

4. Karl Lagerfeld's pink copper rectangular purse is one of many third-party accessories for iPods. Explain what a third-party accessory is. Why are these being created? What does their prevalence say about iPods?

PROBING CONTENT

1. Why have iPods become so important to so many people? What do iPods represent? How do some people feel about their iPods?

2. How was the iPod developed? Why were the original iPods white?

3. What surprises occurred with the sales of iPods? What obstacles has Apple encountered?

4. How do musicians and others in the music industry feel about iPods? Why?

5. In what ways are iPods changing people's listening styles? What one iPod feature has been particularly important to these changes? How?

CONSIDERING CRAFT

1. Locate several sentences or phrases throughout this essay that indicate Levy's attitude about iPods. What is his attitude? How clearly is that attitude communicated here?

2. Although no other manufacturer has achieved Apple's level of success with the iPod, Chris Gorog of Napster says, "The fat lady isn't even on the stage yet" (para. 22). To what operatic expression is Gorog alluding? What does this expression mean? Why does Levy include this quotation when many readers may not know what Gorog is implying? What does the expression indicate about Gorog's attitude?

3. In paragraphs 2 and 11, Levy uses sports terminology to discuss the rise of the iPod. Pick out the baseball and softball language in these two paragraphs. Why does he use this language? How effective is it in advancing his point in the essay?

WRITING PROMPTS

Responding to the Topic   In an essay, examine how iPods have affected your and your friends' relationship with music. Discuss how you hear new music, how you listen to favorites, how you share enthusiasm for certain songs, and how music is marketed now. Interview some of your friends to accumulate information to use in your essay.

Responding to the Writer   Levy believes that the iPod and its successors are the future of music. Write an essay in which you either agree or disagree with his assumption. Be sure to be specific about what alternatives you see for music in the next decade and beyond.

Responding to Multiple Viewpoints   In what ways has the iPod phenomenon impacted people who are — or who would like to be — cultural icons in the music industry? Refer to "Material Girls" by Erika Fricke and other sources from this text and from your own reading to support your thesis.

For a quiz on this reading, go to bedfordstmartins.com/mirror.

Harry Potter and Magical Realism

DANIEL NEXON

The enormously popular *Harry Potter* series has reached far beyond its British roots to become a global cultural phenomenon. One interesting aspect of these books, notes author and professor Daniel Nexon, is how each region of the world seems able to adapt the messages they contain to suit its own culture. Nexon is an assistant professor at Georgetown University. He received his Ph.D. in International Relations from Columbia University and has held fellowships at Stanford University's Center for International Security and Ohio State University's Mershon Center for International Studies. He is coeditor of the book *Harry Potter and International Relations* (2006). "*Harry Potter* and Magical Realism" was published in *The New Republic* in 2007.

> **THINKING AHEAD** How would you explain the entire Harry Potter phenomenon? Why have the books and movies become so popular, inducing even rowdy middle school boys to curl up in chairs and read for hours? What accounts for the appeal of Harry Potter to both males and females and to all age groups?

As the seventh and final installment in J.K. Rowling's *Harry Potter* series hits bookstore shelves this weekend, the frenzy over the young magician and his chums appears set to reach even more spectacular heights. Scholastic, *Harry Potter*'s U.S. publisher, ordered a first-run printing of 12 million copies, which may be the largest in world history. The series has already sold 325 million copies worldwide and been translated into sixty-six languages. And the *Harry Potter* films—the fifth of which was released last weekend—have grossed more than $3.8 billion globally. As a franchise,[1] *Harry Potter* thrills its fans, annoys some prominent literary critics, and generates large sums of money for its author and corporate backers. And its evolution holds any number of lessons for publishers, marketing executives, and other members of the industrial-entertainment complex. But in the course of its spectacular rise, *Harry Potter* has become more than simply a commercial success story: It has become a global phenomenon. 1

Harry Potter, in fact, functions something like a Rorschach Blot: In countries around the world, it captures various national anxieties about contemporary culture and international affairs. French intellectuals, for example, debate whether or not *Harry Potter* indoctrinates youngsters into the orthodoxy of unfettered market capitalism. Some Swedish commentators decry what they perceive as *Harry Potter*'s Anglo-American vision of 2

---

[1] **franchise:** A group marketing goods or services by special permission.

bourgeoisie[2] conformity and its affirmation of class and gender inequality. In Turkey, we find a significant discussion of *Harry Potter* that pivots around issues of Turkish civilizational identity: whether Turkey is part of the West, the East, or a bridge between the two. A few Turkish writers have even asserted that controversies over *Harry Potter* in the United States demonstrate how Turks are more "Western" than Americans. And in Russia, a country whose concern over international status and prestige becomes more apparent each day, the newspaper *Novaya Gazeta* created a minor firestorm when it claimed that the film visage of Dobby the House-Elf was a deliberate insult to President Vladimir Putin.

More fundamentally, reactions to *Harry Potter* highlight the worldwide character of clashes between various forms of traditionalism and modernism. To many religious conservatives, *Harry Potter* represents yet another assault by the mass media, public institutions, and other manifestations of secular culture against their traditional values. In the United States, Russia, Thailand, and Australia, some Christian conservatives have condemned the books for, among other things, promoting occultism[3] and Satanism. Harry Potter and his friends, after all, use magic and witchcraft not only as part of their everyday lives but also as part of their struggle against the forces of evil. Christian critics of *Harry Potter* argue that the Bible makes clear that all magic stems from demonic sources. By teaching children that witchcraft is acceptable and by encouraging them to play with wands and cauldrons, Harry Potter risks seducing them away from Christianity and into occult practices. It may even, the argument goes, bring them into contact with the very real demons that haunt our world. According to the American Library Association, Rowling's books were the fourth most challenged library books from 1990–2004, and the most challenged from 2000–2005. 3

Members of other religious movements also find fault with *Harry Potter*. The series is enormously popular in Indonesia, the Gulf States, and many other Islamic countries. But the Wahhabist tradition, as Peter Mandaville, assistant professor of government and politics at George Mason University, and Patrick Jackson, associate professor of international relations at American University, have noted, strongly opposes "various esoteric and mystical practices that . . . entered popular Islamic practice." For Wahhabists, those who practice such "heterodox" forms of Islam amount to "magicians and witches." Thus, it comes as little surprise that some Wahhabist authorities, as well as adherents to other conservative Islamic traditions, view *Harry Potter* as promoting paganism and undermining Islam. Although the specifics of the doctrinal objections differ from their Christian counterparts, the parallels remain striking. 4

Moreover, the reception of the books also reveals a number of important dimensions of globalization. Americans increasingly see themselves as 5

---

[2]**bourgeoisie:** Relating to the middle class.
[3]**occultism:** Belief in the powers of the supernatural.

objects of economic globalization, whether in the form of "outsourcing" or the impact of Chinese imports on U.S. manufacturing. But we still tend to think of cultural globalization as synonymous with "Americanization." The *Harry Potter* books—with their distinctively British boarding school setting, slang, and cuisine—provide a subtle rejoinder to such impressions and subvert the equation of globalization with relentless homogenization.

In fact, *Harry Potter*'s worldwide popularity owes much to the deliberate and inadvertent adaptation of the series to meet local tastes. The Chinese editions translate aspects of the western folklore in *Harry Potter* into Chinese mythological traditions. Translators of the books wrestle—often unsuccessfully—with how to convert faithfully Rowling's extensive use of puns and idioms into other languages. Unauthorized "sequels" in China and India explicitly recast *Harry Potter* in local settings and using local plot devices. (In the Indian fake novel, for example, he makes friends with a Bengali boy and tours India.) Fans produce a worldwide stream of fiction set in the Harry Potter universe, each extending elements of the novels to reflect their own interests and preferences. For all its often crass commercialization, *Harry Potter*'s success owes something to a process of hybridization[4] familiar to scholars of cultural globalization. 6

The *Harry Potter* books lend themselves well to real-world political debates, because their plots themselves intersect with a surprising number of themes in real-world politics. The evil Voldemort and his Death Eaters, both in their organization and tactics, bear a striking resemblance to transnational terrorists. Their hatred of the impure—particularly those "mudbloods" who, despite their magical powers, lack wizarding parentage—and thirst for power genuflects[5] in the direction of fascism,[6] whether of the traditional or, as some might see it, the "Islamo-" variety. The Death Eaters, at least in the first six books, hide among the general wizarding population and strike with relative impunity against an often hapless Ministry of Magic with its bumbling bureaucrats and politicians. The former Minister of Magic, Cornelius Fudge, spends the last years of his tenure denying and downplaying the Death-Eater threat. *Harry Potter* heroes fight back by forming their own clandestine organization—the Order of the Phoenix—and, when necessary, bending the rule of law as they seek to defeat Voldemort's bid for global mastery. 7

Harry Potter, however, is no Jack Bauer.[7] For those concerned about sacrificing civil liberties and democratic values to the war on terrorism, Rowling has much to offer. Innocents frequently find themselves imprisoned in the dreadful dungeon of Azkaban, which some might read as the Potterverse's own version of Guantanamo Bay. A wide variety of 8

---

[4]**hybridization:** The production of something from two different components.
[5]**genuflects:** Bows one's knee in respect.
[6]**fascism:** A movement whose followers hold nationality and frequently race above the value of the individual.
[7]**Jack Bauer:** The hero of the television series *24*, who rescues the world from danger in each episode.

miscarriages of justice mark the novels. Albus Dumbledore, the moral center of the first six books, often deplores the excesses of the Ministry during the first and second struggle against the Death Eaters. He also condemns the legal inequalities that permeate the wizarding world.

The books tackle not only issues of inequality but also of multicultur-   9
alism. Class antagonism, prejudice against mudbloods, and intolerance of non-human species abound in Hogwarts and the broader wizarding community. Rowling's witches and wizards, however, display almost total indifference to Muggle racial categories. Rowling strives mightily to present a consistent moral vision of equality, but as critics such as Debra Thompson, a doctoral candidate in political science at the University of Toronto, note, she often seems to inadvertently endorse essentialist notions of racial differences. Such tensions, of course, are also endemic in real-world manifestations of multiculturalism and racial politics.

Such themes reflect, at least in part, what we might term the "partially   10
globalized" character of *Harry Potter's* world. Divisions of the Ministry of Magic concern themselves with regulating imports. The Ministry, for example, standardizes cauldron thickness to prevent dangerous and inferior goods from flooding the market. International bodies and legal regimes govern aspects of wizard behavior. The Quidditch World Championship parallels Soccer's World Cup; it simultaneously affirms national differences while providing a focal point for cosmopolitan sporting competition. The Triwizard Tournament that forms the centerpiece of the fourth book, *Harry Potter and the Goblet of Fire*, aims to establish ties "between young witches and wizards of different nationalities"—sort of like an Olympics with flying broomsticks.

At this point, however, the global *Harry Potter* phenomenon has out-   11
grown the specifics of the books. Entrenched as they now are in the public consciousness, the characters have become symbols—abstract representations rather than the specific products of Rowling's imagination. Thus, during his 2002 election campaign, for example, Dutch Prime Minister Jan Peter Balkenende proudly embraced comparisons between himself and Daniel Radcliffe's Harry Potter to help promote his image as, according to Agence France Presse, "reliable and upright but not stuffy." But, when the Belgian Prime Minister, Guy Verhofstadt, described Balkenende as "a mix between Harry Potter and a worthy burgher,[8] a man in whom I detect no trace of charisma," it strained relations between the two governments. Liberals in the United States, for their part, affix bumper stickers such as "Republicans for Voldemort" and "Cheney-Voldemort '08" to their cars. Voldemort may be fast on his way to becoming a general symbol for evil.

Perhaps one day, then, soon-to-be-defeated senators will justify a   12
war not with reference to J.R.R. Tolkien's *Lord of the Rings* but to J.K. Rowling's *Harry Potter*. Indeed, the world might be a better place if future politicians and Supreme Court justices look to Harry Potter, rather than

[8] **burgher:** A solid citizen of the middle class.

24's Jack Bauer, for guidance on the legitimacy of torture. But it will be a long time before we know if Rowling's creations achieve the status of global political currency. It may happen. After all, from Indonesia to Taiwan, the United States to Iran, and Russia to India, *Harry Potter* is already part of the globalizing process, with all its complexities, tensions, and possibilities.

EXERCISING VOCABULARY

1. Record your own definition for each word below in your notebook.

phenomenon (n.) (1)
indoctrinates (v.) (2)
orthodoxy (n.) (2)
unfettered (adj.) (2)
decry (v.) (2)
pivots (v.) (2)
visage (n.) (2)
esoteric (adj.) (4)
adherents (n.) (4)
cuisine (n.) (5)
rejoinder (n.) (5)

subvert (v.) (5)
inadvertent (adj.) (6)
crass (adj.) (6)
impunity (n.) (7)
bumbling (adj.) (7)
miscarriages (n.) (8)
deplores (v.) (8)
permeate (v.) (8)
endemic (adj.) (9)
charisma (n.) (11)

2. According to Nexon, a Russian newspaper "created a minor firestorm" when it denounced the characterization of Dobby the House-Elf (para. 2). What is a firestorm? What reaction does this imagery reveal? Why did this happen?

3. To some religious conservatives, *Harry Potter* is one of many "manifestations of secular culture" (para. 3). What is a manifestation? What kind of culture is secular culture? What are some other representations of secular culture? Why are they objectionable to some groups?

4. In the final paragraph, Nexon notes that only time will tell whether Harry Potter and his cohorts become part of the "global political currency." What does this expression mean? Derive its meaning by examining each word separately and then regarding the entire phrase. What is one indication that this may indeed occur?

PROBING CONTENT

1. Nexon details specifics about the reaction to *Harry Potter* in various countries. Choose one country mentioned in this essay and report the reaction there, as noted by Nexon.

2. Why are J. K. Rowling's books among the most often challenged library books? What does it mean to challenge a library book?

3. In what ways does *Harry Potter* challenge existing ideas Americans may hold about globalization? To what might the worldwide popularity of the books be attributed?

4. In what ways do the *Harry Potter* novels reflect themes in real-world politics? How do *Harry Potter* characters exemplify these themes?

CONSIDERING CRAFT

1. In paragraph 2, Nexon writes that *"Harry Potter*, in fact, functions something like a Rorschach Blot." What is a Rorschach Blot? How is one generally used and under what circumstances? How does introducing that imagery here help the author accomplish his purpose for this essay?

2. In paragraph 8, Nexon refers to "the Potterverse." This is a word he creates for a specific purpose. Of what two words is this word formed? What does it mean? What is the author's purpose in using this word?

3. Nexon writes this essay as though all his readers have also read the *Harry Potter* novels or at least seen the movies. What effect does this assumption have on your reading of the essay? How does making this assumption relate to Nexon's purpose for writing this essay?

4. In this essay, what is Nexon's attitude toward his topic? How does he communicate this attitude? Support your answer with specific evidence from the text.

WRITING PROMPTS

Responding to the Topic   To what extent have you and your friends and family become part of the *Harry Potter* craze? Have you and they read the books and seen the movies? Do you regard *Harry Potter* as more than just entertainment? Interview five to ten acquaintances to record their reactions to these questions and others questions you devise. Then write an essay detailing the impact of *Harry Potter* on their world and yours.

Responding to the Writer   Nexon argues that "the global *Harry Potter* phenomenon has outgrown the specifics of the books" and that "in the public consciousness, the characters have become symbols" (para. 11). Compose an essay in which you accept or reject Nexon's assertion. If you have access to the books, use examples from the books themselves, as well as from this essay, to support your position. If you have not read the books, rely on specific examples cited in this essay or on examples you describe from the film versions.

Responding to Multiple Viewpoints   In "*Harry Potter* and Magical Realism," Nexon notes that certain groups have raised serious objections to the *Harry Potter* phenomenon. How do their objections and actions compare to those of Native Americans who object to certain teams' mascots, gestures, and activities (see Phyllis Raybin Emert's "Native American Mascots: Racial Slur or Cherished Tradition?")?

For a quiz on this reading, go to bedfordstmartins.com/mirror.

Native American Mascots:
Racial Slur or Cherished Tradition?

PHYLLIS RAYBIN EMERT

Phyllis Raybin Emert writes books for the History Compass series, including *Shipwrecks: The Sinking of the* Titanic *and Other Disasters at Sea* and
World War II: On the Homefront. She has also written several books for
the children's series Strange Unsolved Mysteries, including *Mysteries of People
and Places* (1992) and *Mysteries of the Bizarre Animals and Freaks of Nature*
(1994). In "Native American Mascots," which appeared in 2003 in *Respect,* a
publication of the New Jersey State Bar Foundation, she covers the debate
over the appropriateness of Native American mascots in sports. This controversy isn't new, but here Emert relates multiple arguments from both sides that
consider the place of the Native American mascot as a contested symbol of
America.

> **THINKING AHEAD** What was the mascot of your high
> school sports teams? Did you ever consider whether that mascot could
> be offensive to anyone? Why? What do you think about teams that
> name themselves after Native American groups, such as the Atlanta
> Braves and the Florida Seminoles? Why do the schools choose these
> names?

N ative American mascots and nicknames can be seen everywhere in   1
our society. People drive Jeep Cherokees, watch Atlanta Braves baseball fans do the tomahawk chop[1] and enjoy professional and college football teams such as the Kansas City Chiefs and the Florida State University
Seminoles. Are the use of these symbols a tribute to the Native American
people, or as some feel, a slap in the face to their honored traditions?

Across the country, according to the National Coalition on Race and   2
Sports in Media, which is part of the American Indian Movement (AIM),
there are more than 3,000 racist or offensive mascots used in high school,
college or professional sports teams. In New Jersey alone, there are dozens
of schools that use Native American images and symbols, such as braves,
warriors, chiefs or Indians, for their sports teams.

In April 2001, the U.S. Commission on Civil Rights recommended   3
that all non–Native American schools drop their Native American mascots or nicknames. The commission declared that "the stereotyping of
any racial, ethnic, religious or other group, when promoted by our public

---

[1] **the tomahawk chop:** Gesture of the hand to resemble a light ax chopping down on something; used by Atlanta Braves' baseball fans to mark success.

educational institutions, teaches all students that stereotyping of minority groups is acceptable, which is a dangerous lesson in a diverse society." The commission also noted that these nicknames and mascots are "false portrayals that encourage biases and prejudices that have a negative effect on contemporary Indian people."

Harmless Fun?

For years, Native American organizations have opposed the use of such   4
mascots, finding them offensive and a racial slur against their people. Supporters of the nicknames believe they honor Native Americans and focus on their bravery, courage and fighting skills.

Karl Swanson, vice-president of the Washington Redskins profes-   5
sional football team, declared in the magazine *Sports Illustrated* that his team's name "symbolizes courage, dignity, and leadership," and that the "Redskins symbolize the greatness and strength of a grand people."

In the Native American mascot controversy, the nickname "redskins"   6
is particularly controversial and offensive. Historically, the term was used to refer to the scalps of dead Native Americans that were exchanged for money as bounties, or cash rewards. When it became too difficult to bring in the bodies of dead Indians to get the money (usually under a dollar per person), bounty hunters exchanged bloody scalps or "redskins" as evidence of the dead Indian.

In 1992 seven Native Americans filed a lawsuit against the Washington   7
Redskins football club. Suzan Shown Harjo, one of the plaintiffs[2] in the case, wrote in her essay "Fighting Name-Calling: Challenging Redskins' in Court," which appeared in the book titled *Team Spirits — The Native American Mascots Controversy*, that they "petitioned the U.S. Patent and Trademark Office for cancellation of federal registrations for Redskins and Redskinettes . . . and associated names of the team in the nation's capital." In 1999, the Trademark Trial and Appeal Board "found that Redskins was an offensive term historically and remained so from the first trademark license in 1967, to the present." In a 145-page decision, the panel unanimously canceled the federal trademarks because they "may disparage Native Americans and may bring them into contempt or disrepute," Harjo reported. The Washington Redskins appealed the decision and the case is now pending in federal district court.

Demeaning or Entertaining?

Supporters contend that such nicknames are an entertaining part of a cher-   8
ished tradition and were never intended to harm or make a mockery of any

---

[2] **plaintiffs:** Those who bring legal actions against others.

group. There is also a financial side to the issue. The sale of merchandise with team mascots and nicknames on items such as t-shirts, hats and jackets brings in millions of dollars to various schools and sports teams every year. A changeover would cost money and render much of the current merchandise obsolete, the teams contend.

Opponents of Native American mascots and nicknames are not concerned about the cost and use words such as disrespectful and hurtful, degrading and humiliating to describe what they believe is racial stereotyping. They regard the mascots as caricatures of real Indians that trivialize and demean native dances and sacred Indian rituals.   9

"It's the behavior that accompanies all of this that's offensive," Clyde Bellecourt told *USA Today*. Bellecourt, who is national director of AIM, said, "The rubber tomahawks, the chicken feather headdresses, people wearing war paint and making these ridiculous war whoops[3] with a tomahawk in one hand and a beer in the other—all of these have significant meaning for us. And the psychological impact it has, especially on our youth, is devastating."   10

What Is the Price of Entertainment?

What is at stake, opponents of Native American mascots argue, is the self-image and self-esteem of American Indian children.   11

"Their pride is being mocked," Matthew Beaudet, an attorney and president of the Illinois Native American Bar Association, explained in "More Than a Mascot," an article that appeared in the newsletter *School Administrator*. "The Native American community is saying we know you're trying to flatter us, but we're not flattered, so stop."   12

Washington Post columnist Richard Cohen agrees.   13

"It hardly enhances the self-esteem of an Indian youth to always see his people and himself represented as a cartoon character," Cohen wrote. "And, always, the caricature is suggestive of battle, of violence—of the Indian warrior, the brave, the chief, the warpath,[4] the beating of tom-toms[5]."   14

Survey Says

The mascot issue is most controversial at the local level. Although numerous schools have voluntarily taken action to cease using Native American symbols, many school boards have refused to do so. Supporters of Native American mascots and nicknames point to surveys, such as the one published by *Sports Illustrated* in March 2002, which found   15

---

[3] **war whoops:** Battle cries of American Indians, shouted to frighten the enemy.
[4] **warpath:** Route taken by American Indians going to battle.
[5] **tom-toms:** Small Native American drums generally beaten with the hands.

that although most Native American activists found Indian mascots and nicknames offensive, the majority of non-activist American Indians were not disturbed by them.

American Indian activists explained the discrepancy in the *Sports*   16
Illustrated article that accompanied the survey, saying, "Native Americans' self-esteem has fallen so low that they don't even know when they're being insulted."

Harjo, who is president of the Morning Star Institute, an Indian-rights   17
organization in Washington, D.C., stated in her essay, "There are happy campers on every plantation." Harjo implied that although many slaves may have been content with their lives in bondage, the institution of slavery still needed to be abolished and the same reasoning holds true for Native American mascots.

According to the *Sports Illustrated* survey, 87 percent of American   18
Indians who lived off Indian reservations did not object to Native American mascots or nicknames. Of the Indians who lived on reservations, 67 percent were not bothered by the nicknames, while 33 percent opposed them.

In addition to the survey, those who would like to keep the traditional   19
Native American nicknames give examples of American Indian tribes that have openly embraced schools and teams using their names. At Arapahoe High School in Littleton, Colorado, for example, the Warriors' school gym is named for Anthony Sitting Eagle, an Arapaho leader. Every year on Arapaho Day, tribal members come from the reservation to visit with students and teach Arapaho history and traditions. Tribal leaders have also advised the Warriors on how to make their logo authentic, and even persuaded the school to remove a painting on the gym floor because it was offensive to have students walk over it. Similar close relationships exist between Florida State University and the Seminole tribe, Central Michigan University and the Chippewa tribe and the Arcadia High School Apaches in California, who have a relationship with an American Indian tribe in Arizona.

Racial Slur or Cherished Tradition?

The Native American mascot issue has caused debate throughout the   20
country between communities and school boards, students and Native American groups. Although the outcome of the debates has varied from state to state, with some communities refusing to change, the trend in recent years has been to eliminate offensive Native American mascots and nicknames at schools and colleges. Not a single professional sports team, however, has changed its name. Given the strong opinions on both sides and the pending Washington Redskins case, the controversy will no doubt rage on.

EXERCISING VOCABULARY

1. Record your own definition for each word below in your notebook.

mascots (n.) (1)
stereotyping (n.) (3)
slur (n.) (4)
controversy (n.) (6)
unanimously (adv.) (7)
disparage (v.) (7)
demeaning (adj.) (8)

render (v.) (8)
obsolete (adj.) (8)
trivialize (v.) (9)
devastating (adj.) (10)
activists (n.) (15)
discrepancy (n.) (16)
bondage (n.) (17)

2. In 1999, the Trademark Trial and Appeal Board found reason to cancel the Washington Redskins' federal trademarks "because they 'may disparage Native Americans and may bring them into contempt or disrepute' " (para. 7). What does the prefix *dis* mean? What other words have *reput(e)* in them? What then does *disrepute* mean?

3. Native Americans see some team mascots as "caricatures of real Indians" (para. 9). What is a caricature? What does it imply to caricature someone or something? Why would Native Americans find this practice insulting?

4. You already know what the word *rage* means as a noun. How does that meaning change when the same word is used as a verb, as in "the controversy will no doubt rage on" (para. 20)? By using this verb here, what does Emert indicate about those on both sides of the controversy concerning Native American mascots?

PROBING CONTENT

1. According to Emert, how widespread is the concern about Native American mascots? According to the National Coalition on Race and Sports in Media, about how many high schools, colleges, or professional sports teams use "racist or offensive mascots" (para. 2)?

2. As this controversy rages, which mascot is particularly offensive to Native Americans? Why? Explain the history of this nickname.

3. What's really at stake in this controversy? Why is that significant?

4. How do nonactivist American Indians react to these mascot names? Why do they have this reaction, according to Emert?

5. What is unique about Arapahoe High School in Colorado? Describe the relationship between the Native Americans and the students.

CONSIDERING CRAFT

1. Briefly discuss the impact the title of this essay has on your reading of this selection. What does Emert accomplish by being so clear about the two sides in this controversy?

2. Locate and name two of the authoritative sources that Emert quotes in this essay. Why did she add their quotations? Why did she choose these particular people?

3. What role do the subheadings throughout the selection play in your comprehension of the essay? What would be lost if they were deleted?

4. In paragraph 19, Emert discusses a high school in Colorado that has built a close relationship with a Native American tribe. Why would the author choose to include such a positive example when the overall intent of the essay seems to indicate that Native American mascots are demeaning to Native Americans? How does this strengthen or weaken her thesis?

WRITING PROMPTS

Responding to the Topic   From what you have read or seen on television, in movies, or on the Web, describe in an essay your understanding of Native Americans. Be sure to include the specific sources on which that understanding is based. If you know personally or have met Native Americans, detail the circumstances, your reaction to their culture, and theirs to your culture.

Responding to the Writer   Native American organizations find the use of Native American mascots "offensive and a racial slur against their people. Supporters of the nicknames believe they honor Native Americans and focus on their bravery, courage and fighting skills" (para. 4). In an essay, argue for and support one of these two viewpoints.

Responding to Multiple Viewpoints   In "Material Girls," Erika Fricke compares two radically different performers. In "Native American Mascots," Emert describes people who tend to divide up into one of two camps regarding a divisive issue. Would the Dolly Parton supporters that Fricke portrays be for or against a popular American Indian candidate for president? Why?

For a quiz on this reading, go to bedfordstmartins.com/mirror.

Booze, Blood, and the
Star-Spangled Banner

JACK EL-HAI

In the following essay, author Jack El-Hai provides a fascinating lesson about the history of America's national anthem, "The Star-Spangled Banner," by following attempts to change it to what many critics feel is a more appropriate song. El-Hai is the author of *The Lobotomist: A Maverick Medical Genius and His Tragic Quest to Rid the World of Mental Illness* (2005). As a freelance writer, he has contributed articles to the *Atlantic Monthly, American Heritage*, and the *Washington Post Magazine*, among other publications. He is also president of the American Society of Journalists and Authors. "Booze, Blood, and the Star-Spangled Banner" appeared in the *Utne Reader* in 2006.

> **THINKING AHEAD** How many of the words to America's national anthem do you know from memory? When you are at a ball game or a civic affair where the anthem is played, do you sing along? Why? How do you feel when you hear the anthem sung or sing it yourself? How would you react to a movement to change our national anthem to a different song?

In 1992 Anders Skaar, an executive headhunter[1] with negligible musical talent, set up a bare-bones organization called Anthem! America and put out a call for composers and lyricists to submit new songs that could replace "The Star-Spangled Banner," which he found both hard to sing and hard to swallow.

"It ranges an octave and a half," he says. "For most of us, a song should lie within an octave to remain singable. And it's not really our song. Francis Scott Key wrote the words, but the music supposedly comes from an English drinking song. I thought we should have an anthem that was our song." In addition, Skaar hoped to find a national hymn that was inspirational, understandable for people of all ages, and not in the category of what he called "we-drink-our-enemy's-blood type songs."

Dozens of entries, addressed to Skaar's home in Raleigh, North Carolina, poured in from all over the country. A panel of musicians and academics judged the winner of the competition to be "America, My America," a composition by an Indiana music teacher and two lyricists from Tennessee who were inspired by the view from the north rim of the Grand Canyon.

---

[1]**headhunter:** Someone who recruits personnel, especially executives, for businesses.

Skaar immediately went to work promoting "America, My America"   4
and trying to raise prize money for its creators. He circulated tapes of the
winner and nine runners-up to radio stations and record companies, but
no one was interested. It seemed that despite the public's lackadaisical[2] attitude toward actually singing the song, "The Star-Spangled Banner" had
achieved sacred status. Ever since Congress adopted the anthem in 1931,
in fact, many Americans have viewed any attempt to replace it as sacrilegious. "Republicans thought it was a Democratic conspiracy, and Democrats thought it was a Republican conspiracy," Skaar says. He eventually
stopped advocating the new anthem and now serves on the board of a
Raleigh charity that distributes Christian books to prisons, shelters, and
missions.

Francis Scott Key wrote the words that would become the lyrics to   5
"The Star-Spangled Banner" in 1814, after he watched an American force
that was displaying a gigantic battle flag at Fort McHenry in Maryland
withstand a British naval bombardment. Key set his poem to a well-known
tune called "To Anacreon in Heaven," which was a tribute to an ancient
Greek poet who celebrated the joys of eating, drinking, and arguing. John
Stafford Smith composed the piece around 1780 as the signature song for a
gentlemen's club of amateur musicians in London who dubbed themselves
the Anacreontic Society.

Key had previously set at least one other poem to the same tune, and   6
dozens of other lyricists used the music as the starting point of their comic,
sentimental, and bawdy compositions. But Key's version gave expression to
"something important in American history," says Deane Root, a member of the
music faculty at the University of Pittsburgh. "The country had been attacked,
and even though its forces were unable to defend Washington, they were able
to hold this fort. The song represents a successful national defense."

As "The Star-Spangled Banner" grew in popularity, bands made it   7
more playable by changing the key and slowing the tempo. (The tune was
originally quite jaunty and irreverent, and to this day there is no officially
sanctioned version.) Around the turn of the twentieth century, the song was
already used by the military during the raising of the flag, and "The Star-
Spangled Banner" became an institution.

It has since lost its hold on the public. A recent Harris poll showed that   8
61 percent of American adults admit they do not know all the words, and
most who think they do really don't. (The second, third, and fourth verses
are practically unknown.) Among teenagers, according to an ABC News
poll, 38 percent don't know the song's name. Indifference toward "The
Star-Spangled Banner" is so widespread that a coalition of supporters—
including the entire congressional delegation of Maryland and honorary
chair Laura Bush—joined forces in 2005 to unleash the National Anthem
Project, an effort to teach the song to schoolchildren.

---

[2] **lackadaisical:** Lacking life, spirit, or enthusiasm.

After 9/11, the American Coalition for a New National Anthem began   9
advocating Irving Berlin's "God Bless America" as a replacement, but the
Massachusetts-based organization has since gone into hibernation. Public
figures ranging from Ray Charles to Ted Turner have spoken on behalf of
"America the Beautiful," and in the past few years essays about the overthrow of Key's song have frequently appeared in newspaper op-ed[3] pages,
including those of the *Milwaukee Journal Sentinel*, the *Chicago Tribune*,
and the *Boston Globe*. Six times between 1985 and 1995, then Democratic
congressional representative Andy Jacobs of Indiana, a former marine, introduced bills to make "America the Beautiful" the national anthem; all
died quietly. (Before the official adoption of "The Star-Spangled Banner"
three-quarters of a century ago, the Music Supervisors of America, a group
of education professors at Columbia University Teachers College, and the
National Hymn Society publicly opposed it.)

A lot of people find "The Star-Spangled Banner" to be lacking in feel-   10
ing, bellicose (the rarely sung third verse declares of the invading British,
"Their blood has wash'd out their foul footsteps' pollution"), descriptive
of a forgotten event, stale (the same tune served as the national anthem of
Luxembourg before 1864), and difficult to navigate even for professional
singers, who often apprehensively lead the song into "a kind of musical
stream of consciousness," as Balint Vazsonyi observed nearly a decade ago
in the *National Review*.

Even Key's biography is suspect: As district attorney of the city of   11
Washington in 1835, he sought the death penalty for a mulatto slave who
drunkenly yet unthreateningly appeared in a white woman's bedroom one
night holding an ax. President Andrew Jackson ultimately pardoned the slave,
and Key unsuccessfully tried to connect an abolitionist with the crime.

If it ever were possible to dethrone Key's song, finding the right replace-   12
ment will be tricky. The most powerful national anthems—like France's and
Russia's, which give you chills and keep ringing in your ears—tread a fine
line between sentiment and cliché.[4] "You can't be obtuse, and you need to be
direct," says Gene Scheer, a composer whose best-known work, a song called
"American Anthem," was performed at the 2005 inauguration of President
George W. Bush. "You mustn't underestimate your audience—people
aren't stupid, and they know when they're being pandered to. You can't
calculate your way to a good song. It has to be an honest expression of
what you're thinking, and it involves emotion and the best aspects of
your intellect."

"I still get a tingle up my spine when I hear 'The Star-Spangled Banner,'   13
but I feel better when I hear and sing 'America the Beautiful,'" says Lynn
Sherr, ABC news correspondent and author of *America the Beautiful: The
Stirring True Story Behind Our Nation's Favorite Song* (PublicAffairs,

---

[3]**op-ed:** Short for "opposite editorial"; a page of special features often located opposite the
editorial page in a newspaper.
[4]**cliché:** An expression that has become trite through overuse.

2001). "That song fills my eyes with tears, something I don't get from 'The Star-Spangled Banner.'" Many agree with Sherr, but the difficulty is satisfying everyone's view of what America represents. Some citizens want a song that shows defiance in the face of outside threats, as the "The Star-Spangled Banner" does. Others want a tribute to our country's distinctiveness, an evocation of spirituality, or simply a song that feels emotionally gratifying to sing. Is there a substitute anthem that meets all of these requirements?

The top contenders to replace "The Star-Spangled Banner" (see list below) include many lovely songs that, by and large, are falling into disuse. "We Shall Overcome," however—an ode to determination and courage and American ideals if ever there was one—is widely known by children and adults alike. Perhaps that civil rights–era hymn, or some new song that sneaks into our consciousness, will be the one to inspire a future generation to rethink our national tune.

14

American Songbook

Commonly (and uncommonly) cited candidates to replace "The Star-Spangled Banner."

Contenders

"America the Beautiful," lyrics by Katharine Lee Bates, to music by Samuel Augustus Ward. This love song to America's charms has been the chief competitor of "The Star-Spangled Banner" for nearly one hundred years. But its popularity, at least in schools, appears to be fading.

"God Bless America," lyrics and music by Irving Berlin. A favorite after 9/11, this song needs a singer like Kate Smith to make it inspiring. In the hands of mere mortals, it sounds bland.

"This Land Is Your Land," lyrics and music by Woody Guthrie (with musical inspiration from the Carter family). Written in response to the smugness of "God Bless America," this song lacks the weight of a national anthem yet still embodies the ideals of a large swath of America.

"We Shall Overcome," a gospel song, origins unclear. A mesmerizing and powerful work that has already led the country through adversity and continues to sustain Americans in difficult times.

Long Shots

"Columbia, Gem of the Ocean," by T. Becket and D. Shaw. Once a true rival of "The Star-Spangled Banner," this rousing song grows less familiar with each passing generation.

"Ashokan Farewell," by Jay Ungar. Ken Burns used this entrancing tune in his PBS documentary series *The Civil War*.

"My Country 'Tis of Thee" (also known as "America"), lyrics by Samuel Francis Smith to an English melody. Long a schoolchildren's favorite, this song is slowly fading from our collective memory. The tune is the same as "God Save the Queen."

"American Anthem," by Gene Scheer. A lovely contemporary song, to be featured in Ken Burns' forthcoming television documentary about World War II.

"The Battle Hymn of the Republic," lyrics by Julia Ward Howe to the traditional tune of "John Brown's Body." A fierce and grim song with strong religious overtones, sung at the funerals of Ronald Reagan and Robert Kennedy.

Bringing Up the Rear

"America," lyrics and music by Neil Diamond.

"Don't Tread on Me," by James Hetfield and Lars Ulrich.

"We Are the Champions," lyrics and music by Freddie Mercury.

"Theme from *Hawaii Five-O*," music by Morton Stevens.

"Don't Fence Me In," lyrics and music by Cole Porter.

"Louie Louie," lyrics and music by Richard Berry.

EXERCISING VOCABULARY

1. Record your own definition for each word below in your notebook.

    negligible (adj.) (1)   coalition (n.) (8)
    sacrilegious (adj.) (4)   hibernation (n.) (9)
    advocating (v.) (4)   apprehensively (adv.) (10)
    bombardment (n.) (5)   obtuse (adj.) (12)
    bawdy (adj.) (6)   pandered (v.) (12)
    jaunty (adj.) (7)   evocation (n.) (13)
    irreverent (adj.) (7)   gratifying (adj.) (13)
    sanctioned (adj.) (7)

2. "The Star-Spangled Banner" is a secular song, yet El-Hai notes that "many Americans have viewed any attempt to replace it as sacrilegious" (para. 3). What does the word *sacrilegious* mean? In what sense is it usually used? Why would Americans feel this way?

3. When people accuse our national anthem of being bellicose, what is their criticism? What words in the song reinforce this idea? What other words do you know that are related to *bellicose* and begin with the same prefix, *belli*?

4. Balint Vazsonyi observes that the difficulty in singing "The Star-Spangled Banner" leads even professional singers into "a kind of musical stream

of consciousness" (para. 10). What does the phrase *stream of consciousness* mean when it applies to writing? How would this apply musically?

5. El-Hai writes that to replace the national anthem, it would first be necessary "to dethrone Key's song" (para. 12). Who is usually dethroned? What message does the author convey about "The Star-Spangled Banner" by choosing this word?

PROBING CONTENT

1. When and under what circumstances did Francis Scott Key write the lyrics to "The Star-Spangled Banner"? What is the origin of the tune to which Key set the lyrics?

2. As the song gained popularity, what did bands do with "The Star-Spangled Banner" to make it easier to play? When was the song first widely used by the military, and on what occasions?

3. What is the National Anthem Project? Why was it necessary? Who supported this effort?

4. In this essay, El-Hai mentions two other songs as strong anthem contenders. What are these songs? What reasons does he give for considering either of these as the new national anthem?

CONSIDERING CRAFT

1. The original title of this selection was "Booze, Blood, and the Star-Spangled Banner: A Noble Quest to Replace the National Anthem with a Winner." There is, however, very little reference to blood or booze in the essay. Why did El-Hai choose this title? What does the subtitle imply about the essay's intent?

2. Reread the opening paragraph of this essay. What strategies does El-Hai use to grab the reader's attention?

3. In paragraph 11, El-Hai introduces an *ad hominem* fallacy into his discussion of the national anthem. What is an *ad hominem* fallacy? Why does the author insert this information here? What effect does its inclusion have on your reading of the overall argument?

4. Why does the author introduce a second song as a replacement for "The Star-Spangled Banner" in the last paragraph of the essay? What are the benefits and the drawbacks of introducing new material at such a late point in this or any other essay?

WRITING PROMPTS

Responding to the Topic "Some citizens want a song that shows defiance in the face of outside threats. . . . Others want a tribute to our nation's distinctiveness, an evocation of spirituality, or simply a song that feels emotionally gratifying to sing" (para. 13). In your own opinion, what are the characteristics of a good national anthem? What should people feel or think about as they sing it? Write an essay in which you explore these characteristics and explain why they are essential.

Responding to the Writer Choose one of the songs in the "American Songbook" list and write an essay in which you argue for its selection as our national anthem. You may also argue that "The Star-Spangled Banner" should remain America's anthem. Be sure to locate a copy of the words to the song you select to reference in your discussion. Include arguments for the melody as well as for the lyrics.

Responding to Multiple Viewpoints In "Signs of Our Times," Virginia Postrel writes that neon "still exists today largely because of the efforts of enthusiasts, mostly older baby boomers with fond memories of roadside America" (para. 4). Could this same argument be made for the longevity of "The Star-Spangled Banner" as our national anthem? Which of the reasons that account for the preservation of neon may also account for the preservation of our national anthem?

For a quiz on this reading, go to bedfordstmartins.com/mirror.

DRAWING CONNECTIONS

1. In both "Native American Mascots" and "Booze, Blood, and the Star-Spangled Banner," the authors discuss a small group of people who are trying to change tradition. El-Hai quotes Anders Skaar's statement that our anthem should be "inspirational, understandable for people of all ages, and not in the category of what he called 'we-drink-our-enemy's-blood type songs'" ("Booze, Blood, and the Star-Spangled Banner," para. 2). Discuss how Phyllis Raybin Emert might apply this statement to mascots selected for sports teams.

2. Who do you believe builds a better argument for changing a long-held tradition, El-Hai or Emert? Why do you find the argument you selected more valid?

3. Emert cites the financial side of the argument about changing sports mascots. What might El-Hai add to his essay concerning financial incentives for or against changing the national anthem?

4. Compare the ways in which El-Hai and Emert use statistics to support their viewpoints. Whose use of statistics best validates his or her argument? Why?

Material Girls

ERIKA FRICKE

America is the land of *American Idol*, but music icons have been around long before they were judged and approved by Simon, Paula, and Randy. In the following essay, Erika Fricke analyzes the popularity of two of the most enduring American music legends, Dolly Parton and Madonna, and tries to discover just what about these women resonates with American audiences. Fricke is vice president of public affairs for Planned Parenthood of Western Pennsylvania. She previously worked as procedural counselor for Planned Parenthood and as a writer for the *Berkeley Daily Planet* and the *Pittsburgh Post-Gazette*. "Material Girls" appeared in *Bitch* magazine in 2006.

> **THINKING AHEAD** Are you a fan of Madonna or Dolly Parton? Why? What has made it possible for these two women, unlike most other pop icons, to remain popular and maintain a devoted fan base over so many years?

When I summon up a mental picture of Dolly Parton, an indelible 1
image emerges: There she is, hopping out of a stretch limo, her body barely contained by a cling-tight rhinestone outfit and her breasts toppling out, rivaled in pulchritude[1] only by her enormous 'do. She's on her way to the Grand Ole Opry to perform a show with Alvin and the Chipmunks.

It's fitting that my strongest memory of Parton is as a guest star on a 2
TV show about animated rodents; after all, the lines of her femininity are cartoonishly drawn. Her boobs are huge and her waist is tiny, in the classic va-va-voom hourglass style. False eyelashes rim her lids. Her crown of ornately styled white-blond curls boasts a life of its own. Parton has the magical quality of appearing to have retained the same age, size, and demeanor over time. Like those of Alvin and his chipmunk friends, the lines of Dolly's body haven't seemed to change over the years, and no new ones have appeared. ("If I see something saggin', baggin', and draggin', I'm going to nip it, tuck it, and suck it" is a classic Dollyism.) And although her individual outfits may have changed over the years, the overall Parton look has remained remarkably constant, from her original "Tennessee mountain home" to her recent performance at the Academy Awards.

When I try to conjure up a formative image of Madonna, what I get 3
instead is a flash of my little sister at age 8, dressed in the Material Girl's

---

[1]**pulchritude:** Physical attractiveness.

'80s-era can-can dancer/street-urchin togs, complete with flouncy miniskirt and large hairbow. I try to refocus on Madonna, the ex-Catholic working-class girl, in white lace gloves and torn fishnets,[2] but it's quickly eclipsed by Madonna demurely covered with a lace mantilla; Madonna flaunting a Gaultier-designed[3] cone bra and a long blond pony tail; Madonna in a man's suit, jacket open to reveal a lacy bustier;[4] Madonna as a chic, icy Eva Peron; Madonna in a sari with deeply bronzed skin; Madonna in geisha[5] drag; Madonna glammed up like Marilyn Monroe; Madonna as a Burberry-clad British matron. Madonna's image has changed so drastically at so many junctures that to lock her into only one incarnation is to miss the larger picture. For Madonna, the medium—or, in her case, the image—*is* the message.

Over the years, a number of iconic, first-name-basis female musicians   4
have been adored as much for their style as for their music—Janis, Aretha, Dusty, Cher, Whitney, Mariah, Ani, Britney. But there's something special about Dolly and Madonna. For one thing, both have continually released new albums, year after year, building up new audiences as they reassure their longtime fans that they'll always be there for them. A big part of their staying power, however, is that the public continues to respond to them not just as musicians but as icons. There's something in these two women that we'd like to be, and one way we do it is by re-creating their style. (Exhibit A: the vast department-store acreage given over to Madonna-wannabe clothing in the mid-'80s. Exhibit B: the number of drag performers who emulate Dolly.) In their own very different ways, both women make the mutability of fashion and femininity central to their work; for their many and varied fans, parsing[6] the messages is an extended (even lifelong) project that not only has personal meaning but also uncovers crucial ideas and biases about how we define identity, authenticity, and success.

Hello Dolly

Dolly Parton's femininity has always been so overblown it borders on   5
kitsch.[7] And because of this, it's easy to make her the butt (no pun intended) of crass jokes. A popular visual riddle perfectly illustrates Parton's exaggerated, comic qualities: Two vertical lines are drawn, and equal-sized semicircles pop out from both sides. The punch line? Dolly Parton behind a tree.

Kitsch takes sincere art or style and packages it into a ready-to-use con-   6
sumable. Similarly, Parton takes the classic, stereotypical representation

---

[2]**fishnets:** Stockings with an open-weave pattern.
[3]**Gaultier:** Jean-Paul Gaultier, a famous designer.
[4]**bustier:** A tight-fitting top resembling a brassiere.
[5]**geisha:** Japanese female who undergoes rigorous training to be an entertaining companion for men.
[6]**parsing:** Examining in great detail.
[7]**kitsch:** Something that appeals to popular taste but is of low quality.

of femininity and makes it utterly, unavoidably obvious. "It's an almost absurd level of femininity that she is in complete control over," says Duane Gordon, who runs Dollymania.net, the star's unofficial fan site. "She has taken the modern idea of what a woman is supposed to be and blown it up to 100 times its original size." This larger-than-life woman pulls off the neat trick of remaining an idealized object for heterosexual men's desire while also serving as an easily emulated model for other men's adoration—that is, the inspiration for countless drag-queen Dollys.

But although she may be a model of exaggerated femininity, Parton   7
is also, paradoxically, perceived by fans and journalists alike as the very antithesis[8] of kitsch. Articles about her regularly use words like "authentic," "genuine," and "sincere." Tai Uhlmann, who interviewed Dolly fans for her upcoming documentary, *For the Love of Dolly*, says, "She feels like a very honest person who sings about love and family. Any time I've seen her, she's incredibly consistent in her personality; she comes off as very authentic."

Certainly, Parton is committed to her style in a way that neither trend-   8
setters nor trend followers can be. Her adherence to now-dated glamour certainly comes off as genuine—after all, who would keep faking it for all these years? Some of this language of authenticity is simply part of the lexicon[9] of the country-music genre. Just as it's popularly believed that "authentic" rappers should hail from the streets of Detroit or Compton and rhyme about gang life, so an unwritten rule of country music is that the "true" artists emerge from the backwoods, guitars in hand. Parton's country pedigree is the stuff of legend: born in the mountains of Tennessee, an outhouse for a toilet, sleeping several to a bed with her 11 brothers and sisters. Parton's aura of authenticity goes beyond her backstory, however, to include her straight-talkin', aw-shucks onstage demeanor. During shows, she makes eye contact and conversation with individual audience members, and she's a master of self-deprecation.[10] One of her most famous lines is the quip "It takes a lot of money to look this cheap," which she throws out before concerts when thanking her audience for paying admission.

This level of self-awareness implies that Parton is no less deliberate in   9
the construction of her persona than any other pop star. But unlike performers whose "natural beauty" turns out to be the product of science or eating disorders, Parton's acknowledgment of artifice actually reinforces, rather than undermines, her image. At the most basic level, Parton's figure gives her an obvious physical punch line that creates both a sense of humility and an intimate wink-nudge rapport with her fans. Dolly and fans alike are in on the joke. What joke they're getting, of course, depends on the listener.

"[A Dolly Parton concert] is the only place you're going to find gay   10
club kids, Southern Baptist ministers, drag queens, and housewives sitting

---

[8]**antithesis:** The opposite.
[9]**lexicon:** The vocabulary of a group of speakers.
[10]**self-deprecation:** Belittling oneself.

together having a good time," Gordon says. Some see a good Christian girl who loves her mama and daddy; others see an outrageous woman who sings about peace, freedom, and acceptance. These images are not irreconcilable, even if her fans don't always agree. Parton doesn't shy away from social politics, but she manages to ingratiate herself with opposing parties—her Best Song nomination at the Oscars, for instance, was for the song "Travelin' Through," a homey road tune written for *Transamerica*, a film about a pre-op transsexual and her teenage son. Likewise, her musings about controversial issues are jovial home truths rather than soapboxy proclamations ("Why shouldn't they be as miserable as the rest of us?" she recently queried on the subject of gay marriage), and thus she's able to balance a fan base that's strongly conservative along with one that's extravagantly progressive.

At this stage in her career, Parton has her patter down—an arsenal of   11 good-natured Dollyisms that she has deployed onstage, in interviews, and in cherished playing-to-type roles in films like *9 to 5* and *Steel Magnolias*—and one of her best lines is "If I hadn't been a woman, I'd have been a drag queen." Parton readily admits that, as a country girl, she fell in love with the style of the town prostitute. And indeed, her outlandish gear—rhinestones, sequins, tight-fitting clothes—displays a country girl's fascination with glitz and glamour. But no matter how fancy the design of her outfits, this oversized femininity also keeps her firmly attached to Tennessee soil. As she escaped small-town Sevierville and landed in urban metropolises like New York and Los Angeles, Parton held fast to her showy look. I suspect it's served her well as a reminder of her link to her rural past, and the kind of poor girl who falls in love with big hair, shiny buttons, and high heels.

But that also means Parton is never allowed to leave behind her lower-   12 class background—it's in her clothes, in her accent, and inscribed on her body through the breast lifts and collagen injections[11] that keep her looking town-whore beautiful at age sixty. But it's also what her diehard fans seem to desire. After all, when Parton first moved to Los Angeles, Nashville fans despaired. Over time, with her crossover hits like "9 to 5," she lost touch with her country roots, couldn't get airtime on country radio, and had to disband her fan club—a terrible blow for a star who considers herself country. Renewed success only came in the late '90s through returning to bluegrass, the most "authentic" music of her childhood in the Appalachians, which won her new Grammies and renewed attention.

The idea that Parton's flair for feminine artifice provides a link to her   13 impoverished past helps explain why Parton's huge wigs, false eyelashes, and corseted waist only make her more "genuine." The more of Dolly Parton there is—whether it's hair or breasts—the more Dollyesque she becomes. The authenticity comes from the improbably outsized femininity. We never want the wig to come off, the breasts to be shrouded, or the big, lipsticked, and always joyful mouth to close.

---

[11]**collagen injections:** Fibrous protein injected to restore a youthful appearance.

Blond (and Brunet, and Auburn) Ambition

While Parton has built her brand of womanly wiles by maintaining the   14
archetypal[12] persona of the busty blond with a heart of gold, Madonna's
take on femininity is all about reinvention and possibility. There is no
one classic Madonna look, but a dozen; what links them all is the singer's
constant desire to push the boundaries of what she can say, or do, or embody—not as an emblem of womanhood, but as her own performance
project.

Parton is clearly also a world-class performer of femininity, but be-   15
cause her take on femaleness adheres so closely to stereotypes—and because it has been so consistent—she hasn't been embraced by pomo[13]
theorists the way Madonna has. Postmodernists go haywire for Madonna.
Books with titles like *Madonna as Postmodern Myth* and *The Madonna
Connection: Representational Politics, Subcultural Identities, and Cultural
Theory* explore Madonna's message and impact for academic audiences,
while pulp biographies retell her story for popular ones. What feminist
and queer theorists love about Madonna is the way that her deliberately
created looks—whether it's as dominatrix[14] or as Marilyn Monroe—point
out the artifice of gendered images.

Each time she releases a new album or sets out on a tour, Madonna   16
takes on a new persona. Many pop stars adopt thematic changes for
each album, but few are able to construct their images so thoroughly as
Madonna. Over the years she has broadcast all kinds of femininity—from
tramp to vamp[15]—shedding one style to move on to the next. She skirts
across boundaries of class, gender, and race, picking up parts of culture
that she likes and flashing them back at us. Every Madonna reinvention is
a firm cancellation of the last. Unlike Parton, she is loath to acknowledge
her dramatic changes, and never returns to a persona she's abandoned.
Where Parton freely admits her artifice, one gets the sense that Madonna,
through sheer force of will, absorbs her changes fully and brooks no resistance from those around her ("I've always dressed like a cowboy/studied
Kabbalah/talked with a British accent"). And visually, Madonna's presentation of femininity often tends toward the bold, taking the idea of,
say, the large-breasted ideal and bringing it to a grotesque extreme, as the
Gaultier-created conical bra did.

But even the self-styled mistress of shock and awe can go too far. The   17
shakiest time in Madonna's career came when she went too deep into one
identity: gender outlaw. In the early '90s Madonna produced, in rapid
succession, several cultural items exploring her own transgressive sexual
identity. In the controversial 1992 photo book *Sex*, she showed images of

[12]**archetypal:** A perfect example; the model on which others are based.
[13]**pomo:** Short for "postmodern."
[14]**dominatrix:** A woman who dominates and abuses her sex partner.
[15]**vamp:** A woman who uses her feminine charms to seduce men.

herself in potentially exploitative sexual fantasies. In her documentary film, *Madonna: Truth or Dare,* she exposed her cast in a way that later resulted in lawsuits for exploitation. People who'd applauded her previous shape-shifting began to hold the singer accountable for the messages she put into the world—and, invariably, they got pissed.

In her 1994 book, *Outlaw Culture: Resisting Representations,* feminist theorist bell hooks took Madonna to task, accusing her of playing the role of white patriarch in *Truth or Dare* and of acting as a "cultural imperialist," moving amidst black and gay subcultures but never losing "white privilege." Hooks had a point: Madonna worked primarily with gay and black dancers and then positioned herself as a mother figure and savior of those she herself called "emotional cripples." Her appropriation of vogueing, the flamboyant dance long popular among black and Latino gay men and depicted in the 1990 documentary *Paris Is Burning,* brought the show to the mainstream but left behind the sociopolitical milieu[16] from which it originated.

As the '90s wore on, Madonna slowly began to seem less like a revolutionary and more like a poseur, someone whose real talent lay in jumping other people's trains and getting rich from it. Talking about sex publicly no longer seemed daring—instead, it seemed like a commercial ploy.

Madonna saved her career in a rapid about-face, metamorphosing once again. The filming of the 1996 movie *Evita* served as a chrysalis: Madonna abandoned her gender-outlaw incarnation and immersed herself in the character of Eva Peron, even dressing and eating like the star off-set. She emerged after the movie, reborn as a single mother. Later, she married British filmmaker Guy Ritchie and relocated to England. Her most recent incarnation writes sappy,[17] moralistic children's books and masquerades as a member of the British upper crust, complete with a bizarre British accent.

But even this new version of Madonna can't give up cultural cross-dressing completely: There's her commitment to Kabbalah, the study of Jewish mysticism that, in its Hollywood form, looks very much like a celebrity cult.

Longtime Madonna fan Mariam Ayuba, who runs several Madonna fan-club websites, says that it's just this kind of logic-free transformation that fuels her lifelong fascination with the star: "Madonna [acts] like, 'I'm not going to apologize for who I am,'" says Ayuba. "'You don't have to like it if you don't want to.' I feel like that's something girls [need] to hear." This is the message that always leads me to Madonna through the image of my spindly sister as Madonna wannabe. The person looking for the real Madonna misses the point that the only "authentic" thing about the Madonna behind all of these chameleon-like changes is her desire and ability to stay in front of the public and ahead of the press.

18

19

20

21

22

---

[16]**milieu:** Environment or background.
[17]**sappy:** Overly sentimental or silly.

Class Acts

Fans may look to stars for guidance and messages of liberation, and
Madonna and Dolly offer extreme examples of ways that women can succeed
by manipulating femininity—never playing by the rules but not rejecting
them outright either. But perhaps even more important, they offer a powerful
message about the way class works in the United States.

Madonna's ever-shifting image isn't just related to outfits, and if there's
a key to her will to change, it may well lie in her rarely mentioned middle-
class background. In the United States, the mainstream middle class is often
considered to be the "cultureless" class, one that aligns with the dominant
messages in popular culture and is free from limitations like accents, cultural
dress, or manners that might limit one's ability to transform oneself. For
example, in 1982, when Madonna's first single, "Everybody," was played on
R&B stations, people assumed she was black. The video for "La Isla Bonita"
portrayed her as Latina. And in one of her most compelling performances,
she convinced the public that she was a working-class girl who grew up in a
primarily African American neighborhood and struggled against the abuse
of formidable females including nuns and a stepmother. (The reality was
that Madonna Louise Ciccone's father was more of a six-figure type, and the
young Madonna was a cheerleader and straight-A student in a middle-class
school.)

Parton, on the other hand, had the hardscrabble[18] upbringing that
Madonna pretends to. Hers is the classic American success story, bootstraps[19] and all—she grew up in extreme rural poverty; she had talent and
worked hard; and now she's rich and famous. But beneath it all, she's still
a hillbilly. Parton's success is tied to her poor Southern beginnings, and her
music provides a way for mainstream Americans to feel their own phantom
roots, and for true Southern and country folks to admire her gumption[20]
and feel proud of one of their own.

Nobody really believes Madonna is working-class, black, Latina, or
Marilyn Monroe, so it's not a rejection when she moves on, the way it would
be for an artist like Dolly to suddenly turn her back on Tennessee. When
Madonna decides, in a few more years, that she no longer wants to be a
proper British horsewoman/Kabbalah devotee and would rather, say, refash-
ion herself as a Santeria[21] priestess, will anyone truly be surprised?

Dolly Parton is a country girl who became fabulous, while Madonna
is a fabulous fabulist,[22] but both have entertained vast audiences with their
music and their personas. In a time when authenticity and truth are ever
more conflicted, it seems entirely possible that there will never be another

23

24

25

26

27

---

[18]**hardscrabble:** Made difficult due to poverty.
[19]**bootstraps:** From the phrase "She pulled herself up by her bootstraps," meaning to do
   something on one's own without help from others.
[20]**gumption:** Initiative or common sense.
[21]**Santeria:** African-based religion similar to voodoo and practiced in Cuba.
[22]**fabulist:** Someone who creates fables.

performer like either woman. But then again, everything about both Dolly and Madonna suggests that they'll live forever, in our minds, our theories, and — in many cases — our own transformations.

EXERCISING VOCABULARY

1. Record your own definition for each word below in your notebook.

   indelible (adj.) (1)
   rodents (n.) (2)
   rim (v.) (2)
   demeanor (n.) (2)
   formative (adj.) (3)
   togs (n.) (3)
   incarnation (n.) (3)
   emulate (v.) (4)
   mutability (n.) (4)
   crass (adj.) (5)
   adherence (n.) (8)
   aura (n.) (8)
   artifice (n.) (9)
   rapport (n.) (9)
   irreconcilable (adj.) (10)

   ingratiate (v.) (10)
   patter (n.) (11)
   arsenal (n.) (11)
   deployed (v.) (11)
   flair (n.) (13)
   shrouded (v.) (13)
   wiles (n.) (14)
   embody (v.) (14)
   loath (adj.) (16)
   brooks (v.) (16)
   exploitative (adj.) (17)
   ploy (n.) (19)
   spindly (adj.) (22)
   aligns (v.) (24)
   phantom (adj.) (25)

2. Dolly Parton is famous for saying, "If I see something saggin', baggin', and draggin', I'm going to nip it, tuck it, and suck it" (para. 2). To what is she referring? How does such vocabulary reinforce her image?

3. In paragraph 3, Fricke mentions that as she remembers Madonna, one image is quickly eclipsed by another. What is the meaning of the word *eclipse* in astronomy? What does the verb mean as Fricke uses it here? Why is this word choice appropriate?

4. Fricke writes that when Madonna needed to make a career change, she was capable of "metamorphosing once again," finding a film that "served as a chrysalis" (para. 20). What happens when something undergoes metamorphosis? What creatures do this? What is a chrysalis?

PROBING CONTENT

1. According to Fricke, what is so special about Dolly Parton and Madonna? What accounts for their enduring popularity as both musicians and icons?

2. What is ironic about Dolly Parton's persona as "a model of exaggerated femininity" (para. 7)? What other words are frequently used to describe her?

3. How has Dolly Parton managed to keep both conservatives and pro-gressives in her loyal fan base? Why does she appeal to both groups?

4. What does Fricke mean when she describes Madonna as "her own per-formance project" (para. 14)? How does Madonna's behavior reinforce this idea?

5. Compare the environments in which Madonna and Dolly Parton grew up. What part do the background and childhood of each woman con-tribute to her public image?

CONSIDERING CRAFT

1. "For Madonna, the medium—or, in her case, the image—*is* the mes-sage," Fricke contends at the end of paragraph 3. To what classic book about American culture is her statement a reference? Why did Fricke choose to evoke that book when discussing Madonna?

2. Locate the thesis, which in this selection is clearly stated rather than simply implied. Discuss why Fricke chose to position the thesis as she did. How effectively does this thesis statement serve as an umbrella statement to cover the entire essay's content?

3. Fricke's attitude toward Dolly Parton and toward Madonna is steadily disclosed throughout this essay. Locate quotations from the essay that announce Fricke's position on both of these women. How does this clarity about her personal opinion affect your reading of this selection?

4. How does Fricke organize her information in this essay? Why does she choose this approach? How well does this organizational pattern work with her thesis and her purpose for writing the essay? Why?

WRITING PROMPTS

Responding to the Topic   Writing about Madonna, Fricke comments, "She skirts across boundaries of class, gender, and race, picking up parts of culture that she likes and flashing them back at us" (para. 16). Develop such a thesis statement about one of your own favorite per-formers and write an essay in which you support your thesis by specific references to that performer's films, concerts, music videos, or television appearances.

Responding to the Writer   Choose either Dolly Parton or Madonna and write an essay in which you either support or refute Fricke's opinion about that performer. Use specific text from this essay in your paper to establish points to debate; you may use outside source material to validate your assertions, but be sure to cite those sources.

Responding to Multiple Viewpoints   A number of other selections in this chapter — "The Worst Op-Ed Ever Written?," "iPod Nation," "*Harry Potter* and Magical Realism," and "Grand Mall Seizure" — attempt to explain the success of someone or something as a cultural icon. Choose one of these other essays and compare that author's approach to his subject to the approach that Fricke takes to Dolly Parton and Madonna. Include such aspects as the organization of the material, the reader's awareness of the writer's personal feelings, the intended audience, and the intent of the author in developing that particular essay.

For a quiz on this reading, go to bedfordstmartins.com/mirror.

Rockers' Shocker

ANALYZING THE IMAGE

Madonna's career has been punctuated by shocking moments, but this particular moment certainly grabbed the world's attention. Madonna and Britney Spears had just performed "Like a Virgin" and "Hollywood" to open the 2003 MTV Music Video Awards when this lip lock astonished fans and rock stars alike. Later Madonna replayed this same scene with Christina Aguilera.

1. What do you think Madonna was hoping to accomplish?

2. How do you think most of her fans reacted? Why? What is your reaction?

3. During this TV awards show, Madonna wore black while Spears and Aguilera wore white. What might these wardrobe choices represent?

4. Compare this image to Erika Fricke's portrayal of Madonna in "Material Girls."

Grand Mall Seizure

DANIEL ALARCON

Daniel Alarcon is an associate editor for *Etiqueta Negra*, a magazine published in Lima, Peru. He is a Visiting Scholar at the Center for Latin American Studies at the University of California, Berkeley. His novel *Lost City Radio* (2007) appeared on the best-of-the-year lists in the *Washington Post*, the *Los Angeles Times*, and the *Chicago Tribune*. He is also the author of a short story collection, *War by Candlelight* (2005). In "Grand Mall Seizure," published on *Alternet* in 2004, Alarcon chronicles his visit to the Mall of America, the largest shopping center in the country.

> **THINKING AHEAD**   How much do you like shopping at a mall? As a teenager, how often did you go to the mall just to hang out? What did you buy there? What rituals did you observe? Now that you're older, how have your thoughts about malls changed?

It is Saturday at the Mall of America, the nation's largest shopping cen- 1
ter, and the crowds are thick and expectant. A small brass band of high school students parades by, playing a cheerful version of "Sunshine of Your Love." Above the glass atrium, a bank of heavy clouds bruises the Midwestern sky. Inside, it is incongruously bright and warm. I sit on a bench and take it all in. A group of teenage boys with piercings and baggy black jeans pass me, one wearing a red T-shirt that reads, "I Have No Idea What's Going On." A fat woman trundles[1] by carrying an enormous bouquet of colorful cellophane balloons, literally dozens of them—cartoon characters, hearts, smiley-faces. Her own smile is easy and unforced, and I'm struck for a moment with the image of her floating, the whole of her, above this sprawling panorama, upwards to the steel girders that crisscross the Mall's glass ceiling, and then beyond.

Two older gentlemen sit amidst the din and controlled madness of 2
Camp Snoopy, the Mall's indoor amusement park, focusing on the matter at hand: a game of checkers.

I share my bench with a large human size statue of Snoopy, and it isn't 3
long before a group of women asks me politely if I wouldn't mind moving. "It's for my granddaughter!" one of them says, posing for a photograph with an arm draped affectionately over Snoopy, both human and canine smiling broadly. Cameras flash. I sit again, but every five minutes or so another group poses with the big white smiling dog. Eventually I give up my seat for

[1]**trundles:** Moves as if on wheels.

good. A rollercoaster roars overhead. There are whistles and screams, the ambient[2] noise of fun all around.

The men play checkers.   4

Robert is retired and lives in Bloomington. He comes most Saturdays to   5
play. His partner Juma is a darker-skinned, more ragged version of Henry Kissinger,[3] and seems unwilling or unable to answer my questions. Though his English isn't good, I understand he comes every Saturday and Sunday to play checkers. "From 10 to 4," he says, without looking up from the game. When he speaks, I can see that he has only a few teeth still holding on.

They do not banter or chat. They tolerate my questions for a mo-   6
ment, but it isn't long before I can sense their patience waning. Robert explains they've been playing together for close to four years. Both claim to do very little actual shopping at the Mall. Do you bring the checkers set, I ask. They do not. They play on a cloth set provided by Camp Snoopy Outfitters, next to a sign that says brightly, "Checkers set on sale inside!"

They are, in other words, living advertisements for a store.   7

To understand the Mall of America, it is helpful to know how this all began.   8
Southdale, the first enclosed shopping [mall] in the United States opened in Edina, Minnesota, to great fanfare in 1956. It is still in operation today, not even a half hour from the present site of the Mall of America. Its architect was a man named Victor Gruen, an Austrian Jew who fled the Nazi invasion of 1938 and arrived in the United States with $6 in his pocket. A man of European sensibilities, Gruen's Southdale was inspired by the covered pedestrian galleries of Milan and Venice. He saw the enclosed mall, with its walkways and open spaces, as a hedge against the corrosive suburban sprawl that was then just beginning to overwhelm the American landscape. He wrote of shopping centers that not only served a community's physical needs, but its civic, cultural, and social needs as well. In describing Southdale, he grandiosely and unselfconsciously evoked the Greek agora[4] and the medieval city centers of old Europe.

All over the country the Southdale model was replicated, simplified,   9
and the money came in hand over fist. Developers bought farmland at the junctions of highways and the building frenzy began in earnest. By 1964, when Gruen wrote *The Heart of Our Cities: Urban Crisis*, he had watched his creation grow like a hydra and spiral away from its original intent. He blamed local governments and unscrupulous developers for the decay of America's cities. More to the point, he refused to accept any credit or blame for the invention of the enclosed shopping center. "I have been referred to in some publications as The Father of the Mall. I want to take this opportunity to disclaim paternity once and for all."

---

[2]**ambient:** Present on every side.
[3]**Henry Kissinger:** Former American secretary of state.
[4]**agora:** Marketplace in ancient Greece.

Gruen left his adopted country in 1968, and returned to Vienna, where   10
he died twelve years later.

Unlike Gruen, the immigrant developers of the Mall of America, four   11
Iranian-born Canadian brothers surnamed Ghermezian, never seemed at all
torn about the purposes of their project. They are not urban designers, city
planners, or architects. They are showmen. The Ghermezians are mercenary
capitalists, no less visionary than Gruen, but certainly less thoughtful. And the
Mall of America was created to fulfill their baroque[5] visions of festive shopping, where commerce and entertainment would come together in a profitable
union. In 1986, when the Mall was still in its planning stages and meeting
resistance, Nader Ghermezian spoke as if he couldn't understand his
opponents, as if he were baffled by their short-sightedness: "You will have
all the shoppers from New York, Rome, Los Angeles, and Paris coming
here," he proclaimed at a press conference. "I bring you the moon and you
don't want it?"

He was only partially exaggerating. The sheer numbers are staggering.   12
It cost $650 million to build. With 4.2 million square feet, the Ghermezian
brothers' behemoth[6] includes 520 stores on four levels. It has four food
courts, two health clinics, a university, a post office, a police station, and a
store that sells Christmas ornaments year-round. It hosts a weekly church
service, and is the home of Camp Snoopy, a seven-acre indoor amusement
park. The Mall is staffed by more than 11,000 year-round employees,
visited by some 600,000 to 900,000 shoppers each week, depending on
the season. On an average weekend, the Mall is the third largest city in
the state of Minnesota. If you were to spend only ten minutes in each
of the stores, it would take you more than eighty-six hours to complete
your circuit.

Would you like to purchase a decorative ceramic of a smiling cow? Or a   13
sexy dress for your overweight teenager? Perhaps you have come to buy a
CD recording of wind chimes that recall "the long, lazy days of summer"?
Is it leprechaun[7] shoes you want or a microwave bacon tray? A portrait of
the Virgin of Guadalupe in a gold-colored wood frame?

Shoppers laden with bags stroll down each of the themed corridors,   14
past boutiques, in and out of department stores. There are stores called
Stamps Away, Bead It!, Hat Zone, Calido Chili Traders, stores whose
names announce their particular niche in the market economy. Each of the
four corridors of the Mall has a different feel, by design. West Market, with
its gray tiled floors, painted steel benches, and a metallic silver roof above,
is the least attractive, not unlike an airplane hangar with balconies. There
are gaudy golden lamps along the columns, and small ornamental plants.

---

[5]baroque: Extravagant; excessive.
[6]behemoth: Something of enormous size.
[7]leprechaun: A mischievous elf from Irish folklore, the toes of whose shoes curled upward.

North Garden has a more traditional feel, with wooden benches, wrought iron lampposts, small trees in planters, and lots of natural light streaming in through the glass ceiling. This is the kind of design element that would have made Victor Gruen proud: without leaving the climate-controlled environs of the Mall, one has the impression of changing neighborhoods, of crossing boundaries, when, in fact, you are simply walking in circles.

Indeed, I only notice these design elements because I look for them. Most shoppers I talk to seem completely unaware of their surroundings; none expressed any particular attachment to North Garden over West Market, or East Broadway as opposed to South Avenue. It's all the same, and it's all shopping, mostly, though not exclusively, for the kinds of items we could all do without. And so, after an hour or two of wandering, it is with some amazement that I stand to gather my breath in front of the display of hammers at Sears. Shoes, hats, clothes, perfumes, gadgets, jewelry are available in hedonistic[8] excess at the Mall—but hammers? They seem out of place, a wrinkle in the climate-controlled fantasy, a blip[9] in the Mall's matrix[10] of eternal leisure: hammers imply work, imply effort and sweat and all those things that do not exist at the Mall, at least not for the shopper. And yet, there they are: fifty-seven different types of hammers. I count. Fifty-seven varieties of this Stone Age tool, with ergonomic[11] handles and rubber grips, in every size and weight and color scheme. So much commercial esoterica,[12] and perhaps what is most out of place here is a tool.

In his 1986 book *The Malling of America*, sociologist William Kowinski observes that spending any time in contemporary shopping centers is like walking through 3-D television. If this was true then, it is even more true today—the mall today is quite deliberately the physical representation of television's immanent consumer visions.

Television is everywhere, the glow of it calling you. I stroll down the North Garden to Nordstrom's, where Donny Osmond, host of a game show called *Pyramid*, is scheduled to put in an appearance later in the day. In the meantime, a kind of star search is underway: a soundstage, a diverse crowd, looking at once expectant and bored, a slick Osmond look-alike emcee chatting onstage with potential contestants for exactly thirty seconds each before the game began (Two questions: 1. Where do you live? 2. What do you do?). The eager would-be contestants come and go in pairs, leaving us with one sentence summaries of their lives: "I'm Kurt from Bloomington and I'm a janitor," says a man whose tiny legs dangle five inches above the

[8]**hedonistic:** Seeking pleasure as the greatest good.
[9]**blip:** An interruption.
[10]**matrix:** Something from which other things originate.
[11]**ergonomic:** Designed to physically benefit the people using the object.
[12]**esoterica:** Items understood and appreciated only by a small group.

floor. The host smiles enthusiastically and turns to Kurt's partner. The game is played, they lose. We groan and then applaud. Three minutes later, Kurt is replaced by Dee from Apple Valley, mother of two beautiful daughters, who has recently welcomed a Swedish exchange student into her home. The crowd cheers. When Dee's team loses, we all welcome Jody, a claims administrator, who announces proudly that she has been here since 5:30 in the morning.

Black and white, Asian and Latino, fat and thin, tall and short, they step   18
up for their chance to be on television. The host's enthusiastic smile shows no signs of flagging. Every now and then, a pair wins and is selected for the next round. Applause, banter, game show: the myth machine hitting on all cylinders.

To criticize the Mall for being unreal is to miss the point entirely. *Of course*   19
it is unreal: a banner at the entrance blithely reads LOSE YOURSELF. Literal disorientation begins the moment you step into the cavernous mall. The Mall extends outward from your person in every direction, a seeming infinity of shopping possibilities. And what a place to be lost! It is clean, eternally prosperous, a safe, climate-controlled vision of Eden. And then the more narcotic meanings of the phrase LOSE YOURSELF come into play: it is undiluted fantasy, a beating heart of commerce. This is the language of addiction: we gather near it to feel the pulsating warmth of capitalism. We melt into its embrace.

And yet, somewhere outside the Mall of America, the real world does   20
exist. Hundreds of workers spent years building the complex. And all is not well. The day I visit the Mall the local headlines were of a shooting at an area high school and a government report on rising poverty. Minnesota has been spared the worst of the current economic doldrums,[13] and the Mall itself operates as if they didn't exist at all.

Michael Silsby is twenty years old, from Topeka, Kansas. He has a thin,   21
pale face, and dark brown hair pulled back in a ponytail. He finished a two-year program in graphic design in Omaha, Nebraska, and moved to Minneapolis, looking for work. Michael looked for work at computer firms, design companies, but even in Minneapolis, a job isn't easy to come by. "I never thought I'd wind up working at a mall," he says. "I hate malls."

Michael draws portraits on the eastern second floor balcony. When I   22
approach him, he's working on a portrait of his brother, drawing carefully from a glossy headshot. His boss, Kehai, is a Chinese immigrant who has run the stand for only a few months. "Business is slow," Kehai says. People walk by constantly, a few are curious enough to examine the charcoal images of Michael Jordan, Jack Nicholson, and Marilyn Monroe, but most continue on. Michael works a forty-hour week without a fixed salary, earning commission on each portrait. It works out to around minimum wage, without benefits.

---

[13]**doldrums:** Periods of inactivity or downturns.

It is hardly back-breaking labor, at least not in the Third World sense, 23
and there are far worse jobs in the Mall. A veritable army of custodial and
security staff keeps the place gleaming evenings, weekends, and holidays.
In any case, Michael doesn't foresee that he will be here very long. He
doesn't mind drawing with people looking over his shoulder; it's the noise
that gets him. And it's true: the perpetual buzz from Camp Snoopy below is
maddening, bells going off at regular intervals, shrieks of delight from the
log flume,[14] the nauseating music of the carousel. They coalesce into a wall
of sound, so that as we talk, we are both nearly shouting. I sit with him for
nearly an hour while he draws my portrait. I listen to him talk about *Star
Trek*, about his brother, who is looking for work in commercials. People
stream by, looking first at the portrait in progress, then at me, and snicker.
It is a humiliating experience.

From the western third floor Food Court, the gleaming neon heart of Camp 24
Snoopy is on display. There are giant cartoon characters suspended from the
ceiling; pterodactyls[15] built of Legos hover just above. Below, children scurry
about through thickets of trees, along ponds and over streams heavy with
coins and forgotten wishes. But we, on this level, are above it all: it is evening, the lights are low, and romance is in the air. Couples share a bite of Japanese food before heading to the movie theatre. Everywhere there is hushed
conversation over a burrito or a burger, or two straws poking from the same
oversize cup of soda. I watch a young man approach the railing, arm around
his girlfriend, whose eyes are shut tightly. "Now look," he says.

She opens her eyes and it's there: the lights snaking upwards, the elegant 25
Ferris wheel, the pastoral[16] green of the indoor garden. "It's soooo huge!"
she says. "Soooo huge!"

This, I believe, is the essential calculus of American capitalism: big- 26
ger is better. It explains why the Mall's developers are Canadian Iranians,
who seized the opportunity to sell Americans their own oversized dreams.
It explains why it attracts, according to the *New York Times*, more annual visitors than Disney World, Graceland, and the Grand Canyon combined. In the American imagination, there is nothing quite like the allure
and romance of being the biggest. Size is glory and relevance. Chartered
buses ply the route from the airport directly to the Mall. Its size makes it a
destination.

In one very important respect, size apparently does not matter: the spec- 27
tacular size of the Mall of America has not been matched by spectacular
profits. By some accounts, the Mall is now worth about $550 million, or
$100 million less than its original development cost. Many observers say

---

[14]**log flume:** An amusement park roller coaster that travels through water.
[15]**pterodactyls:** Prehistoric birdlike creatures of the Late Jurassic period.
[16]**pastoral:** Reminiscent of rural life.

that the era of the mega-mall has passed. Construction of large, enclosed malls is down 70 percent since 1996. But this is only part of the story: while no new enclosed shopping centers have been built in the Minneapolis area since the opening in 1992 (and more than a few have closed), those that remained have survived through growth, the retail equivalent of an arms race. Southdale, Victor Gruen's creation, has expanded by 30 percent, to nearly 2 million square feet. By the end of this year, there will be seven enclosed malls with over 1 million square feet of retail space in the Greater Minneapolis area. In 1990, there were only two.

The shopping center is America's great safe haven, and it embodies   28
the promise of the American dream. The Mall attracts foreign tourists of course, but also immigrants from all continents who have made new homes in the Minneapolis area: I see women in Arab dress, families of Africans in bright head-wraps, Latin Americans from every corner of our continent. Buying little, they wander around the Mall and inhale its scent. What better place to understand your new country than here? Consumption is a dearly held American right, a pastime and tradition.

Nowhere is this more acutely observed than in *Dawn of the Dead*,   29
George A. Romero's 1978 zombie movie. In the film, a quartet of survivalists flee Philadelphia in a stolen helicopter, escaping the living dead who have overrun all the cities. After a few false starts, they find safety in the relative luxury of an abandoned suburban shopping mall. It has everything they might need: food, clothes, furniture, television, guns. Unfortunately the mall too is seething with zombies, stumbling along the corridors, stiff-legged, gangly, lethal. The intrepid refugees lock themselves inside a closed department store, before clearing the mall in a paroxysm[17] of violence.

Then, once safe, they celebrate by shopping, choosing new watches,   30
trying on clothes, grinding fresh coffee, going ice skating with new skates. They parade around their liberated mall with beaming smiles, loaded with new gear and gadgets. They lose themselves to festive shopping.

In the subdued light of morning, the Mall is a thoughtful place. It is Sun-   31
day, before the stores open, and I wander the empty corridors of the Mall at rest. There are a few resolute elderly walkers, a man reading the newspaper at the open coffee shop, but mostly there is the shuttered quiet of a vacant place of commerce.

I am here for church. Each Sunday at 10:00 AM, the River Church has   32
a service in the rented space of the Great Lakes Ballroom in the southwest corner of Camp Snoopy. I arrive early and watch the eager participants get everything ready. There are twenty or so people milling[18] around, musicians onstage, a technician putting the finishing touches on a PowerPoint presentation about today's sermon. The mood is earnest, yet informal, and everyone, it seems, is under forty.

---

[17]**paroxysm:** A sudden action.
[18]**milling:** Wandering.

More people arrive and the lights dim, and the band launches into a   33
Thelonious Monk[19] tune, with agile soloists and swinging drums. I'm tap-
ping my feet. After a few songs, a white man with a pudgy face asks us to
bow our heads for fellowship. "God," he says serenely, shutting his eyes to
address Him. "You are an awesome God."

For the past few Sundays, Pastor Chris Reinerston's sermons have been   34
breaking down the Lord's Prayer, phrase by phrase. Today he will focus on
"Your Kingdom come, Thy Will Be Done, On Earth as it is in Heaven."
The last two phrases, he says, are pretty self-explanatory, so he asks our
permission to concentrate on the first: God's Kingdom.

Reinerston describes a world of plenty, where children's bellies   35
are bloated not from malnutrition, but from eating so many of God's
wondrous fruits and vegetables. "God will blow our minds!" Reinerston
announces enthusiastically. He gains momentum as he speaks: everything
will be provided for, the stock market will go up and up, and there will be
no single-parent homes. "It will be," he says at one point, "like everyone
sitting around, watching TV, just loving each other!" I can't do it justice of
course, because Reinerston means everything he says, means it intensely,
fervently. But when he says that in God's Kingdom there will be "no more
run-down buildings, no more cracked sidewalks, no more graffiti," that
"everything will be new!" I can't help but wonder if the place he is describing isn't actually the Mall of America, with all its abundant, excessive newness. Imagine the Mall, full of God's Elect lounging at the Bose
Audio Store, watching DVDs of the latest releases, frolicking on God's
trampoline, trying on clothes straight off the Macy's rack. "Imagine," he
says later, voice quavering, "a world without poverty. Imagine never seeing another one of those commercials for starving children in Third World
countries!"

Ultimately, what Reinerston has described is the contemporary American   36
condition: a rarified vantage point, where it is not poverty we decry, but the
televised representation of it, as if the real thing were too far, too distant
and abstract to pierce this pretty, pretty bubble. Poverty, of the American
variety, is on the rise, or so the newspapers are saying. But here?

After the service, I ask Pastor Chris about some of these things. He is an   37
energetic man in his mid thirties, a father of four, he tells me proudly, and
eager to talk. Why a service in the Mall of America, I ask him. "It wasn't my
idea," he says, "It was God's." Bart Holling, another River Church leader,
joins our conversation, and he puts it this way: "The Mall of America is a
river of life. People come here looking for stuff to fill their hearts with. We
believe there is a God-size hole in each person's heart, and they're always
trying to fill it with other stuff, but we're here to help them fill it with God."
I am not convinced. What about Jesus throwing the money-changers out

[19]**Thelonious Monk:** Famous American jazz musician (1920–1982).

of the temple? Haven't you brought the temple to the money-changers? In response, Pastor Chris re-interprets his sermon as anti-consumerist; referencing commercials, he says, is just a way to connect with people.

After the service, I wander into Camp Snoopy and run into Juma, looking   38
uneasily at the empty checkers table. He wears the same clothes as yesterday. His partners haven't come. It is past 11:00 AM, and he is itching to play. He recognizes me and all but drags me to the checkers set.

I am a disappointment. He beats me in a flurry of decisive moves. We   39
set up and he beats me again. In between, I ask him where he is from, and listen over the rising noise of the Mall as he evokes in halting English a faraway African city: Kampala, Uganda. He owned a fabric store in Kampala, before Idi Amin, the murderous, self-aggrandizing dictator, expelled him thirty-one years before. "I have four sons here," he says proudly. "They study." He chose to leave. Here, in the comfort of the Mall of America, Juma doesn't seem to regret his decision—and why would he? "The Mall is good," he says. "No problems."

No war at your front step. No landslides or floods, droughts, strikes,   40
or coup[20] attempts. The Mall banishes all worldly problems, man-made or natural. It is no wonder that so many people come not only to the Mall but to the United States: to be near so much power, so much money is to believe in the possibility of earthly tranquility.

Is it too simple to say that the whole world wants in? In one memo-   41
rable scene in *Dawn of the Dead*, the four heroes stand triumphant on the second floor balcony, decked out with guns, jewelry, and resplendent fur coats. Below are the bodies of zombies, and beyond that the doors of the shopping center, where hundreds more living dead claw and press against the glass, trying desperately to get in. "What do they want?" one of the survivalists asks. Another answers thoughtfully:

They're after the place. They don't know why, they just remember they   42
want to be in here.

What the hell are they?   43

They're us, that's all.   44

EXERCISING VOCABULARY

1. Record your own definition for each word below in your notebook.

expectant (adj.) (1)	mercenary (adj.) (11)
incongruously (adv.) (1)	visionary (adj.) (11)
sprawling (adj.) (1)	baffled (v.) (11)
waning (v.) (6)	staggering (adj.) (12)
grandiosely (adv.) (8)	niche (n.) (14)
replicated (v.) (9)	immanent (adj.) (16)
unscrupulous (adj.) (9)	flagging (n.) (18)

[20]coup: Sudden and highly successful action; often used with the overthrow of a government.

cavernous (adj.) (19)

undiluted (adj.) (19)

veritable (adj.) (23)

gleaming (adj.) (23)

coalesce (v.) (23)

allure (n.) (26)

ply (v.) (26)

embodies (v.) (28)

intrepid (adj.) (29)

resolute (adj.) (31)

agile (adj.) (33)

frolicking (v.) (35)

rarified (adj.) (36)

decry (v.) (36)

self-aggrandizing (adj.) (39)

resplendent (adj.) (41)

2. Victor Gruen decided to construct "a hedge against the corrosive sub-urban sprawl" that had begun to engulf his adopted country (para. 8). Of what is a hedge usually made? What purpose does a hedge serve? What effect does something corrosive have? In what sense can this be applied to suburban building patterns? Rewrite this phrase in your own words.

3. Describe an atmosphere of "din and controlled madness" (para. 2). What does *din* mean? How does this early reference to the Mall of America's atmosphere set the stage for Alarcon's entire essay?

4. In paragraph 9, Alarcon notes that Victor Gruen watched his first mall idea "grow like a hydra." What is a hydra? How does a hydra grow? To what extent is this simile appropriate for the proliferation of malls across America?

5. In paragraph 27, Alarcon likens the struggle of malls to survive as "the retail equivalent of an arms race." What was the arms race? Who participated in it? How was this like the battle each mall undertakes to survive economically?

PROBING CONTENT

1. What is ironic about the location of the first enclosed shopping mall in the United States? Who was responsible for its creation? Where did he get the idea?

2. Who is responsible for the Mall of America concept? Why do you think they chose that name? How successful has their dream become?

3. Why does Alarcon feel that hammers are "a blip in the Mall's matrix" (para. 15)? What is significant about the hammers? Why do they capture the author's interest?

4. Why is the Mall of America so popular with immigrants? What do they gain from wandering past its stores, even if they buy very little?

CONSIDERING CRAFT

1. The title of this selection is a play on words. What is the more commonly heard phrase? To what does it refer? What imagery does Alarcon invoke in the reader by using this title?

2. What does Alarcon accomplish in the first paragraph of this essay? What mode of writing does he use? How effective is his opening? Why?

3. What is the purpose of the occasional one-sentence paragraphs that Alarcon uses? Locate several and discuss their function in the essay. How effective is this strategy?

4. In paragraph 18, Alarcon describes the TV show filming in the Mall as "the myth machine hitting on all cylinders." To which myth is he referring? What ordinary object does the phrase "hitting on all cylinders" evoke? What does Alarcon accomplish by including this phrase here?

5. Why does Alarcon include the description of scenes from *Dawn of the Dead*? How does referencing this movie further his purpose for this essay? Why does he choose to end with a quotation from this movie?

WRITING PROMPTS

Responding to the Topic   Does being in a mall open up for you "the promise of the American dream" (para. 28)? In an essay, describe in detail a recent mall experience you have had. If you haven't been to a mall lately, spend several hours in one. Did you experience any of the feelings Alarcon mentions? What did you see, taste, smell, hear, and touch?

Responding to the Writer   Alarcon asserts that the Mall of America represents "the essential calculus of American capitalism: bigger is better" (para. 26). To what extent does this axiom hold true in America's economy? Take a position agreeing or disagreeing with this assertion. Defend your own position with numerous examples.

Responding to Multiple Viewpoints   In "*Harry Potter* and Magical Realism," Daniel Nexon argues that Harry and his fellow witches and wizards have become symbols that exist beyond the narrow realm of the books and movies. Write an essay in which you explore the symbolism of the mall culture and compare the degree of fantasy offered by the *Harry Potter* universe with that offered by the universe of the American mall.

For a quiz on this reading, go to bedfordstmartins.com/mirror.

Wrapping Up Chapter 8

CONNECTING TO THE CULTURE

1. Choose a person, place, event or object that you would classify as an American icon. Develop an essay in which you state your case for your choice as being representative of American culture and easily recognizable to most Americans. Also explain how this icon would be likely to be received abroad and the impact it would have on other cultures.

2. Choose a technological device like the iPod (for example, the Wii) and write an essay examining its popularity. Be certain to include details about its marketing and its appeal to the public. Has this appeal translated overseas? Why?

3. Since "The Worst Op-Ed Ever Written?" was written, Starbucks has fallen on hard times and has been forced to close a number of its stores. In an essay, track the rise and fall of another uniquely American enterprise. Include reasons for both its success and its demise.

4. Young people today rarely meet at drive-ins like McDonald's or Sonic to see and be seen; now they convene at malls or multiplexes or in Internet chat rooms. Choose one place that attracts teenagers today. In an essay, describe that place in detail. Who hangs out there? Why? Why do they choose that location? What interaction occurs? What is the significance of that place for its congregants?

5. Choose a music star whose career has spanned at least two or three decades. In an essay, explain his or her continued popularity and appeal to multiple generations. What about that person is responsible for his or her elevation to iconic status? If you prefer, you may write about a musical group rather than an individual.

Focusing on Yesterday, Focusing on Today

Music exists at the heart of every culture. The forms may change, the methods of access may alter, the popularity of a type of music may wax or wane, but music is undeniably part of our cultural roots and intrinsic to our cultural expression.

In the photo titled "Movin' with His Boom Box," what do you notice immediately about the relationship between the boy and the music? Describe the young man in the photograph. Why is he smiling so broadly? Describe the setting and the other people present in the photograph. How do they relate to the young man? Why?

Movin' with His Boom Box

Now look at a recent photograph of a woman listening to her MP3 player on a commuter train. Where has she probably been? How do you know that? What is the most striking similarity between this photograph and "Movin' with His Boom Box"? What is the most striking difference? Why do both of these photographs grab the viewer's attention? What does each of them say about American culture? What do the photographs say about the evolution of our culture through time?

Travelin' to Her Own Beat

Evaluating and
Documenting Sources

When you research topics of interest in popular culture, you are going to want to augment your own thoughts and ideas with credible sources that support your position. You may think that it will be difficult to locate such sources. On the contrary, for most topics, you'll find a wide array of potential material to incorporate into your work. You won't be able to use everything, so you will have to make some important choices in order to focus on the most legitimate and persuasive evidence.

As you begin, remember two important things. First, because popular culture involves what's popular, it changes rapidly. Remember 98 Degrees? Old news, right? Consequently, the more recent your source, the more valuable that source is to your research. A *Rolling Stone* article on current music trends isn't current if it was written in 1997, although it may still be useful if you are seeking a historical perspective.

Second, all sources are not created equal. Some publications or Web sites are created specifically to further the writer's own views. Material on the Internet is often posted without being evaluated. Let the researcher beware. You will want to establish certain basic information about any source you plan to rely on for information—for example, its date of posting or publication or the person or organization that is responsible for the veracity of the site's or the magazine's content. Learning to recognize and evaluate the bias embedded in some potentially useful material may require a little detective work, but it is essential to the authenticity and credibility of your own research.

In Chapter 2, we suggested a list of questions to ask as you deconstruct media images. Let's start with a similar list of questions to help you learn to evaluate the usefulness of possible electronic and print sources:

1. Where is the source material located?
2. What is the date of the publication, posting, or update?
3. Who is the author?
4. When the material was written or posted, who was its intended audience?
5. Is the material a primary source or a secondary source?

Just as we do when deconstructing a visual image, let's take the most easily answered questions first.

WHERE IS THE SOURCE MATERIAL LOCATED?

The first important question to ask about potential source material is "Where is it located?" If the article or advertisement is in print form, in which magazine, newspaper, or journal does it appear? What can you find out about this publication? How long has it been in circulation? Who publishes the book, newspaper, or magazine? Who sponsors this Web site? What's the purpose of the Web site or print source? Check the titles of other articles listed in the table of contents. What patterns or similarities do you see? Are different viewpoints represented?

Answers to most of these basic questions can usually be found on a page near the front of the publication. Journals, whose articles are generally closely scrutinized by editors and reviewers before they are published, are even more likely than magazines to provide such particulars. Remember that scholarly journals, unlike popular magazines, are published less frequently, are peer reviewed, and are often written for a select audience of professionals.

If your source is electronic, you may not find this information as readily. Some Internet sources are affiliated with journals, magazines, newspapers, or professional organizations. These sites are generally reliable and may include relevant dates, biographical information about the author, and general information about the site itself. However, remember that anyone can host a Web site and post whatever he or she chooses, whether or not it is accurate. Wouldn't it be embarrassing to find out that you've quoted a seventh grader's Lindsay Lohan site in a college paper? You'll want to reference only reliable Web sources that clearly reveal ownership and other factual documentation.

WHAT IS THE DATE OF THE PUBLICATION, POSTING, OR UPDATE?

How recently was this online information written and published? Magazines and journals usually print a date on the cover. Weekly publications give you more current information about popular culture topics than monthly ones do, and daily newspapers stay ahead of both. Some journals are published only once or twice a year, but they may still provide important background for your research.

Articles on the Internet may have the date of the site's creation or most recent update or may not have any date. You might have to use clues to judge how recently the information has been gathered. Check the information against other dated sources. Read carefully for dates and events mentioned within the article itself.

WHO IS THE AUTHOR?

Book authors' names are readily available, and sometimes a note on the book jacket will list important biographical data. Periodical authors who have established reputations will be identified by name either near the beginning or end of the article. A few lines about the author — other articles or books written, current position held, any literary recognition received, or other specific information that makes the author more credible than others on that subject — may also be included. Tiger Woods's writing about the best golf courses, for example, would automatically carry more clout than the average weekend golfer's. Journals generally offer a great deal of specific information about their authors' professional accomplishments and affiliations.

On the other hand, many magazine articles are written by staff writers who work full-time for the publication, providing material on whatever topic they are assigned. Still other articles are written by freelance writers who are hired by the publication or Web host to contribute one article on one particular topic at a time. Such authors may or may not be named. Whatever you can learn about authors, famous or not, will help you to read the articles more accurately and alert you to any particular bias or viewpoint. Clues about the author's angle and tone may also present themselves in the writing. An author who professes in the opening paragraph of a review to be a great fan of Julia Roberts is not likely to be truly impartial about one of her movies.

Internet sources should list at least the author's name. We suggest treating with caution any Internet article that lists no author at all. Be diligent in trying to find the author of an Internet source. You may need to go back to the home page if the author's name does not appear just before or just after the essay.

As your research on a popular culture topic progresses, chances are good that a few authors' names will appear as references in several different sources. This is testimony to the author's credibility and an indication that this author's thoughts and opinions on this topic are generally sought after and respected.

WHEN THE MATERIAL WAS WRITTEN OR POSTED, WHO WAS ITS INTENDED AUDIENCE?

Do readers of the source belong to a particular age group, ethnicity, interest group, or occupational group? *Teen Magazine*, for example, is clearly marketed toward a certain age group, as is *AARP The Magazine*, one of the publications of the American Association of Retired Persons. Perhaps the publication or site is intended for a special-interest group. Publications like *Dog World* fit this category. Some magazines, such as *Time*, *Newsweek*, *People*, and *Reader's Digest*, are written to appeal to a much wider audience. Knowing the target audience for a publication will help you evaluate any common knowledge, vocabulary, values, and beliefs that its writers expect most readers to share.

Journals tend to be directed to specific target audiences, which frequently consist of people in the same profession. Often in such publications the language and style used will be baffling to the outsider yet easily understood by members of the profession. The medical terminology used in the *American Journal of Nursing* may sound like unintelligible jargon to someone outside the field of medicine. Remember, if you don't understand what you are reading, that material may have little value to you as a source.

In some cases, if the specifics of a complicated journal article are important to your research, you may want to consult a specialized dictionary. These references will help you decipher language unique to one field of study — like law, psychology, or engineering.

IS THE MATERIAL A PRIMARY SOURCE OR A SECONDARY SOURCE?

Determining whether material is a primary or secondary source may not be as easy as finding the date of publication or the author's name, but this distinction isn't difficult. When you see *Star Wars, Episode III: Revenge of the Sith* and then describe in a paper how George Lucas employs technology to develop the character of Yoda, you are using a primary source — the movie itself. When you read an article that compares George Lucas's use of technology in the *Star Wars* trilogy and in the prequels in *Entertainment* magazine and then quote the author of that article in your own work, you are using a secondary source — the article about the movies.

Let's take one more example. If you watch a television interview with Denzel Washington about the role of black actors in American films and refer to that interview in your research, that is a primary source. You saw the interview yourself. However, if you miss the television show and read a review of it in the next day's Life and Arts section of your local newspaper, then you'll be using a secondary source when you incorporate information from the review in your paper.

With primary sources, you are in direct contact with the music, film, novel, advertisement, or Web site. You develop your own interpretation and analysis. With secondary sources, someone else is acting as a filter between you and the CD, the play, the short story, or the painting.

Both types of sources are valuable. After all, not many of us saw the Beatles' last live concert in person. But with secondary sources you will want to be alert for any bias or viewpoint of the author's that could affect the credibility of the source material.

Practice in applying these five questions will help you to become confident about the value and validity of the sources you use to support your own ideas.

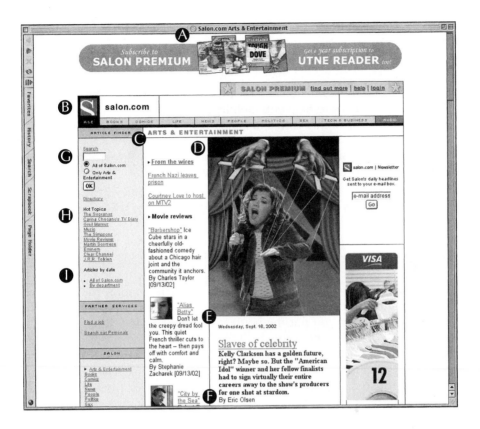

Here is an example of a Web page you might consult during your research into a popular culture topic:

- Item A identifies the group as a company (.com), not a school (.edu), an organization (.org), or a government agency (.gov).
- Item B offers a link to the Web site's home page.
- Item C provides a heading to let you know what part of the site you are viewing.
- Item D uses an engaging graphic image that is related to the subject matter of a general topic.
- Item E provides a date for the issue.
- Item F provides the name of the author below an article title.
- Item G allows for a search function.
- Item H provides links to other topics within the site that might be of interest.
- Item I provides links to additional articles.

EXERCISE

After closely examining the Web screen shot on p. 408, answer the following questions:

1. Who is the intended audience for this Web page? What aspects of this site provide clues to help you identify its audience?
2. What elements of this Web site indicate the reliability or unreliability of its information?
3. What aspects of this site let you know that this Web-based company wants its audience to return to the site often?

Documenting Electronic and Print Sources

Now we are ready to take those sources for which we have established relevance and the proper credentials and think about using them in a paper or other research project.

Attention, please! Always write out a complete citation for any piece of material that you are seriously considering as a source for your research. That way, days after you put the bound volume of periodicals back on the shelf, you won't have to go through all fifty volumes to locate one article that contains just the right quotation or statistic. Also, always print out a hard copy of anything from the Internet that you consider using. The fact that you knew the URL today doesn't mean you'll know it a week from now or that the same information will be posted again in exactly the same place.

Here are some examples of the correct ways to document your sources in the body of your paper. We also provide examples of the correct ways to document your sources in your Works Cited page at the end of your paper. This is a brief listing and isn't meant to be the only reference you should consult. If you need additional information on documenting sources, ask your professor to recommend a text or go to *Research and Documentation Online* at dianahacker.com/resdoc. All the citations here follow the 2009 Modern Language Association (MLA) format. Before writing any paper, check with your instructor to see which format is required.

MLA FORMAT FOR IN-TEXT CITATIONS

You should provide an in-text citation every time you quote from, paraphrase, or summarize an outside source. Your citation should directly follow the sentence or sentences in your paper that refer to the source information. Consult the following models when you cite sources within your essay.

Books or Periodicals

When you use a quotation and do not name the author within your text, you must put both the author's name and the page number in parentheses at the end of the quotation. The complete citation that identifies the book's title, date, and place of publication will be found in the list of Works Cited:

"The fact is that much of advertising's power comes from this belief that advertising does not affect us. The most effective kind of propaganda is that which is not recognized as propaganda" (Kilbourne 27).

If a work has four or more authors, list all of their last names, or list the first author's name followed by et al., which means "and others":

"In another scenario, where a woman gives birth to her own clone, would she be her child's mother or twin sister with a different age?" (Borem et al. 83).

If you mention the author's name in your text, then only the page number needs to be in parentheses at the end of the quotation:

Kilbourne states that "much of advertising's power comes from this belief that advertising does not affect us" (27).

If an article or a Web page does not have an author, either use the complete title in the text or use a short form of the title within the parentheses before the page number. Use quotation marks around titles of essays and other short works.

Fashion companies hope that "by making an ordinary product 'exclusive' they can add a note of urgency to splurge spending" ("Putting a Limit on Labels" 12).

If you *paraphrase*, or express in your own words, an idea from a source, you must still include a citation:

Every day, the average American spends nearly an hour watching, listening to, or reading advertisements (Jacobson and Mazur 193).

Before Title IX's implementation in 1972, fewer than 300,000 high school girls played competitive sports. By 1997, that number had increased to 2.4 million (U.S. Department of Education).

MLA FORMAT FOR WORKS CITED

At the end of your essay, you must provide a list of the sources from which you quoted, paraphrased, or summarized. Put the entire list in alphabetical order using the author's last name and the title as it appears on the title page of the source. If your source has no author, alphabetize it by the first main word of the title. Double-space your Works Cited page, and indent the second line of each entry five spaces. MLA prefers that the titles of books, movies, record albums, television programs, and so on be italicized to clearly distinguish the title from surrounding words.

Books

One Author

Kilbourne, Jean. *Can't Buy My Love: How Advertising Changes the Way We Think and Feel*. New York: Touchstone, 1999. Print.

Two or More Authors

Borem, Aluizio, Fabricio R. Santos, and David E. Bowen. *Understanding Biotechnology*. Upper Saddle River: Prentice Hall, 2003. Print.

Jacobson, Michael F., and Laurie Ann Mazur. *Marketing Madness: A Survival Guide for a Consumer Society*. Boulder: Westview, 1995. Print.

Periodicals

Signed Magazine Article

Will, George F. "Electronic Morphine." *Newsweek* 25 Nov. 2002: 92. Print.

Unsigned Magazine Article

"Women's Dissatisfaction with Body Image Greater in More Affluent Neighborhoods." *Women's Health Weekly* 21 Mar. 2002: 12. Print.

Signed Newspaper Article

Barnes, Steve. "In a World Where Sex Sells, One Group Isn't Buying." *Austin American-Statesman* 5 June 2005: K1, K9. Print.

Unsigned Newspaper Article

"Putting a Limit on Labels." *Wall Street Journal* 14 June 2002: W12. Print.

Signed Editorial

Cohen, Adam. "America's Favorite Television Fare? The Normals vs. the Stigmatized." Editorial. *New York Times* 2 June 2002: WK18. Print.

Journal Article

Birmingham, Elizabeth. "Fearing the Freak: How Talk TV Articulates Women and Class." *Journal of Popular Film and Television* 28.3 (2000): 133–39. Print.

Electronic Sources

Web Site

United States Department of Education. "Title IX: Twenty-Five Years of Progress." United States Department of Education, 9 July 1997. Web. 29 July 2002.

Online Magazine Article

Goldberg, Michelle. "Flag-Draped Voyeurism." *Salon*, 9 July 2002. Web. 1 Aug. 2002.

Other Sources

Published Interview

King, Stephen. "Ten Questions for Stephen King." *Time* 1 Apr. 2002: 13. Print.

Broadcast Interview

Tarantino, Quentin. Interview by Charlie Rose. *Charlie Rose*. PBS. WGBH, Boston.
    26 Dec. 1997. Television.

Personal Interview

Salomon, Willis. Personal interview. 14 Apr. 2001.

Print Advertisement

T Mobile BlackBerry. Advertisement. *U.S. News & World Report* 23 May 2005: 23. Print.

Television Advertisement

Nike. Advertisement. NBC. 7 June 2005. Television.

Sound Recording

U2. *How to Dismantle an Atomic Bomb*. Universal, 2004. CD.

Television Program

"Daddy Knows Best." *Cold Case Files*. Narr. Bill Kurtis. A&E. 6 Sept. 2004.
    Television.

Radio Program

"Natural Santa Claus." *All Things Considered*. Host Robert Siegel. Natl Public Radio.
    WGBH, Boston. 29 Nov. 2004. Radio.

Film

Star Wars, Episode III: Revenge of the Sith. Dir. George Lucas. Perf. Ewan McGregor,
    Natalie Portman, Hayden Christensen, Ian McDiarmid, Samuel L. Jackson, and
    Christopher Lee. Lucasfilm, 2005. film.

Speech or Lecture

Mahon, Maureen. "This Is Not White Boy Music: The Politics and Poetics of Black
    Rock." Stanford University, Stanford. 30 Jan. 2002. Lecture.

ACKNOWLEDGMENTS (continued)

Daniel Alarcon. "Grand Mall Seizure." First posted on www.alternet.org/story/20782. December 20, 2004. Copyright © 2004 by Daniel Alarcon. Reprinted with permission of the author.

Lorraine Ali. "Do I Look Like Public Enemy Number One?" Originally published in *Mademoiselle*. (1999). Copyright © 1999 Condé Nast Publications, Inc. Reprinted by permission. All rights reserved.

Julia Alvarez. "I Want to Be Miss America." From *Something to Declare* by Julia Alvarez. Copyright © 1998 by Julia Alvarez. Published in paperback by Plume in 1999 and originally in hardcover by Algonquin Books of Chapel Hill in 1998. Reprinted by permission of Susan Bergholz Literary Services, New York, and Lamy, NM. All rights reserved.

Dan Barden. "My New Nose." Originally published in *Gentlemen's Quarterly*, May 2002. Copyright © 2002. Reprinted with permission of Dan Barden. Dan@danbarden.com.

David Brooks. "People Like Us." From the *Atlantic Monthly*, September 2003. Copyright © 2003 by The Atlantic Monthly. Reproduced with permission of The Atlantic Monthly in the format Textbook via Copyright Clearance Center.

Mindy Cameron. "In the Language of Our Ancestors." Originally published in *Northwest Education Magazine*, Spring 2004. Copyright © 2004 Northwest Regional Education Laboratory. Reprinted with permission of NWREL. All rights reserved. www.nwrel.org.

David Carr. "On Covers of Many Magazines, a Full Racial Palette Is Still Rare." From the *New York Times Business/Financial Desk*, November 18, 2002. Copyright © 2002 by The New York Times. All rights reserved. Used by permission and protected by the Copyright Laws of the United States. The printing, copying, redistribution, or retransmission of the material without express written permission is prohibited. www.newyorktimes.com.

Michelle Jana Chan. "Identity in a Virtual World." From CNN.com at http://edition.cnn.com/2007/TECH/06/07/virtual_identity/index.html. Posted June 14, 2007. Copyright © 2008 Cable News Network. Reprinted with permission by CNN.

Jay Chiat. "Illusions Are Forever." From *Forbes ASAP*, October 2, 2000. Forbes, Inc. Reprinted by permission of *Forbes ASAPMagazine* © 2008 Forbes Media LLC.

Anupama Chopra. "Bollywood Princess, Hollywood Hopeful." From the *New York Times*, February 10, 2008. Copyright © 2008 by The New York Times. All rights reserved. Used by permission and protected by the Copyright Laws of the United States. The printing, copying, redistribution or retransmission of the material without express written permission is prohibited. www.newyorktimes.com.

John Clark. "Hollywood Clicks on the Work of Web Auteurs." From the *New York Times*, July 23, 2006 issue, Arts and Leisure Secton. Copyright © 2006 by The New York Times. Reprinted by permission of The New York Times. All rights reserved. Used by permission and protected by the Copyright Laws of the United States. The printing, copying, redistribution or retransmission of the material without express written permission is prohibited. www.newyorktimes.com.

Delia Cleveland. "Champagne Taste, Beer Budget." Originally appeared in *Essence* magazine, March 2001. Adapted from an essay published in *Starting with "I"* (Persea Books, 1997). Reprinted by permission of the author, freelance writer, and author of *Fallin' Out*.

The Economist. "The Ultimate Marketing Machine." From the *Economist* print edition, July 6, 2006. Copyright © 2006 by The Economist Magazine. Reproduced with permission of The Economist in the format Textbook via Copyright Clearance Center.

Jack El-Hai. "Booze, Blood, and the Star-Spangled Banner." First published in the May–June issue of *Utne Reader*, pages 51–53. Copyright © 2006 by Jack El-Hai. Reprinted by permission of the author.

Phyllis Raybin Emert. "Native American Mascots: Racial Slur or Cherished Tradition?" First published in *Respect*, Winter 2003 edition, a tolerance newsletter published by the New Jersey State Bar Foundation. Copyright © 2000–2007, the New Jersey State Bar Foundation. Reprinted by permission of the New Jersey State Bar Foundation.

Erika Fricke. "Material Girls: Behind the seams of beloved pop icons Dolly Parton and Madonna." Appeared in the summer 2006 edition of *Bitch* magazine, issue 32. Copyright © 2006 by Erika Fricke. Reprinted by permission of the author.

Bob Garfield. "Taking Cadillac from Stodgy to Sexy: Kate Walsh." Reprinted with permission from the October 1, 2007 issue of *Advertising Age/AdAge.com/American Demographics*. Copyright © 2007 by Crain Communications, Inc. Reprinted with permission.

412

Katrina Onstad. "Horror Auteur Is Unfinished with the Undead." From the *New York Times*, February 10, 2008. Copyright © 2008 The New York Times. All rights reserved. Used by permission and protected by the Copyright Laws of the United States. The printing, copying, redistribution or retransmission of the material withour express written permission is prohibited. www.newyorktimes.com.

Meghan O'Rourke. "The Croc Epidemic: How a heinous synthetic shoe conquered the world." From *Slate* magazine, Friday, July 13, 2007. Copyright 2007 United Media.slate.com and Washingtonpost.Newsweek Interactive Co. LLC. Reprinted with permission. All rights reserved.

Tara Parker-Pope. "Custom-Made." From the *Wall Street Journal*, September 30, 1996, pages R6–R9. Copyright © 1996 Dow Jones & Company, Inc. Reproduced with permission of Dow Jones & Co, Inc. in the format Textbook via Copyright Clearance Center.

Virginia Postrel. "Signs of Our Times." From the *Atlantic Monthly*, September 2006, pages 137, 138, and 140. Copyright © 2006 The Atlantic Monthly. Reprinted with permission of The Atlantic Monthly in the format Textbook via Copyright Clearance Center.

Dr. Edward Rhymes. "Caucasian Please! America's Cultural Double Standard for Misogyny and Racism." Posted on *Black Agenda Report*, June 26, 2007. Printed on August 6, 2007. www.alternet.org/story/52343. Reprinted with permission of the author.

Eugene Robinson. "Tyler Perry's Money Machine." From the *Washington Post*, Tuesday, October 16, 2007, page A19. Copyright © 2007 The Washington Post. All rights reserved. Used by permission and protected by the Copyright Laws of the United States. The printing, copying, redistribution, or retransmission of the material without express written permission is prohibited. www.washingtonpost.com.

Gregory Rodriguez. "Mongrel America." First published in the *Atlantic Monthly*, January/February 2003, pages 95–97. Copyright © 2003 by The Atlantic Monthly. Reproduced with permission of The Atlantic Monthly in the format Textbook via Copyright Clearance Center.

Ron Rosenbaum. "The Worst Op-Ed Ever Written?" Posted on Slate.com, Tuesday, August 14, 2007. www.slate.com. Reprinted with permission of Ron Rosenbaum, author of *Explaining Hitler* and *The Shakespeare Wars* and columnist for *Slate.com*.

Read Mercer Schuchardt. "Swoosh!" From *Re:Generation Quarterly*, Summer 1997. Copyright © 1997 by Read Mercer Schuchardt. Reprinted with permission of the author.

Craig Simons. "Hooters Translates in China." First published in the *Austin American-Statesman*, February 10, 2006, page A22. Reprinted by permission of Cox Newspapers.

Michael Specter. "Damn Spam: The losing war on junk e-mail." First appeared in the *New Yorker*, August 6, 2007. Copyright © 2007 Michael Spector. Reprinted with permission of International Creative Management.

Grace Suh. "The Eye of the Beholder." First published in *Echoes upon Echoes: New Korean American Writings*. Copyright © 2003 by Grace Suh. Reprinted by permission of the author.

Garry Trudeau. "My Inner Shrimp." From the *New York Times Magazine*, March 31, 1997. Copyright © 1997 by Garry Trudeau. Reprinted by permission.

Kelly Tyler-Lewis. "Virtual Humans." Excerpted from NOVA online, "Special Effects: *Titanic* and Beyond." NOVA/WGBH Educational Foundation. Copyright © 2000 WGBH/Boston. Reprinted by permission. www.pbs.org.wgbh/nova/.

Alice Walker. "Beauty: When the Other Dancer Is the Self." From *In Search of Our Mothers Gardens: Womanist Prose*. Copyright © 1983 by Alice Walker. Reprinted by permission of Houghton Mifflin Harcourt Publishing Company.

Rob Walker. "Cleaning Up." From the *New York Times*, June 10, 2007. Copyright © 2007 Rob Walker. Reprinted with permission of the author.

Eric L. Wee. "Shlock Waves Felt across U.S. Campuses." From the *Dallas Morning News*, June 3, 1998. Copyright © 1998 The Washington Post. All rights reserved. Used by permission and protected by the Copyright Laws of the United States. The printing, copying, redistribution, or retransmission of the material without express written permission is prohibited.

Geneva White. "Corporate Names and Products Creep into Everyday Language." First published in the *Northwest Herald*, September 19, 2007. Copyright © 2007 Northwest Herald. Reprinted with permission of the publisher.

Jennie Yabroff. "Girls Going Mild(er)." First published in *Newsweek*, July 2007; updated and retitled "Drag Hags," August 15, 2007. Copyright © 2007 Newsweek, Inc. All rights reserved. Used by permission and protected by the Copyright Laws of the United States. The printing, copying, redistribution, or retransmission of the material without express written permission is prohibited. www.newsweek.com.

Art Credits

Chapter 2: To Have and To Hold. "Le Plus Beau Jour de la Vie," from *Doubletake* magazine, Fall 1997. Photograph © Jean-Christian Bourcart.

Mallard Fillmore cartoon by Bruce Tinsely from the *Austin-American Statesman*, January 27, 2002. © Reprinted with special permission of King Features Syndicate.

Diet Coke ad, Courtesy The Advertising Archives.

Chapter 3: Mother and Daughter in India, © Joe McNally/Getty Images.

Beauty pageant contestants, © Lambert/Getty Images.

Norman Rockwell, *Freedom From Want*. © 2009 Reprinted by permission of the Norman Rockwell Licensing Company. Photography from CORBIS © Swim/Ink.

"One Big Happy Family" © Charlie Powell Illustration.

Chapter 4: American Gothic plastic surgery parody, © Victor Juhasz.

Choi Seang Rak and avatar, Photograph © Robbie Cooper.

"Body Rites" ad, Courtesy River City Tattoo.

"Losing the Trauma" Before and After plastic surgery photos, © Dan Winters Photography.

Girl writing in diary, © Ryan McVay/Photodisc/Getty Images.

Young man at computer, © Freitag/zefa/CORBIS.

Chapter 5: Cheerful technology, © William Whitehurst/CORBIS.

Tourist cartoon, © Jason Love/Cartoonstock.com.

1950's teen on phone, © CBS Worldwide Inc./Hulton Archive/Getty Images.

Teens texting, © Kevin Dodge/CORBIS.

Chapter 6: Corporate American flag, Image Courtesy of www.adbusters.org.

Cover census chart, Courtesy U.S. Census Bureau.

Spam cartoon, © Images.com/CORBIS.

Vintage car ad, Image courtesy of The Advertising Archives.

New car ad, Image courtesy of The Advertising Archives.

Chapter 7: Oscar statue, © Timothy A. Clary/AFP/Getty Images.

Gollum on the NY subway, © Mario Tama/Getty Images News.

Actress Aishwarya Bachchan, © UTV Motion Pictures.

Poltergeist film still, © MGM/Courtesy Everett Collection.

The Ring film still, © THE RING Productions Group 1998.

Chapter 8: New York, New York hotel, © Rudy Sulgan, CORBIS.

Britney Spears and Madonna kiss, © Julie Jacobson/AP Wide World Photos.

Young man and boom box, © Owen Franken/CORBIS.

Commuter and ipod, © Mike Kemp/Rubberball/Getty Images.

Index of Authors and Titles